In Search
of
Personal Welfare

SUNY series in
Chinese Philosophy and Culture

David L. Hall and Roger T. Ames, editors

In Search
of
Personal Welfare

A View of Ancient Chinese Religion

Mu-chou Poo

STATE UNIVERSITY OF NEW YORK PRESS

Production by Ruth Fisher
Marketing by Anne M. Valentine

Published by
State University of New York Press, Albany

© 1998 State University of New York

For information, address the State University of New York Press,
State University Plaza, Albany, NY 12246

Library of Congress Cataloging-in-Publication Data

Poo, Mu-chou
    In search of personal welfare : a view of ancient Chinese religion
  / Mu-chou Poo.
      p.   cm. — (SUNY series in Chinese philosophy and culture)
    Includes bibliographical references and index.
    ISBN 0–7914–3629–2 (alk. paper). — ISBN 0–7914–3630–6 (pbk. : alk.
paper)
    1. China—Religion.   2. China—Religious life and customs.
    3. China—Civilization.   I. Title.   II. Series.
  BL1802.P65   1998
  299'.51'0901—dc21   97–19197
                                                            CIP

10 9 8 7 6 5 4 3 2 1

Contents

List of Figures

Note: all illustrations included in this book are the author's own original drawings based on the original art. Reproductions of the original art can be found as well in the works indicated above.

Preface

What do we know about the religion of ancient China? Besides what we know about Buddhism and Taoism, the two religions that rose to court prominence and popularity at many levels beginning in the third century, relatively little. Students of Chinese history usually have a less than clear view of religions and religious life beyond the Buddho-Taoist horizon. Most books on ancient China include limited discussion about ancient Chinese religion: ancestor worship, nature worship, and the ideas of ghosts and gods. Some might mention the Confucian philosophical aversion to heaven, ghosts and spirits or the Mohist belief in such things, or the grandeur of seasonal sacrifices to heaven and earth performed by rulers. None of these, however, satisfactorily answer the following questions: what were the features of religious life among the common people of ancient China? And can such a question even be asked given the present state of knowledge about the religion of ancient China? This book is an effort to answer those questions. It proposes to turn our attention from state rituals and intellectual discussions to the experience of the people. It takes into consideration newly discovered texts and archaeological materials, and at the same time reconsiders some very old and, at least from the point of view of researchers, familiar texts.

My interest in the phenomenon of religion in ancient China is not in establishing a new interpretive theory, nor does it focus on the relationship between religion and culture—that is, culture in reference to to the intellectual aspects of, for example, Confucianism or

Taoism. As I understand it, the purpose of the historical study of religion, besides explaining the content of the religion one studies, is to try to establish the relationship between the nature of a religious tradition and the life experience of the broad stratum of the populace in that tradition. For a religion to perpetuate itself and thrive among a group of people, it is necessary that it fit in with the life of the people, in addition to any teachings or ethics it might carry. Clearly, even in this modern world, people still observe all sorts of religious beliefs. None can be seen as unrelated to the lives of its practitioners. Since the aim of the study of history is to understand the lives of past people and civilizations, to understand their religious experience is of primary importance.

The concept that I have employed to describe religion in the context of everyday human lives is "popular religion." In the first chapter, I discuss the problems related to this term, especially the confusing field of names and categories, such as big/little traditions and elite/commoner. I also discuss the paucity of materials available for research. The term "popular religion" has often been used to describe religious phenomena in modern societies. Can one use it in the context of ancient societies? It is, to be sure, a controversial concept. One objection that may be raised concerns the fact that the extant materials, especially the texts, are basically the product of the ruling elite. This objection, however, provides a crucial pivot to the argument that this study pursues. I believe that we can draw a picture, albeit a very crude one, of the religious life of the common people through a fresh reading of the texts—between and behind the lines. Some recently excavated texts help to corroborate our new readings. As a result, I offer tentative answers that support the idea that the popular/elite (or commoner/elite) dichotomy is not really useful in discussing culture and religion, and that we can learn quite a bit about everyday religious life from the received materials. With these methodological problems in view, I trace, in Chapter 2, 3 and 4, the development of religious life in ancient China from the Neolithic period to the end of the Warring States period.

Following that, I discuss religion in the Han dynasty. As background to an understanding of the religious life of the common people, I first provide an overview of official religious activities, the organizations and changes within them. The difference between official religion and the religion of the people, as I see it, is not their underlying cosmology, but their paraphernalia and practical objectives. Thus, the official religion focused on its benefit to the state and to an abstract humanity, while the religion of the people concentrated mainly on the personal welfare of worshippers. Furthermore, I discuss some salient aspects of Han religious activities in the daily life of those outside of the ruling or administrative worlds. I focus on practices attached to the agricultural cycle, life cycle, and daily decision making, as well as ideas concerning ghosts, spirits, and life after death. From an analysis of the role of the intellectuals in popular religion, I find that religion was a force that cut across the entire society, adding, by the way, another layer of meaning to the term "popular religion."

I have not dealt with certain subjects pertaining to politics, social history, economics, and even intellectual developments. My excuse is twofold: on the one hand, these problems have already been widely treated by scholars East and West, and on the other hand, I believe it is legitimate and effective to concentrate on religious aspects by themselves. This is not to say that I am entirely justified in concentrating my study thus. Certainly, in the future, studies will have to broaden the field of early China's religion and provide an organic explanation that places the nature of and change in religious beliefs in the context of the above-mentioned areas of history.

The reader will notice that I introduce each chapter with some non-Chinese material. My intention is simple: to remind the reader that although we are dealing with the religious beliefs of China, the problems encountered in China are also human problems.

I am indebted to my former teachers at the Johns Hopkins University, Professors Hans Goedicke, Jerrold S. Cooper, and Delbert Hillers. They gave me a sound training in Near Eastern Studies so that I could have a firm grasp of the religions of some of other ancient cultures. I would also like to thank Professor Kwang-chih Chang of Harvard University for his encouragement and reading of the first draft of this book. Professor Benjamin Schwartz, also of Harvard, made some critical comments on parts of the manuscript; Drs. Howard L. Goodman, John Kieschnick, and Terry F. Kleeman provided detailed readings and corrections that improved my first and second drafts enormously. My colleagues at the Institute of History and Philology gave me numerous comments and suggestions at various stages of my research. Special thanks are due to E. J. Brill for granting me permission to incorporate part of my article published in *T'oung Pao* (1993) into this book. To my two daughters, Cindy and Sheila, I owe special thanks for their tolerance and for being happy and healthy all along. Finally, this task would be impossible without the spiritual, intellectual, and physical support of my dear wife Ping-chen, although my incompetence has prevented me from transforming all her wit and wisdom into written words. The inadequacies and errors that remain are therefore entirely mine.

Abbreviations

BIHP	*Bulletin of the Institute of History snd Philology*
BMFEA	*Bulletin of the Museum of Far Eastern Antiquities*
BSOAS	*Bulletin of the School of Oriental and African Studies*
CS	*Chin-shu* 晉書
HS	*Han-shu* 漢書
HHS	*Hou-Han-shu* 後漢書
HJAS	*Harvard Journal of Asiatic Studies*
JAOS	*Journal of American Oriental Society*
JAS	*Journal of Asian Studies*
KK	*K'ao-ku* 考古
KKHP	*K'ao-ku Hsüeh-pao* 考古學報
SC	*Shih-chi* 史記
SKC	*San-kuo-chih* 三國志
SKCS	*Ying-yin wen-yüan-ko ssu-k'u ch'üan-shu* 景印文淵閣 四庫全書
SPCKCP	*Ssu-pu ch'ung-k'an ch'u-pien* 四部叢刊初編
SPPY	*Ssu-pu pei-yao* 四部備要
WW	*Wen-wu* 文物

Chapter 1 ————————————————

Introduction

Toward a History of the Everyday, Personal Religion of Ancient China

Historians face one of their sternest challenges in the attempt to explain religions and beliefs. This is especially critical when dealing with ancient civilizations: how should religion and belief be defined, who were the participants, and what caused religious change? We often study the formation of religions by analyzing the political, social, economic, and intellectual background of the societies in which they arose. Major disorder and disintegration in social and ethical structures indeed contributed to the development of new religions. For example, the rise of so-called mystery religions during the Hellenistic period, religions that emphasized personal salvation, has been attributed to the disintegration of the city-state system, new hardships in everyday life, and the disappearance of the previous religions.[1]

In the case of China, the situation is further complicated because religious practice was bifurcated wherever it touched upon the central government, which maintained a tradition of imperial ritual programs, sacrifices, and worship whose main features were established, even before the Han (206 B.C. to 220 A.D.), by Ch'in Shih-huang-ti (the "First Emperor" of Ch'in dynasty). It is difficult to determine with certainty how cults and private beliefs outside the imperial court came to be, and which ones were approved, merely tolerated, or expunged by the court. Officialdom, especially during the Western Han period, changed its mind frequently about the underpinnings of its own programs of worship, as well as its relationship with noncourt worship. Furthermore, historians have yet to agree on exactly the relationship between nonofficials and their families (often called "the people," or "the peasantry and artisans") and the families of officials, who became increasingly aristocratic toward the end of Han. It is hard to tell which religious practices might have been universally vilified as vulgar and dangerous and which were deemed so but were nonetheless accepted. Conversely, it is hard to tell which ones spread out everywhere, so that we can state confidently that all under the sway of Chinese civilization participated in them.

Ancient China, into Han times and even later, was an active religious society, with personal religions and beliefs, an official religion, and innumerable links between the culture of royal power, writing, divination, ideas and ideology, art, and magic, on the one hand, and personal beliefs, on the other. This is all the more true in a society like China's, which had no separate priest class until the appearance of Buddhist and Taoist priest lineages in the fourth and fifth centuries A.D. Even then, the active and diffuse world of Chinese religions continued on, adopting and expanding.

Discussions of the religious developments in China of the late Han to Three Kingdoms era (roughly 150–250 A.D.) have generally focused on two factors. First is the combination of social and economic problems, including war, epidemic, and political breakdown; and second, the end of the monopoly of Confucian thought and the rise of Taoist, nihilist, and other intellectual trends. The first factor led to the desire among the common people for a new political dispensation; and the second factor urged the development of skepticism and extremism among the educated elite.[2]

Concerning the establishment of Buddhism in China slightly later in time, historians similarly explain that the turbulent situation of Chinese society created a perfect environment for the spread of a religion that offered the common people a way out of seemingly endless misery.[3] Some suggest that the early proponents of Buddhism attracted Chinese intellectuals by deliberately borrowing distinctly Chinese ideas, especially those from Taoist literature. Thus, it was easier for the Chinese to accept Buddhist ideas in a Chinese guise.[4] Studies on the rise of the Taoist religion, on the other hand, also stress the economic hardship and political struggle of the waning years of the Eastern Han.[5]

2

While these interpretations may all be valid to some degree, one factor remains. In any ancient society, the vicissitudes of ordinary life, from birth to death, and the interplay between natural and human environments already constituted a rich background for the development of religious beliefs. Thus M. P. Nilsson on the religious scene of the Hellenistic period: "The study of the syncretism of late antiquity . . . has concerned itself mainly with beliefs and doctrines, while the spiritual soil from which these growths arose and drew their nourishment has been touched on only in passing and in general terms; yet that is the heart of the matter, its weightiest element."[6] The motivations for the acceptance and development of a new religion (or religions) are found not only in grave social or intellectual crises or in doctrines, but also in the daily life of a stable and prosperous society.[7] By studying relatively "ordinary" factors, one reaches the basic stratum of the religious mentality of everyday, private life.[8] How else might we explain why in times of peace or prosperity religion still constituted an essential part of society, and how it persisted?

This book will examine such a religious mentality in ancient China. It is my contention that the most enduring substrate of religion in China, one that perhaps has tendrils and roots in certain ancient beliefs of the surrounding non-Chinese peoples, is the religion of personal welfare and personal access to mantic knowledge. The context in which this religion, or system of religion, was represented includes, on the material side, religious buildings such as temples and altars that were used for both nature deities and ancestors; funerary establishments, including tombs, funerary objects, tomb paintings, and artistic representations in numerous forms. On the behavioral side were various techniques involving magic, omens, and mantic divination, or prayers for the protection of the individual and family. Finally, we find written documents such as talismans and sacred writings and other texts describing ideas, ideologies, and practices concerning all the above.

These were widely distributed and are to be distinguished from court religious activity, which involved ritual programs of imperial authority and ancestor worship, as well as the textual precedents for them. It is to be assumed that when men of the court went to their homes and estates, they practiced not the imperial religion, whose precinct was narrowly defined, but the religious beliefs of everyday life, often involving their kin, guests, bonded and semifree workers, and the artisans and merchants with whom they came into contact. People of all walks of life, then, shared these general contexts of religious life and instantly recognized the religious goals of other individuals in society.

Important though it may be, a survey of the religious beliefs of everyday life from the beginnings of Chinese history until the end of the Han dynasty is not well represented in the existing scholarly literature.[9] Without such an understanding, any explanation of the successful spread of Buddhism and Taoism in the centuries after the Han, why both religions evolved the way they did, and why so-called popular religion in modern China assumed its present shape would lack a firm foundation. Taoism, as we know, evolved from various types of belief that can be traced to before the Ch'in. Its culmination in a distinct religion at the end of the Eastern Han was not only the result of a long historical development, but also the beginning of an enduring Taoist church; and both were intertwined with divergent elements of everyday religious life. Buddhism, on the other hand, did not enter a religious vacuum when it was first introduced into China. Its acceptance by all social groups depended more upon its ability to cope with various elements of the substrate religion than its theological arguments. It is clear, therefore, that a basic understanding of ancient Chinese religion is important not only for our understanding of the nature of ancient Chinese society, but also for a sound assessment of later religious phenomena. This is a challenging task, because almost all contemporary documents of the period are written by and for the social and governing elite. We are immediately confronted with the familiar problem of how to understand popular culture through texts that are essentially the product of the elite. We shall return to this question later in the chapter.

Similar problems are encountered in dealing with material evidence. For example, archaeological discoveries show that the Han elite often possessed funerary equipment similar to, although of better quality than, that of the nonelite. Does this mean that the elite shared with the wider community the religious ideas represented by the objects? How should one regard the religious ideas reflected in funerary paraphernalia? Should they be considered "popular" (or, of the people, or peasants), or are they "official/elite?" It is indeed difficult to isolate analytically an elite culture from a nonelite, or even "popular," culture.

4

Funerary equipment from rich tombs often represented a religious mentality that had little to do with Confucian ideas.[10] One doubts, of course, whether they can be considered "Confucianists." Yet if we admit that during the Han period Confucian values belonged mainly to the ruling, or administrative, elite who usually possessed the richer tombs, there is good reason to believe that many of the so-called Confucianists were influenced by a wide spectrum of religious mentality.[11] Thus, it is possible to approach the beliefs of the commoners by examining the culture of the elite. Furthermore, recent anthropological discussions on Chinese religion show that there was, or is, no simple division between "elite" and "popular" culture, or "great" and "little" traditions in Chinese society. The interaction between the "upper" and "lower" strata of culture presents a complex problem that should be studied carefully.[12] However, these works have not yet made a serious impact on the study of ancient China. Consequently, the notion of the everyday religion of personal welfare in ancient China still needs to be more subtly articulated.[13]

The present study is a historical investigation of broadly shared religious beliefs and goals in ancient China, from the earliest period to the end of Han. Methodologically, of course, it is practically impossible to conduct a purely descriptive investigation without exercising interpretations. It is expected that, in our inquiry into ancient religion, many questions will arise concerning the origin and nature of the beliefs, and many questions will probably remain unanswered or even unidentified. I have tried to investigate the various aspects of this religion of private life as outlined above. However, since there is no established model for such a history of religion in ancient China, this investigation must be a preliminary one both in the scope of the questions raised and the materials used.

Religion and Extra-human Powers: Working Definitions

First, we must formulate a working definition of "religion" in the proposed context. Then must come a definition of the term "personal welfare," which is at the center of our attention.

Despite a host of existing definitions,[14] the term "religion" is to be understood as referring to belief in the existence of extra-human powers.[15] These powers were seen as exerting upon man and society tangible outcomes concerning human and extra-human events. Under such a definition, extra-human agents, animate or inanimate, natural or supernatural, also exerted certain powers over individual human beings. This agency may have been something other than "the powers," such as royal ancestors, ghosts, or gods. It could also have referred to natural phenomena, although it is not clear if there were beliefs in agents of natural phenomena.

In denoting the central concern of religious belief, writers often use the term "supernatural," the efficacy of which has seldom been questioned. Occasionally, scholars have viewed this term as inadequate and substituted "superhuman. Religion, according to one, is "an institution consisting of culturally patterned interaction with culturally postulated superhuman beings."[16] The terms "culturally patterned" and "culturally postulated" are adequate to denote the nature of religious phenomena. There is also the attempt to avoid touching the nature or mode of existence of religious entities. Instead, the nature of religious action is emphasized: "Religion can be looked upon as an extension of the field of people's social relationships beyond the confines of purely human society . . . in which human beings involved see themselves in a dependent position vis-à-vis their non-human altars."[17] I prefer, however, to use the more modest term "extra-human," instead of "superhuman." "Supernatural" and "superhuman" both betray the world view, or conception, of the modern researcher and are inconclusive and cannot characterize the ancient Chinese contexts. I would argue that, in ancient China at least, the "powers" were recognized as something outside human beings. They were not necessarily "supernatural"—in the sense of "above" or "beyond" the natural world. They were not necessarily "superhuman" either—in the sense of having greater power than man. Some amounted to no more than minor irritations and were effectively checked with the performance of exorcistic acts. While both "supernatural" and "superhuman" entail the sense of "superior," "better," or "stronger," the term "extra-human" only refers to the sphere of existence of the powers without reference to their quality, strength, or nature. "Supernatural" or "superhuman" are terms that hardly find an equivalent in the vocabulary of ancient China. As long as the powers are recognized as extra-human and not to be found among "normal" animals, objects, or sociopolitical groups, they become the concern of man, and actions are to be taken to deal with them. As one scholar says: "Religious beliefs are present when non-human agencies are propitiated on the human model."[18] This is an interesting and important aspect of the Chinese religious experience. Having stated my position, however, I shall often use such terms as ghost, spirit, god, etc., in the following discussions as convenient variants.

Finally, we have the observable evidence of people's effort to express their recognition of and rapprochement with such powers. This, as we mentioned above, may include various kinds of communication, worship, or exorcism that involved magical, ritual, or ceremonial activities in public or private. The objective of all these was mainly personal welfare (that of the suppliant and/or his relatives), which was also a primary motivation for keeping worship and cults alive. In the context of ancient Chinese society, this meant every means that could lead to longevity and comfortable life and a well-provided death. I have, therefore, adopted a loose definition of religion that includes organized and rationalized establishments, as well as localized and unarticulated cults and beliefs. Our present interest, obviously, is mostly in the localized and unarticulated cults and beliefs. However, we should never lose sight of what the more rationalized system offered; thus, where appropriate, mention will be made as well of court religious complexes and ideologies.

The Popular-Religion Paradigm in Earlier Research and Theory

In this study, I prefer to develop a set of terms that will provide analytic room for the inclusion of types and categories, rather than to exclude. My premise is that the substrate of ancient Chinese religion took in members of all areas of economic and political life and a wide variety of elements of belief. The previous two generations of scholarship on Chinese religion, however, perceived the problem differently from the way pursued by modern writers, due mostly to the overwhelming revisions in our perception of early China resulting from archaeology. Before this sea change, the most prevalent way of looking at Chinese religious life posited a division into popular (or commoner) and official (or intellectual, elite, ruling) categories of belief and practice.

Our age is the age of "the people"—anything that can shed light on the laboring, nonelite people of the past is likely to be received with considerable interest. [To see how an ordinary person lived his life may be more interesting than exploring the intrigues of kings and politicians, or the speculations of philosophers.] Further, the religious faith of the ordinary people of another era may help us gain insight into the nature of our own beliefs. "Popular religion," in this perspective, has come to mean the religious beliefs of the common people. Yet the term also arouses suspicion, since it is doubtful that a historian can reach the souls of the commoners of a past era. For, by definition or by common sense, the term "commoners" usually refers to people who were ignored by the educated, ruling ranks of society, and who are often also ignored as subjects of modern scholarship because of the lack of written documents concerning their own thoughts and activities.[19] For the more recent past, this is not too great a problem. Anthropologists, by direct participation and personal communication, describe how the people of a given society live their religious life. Work on "popular religion" in China so far has been done mostly by anthropologists concentrating on modern Chinese society.[20] For the remote past, historians of religion are only beginning to explore the possibility of depicting an outline of the religious life outside the imperial court. For example, Valerie Hansen examines the changing images and status of local pantheons in medieval China.[21] Stephen Teiser explains the circuitous ways in which a Buddhist scripture intermingled with popular beliefs and festivals.[22]

Not only do we doubt even the possibility of studying the religion of commoners, the term "popular religion" itself provokes further questions. "Popular" connotes a relatively wide basis among the total populace, but it does not necessarily imply that only the lower echelon of society was concerned or affected. "Popular religion," therefore, seems to carry an inherent ambiguity concerning the social constitution of the worshipers. If, on the other hand, we define "official religion" as those religious beliefs or doctrines that received the recognition and formal protection, or promotion, of secular rulership, what is the essence of this official religion, and what is its relationship with popular religion? Stephan Feuchtwang maintains that popular religion "is of the common people in the one sense that it contains a crucial relation, a political relation, to official religion and to other claimants to control and therefore orthodoxy in China."[23] This points out the political nature of the relationship between official and popular religions. The question is, are the two different in structure, content, cosmology; different in the relationship between the worshippers and the deities; or simply different in their constituents? Finally, are the terms "official" and "popular" appropriate enough for the investigation of religion?[24] As analytical tools in approaching the subject, these terms may cause difficulty. For what is "popular" might not be confined to non-elite laboring or mercantile people. Moreover, it is unlikely that the non-elite were ignorant of official doctrine. In this study, therefore, I will employ such terms as "popular," "commoner," "the people," or "folk," but only do so for convenience.

To use "popular religion," and oppose it to "official religion," then, admits a basic assumption that for analysis it is possible and useful to divide a culture into two or more strata. Here we enter the often traveled yet still thorny road of "great and little traditions." After Redfield's exposition of the concept of the "great tradition" versus "little tradition,"[25] many scholars in the human sciences used it in various contexts in one way or another. Redfield held that the so-called great tradition was created by the elite who consciously and actively passed it on to their successors. The little tradition, on the other hand, was the culture generally accepted and preserved by the people unwittingly, the so-called peasant culture in a traditional peasant society. While this was not an uncommon concept, Redfield did not dwell on a simple bifurcation of culture and society. Instead, he noticed that in traditional peasant societies, China included, the great and little traditions overlapped and gave rise to mutual influences. This acknowledged the complexity of cultural reality and the provisional nature of the concept as an analytical tool.

Although Redfield presented his theory with reservation, the interpretive power of the "great and little" concept was so attractive that, in a number of subsequent studies on the culture or religion of China, the paradigm of "two traditions" was sometimes carried to the extreme.[26] The religion of the elite was considered far removed, or even very different, from that of the populace.[27] Even some modern Chinese intellectuals share the view that in traditional China the rational literati had no need of religion, while the ignorant populace were blinded by superstition.[28]

Long before Redfield, however, scholars had presented different views on the relationship between the elite and the popular in Chinese religion. Marcel Granet, one of the pioneers in this area, repeatedly expounded his view that the elite culture of ancient China was nourished by, and ultimately derived from, popular religion.[29] Granet's view, despite some valuable insight into the meaning of early Chinese poetry, has since been criticized as giving free rein to imagination.[30] Sifting through the ancient literature and drawing on modern ethnology, Granet claimed to have discovered traces of ancient popular religion, such as the primitive rite of sexual union, in the poems of *Shih-ching* or *Book of Poetry*, traditionally dated to the Western Chou period (c. 1045–841 B.C.).[31] He believed that the poems were originally records of such festival rites and songs, a hypothesis that led to his "popular to elite" theory of the development of Chinese culture. In some respect, his view is similar to the Chinese traditional view that a portion of the poems was collected from the countryside by officials to serve as admonitions to the court. However true this may have been, the act of collection was a conscious political strategy, thus the poems collected could hardly have exerted any significant influence in the development of the established elite culture. This is not to say that court rituals were totally unrelated to folk religion: some may have reflected ancient and already forgotten religious customs. The subsequent political uses and twists of the original meaning of the poems in *Shih-ching*,[32] however, only demonstrate that the ancient "popular culture" as represented there did not really become the foundation of elite culture in the way Granet suggested. That Granet was unable to use the crucial evidence provided by the oracle bone inscriptions and Shang bronze art was also a major drawback for his theory.

An older contemporary of Granet, the Dutch sinologist de Groot, also contributed a major work on the religion of China. In contrast to Granet, he started by collecting materials on beliefs and customs among the non-elite in contemporary southeastern China, i.e., Fukien, in the late nineteenth century. He then compared his findings with ancient texts and concluded that there was little change from the ancients to the moderns.[33] His main assessment of Chinese culture in general and religion in particular was that they were static—devoid of innovations and improvements since the ancient time. Despite the wide spectrum of his effort in collecting relevant materials, de Groot's study was marred by a prejudice against Chinese religion and society, as well as methodological deficiencies.[34] Both Granet and de Groot shared a common assumption: the development of Chinese culture and religion was essentially one-directional, either from elite to popular or from popular to elite.

In reviewing the method and theories of Granet and de Groot, Freedman proposed that peasant culture and elite culture were not two different things, but represent "two versions of one religion that we see as idiomatic translations of each other."[35] This is to say that the basic unity of Chinese culture does not come from a single historical origin or a single social stratum, but from a general system of religious ideas, which developed through continuous exchanges of ideas and customs between elite and non-elite. Freedman did not, however, elaborate how this development came about historically.

In this connection, Benjamin Schwartz, when discussing the ideas of ancient Chinese philosophy, touched upon the problem of "popular culture" from another angle. Although he admits that there were basic similarities between the popular and elite culture, "out of the same broad Neolithic matrix" the later development of the two diverged in crucial ways. Further, the relationship between non-elite and elite is not "an unproblematic 'parallelism' of two versions of the same culture but a constant dynamic interaction involving both mutual influence and mutual tension between at least partially separate realms."[36] He further elaborated on this point by discussing the absorption of *yin-yang* and Five Phases theories into non-elite religion.[37]

Recognizing the mutual influence of the popular and the elite, and trying to demonstrate their complex relationship, David Johnson formulated a kind of grid system by dividing the people of late-imperial China into nine social-cultural groups. He uses literary/educational and political/economic statuses as criteria, with the legally privileged literate group representing the high-elite culture, the illiterate/dependent group representing low culture, and others in between of varying statuses.[38] While somewhat mechanical, Johnson's model helps us see the complex image of Chinese culture.[39]

The complex nature of popular culture and religion is made explicit in a recent study of the local cults of modern China. Jordan and Overmyer point out that Chinese popular culture presents both unifying and divergent aspects. Because of the vastness of China, people of different areas have tended to have different cult practices. Yet through historical as well as political forces, divergent local customs have also shared basic ideas and cultural values. Popular culture, at least in the case of China, was itself a congregation of many different, small, regional cultural circles. The interaction between the popular and the elite depends upon some intermediate elements such as secret religious sects, which, transmitting the ideals of the elite to the common folk, also transform and unify the beliefs and values of the local society into a new social organization.[40] To take another example, Stephen Teiser's study of the ghost festival of medieval China shows how the festival, as well as ideas of hell and salvation, were received by the non-elite, Buddhists, and educated writers of differing perspective, and yet constituting a unified system.[41] This demonstrates the inherent mixture of groups and statuses in the cultural reality. While nonofficials were, by and large, set off legally and socially from officials, they met culturally. Furthermore, to be Buddhist cut across several cultural lines.

The theme of "unity" versus "diversity" was further explored by Robert P. Weller in his study of the Taiwanese ghost festival.[42] While criticizing Weber's characterization of Chinese religions as "traditional" and "rational" for being too simplistic,[43] Weller proposes two different styles of interpretation that he argues existed in non-elite religion: ideologized interpretations, i.e., religion understood in an institutionalized and explicit ideology; and pragmatic interpretations, i.e., less explicit and less tied to specific institutions, and more concerned with everyday social relations. Although still carrying the Weberian imprint of "traditional (pragmatic)" and "rational (ideologized)," Weller breaks away from Weber by emphasizing "the flexibility of interpretation as people remake their religion in changing social conditions," therefore the ideologized and pragmatic interpretations are not mutually exclusive but only "two ways of giving meaning to experience."[44] This observation, one may add, is on the whole in accord with C. K. Yang's proposal concerning "diffused" and "institutional."[45]

Steven Sangren explores a theoretical basis for the holistic under-

standing of Chinese religion. In a study of a local community in contemporary Taiwan, he observed that

> [N]o given supernatural entity means the same thing all the
> time; the nature of its power and meaning depends upon the
> ritual context in which it is addressed, who is worshiping it, in
> what role the worshipper addresses it (as individual, officeholder,
> member of a family or community, and so forth), and with what
> other supernatural entities it is being implicitly or explicitly con-
> trasted.[46]

As will be demonstrated in the following discussions, this observation is particularly relevant to understanding the nature of the religion of the common people in ancient China.

In summary, the political, social, or economic status of a person,
although important, was not necessarily the decisive factor governing his religious beliefs and practices. It follows that members of the
ruling elite could still be believers within the religious system of personal welfare and access to mantic knowledge.[47] Official religion, as I
understand it, is what the ruling class formally announced or practiced as the cult of the state, with a system of cosmology and moral
ethics derived from it. Its purpose was mainly for effecting authority
and for maintaining the orderliness of the state and its subjects. The
vast system of personal religion, on the other hand, had a more direct
bearing upon people's lives; the practical benefit of religion to the
individual was invariably a central concern.[48] The difference between
the official and the nonoffical might even have existed not in basic
cosmology, but rather in the nature of the physical precincts and the
secular problems that concerned each of them. We cannot even be
sure about a distinction based entirely on the content of a religious
element, such as the ideas of ghosts and spirits or the act of ancestor
worship. Rather, it is people's attitudes and goals, as occasionally recorded, or as deduced, that give us subtler clues.[49] Thus, a religious
system could have more than one aspect. As E. Zürcher points out,
Eastern Han Buddhism could be described as having three sectors: a
hybrid cult centered upon the court and the imperial family; the first
nucleus of "canonical" monastic Buddhism; the diffuse and unsystematic adoption of Buddhist elements in indigenous beliefs and cults.[50]

This understanding is an important principle in our study of the world of personal religion in ancient China.

The Sources

Rich archaeological discoveries in the past half-century have provided us with numerous details of the material culture of ancient China.[51] Among these finds, tombs are by far the most frequently encountered kind of evidence. The persistent practice of inhumation provides a basic reference for the belief in certain types of existence after death. Furthermore, the change in burial customs, including the funerary objects and tomb styles, throughout the long period studied here provides us with important clues concerning the change in people's conceptions of death and the afterlife.

The significance of archaeological evidence, therefore, can be weighed in two ways. First, individual finds may be employed to illustrate a specific point concerning the religious belief of the people. Statues of monsters or protective demons found in many Ch'u tombs of the late Warring States period, for example, may be used to indicate a belief that evil spirits attacked tombs. The wall paintings and reliefs found in Han-era tombs, to give another example, are relevant to the conception of the netherworld.

Second, the long-term development or change of cultural styles may be used to illustrate a more subtle shift in people's overall conception about the netherworld, and men's fate after death. For example, the shift from vertical-shaft wooden-casket tombs to horizontal brick tombs, a change that started sometime during the late Warring States period and continued throughout the Han dynasty, may be seen as a material manifestation of a corresponding change in the conception of the actual layout of the netherworld. As I argue later, when it became clear that this netherworld was similar to the world of the living, there was a corresponding increase in people's desire to create for the deceased an environment closer to the world of the living.[52]

An inevitable question in this regard is how to determine what kind of archaeological finds can reflect popular beliefs. First, we need to differentiate at each instance between the archaeological context—whether the object was found in the tomb of a commoner or nobleman, which sometimes is guesswork—and, second, the sociological significance an object or a tomb style carries. We cannot automatically assume that everything found in a rich tomb necessarily reflects the ideology of the elite or ruling class.

The same attitude is also our principle in using literary or inscriptional evidence. Traditional texts such as the Five Classics, the *Tso-chuan* 左傳 and *Kuo-yü* 國語, the works of the Confucianists and other thinkers of the Warring States period, or the histories and essays of Han savants, are doubtless the product of the elites. What they have recorded, however, contains not only philosophical treatises and literary inventions, but also reflections of the feelings and beliefs of a wider population. This latter function of their writings is often not an intended purpose, but is nevertheless marked with the imprint of their time and culture. My reading of these traditional texts, therefore, aims not at reworking the refined arguments about the nature of the Confucian idea of humanity, nor at reconstructing the cosmological structure of the Han scholars, but at discovering those unintentional implications of their statements that pertain to the life and experience of the populace at large. What the elite ridiculed in expounding their ideas is often illuminating for the understanding of beliefs. It is up to the researcher to determine at each instance whether a statement carries such unintentional meanings. He must, however, always be skeptical of recorded thought, even when it is a person's opinion about his or other's beliefs. He must make quite clear whether he is describing something he believes to have been false or cynically manipulated, or something that seems to have been true. He must try his best to determine which speaker in a text is the cynical one and which were innocent believers, if in fact such parties can be differentiated.[53]

Some of the newly discovered texts, such as the daybooks (i.e., almanacs, *jih-shu* 日書) from Shui-hu-ti, or the "Fifty-two Recipes" *wu-shih-erh ping-fang* 五十二病方 from the tomb of Ma-wang-tui, since they treat mundane subjects, seem to bear closer relations with the private life of people.[54] The tombs of Ma-wang-tui or Shui-hu-ti certainly belong to the "ruling class," although the actual statuses of the tomb owners vary. The religious beliefs represented in these texts, however, seem to reveal the characteristics of those of a wider populace. This aspect of textual evaluation constitutes a challenge. Other texts found in Han tombs, such as the "tomb quelling texts," which reveal more directly the popular conception of the afterlife, are also invaluable source materials for our understanding of religion in ancient China.

With a concern for the religious experience of the commoners, and with a special eye on the available evidence, we begin our search for a new page in the history of Chinese religion.

Chapter 2 ───────────────────────

Roots of a Religion of Personal Welfare

Although most men affirm that there are gods, still a few do deny
their existence. . . . And among those who affirm the existence of
gods some believe in the gods of their ancestors, others in those
which have been fashioned to fit the dogmatic systems of philosophy. . . . Accordingly even the rank and file of people differ likewise,
some insisting that there is one god, others that there are many,
differing in shape, so that they even fall into the superstitions of the
Egyptians, who think of the gods as long-faced, hawk-shaped, or
cows and crocodiles and whatever else [strikes their fancy].[1]

Prelude

Inquiries into the religious beliefs of prehistoric people, East and West,
tend to operate under unspoken assumptions. While "primitive" tribes
in any era are without the necessary arts for bearing witness to their
beliefs, ancient civilizations, having the art of writing, provide us with
clues to religion in pre-literate periods. In sketching the shape of prehistoric religion through literary documents, scholars often project
later beliefs into earlier periods. In late-prehistoric Egypt, for example,
the dead were often buried with their faces toward the west.[2] Much
later, Egyptian religion considered the west as the abode of the dead,
and this notion was placed into the service of the early practice.[3] On

the other hand, we know of prehistoric burials in which the dead face other directions.[4] The west, furthermore, was not the only destination of deceased Egyptians.[5] Thus, without concrete evidence it is not entirely correct to suggest that a connection exists between burial positions and a specific religious belief. On the Chinese side, a similar argument has been advanced to explain the burial positions at the Pan-p'o neolithic cemetery of the Yang-shao period.[6] Since the majority of the dead in this cemetery are placed with heads toward the west, scholars have suggested that there was a belief in the west as the destination of the deceased.[7] In other late-neolithic cemeteries, however, the directions of the graves follow different patterns. Hence, the most one can deduce from the evidence is the existence of an apparently uniform burial custom within each particular cemetery.[8] In any case, the later ideal from Confucian classical writing that "burial should be northwards facing; such was the proper ritual of the Three Dynasties,"[9] had not taken form at this time. Clear evidence for the idea of a western land of the dead does not seem to have existed in China before the coming of Buddhism.

[If burial positions tell us only very little about the beliefs of the neolithic inhabitants of China, funerary objects provide a better indication.]An idea that the soul, or spirit, existed after death caused funerary objects to be placed in graves out of reverence or sympathy for the deceased. At least this is what scholars have understood about prehistoric peoples. The urn-burials of the Yang-shao period, for example, have been explained by archaeologists as evidence of the belief in souls. It has been suggested that the small hole found on the urn was made for the purpose of allowing the soul to pass through.[10] The only support of this view is the aforementioned belief in the existence of a primitive idea of soul. Yet the explanation tells us very little:[the hole in the urn does not prove the existence of an idea of soul; it is merely a modern preconception] At best it is wishful thinking: one builds a simple and direct connection between a hypothetical idea of soul and a factual hole in the urn. Another example is that of the red pigment often found on the bones in prehistoric burials; it has been explained as evidence of a symbolic act concerning the soul or possibly the resurrection of the dead.[11] Admitting the existence of the ideas of soul, spirit, or life after death, however, we still do not really know the details of such ideas, much less of any difference among various social groups.

Fig. 2.1 Neolithic pottery drawing.

The fish and bird decorations on Yang-shao pottery (Fig. 2.1) provide room for speculation.[12] On the assumption that primitive artistic motifs are seldom purely decorative, these motifs are explained by some as the symbols of totems.[13] Although the fish symbolized abundance, fertility, or even erotic love in the literature of later eras,[14] it is unlikely that it was ever an important totemic animal in ancient China. Birds, especially the *feng* and *huang*, seem to have been quite prominent in later mythological traditions.[15] Yet considering the fact that among the numerous Yang-shao painted pots, only a relatively few have such designs as fish, birds, or the hybrid animal with a human face,[16] while the vast majority contain geometric patterns, there is no compelling reason to assume that such animal or hybrid designs could have represented a prevailing tradition. It is more probable that they were the product of experimentive craftsmen. To connect these decorations to later myths renders no further help in the understanding of the religious beliefs of ordinary people.

The situation becomes different for the late-neolithic period, especially the Liang-chu (c. 2800–1900 B.C.) and Ta-wen-k'ou (c. 3900–2200 B.C.)

Fig. 2.2 Neolithic jade incisions from Liang-chu.

cultures. On some jade objects (mainly *pi* 璧 and *ts'ung* 琮) and pottery there are a number of inscribed signs with bird or sun-bird motifs (Fig. 2.2). If these signs can be explained as evidence of bird and sun worship in the Eastern Yi 東夷 culture and can be connected with traditions preserved in later documents and art objects since the Eastern Chou period, we may have some concrete evidence of religious expressions.[17]

A similar case could be advanced concerning dragon decorations of the late-neolithic Hung-shan (4000–3000 B.C.) culture in the northeastern province of Liaoning. On both artistic and epigraphic grounds, the dragon design from this culture is seen as having a strong affinity with the later dragon motif of the Shang period.[18] This suggests that aspects of dragon worship in the later era may have existed earlier.[19]

Dragon

20

It remains, however, only a possibility, as the distance in time and space between Hung-shan culture and Shang is very great.

The existence of altars and possibly female cult statues in the Hung-shan sites, on the other hand, certainly indicates an elaborate religious cult.[20] Unlike the dragon motif, however, this cult—a so-called "fertility cult"—can hardly find a descendant in the later period. One author explains the function of the altar as the original "*she* 社," the center of a fertility cult. The argument tries to connect a theory of "primitive cult" to later documents simply by juxtaposition.[21] We are once more left with an empty label—"fertility cult"—without any idea of its actual contents.

Meanwhile, at the Yang-shao site of P'u-yang, mosaic dragon and tiger figures made of shells have been found in a burial site.[22] The scale of the burial suggests that the deceased was of a high social status, and that the dragon and tiger figures must have had important symbolic or religious meaning. Compared with the Hung-shan dragon, the shape of the P'u-yang dragon is closer to the traditional image, with feet and claws.

Both the Hung-shan and the P'u-yang dragons, like the bird and sun motifs on Liang-chu jade objects, are associated with the more powerful members of society. The geographical distance between the two sites suggests that the use of the dragon was widespread. If one assumes that these dragons were similar in symbolic or religious meaning, then it may be the case that the dragon was significant in an area stretching from northeast to southeast China, although there is no way to tell if people actually worshipped it.

One of the more interesting interpretations concerning the P'u-yang mosaic animal figures is provided by K. C. Chang, who suggests that they represent the sacred animals that the *wu*-shaman, i.e., the tomb owner, employed during his ritual ascension to heaven, or when he travelled to the world of the dead.[23] This interpretation assumes that a shamanistic religion already existed in China during the neolithic period.[24] Other evidence from the Yang-shao period, such as an androgynous relief figure on a vase,[25] a "skeletal drawing" of a human figure on a bowl,[26] and a ground painting showing what appears to be shamans performing funerary rituals,[27] are all explained as expressions of different aspects of shamanistic religious activities or ideas.[28]

There are of course other kinds of explanation. For example, one of the rock paintings found in Shih-tzu-t'an, Shansi province, has been explained as a shamaness performing a ritual, while another painting represents a kind of agricultural fertility ceremony.[29] It should be made clear, however, that this "fertility cult" and similar explanations are based mainly upon the assumptions of the researchers, first, concerning what prehistorical fertility cults might have looked like; and second, that the paintings should be explained as religious. Unlike the evidence for shamanistic activities, the explanations that these were fertility cults do not have the support of later or cross-cultural evidence.

In connection with the argument that shamanism existed in the Yang-shao period, K. C. Chang further suggests that the jade *ts'ung* and similar objects found in the burials of the Lung-shan cultures, especially that of Liang-chu in Kiangsu and T'ao-ssu in Shansi, were evidence of shamanic tools employed in ritual performances.[30] Chang's argument provides a consistent explanation of the existence of shamanism from the Yang-shao to the Lung-shan period. This explanation logically extends to the Shang period, when shamanism is documented by abundant evidence, as we shall see below.

Given the possible existence of shamanism and other religious elements, such as ancestor worship in the Lung-shan period[31] and the worship of bird, or sun-bird, it is difficult for us to discern any differentiation of religious beliefs among social groups in the neolithic period. The burials of this period, to be sure, present examples of "rich" as well as "poor" grave goods, indicating the appearance of differentiated social strata.[32] Whether they also imply any difference in beliefs, on the other hand, is impossible to determine. Since the burials differ only in the degree of material richness, not in fundamental conception and structure, it stands to reason that we may assume a more or less homogeneous religious belief among the rich and the poor in society. Despite the fact that several culture centers are postulated for neolithic China,[33] this observation seems to reflect a general situation that is less affected by cultural or geographical differences.

It is noteworthy, however, that although religious belief in a given culture sphere might have been homogeneous, the development of a stratified society and the concentration of wealth and power in the hands of fewer and fewer people also imply a concentration of religious authority. As the Liang-chu burials suggest, the concentration of jade objects in large tombs probably meant that the tomb owners were political as well as religious leaders.[34] Thus, the basically homogeneous religious culture began to differentiate into two strata: the religion of the power-holders, and the religion of the common people. The difference lay not so much in the substance or nature of beliefs, but in the authority necessary for access to the divine world. Those with such authority began to construct ever more complicated rituals and paraphernalia, affordable only by the political elite. Although based on conceptions of the earlier period, the culture of the elite, by virtue of its extravagance and visibility, became the focus of attention in society, and, subsequently, became the primary evidence for use in modern scholarly research. Evidence of the religious expression of commoners, on the other hand, surfaced only in later eras.

The Religion of the Shang People

Archaeological evidence

The era of Shang rule in ancient China was the first to leave behind a body of documentation. Thus, Shang culture has been intensively studied.[35] The religion of the Shang people has received special attention, not least because most of the written documents are religious in nature.[36] A widely accepted view of Shang religion is that it can be characterized as a belief built mainly upon nature and ancestor worship, perhaps reflecting a lengthy extant tradition. According to this view, a Supreme Lord, Ti 帝, presided over the royal ancestors and such gods of nature as Wind, Rain, River, and Mountain. Ti, together with the lesser gods and ancestor spirits, was responsible for the welfare of the Shang rulers and subjects.[37]

Scholars also stress the deeply political as well as bureaucratic nature of this religion. As David N. Keightley points out, the "worship of the Shang ancestors . . . provided powerful psychological and ideological support for the political dominance of the Shang kings."[38] K. C. Chang, on the other hand, emphasizes the monopoly of the ruling class over the means of communication with the divine sphere and therefore the means of political control over the people.[39] The Shang king, according to Chang, was at the same time an arch-shaman (*wu*

巫) who possessed special skills (divination) and instruments (jade *ts'ung* and bronze vessels) in order to communicate with the royal ancestors, the gods, and the Supreme Lord.[40]

The view that the king-shaman was the intermediate agent between the divine and the secular finds evidence in part in the decorative motifs on bronze vessels. A typical motif, the so-called *t'ao-t'ieh* 饕餮 design, is generally considered to be a stylized animal figure. According to Chang, they represent the sacred animals that the shamans employed as mediators or transportation aids in their ritual ascendance to the divine world.[41] To be more specific, he suggests, based on evidence from the aforementioned P'u-yang burials, that the shaman's sacred animals were dragons, tigers, and deer, much like the three animals (*chiao* 蹻) associated with the *wu*-shamans and immortals in the much later Taoist tradition.[42]

Although Chang's theory is plausible, since iconographic evidence from the Warring States period indicates that the idea of humans riding dragons was not uncommon,[43] it contains difficulties. For one thing, it is unclear whether the Warring State dragon-riding figure that Chang refers to can be identified as a shaman. Second, as David Keightley argues, according to the oracle inscriptions themselves, the Shang ruler was not shown ascending heaven during the ritual as were shamans.[44] A third theory, while endorsing Chang's view that the king could communicate with heaven, emphasizes that the most direct and obvious way was for him (or a specialist) to observe the heavenly bodies and decipher their meanings. This is corroborated by the fact that special posts for persons with astrological knowledge were among the most important government institutions in early China.[45]

Jordan Paper accepts the possibility that the *t'ao-t'ieh* design represents serpents or dragons and that shamanic concepts constituted a part of Shang religion, but he concludes that the design depicted a kind of mask-helmet showing the upper part of an animal face.[46] Since the bronze vessels functioned as food containers, Paper claims that the designs on the vessels would have been related to ritual offerings to the ancestors and gods. As Paper puts it, "The horned mask of power combined with the ascending serpent or dragon figure graphically represents the function of the vessels to deliver food to the ancestral spirits, and in part represents the chief sacrificer, the Shang king himself."[47] Although the mask might have possessed such a religious

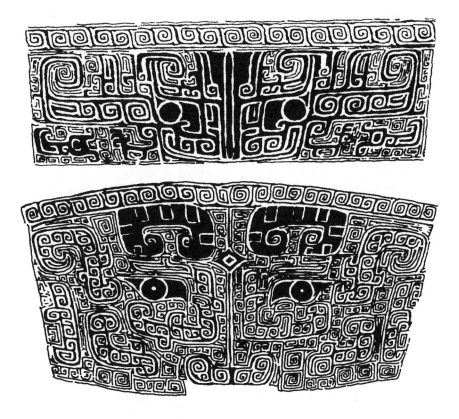

Fig. 2.3 Shang bronze decorative patterns.

function as a tool in shamanistic ceremony,[48] it is arguable whether the mask could have been the origin of the *t'ao-t'ieh* design, and not vice versa. For example, Li Xueqin maintains that a close relationship existed between the *t'ao-t'ieh* and the animal face decorations found on Liang-chu jades.[49] Indeed, modern scholarship has still not determined whether the term *t'ao-t'ieh* and its related myths can be identified with cast-bronze animal designs and thereby help to explain the function of the bronzes.[50] Yet there is no doubt that the bronze vessels and designs (Fig. 2.3) were important in Shang official religion.[51]

It is worth noting that although its meaning and origin are still a subject of debate, by the end of Shang the *t'ao-t'ieh* design had become adopted as a decorative motif on a wide variety of bronze objects. These objects were apparently distributed in a wide area and produced in places other than the central Shang state,[52] such as the predynastic Chou or the eastern state of Po-ku.[53] Thus, regardless of the religious or ritual significance it may have possessed, there is no compelling reason to see every bronze vessel and the decoration on it as having had ritual efficacy. It is perhaps more reasonable in many instances to see the animal designs as simply decorative conventions that befit the status of the owner. On the other hand, it seems to be an overstatement to deny that there is any religious or cosmological significance whatever to them, as Max Loehr once did.[54] A similar situation can be found in ancient Egyptian temple reliefs, which usually represent rituals performed in the temples on various occasions.[55] In the same way, it would be inaccurate to say that *every* scene on the wall must represent a ritual actually performed. There is ample evidence suggesting that many scenes served merely as decorations—decorations, however, with religious and symbolic connotations.[56]

If the bronze vessels and their designs were indeed part of the religious ritual paraphernalia of the Shang ruling class, one is tempted to ask whether we can find similar animal motifs on the objects that belonged to less privileged people, e.g., on everyday pottery. So far the *t'ao-t'ieh* designs have been found mostly on the so-called white-clay pottery, which is usually of meticulous workmanship, suggesting a relatively high social status of the owner.[57] Only rarely are animal or *t'ao-t'ieh* style decorations found on the more common gray-clay pottery.[58] On the crude pottery found in the poorer tombs, decorations are usually made with simple cord impressions or geometric lines. It seems, therefore, that the animal designs such as *t'ao-t'ieh* were used mainly, if not exclusively, on objects that belonged to the royal house or the nobility. Is it reasonable to assume, then, that the religious ideas embodied in the *t'ao-t'ieh* design were not part of the religion of the common people? There is no way either to prove or disprove this argument.

In view of the above, the archaeological evidence for popular beliefs in the Shang is rather inconclusive. This, however, does not preclude making a hypothesis. If we admit that the creation of bronze artifacts was at the hands of craftsmen, and that the importance of the bronzes in religious settings was based on a socially agreed assumption concerning the efficacy of rituals and symbols, there seems to be no compelling reason not to conclude that non-elite shared with the ruling elite a similar religious mentality. As Kesner suggests, the t'ao-t'ieh design might have had different meanings for beholders from different social strata, and its meaning might have changed and developed as Shang civilization grew.[59]

Inscriptional evidence

The use of animal bones for divination started no later than the Lungshan period, and maybe as early as the Yang-shao period.[60] There is no evidence by which to assume that the practice was confined to the ruling class. Discoveries of uninscribed but ritually used oracle bones in areas outside the royal capital indicate that during the Shang such a divination method could have been used by non-royalty.[61] In fact, according to the custom of Shang divination it was not necessary to have inscriptions made on the bones and tortoise shells after each completed divination.[62] The uninscribed oracle bones in and outside the capital most likely indicate less important divinational acts related to the lives of less important people.[63] In the Shang site at Chengchou, for example, uninscribed bones were found in the residential area, which could have been used by nonroyal families.[64] Since the authority of this divinational method was unequivocal, this implies that the religious beliefs represented in the act of divination were shared by the Shang royal elite and the nonroyalty. Otherwise, the political claim of the ruler based on the result of divination would have been weakened. However, since we have no actual example of oracle inscriptions outside the royal household,[65] with the exception of the pre-Chou inscriptions,[66] we can only speculate that the religious beliefs of the common people shared aspects of those of the rulers.

What, then, can we say about those religious beliefs? Obviously, the basic assumption was that man could communicate with extra-human powers. Leaving aside the royal ancestors, who were once human, the nature of the extra-human powers, as revealed in the oracle-bone inscriptions, can be described as sometimes multi-functional, but in general scarcely more than functional. Thus, the rain-god was responsible for sending rain, and the wind-god for sending winds, and so forth.[67] Beyond this, however, there exists little indication of individual characteristics or personalities.

As for the abode of the deities and ancestors, K. C. Chang has suggested that "in the worldview of the Shang people, the difference between the world of deities and the world of ancestors is almost negligible."[68] Moreover, in the inscriptions one senses that the diviner addressed the deities, or ancestors, as if they were immediately accessible. In fact, since man believed so firmly that the deities and ancestors actually extended care and power to the propitiator directly, the world of extra-human powers in the conception of the Shang diviners should be seen as having been either conterminous with the human world or a continuous extension of it. The concept of a "supernatural world," as well as the term itself, was probably foreign to the Shang mentality.[69]

A person's relationship with the powers, moreover, can be described as *do ut des*. The purpose of the communication was mainly for worldly affairs—to solve various practical problems such as war, harvest, sickness, hunting, or to interpret natural disasters and portentous astronomical events that were thought to have grave consequences for human society.[70] There are no tender feelings expressed in the oracle-bone inscriptions. Everything is businesslike. There is, moreover, no problem of morality. The communication between man and the extra-human powers does not, at least on the surface, entail any moral or ethical qualifications. One does not ask, for example, if a certain disaster was connected with one's moral or political behavior. This observation, however, should not lead to the conclusion that there was no piety toward the deities among the Shang people. The nature of the oracle-bone inscriptions was that they were pragmatic records of divination that did not express personal aspects of men's relationships with deities and ancestor spirits.

Besides communicating with the extra-human powers, the oracles also probed the course of future events. The basic belief for the efficacy of divination can be shown by the following assumptions :

1. The fate of human beings was inseparable from the extra-human world;

2. The relationship between the fate of human beings and the extra-human world could be revealed by certain concrete (natural phenomena) or abstract (time, numbers) entities;

3.   Therefore human being's fate and future events were know-
able by learning to read the concrete or abstract signs;

4.   Therefore people could try to change their fate before it happened.

The fundamental belief of all these, that the fate of man is inseparable from the extra-human world, logically leads to the idea that it is
possible to know man's fate and future events by observing the phenomena of the world. Thus it was natural for the king to divine for
the harvest of the coming year, or the catch of the next hunt, among
other subjects.[71] While the kings may have been interested in predicting wars or harvests, the commoners surely would have been eager to
gain similar messages, although perhaps for events on a smaller scale.
This underlying assumption, when we examine evidence from a later
era, remains central in Chinese popular beliefs.

In sum, the oracle-bone inscriptions yield only part of the religious
belief of the Shang people; we have no evidence concerning other religious activities, wherein different aspects of piety might be expressed.[72]
There is, moreover, no evidence as to whether, or how, people would
react when the oracles failed.

The Religion of the Chou People

The animal designs on bronze vessels underwent stylistic changes
from the Shang dynasty to the Warring States period. Most of all, the
stereotyped t'ao-t'ieh gradually became firmly stylized, while a certain realism began.[73] This new realistic style, according to K. C. Chang,
signified an attitude toward the once-sacred animals that no longer
represented reverence.[74] This change in style is symptomatic of the
declining importance of the "shaman culture," a trend with its roots
in the development of the humanistic spirit as well as the changing
ideology of the Chou court concerning the nature of Shang-ti and
"heaven."[75] The general line of argument for this view is as follows.
In order to legitimize religiously as well as politically the displace-
ment of the Shang, the Chou ruling class transformed the Shang idea
of Shang-ti 上帝, or Ti 帝, who, although considered as the Supreme
Lord, was actually more of a figurehead than one who commanded

great reverence,[76] into a supreme deity, known as *t'ien* 天, "Heaven." The deity exercised arbitration over the fate of the people, not whimsically but according to a moral standard.[77] The Chou replaced the Shang precisely because the Shang had violated the moral standard of T'ien, so that the Mandate of Heaven (*t'ien-ming* 天命) was transferred to the Chou.[78]

It is worth mentioning, however, that a change in the conception of heaven from an amoral natural entity to a moral deity, if such was the case, did not came about suddenly. The early-Chou oracle bone inscriptions found at Chou-yüan, the original base of the Chou people, suggest that the religious belief of the early-Chou rulers was basically the same as that of the Shang.[79] Contemporary bronze inscriptions also show that Shang-ti was worshipped by the Chou king, as the Shang rulers had done. Thus, one bronze inscription reads: "(King Wen) first brought harmony to government. The Lord on High (Shang-ti) sent down fine virtue and great security."[80]

The idea of the mandate of Heaven has been interpreted as representing the sprouting of a "humanistic spirit" that emphasized man's own moral effort, because the mandate of Heaven could only devolve to the morally just.[81] Yet if we examine the nature of the texts in which the term "mandate of Heaven" were employed, it can be seen mainly as encompassing political doctrines propagated by the Chou court or its ruling apparatus. The ethics that affected the mandate of Heaven were in fact political ethics, and the so-called humanistic spirit that the documents—principally *Shu-ching* 書經 (*Book of History*) and *Shih-ching* 詩經 (*Book of Poetry*)—revealed was in principle political self-consciousness.[82] One might even suspect that, with such rational attitudes, the religion of the Chou court was more akin to a type of political philosophy. This surely was not the religious concern of the common people.[83]

Unlike the Shang period, from which written documents relating to the life of the people are extremely rare, the religious life of the commoners of the Chou can be gleaned, albeit still fragmentarily, from *The Book of Poetry*. Although heavily edited and perhaps even rewritten throughout the centuries, this work is still our single most important source for the life and thought of the people in the Western Chou period.[84] Their religious life can be divided into two categories. The first includes religious activities mainly related to the agricultural cycle, the other includes various individual cults, beliefs, or ideas.

The yearly life-cycle of the peasant is best represented by the *Book of Poetry* poem entitled "Ch'i-yüeh" 七月, or "The Seventh Month." A passage describes the religious activities of farmers:

> [The ice-house was opened] in the days of the fourth
>   month, early in the morning,
> Having offered in sacrifice a lamb with scallions;
> In the ninth month, it is cold, with frost;
> In the tenth month, they sweep clean their stack-sites.
> The two bottles of spirits are enjoyed,
> And they say, "Let us kill our lambs and sheep,
> And to go to the hall of our prince,
> There raise the cup of rhinoceros horn,
> And wish him long life,—that he may live for ever."[85]

Granet has suggested that the sacrifice of the second month (the fourth month in the poem, according to the Hsia calendar) may reflect the festival of marriage matching, the *kao-mei* 高媒 rite mentioned in *Yüeh-ling* 月令 (*Monthly Ordinances*) and *Chou-li* 周禮 (*The Rites of Chou*). It would be a celebration of the beginning of the agricultural cycle as well as the matching of male and female, i.e., the forces of *yang* and *yin*, in a cosmological sense.[86] While it is only reasonable to assume that the sacrifice was related to the celebration of the coming of spring, it should be pointed out that Granet's view relied heavily on the ethnographical data concerning the customs of minority peoples in southwest China. Specifically, his emphasis on the nature of *kao-mei* and the celebration in the second month as a kind of "sexual rite"[87] cannot be supported by the passage in *The Rites of Chou*, where it describes the duty of *mei-shih* 媒氏, the matchmaker official:

> [I]n the month of mid-spring, to order the gathering of man and women. At this time, there is no restriction on those (couples) who run off (*pen* 奔) together. Those who ignore this order without just cause are to be punished.[88]

The office of *mei-shih* is only seen in *The Rites of Chou*, with no concurrence in other pre-Ch'in or Han texts. In a few related occurrences, the term is either *kao-mei* 高媒, the Supreme Intermediary shrine (or deity) in *Monthly Ordinances,* or *ta-mei* 大祺, the Great Intermediary in *Han-shu (The History of Han).*[89] It is most probably a later bureaucratic name based on an early belief in a certain spirit of marriage and fertility. The "order" to gather the men and women and the punishment of those who do not follow the order (presumably those who do not gather), as described in the *The Rites of Chou* text, are most probably theoretical elaborations. The key word in the interpretation of the whole passage is the word *pen* 奔, literally "to run." Although it might have the overtone of having sexual affairs, the *The Rites of Chou* text does not suggest an organized "sex rite." The text merely passively states that "there is no restriction" on those who run off together Granet's interpretation of *pen* as connoting free sexual intercourse appears to have overstepped the meaning of the word and *The Rites of Chou* text.

In my assessment, the kernel of this passage, if it contains any historical truth at all, at most refers to a relaxation of social barriers between the young men and the girls, and to allow them to have free choice of marriage without prior arrangements, but it hardly indicates a "sexual rite." A passage in *Monthly Ordinances* says:

> In this month (the mid-spring), the dark-colored birds arrive. On the arrival day, one should make a *t'ai-lao* sacrifice at the shrine of *kao-mei.* The son of heaven attends the occasion personally; the queen leads the nine consorts there. Then those who were mounted (*yü* 御, i.e., have had sex with) by the son of heaven are treated with proper ritual. They are given bows, cases, and arrows, in front of the shrine of *kao-mei.*[90]

The whole *kao-mei* ritual described here seems to have been a kind of *post facto* fertility supplication, with hardly any indication of sexual ritual. The bows and arrows could be explained as the symbol of having male offspring, but it would be somewhat farfetched to interpret these as symbols of the sex act, as committed either by the ruler or by the deity of *kao-mei.*[91]

In any case, the most obvious obstacle to the identification of the *Book of Poetry* celebration with the *kao-mei,* or a sexual ritual, is the text itself. Besides the time of celebration, which in fact refers obliquely to the second month, and which might only refer to a kind of celebration for the coming of spring (without mentioning the name of *Kao-mei*), there is nothing there that warrants such an identification. Derk Bodde, in his study of this ceremony and the identity of *kao-mei* in Han times, suggests that it was "a personification of the human life force. . . . Because this life force could be regarded as the common progenitor of all living human beings alike, there was no need to give it more than a generalized appellation like Supreme Intermediary."[92]

As for the festival of the tenth month, no religious sacrifice is mentioned. However, in view of the fact that a religious ceremony was performed during the celebration of the second month that initiated the agricultural cycle, then the end of the cycle, i.e., the harvest, ought to have been accompanied by some kind of religious activities also. The problem is, who were the recipients of the sacrifices? The poem does not say. However, the *Monthly Ordinances* contains records concerning the tenth month:

> In this month great drinking parties are held, the Son of Heaven prays for the coming year to the heavenly clan (*t'ien tsung* 天宗), and great sacrifice is offered. Ceremonies are held at the public altars and at the gates of villages. Five kinds of sacrifices are offered to the ancestors, and the farmers are rewarded with ample rest.[93]

Despite the late date of *Monthly Ordinances* (third century B.C.), the customs and ceremonies related to the agricultural cycle most likely reflect ancient traditions. Thus, heaven and ancestors are probably the objects of farmers' sacrifices and prayers during the tenth-month celebration.[94]

It should be mentioned that the religious activities reflected in the *Book of Poetry* did not involve farmers exclusively. Rather, farmers and aristocrats all followed the same religious schedule, which was only natural in an agricultural society.

In addition to those related to the agricultural cycle, various individual religious activities can also be discerned in the Book of Poetry poems. For example, the divination of dreams, which was often recorded in the Shang-oracle bone inscriptions, was practiced by the Chou people:

> On the rush-mat below, and that of fine bamboos
>   above it,
> Here may he repose in slumber!
> May he sleep and awake,
> [Saying]"Divine for me my dreams.
> What dreams are lucky?
> They have been of bears and grisly bears;
> They have been of cobras and [other] serpents."
> The chief diviner will divine them.
> The bears and grisly bears
> Are the auspicious intimations of sons.
> The cobra and [other] serpents
> Are the auspicious intimations of daughters.[95]

It cannot be denied that the one who sought to have his dreams interpreted belonged to the elite. Yet the fact that divinations were held when a new house was constructed or for an unusual dream suggests that they were impromptu activities common to both peasants and the elite.

In another poem, a shepherd had a dream and his master submitted it to divination:

> The herdsman had a dream,—
> Of multitudes of fishes;
> Of banners with the drawings of tortoise, serpents,
>   and birds;
> The Chief diviner divined the dreams:
> "The multitudes of fishes signify a good harvest,
> The banners with the drawings of tortoise,
> Serpents and birds signify the prosperity of the
>   family."[96]

There is no doubt that the shepherd belonged to the lower echelon. The fact that his dream and the explanation of it were used as the conclusion of the poem, which, after all, was mainly for the blessing of the family of the master, suggests that the divination of dreams was a popular practice in society, and that there was little distinction between the beliefs of the elite and the commoners.[97] The *Rites of*

Chou lists several officials at court for dream divination, which reflects the importance of dream divination in society then.[98]

For such other occasions as marriage, divinations with tortoise shell, bone, or yarrows were employed:

> You had consulted the tortoise shell and the reeds [about the marriage], and there was nothing unfavorable in their response.[99]

This text of *The Book of Poetry* is corroborated by excavations of Western Chou sites in Shensi, where oracle bones were found in the remains of common houses, suggesting divination activities in people's daily lives.[100]

In this connection, it may be appropriate to mention one of the most difficult subjects in the study of ancient Chinese religion, the *I-ching* 易經, or *Book of Changes*. Originally records of yarrow-divinations, *shih* 筮, the texts collected under the sixty-four hexagram headings (*kua-t'zu* 卦辭) and line headings (*yao-t'zu* 爻辭) were, basically, written omens from different times and related to various situations.[101] Recent discussion has recognized that the use of yarrow divination had begun at least as early as the Shang, since evidence of yarrow divination was found on the oracle bones.[102] By the time that they were collected, perhaps during the early-Chou period,[103] they had already been polished in the literary genres of the elite. From the content of the text, however, we can still see some of the subjects divined: visits with high officials, proposals of marriage, crossing the river, defending against bandits, engaging in military operations, travel and animal husbandry.[104] The portents that determined the auspiciousness of events could be directions or time periods, certain natural phenomena such as clouds or rain, or certain actions such as eating salted meat.[105] Thus, although many pre-Ch'in documents show that the *I* was circulated among the elite during the Chou dynasty, and that there probably existed more than one of this kind of divination text, notably *Lien-shan* 連山 and *Kuei-ts'ang* 歸藏, the subjects and methods of divination generally reflect origins in the life of the common people.[106]

Correlations between the movements of heavenly bodies and human activities provided another form of divination. Eclipses of the sun and the moon, for example, were considered omens of worldly disasters, and sometimes connected with political justice:

The sun and moon announce evil,
Not keeping to their proper paths.
All through the kingdom there is no
   [proper] government,
Because the good are not employed.
For the moon to be eclipsed
Is but an ordinary matter.
Now that the sun has been eclipsed—
How bad it is![107]

Similar beliefs had existed in the Shang dynasty, although perhaps without the moral aspect.[108] In later eras, the correlation between astral and human affairs was to become an important aspect of the beliefs of both elite and non-elite.

The worship of ancestors, the hallmark of Shang religion, was of course still practiced by the Chou people:

Where should one set the offering?
Under the window of the ancestral shrine.
Who should be the substitution of the ancestral spirit?
It is the reverent young girl.[109]

The activities of the *wu*-shaman can also be seen in some of the poems, according to the traditional interpretation. One of them reads:

How gay and dissipated you are,
There on the top of Yüan-ch'iu!
You are indeed very pleasant,
But you have not performed the proper sacrifice![110]

Another poem reads:

[There are] the white elms at the east gate,
And the oaks on Yüan-ch'iu;
The daughter of Tzu-chung,
Dances about under them.[111]

The interpretation that this poem refers to the dance of a shamaness is mainly based on *History of Han (Han-shu)*,[112] which says: "[In] the state of Ch'en . . . the females are held in high esteem; they liked to make sacrifice and employ shamanic methods, therefore the people (of Ch'en) were used to shamanism and believed in ghosts." The text then quotes the poem from *Book of Poetry* as proof, although the poem itself does not mention anything except a girl dancing under the tree.

These reflect aspects of the religion of the Chou people, even though the descriptions often concern the life of the elite. There are, however, certain beliefs that can be seen as principally peasant in origin. For example, *t'ien-tsu* 田祖 or "father of the field" was considered the deity for the protection of the crops:

> May the father of the field be powerful,
> Seize them (the pests in the field) and cast them
> into the blazing fire![113]

This *t'ien-tsu*, furthermore, may also be explained as an agricultural fertility deity, since he ensures good harvest. Since examples of clay or stone phalli of this period have been found,[114] it is possible that a human fertility cult also existed, although we do not know the details.[115]

Belief in the existence of evil spirits such as ghosts and the short fox (*yü* 蜮, a type of harmful spirit living in the water that was thought to cause sickness), although rarely mentioned in *Book of Poetry*, must have been widespread. Thus, the poet says to his betraying friend:

> Now I use these three creatures for sacrifice,
> In order to secure a curse on you,
> If you were a ghost or a short fox,
> Then I could not get you.[116]

When all the choices have been exhausted, the people of Chou could still turn to a "heaven" that possessed certain moral will. This is shown in the following poems:

> Heaven protects and establishes you,
> With the greatest security,
> Since you are given abundance of riches,
> What happiness shall be kept away from you?[117]

> Great Heaven, unjust,
> Is sending down these exhausting disorders.
> Great Heaven, unkind,
> Is sending down these great miseries.[118]

37

There is, admittedly, no indisputable evidence to say that the above, and similar poems, reflect the ideas of the common people and not those of the ruling elite. Authorship is unknown, but in any event the poems probably show actual sentiments of commoners regardless of the identity of the author. What is interesting is that while on the one hand the poems reveal a strong need for the protection of Heaven, on the other hand they show a sense of skepticism about the justice of Heaven. Thus, the poet of the last poem protested against Heaven's imparting of disasters to those who did not deserve them. This, I propose, is typical of the mentality of Chinese popular religion, and is not to be found in the official doctrine preserved in *Shu-ching* 書經 (*The Book of History*), or the more formal writings such as bronze inscriptions, where Heaven's justice was never questioned. That there is a different orientation between the mentalities of the common people and the court is also vividly described by another poem:

> They flit about, the yellow birds,
> And rest upon the jujube trees.
> Who followed duke Muh (to the grave)?
> Tzu-chu Yen-hsi.
> And this Yen-hsi,
> Was a man above a hundred.
> When he came to the grave,
> He looked terrified and trembled.
> The azure Heaven there,
> Destroying our good man.
> Could he have been redeemed,
> We should have given a hundred lives for him.[119]

Human sacrifice at royal funerals was a centuries-old custom; an underlying assumption was that there was a life after death. The practice of human sacrifice is only the logical result of this belief. The poet here, however, voiced a different view: the "people" did not consent to this practice. Yet this should not be seen as a certain skepticism concerning life after death and the existence of ghosts and gods. Rather, it should be understood as an idea based on practical experience and the need of self-protection: no one really saw the returning dead. To carry the observation a step further, it seems that the people mourned the death of Tzu-chu not because they unconditionally opposed the idea of human sacrifice, but because they felt that Tzu-chu did not deserve to die in such way. The last sentence of the poem, that they should have given a hundred lives for him, though perhaps only rhetorical, suggests that the idea of human sacrifice was acceptable if the "right" person was chosen. In any case, it is clearly a protest against the way the ruling class handled human sacrifice.

The story contained in "The Yellow Birds" is also recorded in *Tso-chuan* 左傳, *Commentary of Tso*;[120] thus, we are actually in the Eastern Chou period. Politically, a major decline of royal power occurred after the transition from the Western Chou to Eastern Chou. Religiously, however, the change can only have been gradual. That the custom of human sacrifice lasted until the Warring States period is clear proof of this gradual nature.[121]

The archaeological and textual evidence of the Western Chou period suggests that what little we know of the religion of the Chou can be said of the Shang. It was a belief system built around agricultural life, with deep reverence to natural deities and ancestor spirits, and the roots of this system must have been in the prehistoric period. Throughout the Shang and Western Chou periods, the main contour was constant and compatible with the religion of the ruling class. Toward the end of the Western Chou, as evidence in the *Book of Poetry* suggests, nonruling members of society expressed skepticism toward the older presumed piety regarding an ultimate justice dispensed by Heaven. People were realizing the possibility of injustice in the will of Heaven. If or how this realization affected people's attitudes in other religious activities, however, is difficult to estimate. In any case, it reveals an aspect of the religious mentality: for personal welfare the will of Heaven was not necessarily benevolent and according to expectations. This is based on the available evidence, and does not preclude the existence of the same or similar mentality in earlier periods. The ruling elite, on the other hand, also changed beginning in Western Chou: they produced ideas about a moral heaven. Although perhaps at first only a political claim to legitimize changes of dynasty, it is significant that such thinking found momentum and created a schism within the religion of the ruling class. Later developments in the Eastern Chou show that the rulers and the court tended to hold on to the old style, i.e., the worship of ancestor spirits and natural deities, handed down through the Shang court, while (the new idea of a moral heaven was gradually adopted and advocated by the elite, or intellectuals.)

[In the subsequent Ch'un-chiu and Warring States periods, despite turbulent social and economic change and the existence of various schools of thought, the tone of popular religious expression remained basically similar.] On the other hand, precisely because of the appearance of new factors versus the factors of conservatism, the changes in religious attitudes that began in the Western Chou, both in the ruling elite and the non-elite, continued to develop into more clearly recognizable trends, as I will discuss in the next chapter.

Chapter 3 ─────────────

Personal Welfare in the Context of Mantic Technique

> If oxen and horses or lions had hands, and could paint with their
> hands, and produce works of art as men do, horses would paint the
> forms of the gods like horses, and oxen like oxen, and make their
> bodies in the image of their several kinds.[1]

Chou dynastic rule lasted, at least in ceremonial form, from around
1045 to 256 B.C.,[2] and is often deemed as the longest dynasty in Chinese
history. During the Chou period major enduring characteristics of
Chinese culture were formed: political ideology, philosophy, art, and
religion. Chou rule, however, can hardly be regarded as successful on
the political level. Except for a brief period of stability in the early
part of the dynasty, of which we know very little, the Chou was plagued
by both the invasion of barbarians from all sides and political problems
within.[3] In 770 B.C., following an invasion of the Ti people from the
west, the Chou court was forced to move from Tsung-chou, near
present day Sian, to the eastern capital Ch'eng-chou, near present
day Lo-yang.[4] Thus began the Eastern Chou period. The Eastern Chou
was further divided into two periods according to traditional historiography: the Spring and Autumn period, according to the name of a
work attributed to Confucius, and the Warring States period. The

story of political and social change throughout these periods, a complicated subject by itself, cannot be told here.[5]

Although the political power of the Chou court was constantly diminished by the various feudal lords, the official religious cults practiced by the Chou court and the feudal states basically followed the same pattern established since the Shang period and were still closely related to agricultural cycles.[6] A passage in *The Commentary of Tso* states the principle of sacrifice:

> With regard to the sacrifices in general, at the season of *ch'i-chih* 啓蟄 [the emergence of insects from their burrows], the border sacrifice [to Heaven] was offered; at the season of *lung-chien* 龍見 [the appearance of the Dragon], the sacrifice for rain; at the season of *shih-sha* 始殺 [commencement of death] the sacrifice of first fruits; and at the season of *pi-chih* 閉蟄 [the closing of insects in their burrows], the winter sacrifice. Any disagreement with this rule should be noted [by the official historian].[7]

The rule described here is obviously related to animal and plant cycles, although much simplified. To characterize generally the official cult in the Eastern Chou period we turn to a passage from *The Book of Rites* depicting the principle of sacrifice:

> With a blazing pile of wood on the Grand Altar they sacrificed to Heaven; by burying (the victim) in the Grand Mound, they sacrificed to the Earth, (in both cases) they used a red calf. By burying a sheep and a pig at the Mound of Grand Brightness, they sacrificed to the seasons. They prayed to winter and summer at the pits and altars, they pray to the sun at (the altar called) The Palace of the King, to the moon at the (pit called) Light of Night; to the stars at the (altar called) Dark Altar; to the flood and drought at the (altar called) Rain; to the four directions at the altar called Four Pits. Mountains, forests, streams, valleys, hills and mounds, which are able to produce clouds, create winds and rain, and generate monsters, are all considered to have spiritual power. The one who possesses the world shall sacrifice to all the deities. The feudal lords make sacrifices when [the mountains

and rivers] are in their territory, and do not offer sacrifice when
[the mountains and rivers] are not in their territory.[8]

Since Heaven, Earth, the four seasons, the sun and moon, the four
cardinal directions, flood and drought, as well as powers inhabiting
natural places and events are all included in the sacrificial program,
one might say that this passage illustrates the "natural religion" character of Chou official cults. A detailed description of the various officials in charge of religious affairs of the state is provided in *The Rites
of Chou*.[9] Although it is difficult to prove beyond doubt that the records
in *The Book of Rites* and *The Rites of Chou* represent the actual
practices of Chou institutions, it is generally agreed that part of the
material in them may be dated to the Eastern Chou period.[10] It is also
noteworthy that worship of royal ancestors was another important
aspect of the official religion at this time.

As more and more documents become available from this period,
religious contours begin to emerge. This chapter attempts to probe
religious beliefs in several aspects: concepts and attitudes toward
omens, divination, witchcraft, and exorcism; the nature and images
of ghosts and spirits; as well as ideas concerning the soul and the
netherworld. I will try to demonstrate from available, yet fragmentary, evidence a few details of this personal, private piety. Although
little direct evidence can be found, the sheer amount of pre-Ch'in
texts greatly increases the possibility of finding indirect references or
allusions to religious ideas and beliefs related to the areas just mentioned. I cannot encompass the entire corpus; and it is impossible to
make a complete examination of each of the texts. Suffice it to say
that, when using the texts, one should bear in mind that recorded
events can be read either at face value or as authorial judgments and
constructions. The historian needs to bring into play principles of
text reading. For example, in using material from The *Commentary
of Tso*, one of the most important documents to reflect ancient ideas
and culture, one should be aware that although many events might
have been based on accurate records, the dialogues of the various
characters are likely to have been created by the author for various
intents and effects. Thus, using the "words" of the characters in *The
Commentary of Tso* as evidence of their thoughts can only be allowed
with the understanding that they reflect a reconstruction of an ethos,

rather than what actually had been said.[11] When dealing with materials concerning the beliefs of people, furthermore, we have first to admit that although for many readers today the gods or spirits do not exist, they were experienced in some way by the ancients, and this constitutes a historical reality. The historian's responsibility is twofold: on the one hand he should try to explain ancient beliefs as they were experienced, on the other hand he needs to examine the context in which records of these beliefs are preserved. He can neither take his sources for granted nor dismiss them as purely literary tools used for political or social manipulation.

Omens

In ancient China, one of the more conspicuous aspects of the religion of personal welfare was the role given to prodigies. It was not only the privileged who believed that natural places produced meaningful clouds and winds and generated monsters; it was a common, everyday belief. A passage in *The Commentary of Tso* records the following:

> Earlier, the snakes living within the city and those from outside had engaged in battle in the middle of the southern gate to the capital of Cheng. The snakes living within the city died. Six years later, Duke Li of Cheng returned to the capital [from exile]. When Duke Chuang of Lu heard of this, he questioned his minister Shen Hsü 申繻 about it, saying, "Are there really such things as portents?" Shen Hsü replied, "When people have something they are deeply distressed about, their vital energy flames up and takes such shapes. Portents arise because of people. If people have no dissensions, they will not arise of themselves. When men abandon their constant ways, then portents arise. That is why these particular portents came about."[12]

The snake fight was understood as an omen: the city snakes represented the usurpers of Cheng rulership, and the outside snakes represented Duke Li. The victory of the outside snakes was therefore a sign of Duke Li's future return to power from exile. The fact that this event was noticed six years before Duke Li's return, assuming that it was not a fictitious account by the author, indicates that people regarded the snake fight as unusual and ominous, although they could not have realized its implication. When Duke Li did return, the recorded omen was brought out and interpreted, its meaning "revealed." It was with such an understanding that the Duke of Lu posed his question. Shen Hsü's answer was rational to the extent that he played down the importance of ominous events and stressed the power of virtue: it was when men abandoned their constant ways that portents arose. Yet the whole incident indicates a prevalent belief in the efficacy of such portents and omens. It was unlikely that the original notice of the "abnormal" fighting of the snakes was random. The Duke of Lu was suspicious of its ominous intent, though apparently he was preparing to accept the mere event as true. Even Shen Hsü was obliged to admit the existence of prodigies and abnormal events, but coupled it with a moralistic explanation of their origin. The author of *The Commentary of Tso* was obviously sympathetic to Shen Hsü's position, provided he did not in fact invent Shen's speech or the report about the snake fight. Whether he himself believed in the efficacy of the omen is another question. This example quite clearly reveals the constituents of an everyday, common belief regarding omens. The people, the ruler, and the court elite were all participants.[13]

Abnormal astronomical phenomena were another important type of omen. Thus records the *The Commentary of Tso*:

> In winter there was a comet on the west of Ta-ch'en, which traveled to the Milky Way. Shen Hsü 申須 said: "This broom-star serves to take away what is old and arrange something new. The doings of Heaven are constantly revealed by such appearances. Now the Huo (star of Fire, Mars) is not seen. When Huo appears again, fire will certainly spread. May we therefore conclude that the states are going to have the calamity of fires?"[14]

Again, in the twenty-sixth year of Duke Chao, a comet appeared in the state of Ch'i. The Duke of Ch'i wanted to make a sacrifice to the comet, but was dissuaded by Yen Tzu 晏子, on the grounds that Heaven punishes the wicked and rewards the virtuous regardless of material sacrifices:

> It is of no use: you will only practice a delusion. There is no uncertainty in the ways of Heaven; it does not waver in its purpose:

why should you offer a deprecatory sacrifice? Moreover, there is a broom-star in the sky; it is for the removal of dirt. If your lordship has nothing in your conduct that can be so described, what have you to supplicate? If you have, what will it be diminished by your supplication?[15]

These stories show that it was common to discuss human affairs in terms of correlated astronomical phenomena. Yen Tzu's opposition represented some educated elites' more rational and humanistic attitude toward the way of Heaven, although his attitude was likely among the minority. Shen Hsü, on the other hand, was one among those who believed that the movement of the heavenly bodies was ominous of human destiny. It is revealing to note that, during the Eastern Chou, the Chou court obviously still possessed the most prestigious and knowledgeable official diviners, and questions concerning astronomical portents were sent there from the feudal lords for explanation.[16]

Natural calamities were also portentous. The text of *Kuo-yü* records:

In the second year of King Yu 幽王, earthquakes occurred at the three western rivers. Po Yang-fu said: "The Chou dynasty is going to be destroyed. The spirit (*ch'i*) of heaven and earth should not lose its order. If order is disturbed, people will be rebellious. If the spirit of Yang is suppressed and cannot be released, and the spirit of Yin is hiding under and cannot evaporate, earthquakes are bound to occur."[17]

The event described here refers to the end of the Western Chou. Considering the date of the text and the elaboration on the idea of *yin* and *yang*, however, there is no doubt that the interpretation of the earthquake, although put in the mouth of Po Yang-fu, reflects an Eastern Chou or even later conception. In the Han dynasty, the application of the ideas of *yin-yang* and Five Phases, although based on similar assumptions about the relations between man and nature, became a highly complex religio-philosophical system.[18]

According to the same mentality, i.e., human fate as somehow related to natural or astronomical phenomena, any unusual event could be regarded as ominous. We mentioned snakes above. The appearance of special birds (e.g., the grackle) was also ominous. It was mentioned in children's rhymes as an omen of the expulsion of the ruler. One such rhyme was recorded in *The Commentary of Tso*, in the speech of Shih Chi 師己 to explain a coming disaster:

> Here are grackles apace!
> The duke flies in disgrace.
> Look at the grackles' wings!
> To the wilds the duke flings.[19]

That children's rhymes were understood as oracles or satires concerning political events was also a long-established tradition.[20] The author of *The Commentary of Tso* was simply a participant in this belief.

In another incident, the falling of meteorites and the backward flight of *I*-birds were the subject of an inquiry by Duke Hsiang of Sung: "What are they ominous of? What good fortune or bad do they portent?" Shu Hsing answered: "This year there will be the deaths of many great persons of Lu. Next year Ch'i will be entirely in disorder. Your lordship will get the presidency of the states, but will not continue to hold it." When Shu Hsing retreated from the court, he told someone else:

> The duke asked me an improper question. These are only matters concerning Yin and Yang, which are not how good or bad fortune came about. They are produced by men themselves. I so answered because I did not dare to oppose the duke.[21]

Shu Hsing's words, seen together with those of Yen Tzu, show that at least some among the educated elite did not really believe in the relationship between natural phenomena and human affairs. Yet that omens were recorded and taken seriously by the court, and that Shu Hsing did not venture to express his real opinion but instead "interpreted" the portent quite elaborately to satisfy his lord, shows that such belief prevailed. In view of the similar case of the children's rhymes, such belief can hardly be attributed to the ruling and royal elite alone.[22] As for the author of *The Commentary of Tso*, his inclusion of Shu Hsing's "words" in the text seems to indicate that, on the one hand, the "art" of portent interpretation could have by this time become mere technique, and, on the other hand, he held a critical view of the duke's interest in portents.

In another instance, during a great flood, dragons were reportedly seen fighting in the pool outside the gate of Cheng. People in the city therefore demanded to make sacrifice to the dragons to appease them. Tzu Ch'an, however, refused to make such a sacrifice, saying:

> If we are fighting, the dragons do not look at us; when dragons are fighting, why should we look at them? We may offer a sacrifice, but that is their abode. If we do not seek anything of the dragons, they will not seek anything from us.[23]

Here again Tzu Ch'an the intellectual held an opinion different from that of the common people. Although he did not deny the existence of the dragons or the efficacy of apotropaic sacrifice,[24] nor deny the existence of souls and avenging ghosts, as we see below, he considered that it was improper to make the sacrifice, for the dragons did not invade the human sphere.

From the above examples concerning omens, we can trace the development in the Eastern Chou period of a trend wherein some court thinkers such as Shen Hsü, Yen Tzu, and Tzu Ch'an began to break away from the general religious background and opted for a more rational, moral, and secular perspective on prodigies. Confucius and his disciples were undoubtedly among them. This is of course not to say that they were "rational" in the sense of "non-religious." In the case of Tzu Ch'an, for example, the reason for his refusal to make sacrifice to the dragons was not because he did not believe in the existence of dragons, but because it was improper to make the sacrifice. The religious mentality of most of the ruling and nonruling members was basically a shared one as far as the nature of beliefs was concerned. The subsequent rise of omenology during the Han dynasty, however, led to works of *tsai-i* 災異 (calamities and curious events) and *ch'en-wei* 讖緯 (oracle texts), the latter being explanations of natural and textual omens that were encased in scholastic interpretations. This mixture of everyday and learned elements is an important characteristic of Han religious phenomena.[25]

Divination

Divination is closely related to the belief in omens. In contrast to the passive role of receiving ominous signs, in divination men actively search for answers to events through various techniques. Belief in omens and in divination, however, both shared the basic assumption that it was possible for man to comprehend events and relate them to fate.

In the Shang dynasty, the art of divination was probably not monopolized by the royal court, as discussed above in Chapter 2. It is reasonable to assume, however, that the divinations performed at court might have been concerned with problems different from those that arose in private situations. Chou sources reveal that divination by tortoise shell, ox scapula, and lots was commonplace among all sectors of society. Evidence of it during the Eastern Chou and the Warring States period is plentiful. A survey of the examples found in *The Commentary of Tso* shows that the objects of divination included questions concerning marriage, childbirth, war, sacrifice, illness, even moving the capital.[26] These are of course still closely related to the political concerns of the ruling class. On the other hand, items such as illness and childbirth could concern both elite and non-elite private life. Moreover, some of the diviners did not act in an official capacity, indicating the private nature of the activity.

For example, *The Commentary of Tso* records that the prince of Ch'en once had a drinking party with Duke Huan of Ch'i. Duke Huan invited him to extend the party into the evening. The prince of Ch'en replied: "I divined about the day (for attending the party); but I have not divined about the night; I dare not do it."[27] Even if his statement was an excuse, and we have evidence to show that it was probably not,[28] the story shows the wide application of divination in private situations. There was even a saying that "In buying a concubine, if you do not know her surname, consult the tortoise-shell for it."[29] That the author of *The Commentary of Tso* repeatedly recorded instances of divination that, not surprisingly, were basically efficacious shows not only his own attitude toward divination, but also that it was a common affair in his time.

Recent archaeological finds of the Warring States Ch'u tombs have also provided evidence for divination that used tortoise shells and yarrow stalks. These are mainly records of the results of divinations written on bamboo slips.[30] From these records, we know that professional diviners at the time would serve different customers, both high and low in social status. In general, only people with higher status could use both shell and yarrow stalks; those of lower status used only yarrow stalks.[3] This explains why little physical evidence of the divination activities of the latter is preserved.

The prevalence of divination is also reflected by the negative criticism toward it that flourished. At the end of the Warring States period, the famous philosopher Hsün Tzu once commented on the practice of divination and magic:

> You pray for rain and it rains. Why? For no particular reason, I say. It is just as though you had not prayed for rain and it rained anyway. The sun and moon undergo an eclipse and you try to save them; a drought occurs and you pray for rain; you consult the arts of divination before making a decision on some important matter. But it is not as though you could hope to accomplish anything by such ceremonies. They are done merely for ornament. Hence the gentleman regards them as ornaments, but the common people regard them as supernatural (*shen*). He who considers them ornaments is fortunate; he who considers them supernatural is unfortunate.[32]

The phrase "the gentleman regards them as ornaments, but the common people regard them as supernatural" points out clearly the different attitudes of the elite and the non-elite. The legalist philosopher Han Fei-tzu also attacked those who believed in the efficacy of divinations: "Those who employ the date-formula, serve the ghosts and spirits, believe in divinations and enjoy making sacrifices, are ill-fated."[33] He adds,

> When the shaman priests pray for someone, they say, "May you live a thousand autumns and ten thousands years!" But the "thousand autumns and ten thousand years" are only a noise dinning on the ear—no one has ever proved that such prayers add so much as a day to anyone's life. For this reason people despise the shaman priests.[34]

Toward the end of the Warring State period, the author of *Master Lü's Spring and Autumn Annal* (*Lü-shih ch'un-ch'iu*) remarked that:

> Nowadays people consult oracles and pray and make sacrifice (to treat illness), which only incur more illnesses. This is like

50

the archers who fixed the target when they missed it, which is of no avail for their marksmanship. It is also like adding hot soup to boiling water to stop the boiling, which only perpetuates the boiling. When one takes away the fire, however, the boiling will then stop. Therefore to employ *wu*-medicine man and to apply the poisonous drugs to expel the illness was despised by the ancients, for it was not the proper way.[35]

Lü-shih ch'un-ch'iu here exhorts the way of the sages for observing the proper relationships between nature and human destiny and physical well-being. The passage only demonstrates, however, the difficulty in rectifying an idea of everyday religions that was handed down through ancient traditions. The "ancients" most probably did not despise *wu*-medicine men but, on the contrary, believed in their abilities.

Despite such criticism, Hsün Tzu, when describing the structure of ideal government, stated that

To observe the *yin* and *yang*, judge the meaning of portents, divine by the tortoise and milfoil, conduct exorcisms, fortune-telling, and divination by the five types of signs, and understand all that pertains to good and bad fortune—these are the duties of hunchback shamanesses and crippled shamans.[36]

The *wu*-shamans were just as necessary in the constitution of a proper government as the master engineer (*kung-shih* 工師), the master of trades (*chih-shih* 治市), or the chief of police (*ssu-k'ou* 司寇).

Along the same lines, it is noteworthy that the Confucian classic *The Book of Rites* considered the act of divination as carrying positive significance:

Divination by the shell is called *pu* 卜; by the stalk, *shih* 筮. The two were the methods by which the ancient sage kings made the people believe in (the auspiciousness of) seasons and days, revere spiritual beings, and stand in awe of their laws and orders; the methods by which they made them determine their perplexities and settle their misgivings.[37]

This view incorporates the act of divination into a larger framework of political and pseudo-historical explanation. The author might have represented only one strand of Confucian opinion, yet there is little doubt that this also reflected the way courts utilized social customs and beliefs to establish a theoretical basis for a harmonious society. This can be corroborated by *Rites of Chou*'s listing of divination and sacrificial officials and the *wu* personnel.[38] Although one may question how much of *The Rites of Chou* reflects the historical reality of the Warring States period, it at least shows that the ruling elite did not exclude religious personnel from the government, as also evidenced in *The Commentary of Tso* as well as Hsün Tzu's statement.

As we shall see in Chapter 8, the relationship between the religion of the court elite and that of the non-elite was a complex one; the elite were not only critics and reformers, but could also be participants in the everyday religion of personal welfare. Consider in this regard the ancient text of *Ch'u-tz'u* 楚辭 and its author. It has been suggested that not only does *Ch'u-tz'u* (especially its sections "Nine Songs" and "Soul-Calling" (*Chao-hun* 招魂) reflect shamanistic activities, but that Ch'ü Yüan, an official at the court of Ch'u, might also have been a shaman.[39] Yet because its literary renditions of local shamanistic activities are not totally dependable, we shall use material from *Ch'u-tz'u* in the following discussions only when it illustrates what scholars seem to agree to be religious notions that were relatively widespread.

Witchcraft and Exorcism

Although shamanism in political contexts grew less important after the Western Chou, witchcraft and *wu*-personnel continued to be used in society. *The Commentary of Tso* records an example of black magic. After Ying K'ao-shu was killed, the duke of Cheng ordered that a pig, a dog, and chicken should be used to cast a curse against the killers.[40] It was very likely a form of "sympathetic magic" that employed a "law of similarity": by killing the animals, the enemy was stricken in parallel. It is worth noting that the magic was performed with animals contributed by soldiers. This indicates that the performance of magic, in this example at least, could be a communal action and thus an act of popular belief. The author of *The Commentary of Tso* did not approve of this use of magic. He pointed out that because the duke of Cheng lacked proper virtue the curse was improper. The efficacy of magic, however, was not questioned.[41]

Exorcism was another function of shamans. A story in *The Commentary of Tso* describes the use by *wu*-shamans of peach twigs as tools for exorcism in connection with a funerary rite.[42] This story reveals not only the method of exorcism, but also the common belief that[evil spirits were present at funerary rites.] As perhaps a local practice accompanying funeral exorcism, many Ch'u tombs of the Warring States period have been found equipped with statues of demonic figures, often identified as "tomb guardian beasts (*chen-mu-shou* 鎮墓獸)." While the exact identity of such statues is still uncertain,[43] they are probably[apotropaic figures for the protection of the tombs against evil intruders.]

The Commentary of Tso also mentions other exorcist methods such as cutting mountain mulberry trees to induce rain,[44] or setting up *she*-altars and making sacrifices to the four directions to ward off fire calamities.[45] At times, the shamans who performed exorcist rituals would themselves become the victims of witchcraft-like sacrifices, in some sense an indication of their low social status. Several ancient sources mention a killing-sacrifice. In one instance, during a serious drought the Duke of Lu planned to burn a *wu*-shamaness as a sacrifice to heaven for relief. This apparently followed a contemporary custom.[46] These cases, however, show such sacrifice being stopped by rational intellectuals. In fact, this kind of rite may have been an ancient form of rain-inducing magic.[47] In an oft-recorded tale, King T'ang of Shang once proposed to offer himself as a sacrifice in prayer for rain.[48]

Ghosts and Spirits

The nature and behavior of ghosts and spirits

Although the everyday, personal religious practices during Shang and Western Chou incorporated ghosts and spirits as well as their powers, little can be said concerning the nature and behavior of those beings. This might be attributable to the paucity of evidence, rather than to a historical lack. For the Eastern Chou and the Warring States periods, however, information can be gleaned from the traditional sources. An abstract view of the nature of spirits and ghosts is recorded in *Book of Rites*:

> The Master said: "How abundant and rich are the powers possessed and exercised by Spiritual Beings! We look for them, but do not see them; we listen for, but do not hear them; they enter into all things, and nothing is without them. They cause all under Heaven to fast and purify themselves and to array themselves in their richest dresses in order to attend at their sacrifices. Then, like overflowing water, they seem to be over the heads, and on the left and right of their worshippers. It is said in the *Book of Poetry*: 'The Spirits come, but when and where, no one beforehand can declare. The more should we not Spirits slight, but ever feel as in their sight.'"[49]

According to this view, ghosts and spirits were formless beings, undetectable by human senses. This differs considerably from the concrete and tangible spirits that were boldly and frequently depicted in everyday funerary culture in ancient times. The concrete nature of the spirits formed a basis for most religious sacrifices and reflected a primordial belief in the physical similarity between man and spiritual beings. This common attitude is aptly expressed in the text of *Mo-tzu*, which attempts a proof of the existence of ghosts and spirits:

> If one holds that there is no ghost and yet tries to learn about the ritual of sacrifice, it is just like learning to show hospitality to the guest while no guest exists.[50]

He further states that:

> The way to determine whether something exists or not is to find out whether people actually know from their own ears and eyes whether it exists, and use this as a standard. If someone has actually heard it and seen it, then we must assume that it exists. But if no one has heard or seen it, then we must assume that it does not exist. If this is to be our method, then why don't we try going to some village or community and asking? If from antiquity to today, from the beginning of mankind to the present, there have been people who have seen ghost-like and sprit-like beings

and heard their voices, then how can we say they don't exist? But if no one has seen or heard them, then how can we say they exist?[51]

There follow cases of people who "saw" ghosts, including the story of Tu-po. This was a "commonsense" approach to the idea of ghosts and spirits that was quite different from the Confucian idea about them. The Confucian idea, as represented by the passage in *The Book of Rites* quoted above, considered the spirits and ghosts as elusive beings, to be kept at a distance. Thus, Confucius said: "to give one's self earnestly to the duties due to man, and while respecting spiritual beings (*kuei-shen*), to keep aloof from them, may be called wisdom."[52]

The belief in the existence of ghosts is again illustrated by the following story. In the fifth year of the duke of Hsüan, it is recorded that Tzu-liang, the minister of war of Ch'u, had a son. His brother Tzu-wen, however, advised him to kill the infant lest the entire clan be extinguished, since the infant looked like a fierce animal and cried like a wolf, and a saying held that "a wolf-like child will have an evil heart" and will endanger the family. When Tzu-liang refused his proposal, Tzu-wen was distressed and said to his family: "Even ghosts must seek for food; (I am afraid) that the ghosts of the Jo-Ao clan might be famished."[53] Tzu-wen was not discoursing on the nature of ghosts but was simply concerned about a coming disaster. Thus the expression ("even ghosts must seek for food" can be seen as an unintentional, therefore trustworthy, evidence for a common conception about ghosts.)

The Commentary of Tso author's underlying intent was to explain the fall of the powerful Jo-Ao clan of Ch'u as stemming from the refusal of Tzu-liang to heed the ominous features of the infant. Ultimately, Tzu-liang failed to understand the everyday belief system. The author would not have fabricated an element of the belief system since he was striving to convince his readers. The inclusion of the story, whether true or not, confirms a specific aspect of the wider religious mentality.

Not only did people seek the meaning of omens and the shape of future events via divinatory methods, the deities were also able to reveal their messages directly. We read in *The Commentary of Tso*:

In autumn, in the seventh month, there was the descent of a certain spirit in Hsin. King Hui asked Kuo, the diviner in the private service of the king, the reason of it, and he replied: "When a state is about to flourish, gods and spirits descend in it, to survey its virtue. When it is going to perish, spirits descend again, to behold its wickedness. Thus there have been instances of states flourishing from spirits appearing, and also of states perishing; cases in point might be adduced from the dynasties of Yu Hsia, Shang and Chou." The king then asked what should be done in the case of this spirit, and Kuo replied, "Present to it its own proper offerings, which are those proper to the day on which it came."

The spirit stayed in Hsin six months, whereupon the duke of Kuo caused the prayer-master Ying, the superintendent of the ancestral temple Ch'u and the historiographer Yin to sacrifice to it, and the spirit promised to give him territory.[54]

The same story is preserved in *Kuo-yü*, where Master Kuo is described as elaborating on the various deities as well as sacred animals that historically had descended to earth in correspondence to the rise and fall of dynasties. The particular spirit that descended in Hsin was said to be "someone like the god Tan-chu (丹朱)."[55] Here, we are not concerned with exactly which god or spirit had descended. Most important is that people believed that the deities would actively reveal themselves to the world and by so doing indicate coming changes in politics. Second, according to the *The Commentary of Tso* version, there seems to be some uncertainty concerning the identity of the spirits; thus, one sacrificed to it according to the days that it descended. The uncertainty indicates that the form of this belief was more important than its actual content: while the exact names of the spirits or gods might have been a matter for explanation, as the *Kuo-yü* version shows, the basic theme of divine revelation was nevertheless certain. What was curious in this story was that the spirit "stayed in Hsin for six months," received offerings, and even promised to give territory. But what was the actual image of this spirit? Through what medium was its promise made? What became of it after six months? The authors of *The Commentary of Tso* and *Kuo-yü* were not concerned with these questions, and may not have actually believed in the story they recorded. There is no doubt, however, that the purpose of including this story in both works was the same: to admonish those in power. For such admonition to have effect, one assumes that the audience believed in the validity of the active involvement of ghosts and spirits in human affairs. That the names of the spirits had to be explained by some "learned" person such as Master Kuo, furthermore, indicates that there did not exist any "official doctrine" concerning the spirits and their messages. Those who specialized in collecting stories and legends of this nature presumably were those often related to the office of divination and thus entitled to proffer their personal interpretations.

Images of ghosts and spirits

Because they were considered concrete entities, ghosts and spirits must have possessed physical attributes. As Mo Tzu put it: "The ghosts and spirits of past and present are of three kinds only: the ghosts of Heaven, the ghosts of the mountains and rivers, and the ghosts of men who have died."[56] Formerly human spirits, such as Tan-chu or the ghost of Tu-po,[57] had the appearance of human beings. It was also possible that the ghost of a person could be seen in the form of an animal. For example, when the duke of Ch'i was hunting in the field he saw a large boar. His attendant said that it was the ghost of P'eng-sheng, who was executed unjustly by the duke of Ch'i eight years earlier. The duke was enraged and said: "How dare P'eng-sheng show himself!" He then shot at it, whereupon the boar stood upright like a man and howled.[58] This indicates that the facial features of the boar were associated with demons. An evil spirit of the west, to give an example, was described in *Ch'u-tz'u* as "with the head of a swine, slanting eyes and shaggy hair, long claws and serrated teeth."[59]

For other deities a mixture of human and animal forms was not uncommon. Kou-mang, according to the description given in *Mo-tzu*, had the body of a bird with a human head.[60] Ju-shou, the punishing spirit of heaven, had a human face with white hair and tiger's claws.[61] Other examples give evidence of nonhuman images. The spirits or demons, moreover, often appeared in dreams. For example, the duke of Chin dreamt about a giant demon with extremely long, dishevelled hair,[62] and in another story he dreamt about a yellow bear that was thought to be a vicious demon.[63] As in the example from *The Book of Poetry*, discussed in Chapter 2, the identities of these spirits had to be explained by a shaman in the first case, and a learned diviner in the second.

From such descriptive details, one gains an impression that in everyday religious attitudes, there was little difference between gods, ghosts, and spirits. These usually appeared with strange or ferocious features, although ones not completely beyond imagination. Yet it was also because of the uncertainty of such images that people's imaginations were released in all directions. A famous story in *Han-fei-tzu* mentioned a painter who once remarked that it was much easier to draw a ghost than dogs or horses, for no one had really seen a ghost.[64]

Another anecdote from *Han-fei-tzu* concerns a man of the state of Yen named Li Chi, who travelled frequently. In his absence, his wife had an affair with another man. One day Li Chi came home unexpectedly when the man was with his wife in the inner chamber. His wife was frightened but her servant advised the following:

> "Let the young gentleman be naked with dishevelled hair and rush straight out through the door. Then we will pretend to have seen nothing." Thereupon the man followed her advice and ran out through the door. Chi said: "Who is that?" "Nobody," replied everyone in the house. Li Chi asked, "Have I seen a ghost?" His wife replied: "Certainly!" "What shall I do then?" "Take the excrement of five kinds of animal and bathe in it." Chi said: "All right!" So he bathed in the excrement. [Another version says (the man) bathed in orchid soup.][65]

Here we see two characteristics often related with the image of human ghosts: nakedness and dishevelled hair. To use animal excrement to expel the ghosts or evil spirits was another common practice in popular wisdom.

A passage in *Hsün-tzu* further illustrates the everyday ideas about ghosts and spirits:

> There was a man named Chuan Shu-liang who lived south of Hsia-shou. He was stupid and easily frightened. One night he was walking in the moonlight when, glancing down and seeing his shadow, he took it for a crouching ghost. Looking up, he caught sight of his own hair and took it for a devil standing over him.

Fig. 3.1 Figure of a protective demon on the coffin of
Tseng Hou I. Warring States.

He whirled around and started running, and when he reached
his home he fell unconscious and died.[66]

Archaeology has given us images of ghosts and spirits in the context
of tomb-protection demons. In the great tomb of Tseng Hou I from
the early–Warring States period, strange-looking creatures were found
painted on the coffin (Fig. 3.1).[67] Judging from the positions of the
figures, it is possible that they also served as protectors of the deceased.
Even more fantastic figures are found painted on a silk manuscript

Fig. 3.2 Figure of a god on a Ch'u silk manuscript.
Warring States.

found in a Ch'u tomb of the Warring States period (Fig. 3.2).[68] Although there is yet no final answer to the identities of these figures, they at least give us concrete details of the images of spirit-beings.[69]

Images of spirits, as reflected by the above traditional texts and archaeological finds, are similar to those found in *Shan-hai-ching* (*Classic of the Mountains and Seas*) or in the *jih-shu* (almanacs) of Ch'in. As we shall see in the next chapter, such texts reveal a horde of spirits and gods that must be considered as part of the world of extra-human powers in popular conception.

Interactions between humans and extra-human powers

By worshipping deities or spirits, people usually expected to gain welfare and avoid disasters of every kind. The belief that the deities held certain moral criteria in judging the behavior of human beings, however, corresponded to the idea of a moral Mandate of Heaven that gained influence after the establishment of the Chou. The idea that a person's moral behavior was the sole reference by which the supernatural beings judged his supplications became popular among intellectuals of the Eastern Chou period. *The Commentary of Tso* has the following passage:

> (Chao) Ying dreamt that a messenger of Heaven told him: "Make sacrifice to me, and I shall bless you." He then sent for Shih Chen-po and asked him about the meaning of this dream. Chen-po said: "I do not know." Afterwards, Chen-po told his followers: "The gods bless the virtuous and punish the indecent. If one is indecent yet is not punished, it is (already) a blessing."[70]

Here, the idea that one who sacrifices to the deities will be blessed is close to the idea of *"do ut des,"* a term historians of religions in the West have often employed in characterizing the religious mentality of early civilizations. The words of Chen-po, on the other hand, brought a sense of moral judgment into the relationship between human beings and gods.[71] Other intellectuals even went so far as to claim that "people are the hosts of the spirits,"[72] or, "when a country is about to rise, (its ruler) listens to the people; when a country is about to perish, (its ruler) listens to the gods."[73] The former implies that people are more important than gods, and the latter sarcastically points out that humanity (the voice of the people) is more important than piety.

These different understandings of the relationship between human beings and spirits, therefore, represent the difference between the religious mentality of average persons and that of the more reflective intellectuals and writers. In the Eastern Chou period, as the records of *The Commentary of Tso* show, the idea of *"do ut des"* was obviously still a widely accepted attitude amongst the ruling class concerning the relationship between human beings and gods. When Ch'u and Chin were about to engage in a battle, the duke of Ch'u dreamt that the River God told him to make sacrifice so that he might be granted victory over Chin.[74] Even a disciple of Confucius was reportedly to have also accepted the idea that prayers to the spirits could help one recover from sickness.[75]

In discussing the method and the meaning of sacrifice, the text of *Mo-tzu* expounded a view that what heaven and the spirits deemed important was abundant material offerings and the social welfare of the people.[76] Mo Tzu is known to have arisen from socially low origins; he vehemently denounced the luxurious living styles of ruling society, and propounded a simple and practical way of living that reflected the everyday world of the ruled.[77]

Souls, Spirits, and the Abode of the Dead

The oracular inscriptions of the Shang seem not to contain words related to *hun* and *p'o*, which are approximately the equivalents of "soul." Yet this does not necessarily mean that the Shang, or earlier, people did not possess the idea of "soul." The royal ancestors were thought to be able to "be guests with Ti" and to protect descendants. There is no doubt that these ancestors were thought to have had a kind of existence after death, which, furthermore, was not exclusive to royalty. If rulers did not believe in the postmortem existence of servants and slaves, the practice of human sacrifice around the royal tombs would have been meaningless. Although no contemporary source indicates that during Shang nonrulers believed in postmortem existence, there is no evidence to disprove it.

In the bronze inscriptions of the Chou dynasty, two characters, *yen* 嚴 and *yi* 翼, according to a study, may be read as the equivalents of *hun* and *p'o*, the traditional two-part "soul."[78] These characters were used mainly in connection with the royalty, for bronze objects were usually gifts from the Chou kings to lesser nobles. As above, we cannot be sure if nonrulers were thought to possess similar kinds of souls. It was pointed out long ago, on the other hand, that the character *p'o* is related to *pa* in the bronze inscription, with the meaning of "white" or "bright light"—originally the light of the moon.[79] This connection with lunar waxing and waning, according to Yü Ying-shih, "eventually came to associate . . . the life and death of a man with the presence or absence of his *p'o*."[80] Yü believes that this concept came into being around the sixth century B.C. The evidence for this view comes from *The Commentary of Tso*, where the expressions *hun* and *p'o* have their earliest appearances.

What are the natures of *hun* and *p'o*? Is there any difference between them? Tzu-ch'an discusses it in *The Commentary of Tso*:

> When a man is born, that which is first created is called the *p'o*
> and, when the *p'o* has been formed, its positive part (*yang*) is
> called *hun*. If one is well provided, his *hun* and *p'o* grow strong,
> and possess intelligence and clear mind, even can reach the divine
> luminaries. When ordinary men and women die of violent death,
> their *hun* and *p'o* can still attach to the living and became licen-
> tious demons.[81]

Three points must be noted. First, Tzu-ch'an thinks that ordinary people can have both *hun* and *p'o* while alive as well as after their death. Thus, it is certain that *hun* and *p'o* were considered as soul-like properties, regardless of social status. Further, *p'o* was the negative or *yin* part, while *hun* was the positive or *yang* part of this spiritual existence. Third, both *hun* and *p'o* could attach to the living and cause harm. In a sense, Tzu-ch'an was explaining the possibility of dead people's becoming ghosts—a concept intertwined with that of *hun* and *p'o*. From Tzu-ch'an's description, furthermore, there perhaps was little distinction between postmortem *hun* and *p'o*, since both could attach to the living and cause afflictions.

On the other hand, according to a passage in *Han-fei-tzu*:

> The condition of one who is possessed (by a ghost) was that his
> *hun* and *p'o* left him and his spirit was disturbed. When his spirit
> was disturbed, he possessed no virtue (*te*). If the ghost does not
> afflict a person, his *hun* and *p'o* will not leave him, if *hun* and
> *p'o* do not leave, his spirit will not be disturbed. When one's
> spirit is not disturbed, it is considered as having virtue (*te*). If
> the ruler actively accumulates (virtue) and the ghost does not
> disturb his spirit, then his virtue will be entirely beneficial to
> the people.[82]

Here *hun* and *p'o* seem to be the essentials of the living spirit, and the context does not suggest any difference between *hun* and *p'o*.

We have not, however, answered the question of the difference between *hun* and *p'o*. A passage in the *Book of Rites* states that *hun* ascends to the heaven and *p'o* descends into the earth.[83] In the religious beliefs of the Shang and Chou, the deceased kings were said to be at the left and right of Ti, which means that they went up to the heaven after death. No evidence on this aspect exists regarding nonrulers. Judging from the custom of human sacrificial burials, however, there is reason to maintain that people then believed that the ruled could follow the ruler after death, if not in heaven then perhaps under earth. Thus, the idea of the *hun*'s ascending and *p'o*'s descending seems to be supported by the customs and evidence of ancient China.

It is to be expected, however, that the clear description of *hun* and *p'o* in the Confucianist *Book of Rites* may have reflected a systematized version of the ideas current in later society.[84] In the "Chao-hun" section of *Ch'u-tz'u*, for example, there are passages recalling the *hun*-soul of the departed dead, such as: "O soul, come back! In the east you cannot abide. . . . In the south you cannot stay. . . . For the west holds many perils, . . . In the north you may not stay. . . . Climb not to the heaven above, ... Go not down to the dark city."[85] This poetic description implies that the *hun* could either ascend into heaven or descend under the earth, or to any other direction. Actually, one passage in *The Book of Rites* also expresses the view that the *hun* could be anywhere after one's death.[86] This evidence implies that *p'o* might not be destined to go down the earth alone. A more down-to-earth picture of the *hun*'s location after death is found in Mo Tzu's sarcastic description of the Confucian funerary ritual of recalling the soul:

> *soul calling*
>
> When a parent dies, the Confucians lay out the corpse for a long time before dressing it for burial. They climb onto the roof, peer down the well, poke in the rat holes, and search in the washbasins, looking for (the soul of) the dead man.[87]

Mo Tzu might not have done full justice to the Confucian ritual, but since the ritual of soul-calling was common, the situation he described may have reflected certain contemporary practice.[88]

Besides their different destinations, it is still difficult to distinguish the nature of *hun* from that of *p'o*. The idea of *yin* and *yang* in relation to *p'o* and *hun* as stated in Tzu-ch'an's speech is too general for our purpose. On the other hand, considering the ancient belief in ghosts and spirits, discussed before, we may perhaps surmise that, since people had a more vivid idea of ghosts and spirits, and since *hun* and *p'o* are but different designations for ghost, as evinced the expression *kuei-hun* 鬼魂, their idea of the nature and image of *hun* and *p'o* might not be too far from that of the ghosts and spirits.

If the existence of the two-part soul was more or less certain in the mind of the people in the Eastern Chou and the Warring States period, the place where *hun* and *p'o* were supposed to go is not at all clear to us, or, for that matter, to people then. That the king could ascend to a heavenly court to meet his ancestors is a well-established belief, although the exact picture of this court is little known. In the eastern Chou period, dead members of the Chou royal court were thought to be "underneath." An inscription on a *ting*-tripod belonging to a noble of the Chou court, dated to around 560 B.C., states that the owner, Ai-ch'eng-shu 哀成叔, was to "die underneath the earth to serve prince Kang-kung."[89] Here, the souls of both lesser and higher nobles were thought to go under the earth. For the *hun* or *p'o* of the ruled, postmortem location was just as dark. In the Eastern Chou period, the abode of the dead was often referred to as the "Yellow Spring."[90] A famous story in *The Commentary of Tso* tells about Duke Chuang of Cheng, and his oath not to see his mother until they were both in the Yellow Spring—which signified death. Later, in repentance, he had an underground tunnel dug and reached as far as the underground water. This way he finally reunited with his mother inside the tunnel.[91] From an archaeological point of view, the term could very well have originally referred to the underground springs occasionally tapped when digging graves, and might subsequently have become a metaphorical expression for the abode of the dead. For example, there is a passage in *Mencius*: "The earth-worm eats the rotten wood and dirt above and drinks the yellow spring below."[92] Here it would be difficult to interpret the term yellow spring as the world of the dead. In the story just mentioned, the advice to Duke Chuang was: "If you dig the ground and reach the spring underneath, and meet (her) in the tunnel, who shall say that this is wrong?" This indicates that, even then, people could and did accept the meaning of "yellow spring" literally, i.e., the yellow water underground. In any case, there is as yet no precise evidence concerning the details of the postmortem Yellow Spring. We know nothing about the structure or likeness of this place, let alone any activities or characters (save the dead themselves) that could have existed there.[93]

For the Warring States period, we have much more substantial knowledge of the postmortem underground. The passage of *Ch'u-tz'u* quoted above mentioned a "dark city," with a "governor of the earth (*T'u-po* 土伯)" whose ferocious appearance was recited to dissuade the dead from entering. This description of the netherworld suggests that people began to express in a more realistic way the likeness of this place.

A text recently discovered in a Ch'in tomb in Kansu province provides new material for our understanding of the idea of afterlife and the soul. The text is an account of the resurrection of a man named Tan.[94] Here is early evidence for both the idea of postmortem revival and acknowledgment of the control exerted by the deity Ssu-ming 司命, who possessed authority over life and death. The high god Ti did not seem to have been involved in such decisions. The resurrection of Tan was granted when his master objected to Ssu-ming that Tan did not deserve to die because of a minor offense. Moreover, the story explains that after death, one's ghost needed food and possessed various desires. According to the story, the dead lived continuously in the tomb, suggesting location itself of the world of the dead. Resurrection stories used to be datable only as early as Six Dynasties *chih-kuai* 志怪,[95] stories of the strange, thus the unearthing of this new text pushes back the notion to the Warring States period. The idea of resurrection, however, should be viewed as an idea having had a long prehistory in the everyday religion of ancient China. The saying "the spirit of *hun*-soul returns to heaven; the form of the body-*p'o* returns to the earth," seems to be the result of scholarly rationalization as found in *The Book of Rites*. In any event, the ideas of the Yellow Spring and the Dark City were to develop into the netherworld of Han religion, as we shall see in Chapter 7, and finally merged with the Buddhist concept of hell to become one of the most important aspects of Chinese religion.[96]

Summary

It is difficult to discern for the Shang period any difference, if there was one, between the religious ideas and practices of the ruling class and that of the ruled, except in the degree of elaboration and the specific contents of rituals. This impression, one should admit, may be due to a paucity of documentation. In the Western Chou period, besides universal ideas concerning spirits and ghosts and the practice of ancestor worship, the ruling class developed the idea of a mandate of heaven that formulated the will of "heaven" according to human moral standards. This was originally employed by the Chou court to legitimize their overthrow of the Shang regime. It was, however, gradually adopted by intellectuals and writers of the type who composed and edited the texts of *The Book of Poetry*. We have seen examples of their efforts to persuade rulers that virtue was weightier than ritual. The ruled (or peasants), on the other hand, maintained a religious life according mostly to the agricultural cycle, which was shared by the ruling elite insofar as they shared the same agricultural background. Toward the end of Western Chou, therefore, we could detect a split in the religious attitudes among the rulers, the intellectuals, and the peasants.

This religious split includes two aspects. First, among the ruling elite there was the appearance of the moralistic mandate of heaven, which became embedded in the cosmological assumptions of the leading intellectuals of the Eastern Chou and the Warring States period,[97] although their social and political philosophies differed. The formation of an "intellectual" genre of thought and writing during this period,[98] of course, inspired rational discussions of the mandate of heaven and the old religious practices in general. In the case of the Confucians, the mandate of heaven was transformed from political ethics into personal moral conviction.[99] Second, there is a break between the ruling elite and rest of the population. Various shared beliefs received different treatment, as seen in the differing attitudes toward human sacrifice expressed in the "Yellow Bird." On the whole, however, ancestor worship and the belief in ghosts and spirits remained widely held among both social parts. The differences were mainly in the outward paraphernalia, not in the form or nature of their beliefs. Moreover, what concerned the rulers in worshipping spiritual beings was political matters, while the peasants were concerned mostly with personal well-being. Only some intellectuals reflected upon the nature and efficacy of the contemporary practices and launched numerous criticisms. Thus, by the time of the Warring States period, one could delineate a religion of the intellectual, as opposed to a religion of the non-elite, as well as an official religion, or the religion of the court. Nevertheless, it should again be made clear that such distinctions are only conveniences for discussing the development of religious expression among different social and political groups. There are elements of popular belief in the official cult as well as in the beliefs of the intellectuals. Lastly, although our examination of the traditional texts and archaeological finds in this chapter has revealed but a glimpse of ancient beliefs, important discoveries of documents discussed in the next chapter shed further light on the picture of the religious mentality of both elite and non-elite Chinese at the end of the Warring States period.

Chapter 4

Newly Discovered Daybooks and Everyday Religion

The sons of God came to present themselves before the Lord, and Satan came also among them. And the Lord said unto Satan, whence comest thou? Then Satan answered the Lord, and said, From going to and fro in the earth, and from walking up and down.[1]

The Jih-shu or Daybooks

In the previous two chapters our discussion of the religion of the commoners was based primarily on traditional documents edited as Confucian classics. This kind of material was not meant to preserve or to describe the religious practices of everyday life. Even so, we still gain glimpses of the world of the spirits and ghosts through the sophisticated arguments and high-flown language of influential thinkers and writers. Yet if not for the archaeological appearance of new primary material, this religious world would remain largely a subject of speculation. Here, I am referring to the *jih-shu* 日書 (daybooks) discovered only two decades ago.[2]

Jih-shu, or literally "Book of days" (henceforth daybook), a name appearing at the end of a roll of bamboo slips found in a Ch'in tomb (c. 216 B.C.) at Shui-hu-ti, Hupei province, also stands for a whole genre of divination texts for determining auspicious days and hours. In effect it represented a kind of handbook, or almanac, for use by a variety of people probably outside the context of court ritual. We see this genre in circulation even today as "almanac" (*t'ung-shu* 通書), "yellow calendar" (*huang-li* 黃曆), or "farmer's calendar" (*nung-min-li* 農民曆).[3] The pre-Han and early-Han daybooks are the earliest extant evidence of this literature and are of primary importance for the understanding of China's ancient religious practices. So far, seven discoveries of daybooks have been made in tombs from the Warring States period to the Han Dynasty.[4] Since the contents of these daybooks are more or less similar, I shall use the most extensive text, i.e., the daybook version A from Shui-hu-ti, as the source of the following discussions.

The contents of the daybook can be divided into two analytic categories. One deals with the auspiciousness of days in a general manner: whether a given date is suitable for particular activities. The other can be characterized as "issue oriented."[5] An example of the first category is such sections as "*ch'u* 除" or "*Ch'in-ch'u* 秦除"; there, the days are grouped into twelve categories according to the order of the twelve earth-branches. The operating principle for this divination method is, within a certain month, days that share the same earth-branch also share similar fortunes. The earth-branch in every month, furthermore, is categorized into different kinds of days. Thus, under the "*ch'u*" system, in the eleventh month for example, every *tzu* 子 (the first earth-branch) day is called *chieh* 結-day, and every *ch'ou* 丑 (the second earth-branch) day is called *yang* 陽-day. In the twelfth month, however, every *ch'ou* day is now called a *chieh*-day, and every *yin* 寅 (the third earth-branch) day is called a *yang*-day. The *chieh*-days are described as:

> Unsuccessful in doing things. If one makes sacrifice, it will not be auspicious. If a son is born, he shall have no younger brother; if he should have one, he (the younger brother) will certainly die. If one allows someone to stay in his house, this person will certainly forcefully occupy the house of the owner.[6]

Since in the sexagenary dating system every day must contain one of the twelve earth-branchs, there are only twelve kinds of day in the whole year, and their sexagenary order cycles repeatedly, according to the "*ch'u*" method. In other sections, such as "*chi-ch'en* 稷辰," the

70

days are grouped into only eight categories; while sections *hsüan-ko* 玄戈, *sui* 歲, and *hsing* 星 use the positions of the constellations as indicators of auspiciousness.

The above are general predictions of the auspiciousness of days in a whole year, in the sense that they present the general principle (for example, *yin* and *yang*). They are found at the beginning of the daybook, serving as introductions. After these comes the second category. Passages in this category deal with everyday occurrences, for examples, "illness," "offering to the parents," "sacrificing for travel," "taking a wife," "childbirth," "thieves," "dreams," "making clothes," "horses," "prohibitions for building houses," or "prohibitions for farming." We shall examine some of these in order to cast light on people's lives in the context of a system of belief.

Marriage

What did people need to know when contracting a marriage? Probably its overall results as well as the wealth and physical features of the future wife. Various passages in the general category mention the auspicious and inauspicious days for getting married, with a special section on marriage itself.[7]

Except for the simple statements "good" and "bad," most predictions of marriage in the daybook are unfavorable. Concerning the character of the wife, for example, we find such expressions as: "the wife will be talkative," "the wife will not be quiet," "the wife will be jealous," or "the wife will be shrewish."[8] One may surmise, therefore, that the character of an ideal wife was the opposite of these apprehensive descriptions. These predictions also reveal that there was litttle contact between man and wife before their marriage.

The duration of marriage seems to be another concern: on such and such day, "when taking a wife, the wife will not be present," "the wife will surely be deserted," "if (the wife) is not deserted, she will certainly die because of childbirth," "within three years (the wife) will be deserted or dead."[9] It is overwhelmingly obvious that desertion by the husband was a major concern of the would-be bride. Thus, the daybook must have been consulted by anxious parents of both families. We are not told the reasons for a husband's desertion of his wife, but

71

since producing offspring was a major function of marriage, it was likely an important criterion of the overall success of marriage. Thus, [auspiciousness in a marriage depended to a considerable degree upon the ability of the wife to produce children.] One passage reads: "When the constellation is *Tung-ching* 東井, everything is inauspicious. . . . When taking a wife, she will give birth to many children; if a child is born on this day, it will die in ten days."[10] Thus, this is a day suitable for marriage, but unsuitable for childbirth. Again, concerning another day, "One should not take a wife, for she will not bear a child; or if she does, it will not be a son."[11] An entire section is devoted to auspicious days for childbirth (see below).

[The wife's personal or family property was also among the concerns of the users of daybooks.] We read: "When taking a wife, the wife will be poor."[12] Such poverty ought to refer to her situation after marriage. If the wife is poor in the future, the husband also will be; therefore the action is inauspicious. From the vantage point of the wife's family, there could be further anxieties about the imminent marriage. The parents would have liked to know, for example, whether: "when marrying off a daughter, the house will be depleted,"[13] or, "when marrying off a daughter, the parents will have bad luck."[14]

In a few daybook passages, the outcome of a marriage was pronounced favorable.[15] But favorable in which respects? Whenever stated, we find a surprisingly consistent attitude; i.e., they all refer to the loving relationship between the man and the wife: "when taking a wife, the woman will be loved,"[16] "when taking a wife, the man will be loved,"[17] or "(when taking a wife) on the *k'uei* 奎-day, the husband will love the wife; (when taking a wife) on the *lou* 婁-day, the wife will love the husband."[18]

All these notwithstanding, that such predictions are from the vantage point of the husband or the parents of the wife shows the subordinate position of women at this time. Also, since the number of unfavorable predictions about marriage far exceed the favorable, it may reflect a pessimistic attitude toward marriage or toward women. In fact, the whole range of the unfavorable situations in daybooks surpasses that for the favorable ones. This suggests that, in the mind of the users or the compilers of daybooks, undesirable situations were many, while favorable marriages were limited in their scope of enjoyment.]

Childbirth

Various predictions about the fate of the child, collected in a section called "childbirth,"[19] help illuminate people's hopes and fears. The kind of prediction most commonly found concerns the material well-being, social status, character, and temperament of the child.

Along with the statements "rich" and "poor,"[20] there are a number of more complicated forecasts, such as "(the child) will become sick, and will lose his parents, but will become rich in the future," or "(the child) will become alcoholic and incur sickness, but will become rich in the future."[21] This reveals the idea that the life of a person was subjected to the ups and downs of fortune, and did not necessarily follow a linear development. This, however, is still a very simplified way to present potentially much more complex situations.

Optimistic predictions concerning the social status of the child include: (when a child is born on such and such day) "he will become an official (*li* 吏),"[22] "he will become a high-official (*ta-fu* 大夫, *ta-li* 大吏),"[23] "he will become a messenger,"[24] "he will be bestowed with noble title (*chüeh* 爵),"[25] or "he will be favored by the lord."[26] Relatively undesirable situations include: "when a child is born (on this day), no matter whether male or female, he or she will become a thief," "when a child is born (on this day), he will become an orphan, and will dress in rags," or "when a child is born (on this day), he or she will surely become someone's servant."[27]

These different prospects show something of the social status of the users of daybooks. The greatest hope for any male child was appointment as a "high official." For most children, however, eventual social status would have been lower echelon. Considering the fact that people usually hope that their children do better, the social status of the users of daybooks was most probably not very high. Evidence for this observation comes from the professions of the users themselves. We can say this partly because predictions of auspicious days mention work related to farming, trading, and the military, and mentions government offices no higher than *se-fu* 嗇夫, or local bailiff.[28]

Predictions concerning the character and temperament of children give quite a few examples heralding a warlike or aggressive character for the son.[29] In some other cases, indulgence in wine, hunting, and womanizing are mentioned.[30] These of course do not constitute the full range of character or temperament, but are simply common expectations about personalities. It is striking that nothing "sophisticated" or "literary" is detected among these examples. Some scholars have maintained that this fact reflects a ruthless and militant society, one identifiable with Ch'in culture. However, to validate this view, the larger problem of the social and cultural background of the daybooks has to be clarified. We shall deal with this in a later section.

Daily life

The extent to which divination entered the mundane activities of the ancient Chinese is amply attested in the *jih-shu* daybooks. Auspicious days are prescribed for eating and drinking,[31] for slaughtering farm animals,[32] for various construction works,[33] for travelling,[34] for making garments,[35] or for seeking entertainment.[36] Minor or major disasters will occur if one does not follow the instructions.[37]

For example, a passage says: "It is not permitted to make new garments on the *ssu-wei* 巳未 days of the sixth month; violators will surely die."[38] As the making of new garments was often mentioned together with ritualistic capping, i.e., the adult initiation ceremony, it is possible that the making of new garments had religious and ceremonial significance. Similar customs were maintained in the Han era.[39]

In choosing a date for construction projects, a daybook passage warns the reader:

> On the days of (not) building houses, one should not build houses. If the inner chamber is built, the parents will die; if the right chamber is built, the wife of the eldest son will die; if the left chamber is built, the wife of the middle son will die; if the outer wall is built, the son of the grandson will die; if the northern wall is built, the cattle and sheep will die.[40]

Not only are there favorable dates for commencing construction, the positions of the buildings themselves are also related to the fate of the owner. A separate section of the daybook deals with the problem of geomancy in house construction. The direction, height, and width of a house, as well as its position relative to surrounding structures

74

such as pools, storage facilities, wells, pigpens, gates, or roads, are all related to the fortune of the owner.[41] This is the earliest example of Chinese geomancy in its practical application.[42] The idea of the five elements also appeared in connection with the five directions: "The east is wood, the south is fire, the west is metal, the north is water, the center is earth."[43] However, the metaphysical concepts of the five elements had not yet been integrated.

It is interesting that the daybooks paid relatively extensive attention to the auspicious days for travelling, including days for setting out as well as returning home. Several sections are devoted especially to proper days for making sacrifices before travelling.[44] Exorcism and talismans for expelling evil spirits that obstruct the way are also included. One such is "the pace of Yü":

> When you reach the gate of the district, you should stop, make three Yü-steps, shout loudly saying, "I am going to set out. I hope that there is no danger. (I shall) first clean the way for Yü." Then you should draw five lines on the ground and pick up the dirt in the middle of the lines and carry it.[45]

The "pace of Yü" is also mentioned in the early-Han medical text found in the Ma-mang-tui tomb no. 3, where it was employed in exorcism for patients with inguinal swellings.[46] It is later found in the Taoist texts as one of the exorcist rituals, thus demonstrating the deep roots of the Taoist religion.[47]

When we read in *The Commentary of Tso* about the prince of Ch'en's divining before attending a party, it might sound somewhat strange.[48] The material in the daybooks, however, provides ample evidence that people often divined for auspicious days for "hiking in the mountains, eating and drinking, and hunting in the fields," or for "drinking and singing," etc.[49] In a word, recreation was considered significant in the cosmological order and had to be conducted accordingly.

Regarding eating and drinking, the daybooks reveal that sickness was often caused by the food one took. For example, it is said that "meat," "rooster," "red meat," "wine," "dog meat," "fresh eggs," "yellow fish," and "dry meat" could all cause sickness. This may suggest that people already knew that rotten or spoiled meats could be toxic. However, sickness was also often thought to have been caused by dead ancestors or malicious demons, a long tradition that can be traced back as early as the Shang dynasty. A typical passage reads:

> When one falls ill on the *chia-i* 甲乙 days, it is caused by the ghosts of the parents. It is acquired through meat, which comes from the east, and is placed in a lacquer container. . . .[50]

As the text shows, although people attributed the cause of sickness to spirits and ghosts, experience also showed them that certain kinds of food, especially spoilable meats, were responsible for sickness. This reflects a type of medical knowledge at this time. Compare this with views transmitted in other documents, where sickness was thought to be the result of the imbalance of the six *ch'i* or climatic conditions, i.e., *yin, yang,* wind, rain, darkness, and brightness, as presented in *The Commentary of Tso*,[51] or in the medical classic *Huang-ti nei-ching*.[52] The difference is revealing. The ideas found in *The Commentary of Tso,* and especially in *Huang-ti nei-ching,* tried to give a systematic and naturalistic explanation of the cause of illness. This is the natural outcome of an intellectual systematization of cosmological-physical theory. The daybooks, on the other hand, insofar as they were practical handbooks, identified the source: dead ancestors, malicious demons, and certain food. However, the texts do not identify symptoms, nor did they provide medical solutions. Presumably, actual treatments were dispensed by other means. The daybooks only provided predictions of the outcome of illness, and exorcistic methods to drive away haunting spirits, as covered below in the section on demonography. Thus, the daybook passages represented a popular view of sickness, which was still intertwined with beliefs in ghosts and spirits, while those in *The Commentary of Tso* and *Huang-ti nei-ching* represented the views of the literate elite, which were based on naturalistic cosmology.

Social Problems

Because of the political situation of the Warring States period, military affairs were among the concerns of the users of the daybooks. In the general predictions of days, such as the section called *chi-ch'en* 稷 辰, we found such predictions as "good for fighting in the field, certain to catch marquises and kings," or "fighting and sacking a city."[53] These indicate that the predicted military actions were of rather large scale. In fact, the prediction of military outcomes is a regular feature in the *chi-ch'en* section, where at the end of the description of each kind of day, the text would conclude with expressions like "there will be war," "there will be no war," or "there will be intensive war," etc.[54] Rather than advising the military commanders, who presumably made major decisions for war, most texts probably served as references for the lower level officers and soldiers who at the end of the Warring States period were the main constituent of the fighting force.[55] That these predictions became regular features in the daybooks illustrates vividly the socio-political situation. In another text discovered in the same Ch'in tomb as our daybook, thirty-five battles are recorded for a fifty-six-year period. If one adds the records provided by traditional histories, the total number reaches fifty-five, or nearly one every year.[56] No wonder one had to inquire regularly about the possibility of warfare.

The sufferings of the people, however, included not only wars, but other kinds of social unrest as well. One had to be prepared when travelling in the countryside, for one might encounter bandits:

> On a day of "outside-harm" (*wai-hai* 外害), you should not travel. When going to the countryside (on such a day), it is certain that you shall meet bandits, and encounter military actions.[57]

There seems to have been no effective means to solve the problems of banditry and theft. Thus, one of the more interesting daybook sections concerns catching thieves. The section describes the facial features of a thief, whether he was tall or short, and where he was hiding, all according to the day that the burglary happened.[58] It is interesting that, in the various Ch'in codes found in the same tomb, rather harsh laws are given against criminal activities. In a lengthy tract entitled "Laws on Robbery,"[59] cases involving the stealing of even less than "one coin" were prosecuted.[60] With all the laws against robbery, that people still needed a "formula" for thief-catching, as provided in daybooks, only vindicates the observation in the *Lao-tzu* that "the more comprehensive the laws are, the more active the robbers and thieves."

Another important social issue in the daybook concerns desertion. Just as in the predictions concerning military activities, desertion was also among the questions asked daily by the user. Examples include: "(On such a day), if one runs away, he will not be caught," "(on such a day), if the servant or concubine runs away, they will not be caught," "the one who deserts will come back by himself," or "the deserter will be caught."[61] There is also a special section entitled "Days for desertion." A passage reads: "The seventh day of the first month, and the tenth day of the second month, . . . Those who desert on these days will certainly be caught, if not, they will certainly die."[62]

The phenomenon of desertion, whether of household servants and concubines, or of slaves, farmers, or soldiers, seems to have been a widespread one at the end of the Warring States period. *Han-fei-tzu* once mentioned the desertion of soldiers:

> One exacts taxes and revenues and concentrates the people's forces to provide against eventualities and fill up the public storehouses and the state treasury. Officers and soldiers who desert their posts and hide will find shelter in the residences of powerful men, and thereby evade taxation and military service. If the superior fails to catch them they will number in the tens of thousands.[63]

The reason for the desertion of soldiers and farmers, according to *Han-fei-tzu*, was to evade heavy taxation. Other legal documents found in the Shui-hu-ti tomb also contain cases on the desertion of servants and slaves.[64] The daybook text, however, does not clarify the reason for desertion. The way that the predictions appear in the daybook suggests that it was a common phenomenon that needed no explanation. But for whom were the predictions concerning desertion days made? It has been suggested that they were made for the deserters themselves, to help them choose an auspicious day to run away.[65] Considering the context in which the predictions appeared, however, it is unlikely that they were for the use of anyone other than the head of a farming or merchant family. Just as in the section on catching thieves, predictions concerning desertion were mainly to help the user make an arrest.

These problems, as well as issues pertaining to daily life, marriage, or childbirth, reveal not only the living conditions of the people, but also how they coped with them in the context of their beliefs. As mentioned in Chapter 3, such concerns for daily life are also reflected in the lines of the classic *Chou-i*, which suggests a common religious mentality. There is, however, another category that has more to do with the internal, or spiritual, living conditions. This is the material contained in a daybook section that deals with ghosts and spirits.

Ghosts, spirits, and gods

In previous chapters we discussed ideas concerning ghosts and gods maintained by the people of the Eastern Chou and the Warring States period. Due to the narrow focus of the traditional documents, the ghosts and gods found there represent only a small portion of the extra-human powers that existed in the minds of the people. This is confirmed by the Shui-hu-ti daybook, in which a host of ghosts and spirits is described. Most are found in a section called "Inquiry" (*chieh* 詰), which is actually instructions for handling various evil ghosts, spirits, and even gods. In the "Inquiry," evil ghosts and spirits are first identified. The text then provides exorcistic methods to expel each of them. Thus, it could be regarded as a certain kind of demon-ography.[66] Some of the ghosts are zoomorphic, such as "the sacred dog" (*shen-kou* 神狗):

> When a dog continuously enters a person's house at night, seizing the husband and sporting with the wife, and it cannot be caught, it is a sacred dog disguised as a ghost. Use the bark of a mulberry tree . . . roast it and eat it. This will stop it.[67]

Or it might be a "sacred serpent" (*shen-hui* 神虫):

> When a ghost persistently follows a person but goes away upon seeing other people, it is a sacred serpent disguised as a human being. Use a sharp sword to stab its neck, then it will not come again.[68]

Although the word *shen* (god, sacred) is incorporated in the names of these two apparitions, it is clear from the context that they were seen as malicious demons. The word *shen* here is only an adjective describing their supernatural nature.

Some other evil ghosts might have originated from plants, e.g., a certain "thorn demon" (*chi-kuei* 棘鬼):

When in one house without reason all inhabitants fall victim to a plague, some die and some suffer illness, this is caused by the presence of a thorn demon (in the house). It is buried upright and the earth above it is damp during a drought, and dry during a flood. If you dig it out and throw it away, this will stop.[69]

[Because the ancient Chinese believed that certain plants, such as peachwood and thorn,[70] possessed powers, it is not surprising that some transformed into evil demons.]

[Natural phenomena were another source for the formation of evil powers,] e.g., "heavenly fire":

When heavenly fire burns a person's houses and is unstoppable, it will stop if it is quenched using white sand.[71]

Similarly, malicious powers of nature such as "thunder," "cloud," "cold wind," "swift wind,"[72] etc., were also curbed by various methods of exorcism.

Lastly, the dead were, of course, thought to become ghosts, especially when they died an untimely death. Thus, there is the "hungry ghost":

Whenever a ghost holds a basket and enters a person's house, saying: "Give me food!" it is a hungry ghost. If you throw a shoe at it, it will stop.[73]

The "young dead" could also haunt people if they had not been buried:

When a ghost continuously enters a person's house naked, it is someone who died young and was not buried. If you spread ashes on it, it will stop.[74]

Of the seventy entries in the *chieh*, almost half of the ghosts and spirits are anthropomorphic; more than ten entries concern zoomorphic (including insects) demons, and in nine cases, the forces of nature are the source of trouble. [Even inanimate objects are considered possible sources of demonic spirits.]

When throughout the house there is the sound of a drum but one does not see that drum, it is a ghost-drum. It will stop if you answer it with a human drum.[75]

This thriving ghostly community, one surmises, constitutes the object of worship on occasions of "ghost worship 鬼祠," or "sacrifice to the multitude of gods above and below 以蔡 (祭) 上下群神,"[76] as mentioned in other chapters of the daybook. The nature of gods, furthermore, is basically similar to that of the ghosts. Thus, we read that there is the Great God (*ta-shen* 大神):

> His place cannot be passed through because he is adept at harming people. Make balls from dog's excrements and take them along when you pass through that place. When you see the god, hit him with these, and it will not harm anyone anymore.[77]

The use of excrements as means of exorcism reminds us of the story of Li Chi mentioned in the previous chapter, and we will come back to it later in this chapter. There is also the "god on high" (*shang-shen* 上神):

> When a man with the form of a bird or a farm animal continuously walks into a person's house, it is the god on high, . . . If you strike the drum and sound the cymbals and scare it with noise, it will not come anymore.[78]

There is practically no difference between these "great" and "high" gods and malicious demons, either in the nature of their deeds, or in the treatment to which they were subjected.

The idea that there is little difference between the nature of gods (*shen*) and ghosts (*kuei*) is, of course, not peculiar to the daybook.[79] The two characters "ghost" and "god" (*kuei, shen*) often refer to the same spiritual beings in pre-Ch'in documents. The general meaning of *shen* is clearly stated in this passage from the *Book of Rites*:

> Mountains, forests, streams, valleys, hills and mounds, which are able to produce clouds, create winds and rain, and generate monsters, are all considered as having spiritual power (*shen*).[80]

Thus, the word is sometimes better rendered as "spirit" rather than "god." This idea was not confined to Confucianist circles. One passage in *Han-fei-tzu* states that:

> When the world is ruled according to the Tao, the ghosts will not be powerful (*pu-shen* 不神). The people of an orderly age

81

and ghosts and gods do not harm each other. Therefore it is said that it is not because their "ghosts" (*kuei*) are not powerful (*pu-shen*), it is because their "spirits" (*shen*) do not harm people.[81]

Here, the word *shen* is used as a description of the nature of the ghost, and *shen* and *kuei* are interchangeable terms.

Although there is a paucity of information concerning popular conceptions of gods, spirits, and ghosts in traditional sources, as discussed in the last chapter, one can still discern that the concept of spiritual beings in the daybooks does not differ. For example, *Chou-li* records the following method to expel the "god of the water-bugs":

> The Hu-cho-shih 壺涿氏 is responsible for the elimination of water-bugs. To expel them use a drum made of earth, throw burnt rocks at them. If one intends to kill their god, one should use elm wood (?) pierced with ivory and sink it into the water, then their god shall die.[82]

This example could very easily be incorporated into the *chieh* section of the Shui-hu-ti daybook, as the style of language and method of exorcism are quite close. It is especially worth noticing that the "god" can also be "killed." The idea of killing a god or spirit reveals another aspect of the early Chinese understanding of spiritual beings. Since they could be killed, it follows that they were mortals also. The distinction between spiritual and natural, therefore, was probably not obvious, especially with regard to the lesser spirits and demons. In other words, in the popular conception as revealed in the daybook, the worlds of men and spirits were not separate, but formed a continuous whole. This is in contrast to the famous exposition by Kuan I-fu 觀射父, to the effect that earth and heaven were separated by Ch'ung and Li by order of the emperor Chuan Hsü.[83] The world of the daybook, to use Kuan I-fu's words, was still one in which "people mingled with gods and spirits" (*min-shen tsa-jou* 民神雜糅).

As pointed out above, gods, ghosts, and demons in the daybooks did not act as arbiters of morality and ethics. They were not part of the *mores*, i.e., the moral standards and behavior of the people using such handbooks. Their actions were therefore not responses to human behavior but expressions of extra-human intention, for good or for ill.

Gods, ghosts, and demons could cause annoyances[84] affecting people's psychological balance,[85] or cause all kinds of diseases.[86] These were, indeed, unfriendly ghosts. Yet it seems that in the end they posed no real threat to the users of the daybook. It was always possible to counteract a demon, as illustrated by the examples of exorcism mentioned above. I shall examine this mechanistic and optimistic world view of the daybooks in a moment.

Augmented by the gallery of various demons and spirits mentioned in our daybook, we gain the impression of a world inhabited not only by men and animals but also by a host of extra-human powers. This host of extra-human powers may be categorized. The lowest order, it seems, included forces close to natural phenomena, such as wind, thunder, or heavenly fire. The highest order, on the other hand, might include such deities as the "Lord on High" (*shang-ti*), the "Emperor on High" (*shang-huang* 上皇), the "God on High" (*shang-shen*), "Heaven" (*t'ien*), or the "Red Emperor" (*ch'ih-ti* 赤帝). Between the highest and the lowest orders were various demons, ghosts, and spirits, such as the "Earth God" (*t'u-shen* 土神)[87] and others already mentioned. Some scholars are inclined to see the various deities in the highest order as only different names for a single "supreme god."[88] This view, however, is untenable, at least in the case of the chromatic and directional emperor-deities of the Ch'in and Han courts.[89] They were not the same as the "God on High" or "Emperor on High" found in the daybook.

The order of spiritual beings is broadly consistent with that found in classical texts: the spiritual world reflects the human world, and the relative positions among the spiritual beings are comparable to those in human society. However, what is special in the case of the daybook is the preoccupation with beings from the lower echelon of the spiritual power structure. While the high gods are rarely mentioned, the text abounds with minor demons and spirits, as discussed above. This is seldom found in the classical texts, which are documents pertaining primarily to the literate ruling elite, and which usually perceive the world order on a grandiose scale. This naturally leads to the next question: what kind of religious mentality does this preoccupation with the minor demons reflect? And how does it differ from the picture gained from classical texts?

83

Religious mentality as reflected in daybooks

[Generally speaking, the main object of religious belief is to explain the relationship between human beings and spirits and to find ways to achieve a happy life] The divinational and demonographical treatises contained in daybooks provide us with substantial evidence of particular beliefs in this regard. Furthermore, from the methods that the people employed to deal with extra-human forces and beings, and thus to survive, it is possible to investigate the mentality that supported this belief.

The cosmos reflected in daybooks is of a double nature. On the one hand, it is predictable, for every phenomenon in it is already fixed according to its correspondence with the nature of the days and hours prescribed in the divination schemes. In other words, things move in a predetermined direction. Even the identification of thieves, for example, can easily be achieved by referring to the time when the burglary happened. On the other hand, it is also a world full of capricious spirits and demons, whose actions are often beyond human comprehension. Yet, since the world is basically predictable, the role of the demons and gods is also fixed. Unwelcome spiritual beings can be thwarted by exorcistic methods. For example, certain days are suitable for "removing the disastrous and expelling the inauspicious."[90] The "Inquiry," or "Demonography," discussed above, provided the user with all sorts of methods for the successful handling of an attack of unfriendly demons.

What one can deduce from this is a mentality that recognizes as such the unpredictable elements of the world, but at the same time contains them by conceptualizing them as part of a predetermined structure, akin to the regularity of the changing seasons.] Thus, the user of the daybook had reduced the anxiety of having to face chaos in life, for chaos is the origin of uncertainty and fear.

The rationale of the daybooks is based precisely on this world view: every phenomenon in the world has a one-to-one correlation with a certain day or hour, and the auspiciousness of the day or hour is a known fact. This, however, is not the same as determinism. A person has to follow the prescribed instructions to find his way through perils; he can still move freely within the fixed structure, as in the playing of chess according to rules. Yet, since he has only to select the appropriate timing of events according to prescribed days and hours, with their inherent natures, there is no way, or no need, for him to apply subjective and independent intelligence and willpower beyond a limited and conventional value system. In order to enjoy a comfortable and prosperous life, one does not have to exert any personal effort, but only to choose the correct day and hour to undertake things. There is no need for moral reflection, since the nature of neither the days nor the gods and spirits is correlated with ethical or moral values. In the "Inquiry," for example, no explanation is given for infection by unfriendly demons and ghosts. In many cases, the text plainly states that the reasons are unknown:

> When a person is constantly attacked by a demon for no reason, it is the thorn demon. If you make a bow from peach wood and arrows from jujube and feather them with cock feathers, and shoot it when you see it, it will be gone.[91]

In a sense, this reflects an optimistic mentality: there is no unsolvable dilemma in the world, one needs not search one's conscience before finding a simple solution from a daybook.

This world view, it should be made clear, is not unique to daybooks. *Yin-yang* and Five-Phases theories, which gained wide influence during the Warring States period, also reflect a cosmology based on the mechanical movements and interdependence of various elements. The structure of the chapter "Monthly Ordinances" ("Yüeh-ling") in *Book of Rites*, for example, resembles certain parts of daybooks because the characteristics of days are defined according to a predetermined scheme, a scheme that applies the *yin-yang* and Five-Phases theories.[92] Although the daybook does not fully employ such theories,[93] and although its scope, encompassing the relatively mundane concerns of nonrulers, is not as commanding as the concerns for the welfare of the entire society and state expressed in "Monthly Ordinances," both show a rather similar mentality. The universe, according to this mentality, is inhabited by autonomous numinous forces the nature of which, nevertheless, is recognizable and therefore subject to manipulation. Thus, by consulting daybooks, an ordinary person tries to avoid disaster and gain a better life; whereas, by conforming to the instructions in "Monthly Ordinances," the head of state is able to guide his subjects in the proper manner of all social, political, and economic undertakings. It seems, therefore, that the cosmology of the daybook grew out of the same cultural milieu as that which produced the "Monthly Ordinances."[94]

Unlike the highly systemized and idealized "Monthly Ordinances," however, our daybook is not an integrated, homogeneous work. The very fact that there are two versions of the daybook in the corpus at Shui-hu-ti, plus a recent discovery in Kansu and some earlier cases of similar ones,[95] demonstrates that we are dealing with a kind of "miscellanea" of individual divinational methods then in use and frequently appearing as part of a collection.

Furthermore, the contents of the various treatises often contradict each other even within the same collection.[96] It is obvious that if we are to accept that these different sections have an inner coherence, then they ought to be seen as originally separate divinational treatises that are not necessarily of the same tradition.[97] A passage in *Shih-chi* illustrates well this situation:

> In the days of Emperor Wu, the diviners were once gathered together and asked if a certain day was suitable for taking a wife. The *Wu-hsing* 五行 diviner said "yes"; the geomancer said "no"; the *Chien-ch'u* 建除 diviner said "inauspicious"; the *Ts'ung-ch'en* 叢辰 diviner said "great disaster"; the *Li* 曆-diviner said "minor disaster"; the *T'ien-jen* 天人 diviner said "somewhat auspicious"; the *T'ai-i* 太一 diviner said "highly auspicious." They could not come to a conclusion in their heated debate, and a petition was sent to the Emperor. The Emperor replied: "To avoid the various death taboos, follow the *Wu-hsing* method in principle."[98]

Although this incident occurred in the Han dynasty, it certainly reflects the chaotic situation among diviners of earlier periods, and corroborates our observation on the miscellaneous nature of the material in daybooks.

What principle or strategy, then, should the user of daybooks follow? We do not really know. But a clue is found in a passage in the section "Travels" (*hsing* 行):

> Whenever one plans to do something, it is necessary to choose the leisure days within a month, as long as they are not the days

for the descent of the Red Emperor. Even if those other days bear inauspicious labels, there would be no great harm.[99]

In other words, even if "those other days" in the "Travels" section are inauspicious according to other sections, one could still consider them harmless in a travel context. This instruction tells the user that under certain conditions certain inauspicious days can be safely ignored. It also shows that people recognized the existence of inconsistencies among the various divinational treatises contained in daybooks, and that they considered it impossible or impractical to follow all the instructions at once.

The users of such works, therefore, did not concern themselves with whether instructions for daily activities constituted a logical system. What interested them was whether they could use one of the divinational methods to solve their immediate problems. In a sense, the contradictions in systems actually provided the user with loopholes. Is it fair to assume, then, that contradictions in divination systems reflected either a lack of logic or opportunism? Modern overviews tend to use such terms as "immature," "superstitious," or "primitive," but the most compelling view is that the different divinational treatises were simply different methods used to safeguard life and expel noxious forces. Their primary concern was not to construct a comprehensive model of the working of the universe, as did the "Monthly Ordinances" authors. The daybooks provided solutions to practical problems on a limited basis. This is not unlike the religious beliefs of ancient Egyptians and Mesopotamians. They maintained a host of deities whose functions and natures often contradicted each other and yet still coexisted. An explanation about a certain deity, a natural or social phenomenon, or even the origin of the universe, was intended to do no more than solve particular problems.[100]

The spiritual world of the daybooks, like those of other classical texts, contained gods, ghosts, and spirits of a more or less anthropomorphic nature. This differs greatly from the conception of *t'ien*, a Confucian abstraction derived from moral reasoning.[101] Furthermore, the mechanistic cosmology differs from the organismic cosmology that, later in the Western Han period, became the predominant ideology of the official and elite segments of society. Organismic cosmology saw the universe as a harmonious entity comprised of Heaven, Earth, and

Man. The three elements were intertwined and influenced each other through the binary *yin-yang* and cyclical Five-Phases theories.[102] Nevertheless, such organismic cosmolgy was so complex that it would be incomprehensible to many whose daily life was never completely out of the influence of the mechanistic cosmology of the down-to-earth daybooks. The proliferation of various divination and mantic works cited by the "Bibliographical Treatise" (*I-wen chih* 藝文志) in the *History of Han*, under the *shu-shu* 數術 (magic and fortune-telling) section,[103] as well as those "superstitions" that Wang Ch'ung and other intellectuals tried hard to rebuke (see Chapter 8 below), suggest that most people, from courtiers to farmers, availed themselves of practical methods as needed.

The significance of daybooks as documents of everyday religion

Daybooks were a kind of guidebook for daily life, but they did not cover everything. Problems related to literature, social ethics, or statecraft find little mention in them. They are about marriage, business, farming, meeting with officials, and starting any project.[104] The concerns contained in them cross social lines. For example:

> *Yin* 陰-days: favorable for the household, for making offerings, for marriage, very auspicious for buying merchandise. When paying a visit to high officials, the results should be fine and no problem should arise.[105]

Or:

> *Ta* 達-days: favorable for marshaling the troops, for setting out to combat, for meeting with people. When making offerings to (the gods and ghosts) high and low, all will be favorable. If a son is born, favorable; if it is a girl, she is destined to leave the country.[106]

In another section, the statements are even more elaborate:

> *Hsiu* 秀-days are the so-called "double-bright (days)": favorable for fighting in the field, certain to be able to capture kings and dukes, when a son is born he will be handsome and tall and

wise. Favorable for meeting with people and to raise cattle. Good for getting married, for marrying daughters off, for making garments, for making offerings. Suitable for eating, drinking, singing and making merry, and for approaching officials. Favorable for changing official jobs.[107]

What is noteworthy here is that the interests of various social groups, including military personnel, farmers, and bureaucrats, were all integrated into a single formula.

However, it remains to be demonstrated whether daybooks, particularly that discovered in the Shui-hu-ti tomb, reflect the characteristics of Ch'in culture. Based on the contents of the text, it is unconvincing to argue that they represented only the Ch'in, since the mundane concerns could have belonged to many regions of China, as other evidence discussed below shows. Moreover, it has been argued that the existence of a conversion table of the names of the months in the Ch'in and Ch'u calendars suggests that the text was used by the local Ch'in ruling class as a reference for Ch'u customs, and that the *ch'u* 除 section is actually a Ch'u divination text.[108] This can be corroborated by the fact that, on a silk manuscript discovered in a Ch'u tomb of the late Warring States period at Ch'ang-sha, there is a brief treatise on inauspicious days closely resembling passages in our daybook.[109] It has also been suggested that the method of using the position and movement of the planet Jupiter to predict fortunes was a Ch'u custom.[110]

Many historians have viewed Ch'in culture as vulgar, uncouth, and utilitarian. One argument that the daybook is a product of Ch'in culture emphasizes the fact that no special attention is paid to either the larger issues of social justice (*i* 義), or the ideals of humanity (*jen* 仁), or (Confucian) ritual and music, the hallmarks of the Ch'i 齊 and Lu 魯 culture, but only to those matters concerning the everyday life of the people. It is an opinion already shared by ancient texts such as *The Commentary of Tso* and writers such as Chia I.[111] This errs, however, by comparing the world view and religious beliefs of the lower echelon of society with the culture of the elite of Ch'i and Lu. To say that the daybooks reflected a utilitarian and vulgar spirit is one thing; to say that this spirit belonged only to the Ch'in people is another. The ordinary people of the states of Ch'i and Lu might have had more in common with their counterparts in Ch'in or Ch'u than with the elite culture of their own states.

The recent discovery in T'ien-shui, Kansu province, of two more versions of the daybooks, although adding to the academic debate, also provides the possibility for the emergence of new perspectives on such texts.[112] From the published text and descriptions, it is certain that there are similarities as well as differences among the two T'ien-shui daybooks and that of Shui-hu-ti described thus far. Some propose that the T'ien-shui ones represent Ch'in culture, and that of Shui-hu-ti, Ch'u culture. The T'ien-shui versions, it is argued, contain little information concerning ghosts and spirits, which seems as a generalization, to have less interested the Ch'in people. In contrast, the Shui-hu-ti text contains far more information about spirits and ghosts, as well as themes for ritual behavior, thus reflecting the more mystical Ch'u religion.[113] It is interesting to note that some, however, considered the descriptions of ghosts and spirits in the Shui-hu-ti daybook "lacking in imagination," and claimed that they represent Ch'in religious ideas.[114]

There is no need to judge between the two parties at this point. It seems that both may be asking questions in the wrong direction: the issue is not whether the text reflects Ch'in or Ch'u culture—it may contain both elements, or even more. What would be more significant is to consider that the Shui-hu-ti daybook might contain elements of popular culture shared by people from a wide area, an area touching several major regions of China. The story about the adulterer mentioned in *Han-fei-tzu*, discussed in Chapter 3, is of special interest. Although it concerns the popular notions of Yen, a state located to the north of the Central Plain, it is in fact echoed in the daybooks. One passage in the daybook reads:

> When a ghost continuously follows a person's wife and cohabits with her, saying, "(I am) a son of the Lord on High (*shang-ti*) who has come down to take my pleasure." He will die if one bathes with dog's excrement and beats him with a reed.[115]

The similarity in the situations suggests that the Shui-hu-ti text reflects not merely a local (either Ch'u or Ch'in) custom or belief, but something from a wider cultural basis. It suggests that this and possibly other exorcistic methods in the daybook were widely practiced in Warring States China. Another example is the sacrificial rituals to the spirits of distant mountains described in *Shan-hai-ching*. These likely stem from the same religious milieu as the daybook, which has various paragraphs for choosing auspicious days and making proper offerings before travel, such as "auspicious days for sacrificing for travel" (*ssu-hsing liang-jih* 祠行良日),[116] "days for sacrificing for travel" (*ssu-hsing jih* 祠行日) ,[117] "sacrificing for travel" (*hsing-ssu* 行祠).[118] We shall return to *Shan-hai-ching* later in this chapter.

Diviners practicing various divinational methods collected in day-books were not a phenomenon restricted to Ch'in or Ch'u. In *Mo-tzu*, for example, we read that once when Mo Tzu travelled to the state of Ch'i, he met a diviner (*jih-che* 日者) who advised him not to go north, for it was a day that the Lord (Ti) was going to slaughter the black dragon, and black was a synonym of *mo*.[119] In *The Records of History* (*Shih-chi*), Ssu-ma Ch'ien wrote that "the diviners of Ch'i, Ch'u, Ch'in and Chao each have their own customs."[120] The diviners were there-fore scattered among the Warring States. The differences between the Shui-hu-ti and the T'ien-shui versions may be explained as due to local customs, cultural characteristics, the idiosyncrasy of individual practitioners, or simply pure chance regarding textual survival. A detailed study of these points has yet to be undertaken. But the basic similarity of the craft of the diviners and whatever cultural phenomena they represented probably means that the users of daybooks were a stratum common to all states at the end of the Warring States period.

In the Han dynasty, moreover, fragments of daybooks are found both far away, as in Wu-wei on the western frontier, and Hopei.[121] The custom of consulting daybooks became a deep-rooted part of popular culture in the subsequent centuries. Even the Ch'ien-lung emperor of the Ch'ing dynasty ordered a great collection of this kind of literature— *The Book of Harmonizing Heavenly Revolutions and Distinguishing Directions* (*hsieh-chi pien-fang shu*).[122] The modern descendants of the daybook, i.e., *huang-li* 黃曆, *t'ung-shu* 通書, or *nung-min-li* 農民曆, still are pieces of folk literature that are very widely distributed.[123]

It is also worth noticing that although daybooks were a product of popular culture, they cannot be seen as a comprehensive "mirror" of the culture of the people that produced it. The culture or mentality of any people is built on a structure far more complicated than can be represented by a single type of text. There is ample evidence for this statement. From the similarity between the structure of passages in the daybook and the *Yüeh-ling*, one can see that both shared a basic cosmology, and this rules out a clear-cut differentiation between the so-called popular and elite cultures. An examination of the archaeological contexts in which daybooks are found—usually with legal texts—shows that during the Ch'in and Han period it was customary for local officials to practice law and divination conjointly.[124] The local officials therefore served as a cultural bridge between the elite and the people. The owner of the Shui-hu-ti text, moreover, can hardly be seen as a person lacking in sophisticated thought when we consider another text found in his tomb, *Wei-li chih-tao* 爲吏之道 (*The Way of Serving as an Official*), which intermixes Taoist, Legalist, and Confucian ideas.[125] It would be problematic to judge the cultural background of this particular user of the daybook based on the daybook alone.[126]

The world view and religious mentality reflected in our daybook may not be totally alien to those of the upper stratum of society, yet they demonstrate a keen concern for the daily lives of the non-elite. To say that the religion reflected by daybook texts was "immature" or "primitive," however, is to judge from an evolutionist point of view and a narrow concept of the nature of religion. Not all religions possess the same nature and undergo the same development. The truth is, despite the fact that the religious mentality of the daybook seems illogical, amoral, and utilitarian, this "immature" religion was in itself a self-contained form of belief. In addition, the existence of various daybooks from the Han dynasty as well as the unbroken tradition of the *huang-li* for more than two thousand years, forcefully demonstrate that a good part of the popular mentality of the Chinese people had been formed even before China entered the imperial period. If, indeed, before the Ch'in dynasty united China politically, the people in various parts of the country already shared large elements of culture, as reflected in the daybooks, it is very likely that this shared culture facilitated the unification and subsequent sustenance of the Ch'in-Han empire.

Elements of Religion in the Classic of Mountains and Seas

One of the most important sources of the myth and religion of ancient China is *Shan-hai-ching*, or *Classic of Mountains and Seas*. The text is traditionally divided into two parts: a *Shan-ching*, or *Classic of Mountains* (henceforth *Mountains*); and a *Hai-ching*, or *Classic of Seas* (henceforth *Seas*). The *Mountains* relates local oddities, including monstrous animals and spirits, of mountains of the five directions (i.e., the four cardinal directions and the middle.) The *Seas*, on the other hand, relates similar subjects concerning countries bordering the seas surrounding the middle kingdom. It is commonly assumed that at least part of the material can be dated to the Warring States period, and that it was not until the Han dynasty that it had assumed the format, or its prototype, that we see today.[127] Scholars of mythology have studied the mythological elements, which I will not try to tackle here.[128] For our inquiry, the central problem lies in the purpose of this text rather than its actual content. Why was it composed, and what did it reflect of the religious mentality of contemporary society? Of particular importance are the images of spiritual beings, their nature and power, their relationship with human beings, and the religious implications of these issues.

The images of spiritual beings and monsters

Classic of Mountains and Seas refers often to spiritual beings and monstrous animals. Some are given the status of *shen*, i.e., "god" or "spirit," and their basic characteristic is one of hybrid forms.[129] Human figures, or parts, are combined with animal figures to create outlandish beings. For example, there are spirits with "the head of a dragon and the body of a bird," "the head of a bird and the body of a dragon," "the body of a dragon and the face of a man," "the face of a man and the body of a horse," "the body of a tiger with nine tails and the face of a man with tiger's claws," "the body of a goat with the face of a man," or "the likeness of a man with two heads."[130] The most famous of these spirits is the Queen Mother of the West, who is described as having "the likeness of a person, with the tail of a leopard and the teeth of a tiger."[131] It is worth noting that the figure of dragon is also used in a way similar to that of an ordinary animal in this puzzle game. Given the ubiquitous role of the dragon in ancient China's beliefs, to use it to create hybrid figures implies a self-conscious artificiality that was probably not an ancient tradition.

The *shen*-spirits described in the *Mountains* part appear to be different from those in the *Seas* by the collective nature of their image; no individual characteristics can be discerned. For example, in the *Southern Mountains* (*Nan-shan-ching* 南山經) section, at the end of the enumeration of the mountains and rivers, we read: " . . . There are altogether ten mountains, 2950 *li* long. The shape of their gods all have the body of a bird with the head of a dragon, ..."[132] Here, as in the rest of the *Mountains*, the *shen*-spirits of a group of mountains share one image. By contrast, in four sections of *Seas*, the four gods for the four cardinal directions are described individually, although still of hybrid forms consisting of a human face with the body of an animal. In the rest of *Seas*, a number of spirits are mentioned irregularly but individually, with hybrid forms.

Those not called *shen* have even more complicated forms. One passage describes a monster as "having the form of a tiger, with white body, dog's head, horse's tail, and pig's mane."[133] The form of a strange bird "is that of a snake, with four wings, six eyes, and three feet."[134] Yet the principle of hybrid composition is the same. It is interesting to note that these monsters are usually referred to as *shou*, which literally means "beast." Thus, they were not considered as having the same status as the spirits, although their images often resemble those called "*shen.*"

Hybrid images of the spirits and monsters are found not only in *Classic of Mountains and Seas*, (Fig. 4.1) but also in other documents. For example, we have seen that the god Ju-shou 蓐收 in *Kuo-yü* is described as "having the face of a man, with white hair and the claws of a tiger." In *Classic of Mountains and Seas* he is described as "having a snake in the left ear, and riding on two dragons."[135] According to *Mo-tzu*, the god Kou-mang 句芒 has a bird's body and a square face, which agrees with the description given in *Classic of Mountains and Seas*.[136] On the Ch'u silk manuscript mentioned above, twelve "gods" are depicted, each possessing a hybrid form. Some of them resemble the spirits in *Classic of Mountains and Seas* or other ancient documents.[137] The painted coffin of Marquis I of Tseng (曾侯乙), of the early Warring States period, portrays hybrid spirits or monsters.[138] Monsters such as the nine-headed serpent, the elephant-sized moth, the nine-headed giant, and the famous tiger-headed and bull-like River Lord Ho-po described in *Ch'u-tz'u*, furthermore, provide literary cor-

Fig. 4.1 Imaginative drawing of a god in *Shan-hai-ching*.
Ch'ing.

roboration of the archaeological evidence.[139] Later, in the Han dynasty, we have the painting on the coffin of Ma-wang-tui tomb no. 1, with its spirit-like monsters swirling in clouds.[140] A silk painting found in the same tomb depicts a number of monstrous deities that reminds one of the twelve gods on the Ch'u silk manuscript (Fig. 4.2).[141] As late as the Eastern Han period, stone-reliefs show monster-spirits as still inhabiting the public imagination.[142]

All this evidence suggests that the hybrid images of spirits in *Classic of Mountains and Seas* are not the creation of a certain author, but originated from a mental background common to the Warring States, and even earlier.[143] The idea of creating composite animal figures was certainly present in the Shang bronze artifacts, although no half-human animals are found there.[144] It is reasonable to conclude

Fig. 4.2 Figures of gods on a silk
manuscript from Ma-wang-tui.
Western Han.

that these hybrid images were the way people of this time pictured
spiritual beings. An exotic image composed of parts of known animals
would be one of the possible results of this effort to portray the fantastic and the mysterious. Thus, there is "bird's body with dragon's
head" and, conversely, "dragon's body with bird's head." The hybrid
images, therefore, are more the result of reasoned imagination than
recollections of vague and ancient legend. As the possibilities of different combinations were limited, it is natural that repetitions should
have occurred. Thus, the figure of "bird's body with dragon's head"
appeared twice, as did the "human's face with beast's body," or
"human's head with bird's body," etc.

This view, of course, does not propose to say that every "hybrid"
animal in *Classic of Mountains and Seas* was the product of imagination without any factual support. The four-horned sheep,[145] for
example, could refer to a kind of animal that lives on the high plateau

to the west of China even today.[146] Just as there are identifiable plants or places in *Classic of Mountains and Seas,* it should not be surprising if some of the monsters turned out to be rare animals that people of ancient China might have encountered with awe and remembered as something supernatural.)

The nature and abilities of ghosts and spirits

It is noteworthy that in the entire extant text of *Classic of Mountains and Seas* the character *kuei*, usually rendered as "ghost," appears only twice, and does not refer to "ghost" directly.[147] Spiritual beings instead are referred to as *shen*, i.e., "spirits" or "gods," or *shen-jen*, "god-men.") Some of these spirits are related to ancient myths, and are used either as etiological explanations of places or phenomena, or for the intrinsic interest of the myths themselves.[148] Those not part of a traditional, recorded myth, which in fact are the majority, may or may not have been the subject of lost myths. The texts in which they appear usually do not exceed simple descriptions of images and names. No elaboration on the nature of the spirits is supplied. For example, a passage states that, "in the valley towards the sun, there is a god whose name is T'ien-wu. He is the lord of the river."[149] We are not informed of the nature of this god or any story about him except that he may have controlled the river. The Spirit of Thunder, Lei-shen, in another case, is said to "have the body of a dragon and the head of a man, and drummed his belly to the west of Wu."[150] The spirits in the *Mountains* are even less distinct: we know nothing except their images, not even their names.

The description of the *shen*-spirits in the *Seas* section differs from the *shen*-spirits in the *Mountains* in another respect: there is no description of any sacrifice to them. This is further evidence suggesting that the textual use of *Mountains* differed from that of *Seas*. The former was probably a handbook for travellers, who had to know the sacrifices to the various local gods wherever they travelled. Thus, after a simple description of the figure of a spirit there usually follows a detailed instruction for making sacrifice to it. The *shen*-spirits, as well as other items in *Seas*, on the other hand, read more like a catalogue of faraway lands not on a usual itinerary; therefore there is no need to learn the sacrifices.] The detailed mileage between each geographical area given in the *Mountains* is another significant feature that is lacking in the *Seas*.

In general, the *shen*-spirits described in *Classic of Mountains and Seas* are neutral; they are neither hostile nor benevolent. The fact that the word *shen*, not *kuei*, or ghost, was used most often to identify them says something of their benign nature. A few of them, to be sure, were portentous: when people saw them, great disasters such as war,[151] drought,[152] flood, or excessive rain would strike.[153] But by and large the *shen*-spirits are passive: they do not actively plague people. One common characteristic of the spirits and monsters is that they are locally confined, thus, their sphere of influence does not exceed their locality. There is almost no mention of such divine personages as the Shang-ti or Shang-huang found in the daybooks. Huang-ti, the Yellow Emperor, was mentioned mainly in situations where the genealogy of a certain god or ancient ruler was traced to him.[154] Huang-ti, in any case, was not in the same rank as Shang-ti, God on high.

At times it is even doubtful if the designation "*shen*" in *Classic of Mountains and Seas* meant anything more than "monstrous," with hardly any of the sense of "divine" or "sacred" that usually characterizes the word. Many of the "*shen*-spirits" are seen more as monsters than as exalted beings. For example, we read in *Seas*:

> There is a *shen*, with the head of a man and the body of a snake. Its length is as long as a wheel, with heads to the left and the right, dressed in purple garment and red cap. Its name is Yen-wei 延維. If a ruler could make sacrifice to him, he (the ruler) would rule the world.[155]

Yen-wei is described in the text in practically the same way as other monsters that bring disaster or good fortune.[156] Moreover, the *shen* could also be "killed" in certain instance. In the *Western Mountains* section, for example, a son of the god Chung-shan 鍾山 named Ku 鼓 was killed by Ti—presumably the Supreme God—for an alleged crime against another god, Pao-chiang 葆江.[157] As in the daybook text, a *shen*, or god, can actually be "killed." [158]

The text of *Classic of Mountains and Seas* yields little information on the relationship of *shen*-spirits with human beings. In the *Mountains* section the *shen*-spirits are basically mountain guardians. Their relationship with people is defined by and confined to the method used in sacrificial offerings. No information is provided concerning their possible reaction to offerings not delivered. As for the *shen*-spirits mentioned in the *Seas* section, there is little indication as to their participation in worldly affairs.

Although we cannot be sure of the original purpose of *Classic of Mountains and Seas*, it appears most of all to have been a geographical survey of elusive places, or a handbook for travellers.[159] The spirits and monsters are but part of the collected information. It has been suggested that the text originally included pictures, and that its prototype might be the famous nine Hsia *ting*-tripods, with the figures of "hundreds of monsters" (*pai-wu* 百物) on them. The purpose of these figures on *ting*-tripods was to distinguish the harmful spirits and monsters from benevolent animals.[160]

Thus, the main concern of the reader of *Classic of Mountains and Seas* was not in myth and stories, but was to recognize the figures of spirits and, in the case of *Mountains*, to make proper sacrifice to them. After providing such information, the text does little else.[161] We cannot determine, however, why many of the places are unidentifiable. It is therefore unlikely that the book was ever used in a practical sense, as were the daybooks by their owners.

Jih-shu and Shan-hai-ching: Dealing with Domestic and Foreign Environments

Although not a systematic exposition of religious beliefs, the older portion of *Classic of Mountains and Seas* nevertheless reflects beliefs that could have formed the basis of the everyday religion of the Warring States period. However, given the fact that the spirits and monsters in *Classic of Mountains and Seas* were rooted in the beliefs of the people with a practice-oriented context, it is doubtful that we can ever grasp an overall picture of their beliefs just from this material. Moreover, the spirits' functions and natures are frequently not mentioned at all. A comparison with the Shui-hu-ti daybook, however, may shed light on the problem. In the first place, the spirits and monsters are described in a rather clear and affirmative tone. Whenever the text actually gives information on the distances, images, or methods of sacrifices, such data are all plainly and unambiguously stated. This is comparable to the daybook, where things were fixed and certain enough to be comprehended by ordinary people. While it is true that *Classic of Mountains and Seas*, especially the *Seas* section, contains fragments of mythological figures or stories, just as the Shui-hu-ti daybook does, its main purpose is not to collect or retell such stories, but to use them to explain the origins of certain names.

Another aspect that bespeaks the common background of the daybooks and *Classic of Mountains and Seas* is the low level of status of the *shen*-spirits. Not only could they be expelled, they could even be "killed." This concept of "killing" a spirit, although a minor spirit to be sure, is most revealing as an indication of the religious mentality: in order to obtain maximum benefit, the spiritual world is dealt with in a not-so-spiritual way. People sacrificed to the spirits when they needed to propitiate them, and found ways to expel them when possible. The spiritual world, in fact, is little different from the mundane world. The difference between the *shen*-spirits and the monsters in *Classic of Mountains and Seas*, indeed, is difficult to discern in all respects except the label "*shen*." They all lived *in* a definite place in the world of man, not unlike the spirits in daybooks, who roamed variously through people's houses.

Finally, it is particularly interesting to compare the sphere of influence of *Classic of Mountains and Seas* with that of daybooks. For example, the Shui-hu-ti daybook contains several parts devoted to "travel," or "sacrifice for travelling." These are lists of auspicious days for setting out or for making sacrifices to the protecting spirits.[162] Compared with *Classic of Mountains and Seas*, the daybook text can be regarded as a general preparation for travel, and *Classic of Mountains and Seas* text, or at least the *Mountains* section, as a handbook for dealing with the spirits and monsters to be encountered along the way through mountains and countries. The *shen*-spirits in *Classic of Mountains and Seas*, however, are not the kind to be encountered in ordinary journeys, and descriptions about them have no reference to direct involvement with daily life. Therefore, it is reasonable to assume that the daybook is oriented toward domestic daily activities, while *Classic of Mountains and Seas* is designed to deal with the often strange surrounding world. Together, they present a picture for us of the entire world with which common people concerned themselves. The two texts are congruent parts of a common religious mentality.

To conclude the images of ghosts and spirits as seen in the Shui-hu-ti daybook and *Classic of Mountains and Seas* are basically concrete, anthropomorphic, and zoomorphic. This is unlike the abstract ideas of "heaven" or "mandate of heaven," which developed around the Confucian school of thought after the Western Chou period. On the other hand, the ideas of ghosts and spirits were not confined to the so-called world of "common folks," since, as the traditional documents discussed in the last chapter demonstrate, similar concepts were held by the educated and literary elite. The composition of these works required the active involvement of literate diviners, scribes, and perhaps intellectuals. Yet the two texts provide us with a rather detailed picture of what the basic spiritual world at the end of the Warring States period looked like. Through this picture, we can gain understanding of the religious mentality operating in the background.

Chapter 5 _____

Emperors, Courtiers, and the Development of Official Cults

Enlil, whose command is far-reaching, whose word is holy,
The lord whose pronouncement is unchangeable, who forever
decrees destinies, . . .
who perfects the decrees of power, lordship, and princeship,
The earth-gods bow down in fear before him,
The heaven-gods humble themselves before him.[1]

The relationship between developments at court and those in the wider culture is at once obvious and difficult to fathom. In China's imperial system the sovereign affected the lives of his subjects through direct rule. This was also true in other parts of the ancient world. The heretic pharaoh Akhenaten, for example, inaugurated the Amarna Period by promoting the belief in a single god, the sundisk Aten. His personal artistic taste was also forcefully expressed through the peculiar "Amarna style,"[2] and his rulership in general was a major force in the social change of the late Eighteenth Dynasty of pharaonic Egypt. Yet if we wish to know where or how Akhenaten obtained his inspiration and why he wanted to implement his ideas, we must study Akhenaten as the product, rather than the cause. A similar "monotheistic" religious idea was present in a number of "Hymns to Amon" written before Akhenaten assumed the throne.[3] Thus, his rulership was not only a cause of social change, but can be seen as an elaboration of existing tendencies. The failure of the Aten cult after his death, on the other hand, forces us to reassess the extent and nature of his influence.[4] The relationship between imperial rule and the noncourt culture must be seen as a complex of interdependent causes and effects working among different social strata. As we shall see in the following discussion, the example of Akhenaten and his cult is not without relevance for understanding Han emperors and the state cults that they promoted. An overview of the official cults of the Ch'in-Han empire, furthermore, is necessary for any inquiry into the religion of this period: to delineate what is official simply clarifies what is the noncourt culture.

The Establishment of the Official Cult of the Ch'in Empire

Ssu-ma Ch'ien comments at the beginning of his "Treatise on Ceremonies" as follows:

> Since the ancient times, which of the emperors or kings did not perform the grand ceremony for the worship of Heaven and Earth at Mount T'ai when they received the mandate of heaven? There may be those who gained power without corresponding oracles, but never did those who had seen the appearance of auspicious omens fail to ascend Mount T'ai.[5]

Ssu-ma Ch'ien's words point out that court religious activities and the establishment of political authority are two sides of one coin. For example, the Chou kings proclaimed their political authority on the basis of their having received the mandate of heaven. Although a certain degree of moral value was injected into this belief, it is nevertheless clear that the main purpose of this was to achieve and secure political control. The classic text *Book of Rites* also states that "he who owns the world should sacrifice to the hundred gods; those enfeoffed lords whose territory encompass [the mountains and rivers] should make sacrifice; those who do not [possess mountains and rivers], should not sacrifice."[6] The political authority of the "son of heaven" and the lords corresponded to the levels of their duties in religious ceremonies. The ceremony of *feng-shan* 封禪, i.e., the grand ceremony for the worship of Heaven and Earth held at Mount T'ai, was just such a ceremony, by means of which the emperor proclaimed the legitimacy of his authority.[7] On the other hand, the ceremony was also designed for the emperor to seek immortality. There was therefore a strong personal motive behind the act. We shall return to this point a little later in this chapter.

Not long after the Shui-hu-ti daybook was entombed with its owner, China came under the rule of the western state of Ch'in. Thus began a new era, accompanied by drastic changes in political and social organization.[8] As the major military tasks of state were completed, the other major state task—religion—was attended to. The attention of the First Emperor to religious affairs focused on organizational aspects.

The first religious act of the First Emperor was to formally recognize the idea of the Five Phases. This theory maintained that everything in the universe was related to five powers (*te*) or elements—metal, wood, water, fire, earth—which overcome one another in a cyclical fashion. Thus, metal overcomes wood, fire overcomes metal, water overcomes fire, earth overcomes water, and wood overcomes earth. It has also been translated "Five Phases," for each of the five elements represented a different phase of totality.[9] According to this theory, the First Emperor proclaimed that the "power of water" of Ch'in had replaced the "power of fire" of the Chou Dynasty.[10] This indicates a new development in court religious theory.[11] In addition to his mandate of heaven, the "power" of a new dynasty had to be "cosmologically correct," i.e., in a position to replace the "power" of the former regime according to appropriate metaphysical criteria. Many have argued that such ideology was mere political expediency, created as a legitimizing excuse after power was already gained. Yet the fact that a theory was needed at all suggests that it had a rather prominent role in society at large, especially in the circles of power. Furthermore, because the theory of Five Phases became axiomatic in establishing political authority, concomitantly, *yin-yang* and Five-Phases theories influenced the official religion and political ideology.

A further act of the First Emperor was the systematic organization of all religious cults in China. He ordered the setting of schedules for spring and autumn sacrifices to "heaven, earth, the famous mountains and rivers, and ghosts and spirits." Further, there were to be fixed amounts of offerings to deities, each according to status.[13] However, the government could not possibly have controlled all the various local cults outside the center of authority, and such cults continued on their own.[14] The most prestigious cults managed by the central government were the Four Emperors worshipped at the capital of Hsien-yang. Surrounding these four cults were more than a hundred cult shrines, including shrines for the worshipping of the sun, the moon, and various constellations, and for natural forces such as the Lord of Wind, the Master of Rain, the Four Seas, as well as the Nine Ministers, the Fourteen Ministers, etc.[15] Seen in parallel with the human state, the deities were thus officials constituting a divine "central government." At the local level, on the other hand, existed the so-called "famous mountains and rivers," which were analogous to local government, or feudal lords. There were also minor rivers, which, because they were close to the capital, were given their own cults:

> [The rivers] such as Pa, Ch'an, Ch'ang-shui, Li, Lao, Ching, Wei, were not big rivers. It was because they were close to Hsien-yang that they were all given cultic status comparable to the [famous] mountains and rivers, without the extra sacrificial offerings.[16]

The positions of these minor geographic entities in relation to the major rivers and mountains were described in a way comparable to those between the royal relatives and family members and the emperor. Thus the structure of the official cult can be seen as a reflection of the political administration.[17]

It is worth noting that the official cult was not a coherent structure based upon a systematic classification of cults, especially the minor ones lower down in the scale. Besides the abovementioned minor rivers and mountains, which gained official status only because they happened to be close to the capital, the following example also illustrates the nature of the problem. Among the official cults near Hsien-yang, there were shrines dedicated to a certain General Tu of the Chou dynasty. According to *Record of History (Shih-chi)*, he was "one of the minor ghosts worshipped in central Ch'in."[18] The cult originated from a story that began to circulate in the Spring and Autumn period. The revenging ghost of Tu-po, it was said, shot King Hsüan of Chou.[19]

Later, the ghost of General Tu was worshipped by the inhabitants of central Ch'in. It seems that the Ch'in government conferred official status based on no criteria other than geographical proximity. Needless to say, most local cults were not officially managed by the imperial court: "Those shrines of distant provinces and prefectures were worshipped and supported by the local people. They were not governed by the royal office of Supplicator (*t'ai-chu* 太祝)."[20]

[Because it is somewhat difficult to draw a clear line, based on their nature alone, between local cults that were given official status and those that were not, there exists an inherent ambiguity between the official and the nonofficial cults] This aspect became a salient one in the Han state religion.

According to *Record of History*, [the First Emperor was, toward the latter part of his reign, preoccupied with the search for immortality[21] and even proclaimed himself a *chen-jen* 眞人, i.e., a "Perfected."[22] His infamous extermination of scholars was at least partly triggered by their failure to satisfy his request for the elixir of immortality.[23] He also believed in dream oracles as well as magical methods for expelling evil forces.[24] While such activities may not seem to us to be part of an "official cult," in fact they were, and they illustrate the personal religious attitude of the First Emperor, which in turn influenced the official cult. When the First Emperor travelled east, he paid homage to the famous mountains, rivers, and the long extinguished cult of the Eight Deities, and tried to seek out immortals.[25] It was most likely the emperor's personal interest that placed these activities within the official cult system. Thus, *Shih-chi* mentions that "as for the other famous mountains and rivers, the various ghosts and the Eight Deities, the emperor made sacrifice to them whenever he travelled by. And these sacrifices were discontinued when he left."[26] As we shall see below in connection with Han Wu-ti, the First Emperor's plan for the *feng-shan*, the most important ceremony for proclaiming imperial sovereignty, was mostly based on his own ideas.

The Establishment of the Han Official Cult

According to *Record of History*, [the religious policy of the Ch'in empire was inherited by the Han:]

In year two, (the emperor Kao-tsu) returned to the capital after a campaign against Hsiang-chi. He asked: "Which emperors on high were worshiped formerly in Ch'in times?" The reply was: "There were four emperors. There were shrines for the White, the Azure, the Yellow, and the Red Emperors." Kao-tsu said: "I have heard that there are five emperors in heaven, now there are only four. Why?" No one knew the answer. Therefore Kao-tsu said: "I understand now. It has fallen to me to complete the fifth." So the shrine of the Black Emperor was established and was named the Northern Altar. The ceremony was carried out by the responsible officials; the emperor did not attend personally. All the former (religious) officials were recalled, and the office of the Great Supplicator (*t'ai-chu* 太祝) and the Great Steward (*t'ai-tsai* 太宰) were reestablished, performing the ceremonies as before, while prefects were ordered to establish public altars. Then the emperor issued a decree: "I am very concerned about sacrifices and offerings. Now the offering to the Supreme Lord and the deities of the mountains and rivers who ought to be revered should be performed properly on the appropriate moment as before."[27]

It is obvious that by this time Five-Phases metaphysical theory was already widely known. Therefore, Kao-tsu's promoting the Black Emperor was an expected act. However, one may question the historicity of the story about the Black Emperor, as it might have been a later addition to a whole cycle of Kao-tsu myths. These included the dream of an old woman that Kao-tzu killed the white serpent (i.e., the son of the White Emperor).[28] Furthermore, the question of what the power of Han should be was not even settled until the reign of Wu-ti.

It is difficult for us to tell what personal influence Kao-tsu could have exerted on the establishment of the Han official cult, since he basically followed the Ch'in model. However, his decision to promote the local altar at Fen-yü, the place of his origin, and to establish in Ch'ang-an the shrine of Ch'ih-yu, the god he made sacrifice to when he was the bailiff of P'ei,[29] shows that he did not forget to promote the local cult of his native province.

Meanwhile, another Kao-tsu policy had various *wu*-shamans from all over the country assembled in order to perform their respective cultic functions in the capital. They came from such former states as Liang, Chin, Ch'in, and Ching, and were to perform their sacrifices according to seasonal schedules.[30] Officials for supplication and sacrifices, as well as female shamans, were subsequently stationed in Ch'ang-an.

The objective of this policy was probably to absorb local traditions and to symbolize the establishment of a universal empire. On the other hand, it was also a way to appease parochial sentiments and to consolidate and legitimize imperial rule at the local level, since to perform a local cultic ritual at the central court amounted to official recognition of the local tradition and the association of the ruling culture with local culture.[31] In any case, it can be surmised that at this time Ch'ang-an (formerly called Hsien-yang) was a place where shamanic practices could be seen and learned, and thus they exerted a deep influence on the life of the people around the capital area.

It seems that Kao-tsu was also quite relaxed with regard to the control of local cults. *Record of History* says:

> In the tenth year of Kao-tsu, in the spring, the official in charge of religious matters proposed that the county government should make sacrifice to the earth (-god) and grain (-god) in the second month of spring and in the twelfth month. The local earth shrine should be provided with contributions by the people themselves. The decree read: "Approved."[32]

Thus, at the prefectural level the government still controlled religious activities, while below this level people were free to manage their own cult activities.

The above situation amounts to the official religious policy of the Han dynasty: the addition of new shrines and the accommodation of local cults. This policy, however, was not entirely based on rational, political, or theoretical considerations. As will become clear, personal opinions of emperors were oftentimes the decisive factor in the establishment or abolition of cults, as is inevitable when what was "official" was in fact the "private" affair of the royal house.

In the time of Emperor Wen, a certain Hsin Yüan-p'ing presented a theory of watching the ethers (*wang-ch'i* 望氣) that was approved by the emperor.[33] Subsequently, a temple to the Five Emperors was build at Wei-yang and an altar to the Five Emperors was established outside the Ch'ang Gate of the capital, all under the advice of Hsin Yüan-p'ing.[34] When Hsin's ether-watching theory proved false and subversive plots by him were discovered, he was promptly executed. The emperor thenceforth lost interest in worshipping gods and spirits.[35] This incident, contrary to one's expectation, did not prompt the emperor to abolish Hsin's innovations. Once established, shrines and temples seem to have maintained their existence for quite a long time.

Emperor Wu's religious policy contained many examples of personal and casual impetuses for establishing new cults. The first new cult of his reign was established when a certain Miu Chi presented a method of worshipping the god T'ai-i (Grand Unity):

> The most exalted of the gods of heaven is Grand Unity, Grand Unity's assistants are called the Five Emperors. In ancient times the son of heaven made sacrifice to Grand Unity in the southeastern suburb with a *T'ai-lao* (a cattle, pig, and sheep).[36]

Wu-ti promptly ordered the Grand Supplicator to establish a shrine to Grand Unity southeast of Ch'ang-an and to make sacrifice according to the method suggested by Miu Chi. Later on, perhaps to counteract the importance of Grand Unity, someone made the claim that "in ancient times the Son of Heaven sacrificed every three years to the Three Ones—the Heavenly One, the Earthly One, and the Grand One—using the *Tai-lao* sacrifice." The emperor accepted this suggestion and ordered the Grand Supplicator to administer the sacrifice on the altar of the Grand One accordingly, although neither Grand Unity nor the Three Ones were considered ancient cults.[37]

On another occasion, a certain "Divine Lady," a commoner of Ch'ang-ling who had died during childbirth and whose ghost appeared to her sister-in-law, was worshipped by the latter and gained a local reputation. Wu-ti's maternal grandmother Ping-yüan-chün used to pray at her shrine when she was still a commoner. When Wu-ti ascended the throne, he ordered that this "Divine Lady" be enshrined in the royal Shang-lin Park, in order that he himself might also meet her.[38] In this way, a local cult was easily conferred with official status. When Nan Yüeh 南越 was conquered, a man from Yüeh named Yung-chih said to the emperor:

110

The people of Yüeh believed in ghosts, and the ghosts seen in their shrines were effective. Formerly the king of Tung Ou revered ghosts, and lived to one hundred and sixty years of age. Later people became negligent (in revering the ghosts); therefore (their lifespans) were diminished.[39]

This prompted Wu-ti to order the shaman of Yüeh to establish a Yüeh-style shrine to worship gods and ghosts.

We may surmise that Ssu-ma Ch'ien does not distort the actual situation, but it seems that Wu-ti often made such decisions in a spirit of haste and credulity. Other cults were established only after serious consideration, but in Wu-ti's reign such cases were rare. The most famous was the *feng-shan* ceremony, the grand sacrifice to Mount T'ai.[40] Formerly, the First Emperor of Ch'in performed this ceremony once at Mount T'ai. But since he did not trust the scholars from Ch'i and Lu, who were undecided about ritual procedures, he adopted the old Ch'in ritual of sacrificing to the Supreme God (*shang-ti*) at the cult site of Yüng. The actual content of the ceremony was purposely not revealed.[41] Thus, although performed in an official capacity, it was not an institutionalized ceremony. When Wu-ti rekindled interest in the rite, preparation and execution required a series of debates and discussions among court officials, scholars, and diviners before implementation.[42] The establishment of the shrine and cult of *Hou-t'u*, or Queen Earth, was also initiated by Wu-ti and implemented after lengthy discussions at court.[43]

On the whole, however, Wu-ti's personal whims and his fascination with immortality resulted in a rather confused state of affairs for official cults, since many were established for the sole purpose of assisting the emperor's quest for immortal and divine elixirs.[44] Even the most grandiose ceremony, the *feng-shan*, took the immortality of the emperor as its central concern:

A ninety-year-old, Ting-kung from Ch'i, said: "*feng-shan* is the name for achieving immortality. . . ." Thus the emperor ordered scholars to practice shooting the bull and draft the procedure for the ceremony of *feng-shan*. . . . As the Son of Heaven heard the sayings of Kung-sun Ch'ing and the diviners that the Yellow Emperor had communicated with the deities and the prodigious beings because he performed the *feng-shan* ceremony, he intended to imitate the Yellow Emperor and to approach the immortals. . . .[45]

Wu-ti was of course not the only Han emperor interested in immortality. Emperor Hsüan established a shrine for the skin, teeth, and claws of a white tiger simply because it was offered by a southern commandery. He later followed the advice of diviners and founded four shrines in the Wei-yang Palace for the Jade of the Duke of Sui, the Treasure of the Sword, the jade *Pi*, and the *ting*-tripod of the Chou king K'ang. On another occasion, certain diviners mentioned that the divine treasures of the "golden horse and green rooster" in I-chou 益州 (Szechwan) could be obtained by offering sacrifice. Emperor Hsüan promptly sent a special envoy to the province of I-chou to make sacrifice.[46] A host of other shrines were also established as official cults in various places around the country, including shrines to the Sun and the Moon, the Four Seasons, the Five Emperors, the Eight Gods, the Immortals, the Jade Lady, the god Ch'ih-yu, and the Yellow Emperor.[47] Some of these, which were originally only worshipped in the capital, thus became "local cults."

In this kind of exchange between local and official cults, the actual number of cult centers supported by the government at various levels grew rapidly. In the reign of Emperor Ch'eng, a group of scholar-officials headed by Prime Minister K'uang Heng found the situation unbearable and questioned the legitimacy of the existing cults. Because many of the cults established since the founding of the empire did not conform to "ancient" rituals, as understood by these reformists, they demanded abolishment of such prominent cults as the *T'ai-chih* 泰畤 of Kan-ch'üan and the Queen Earth of Ho-tung, established by Wu-ti. Emperor Ch'eng followed their advice and moved these two cults to the southern and northern suburbs of the capital.[48] K'uang Heng further requested that 475 out of the 683 shrines in the various commanderies and kingdoms supported by the court be abolished, since they went counter to various *li*, or ritual codes. Out of the 203 shrines at the ancient cult site of Yung, only fifteen shrines worshipping the mountains, rivers, and constellations were to be preserved. Emperor Ch'eng granted this request; and those shrines established by Kao-tsu, Wu-ti, and Emperor Hsüan mentioned above were all suspended.[49]

It should be pointed out that the reform did not represent an effort toward a rational assessment of the former emperors' cult activities. It was simply a stand against luxury and excessive display of wealth, as well as support for the authority of the classics presented by K'uang Heng. When K'uang Heng fell from power, emperor Ch'eng reestablished the shrines of Kan-ch'üan, Fen-yin, and many others.[50] After Emperor Ch'eng died, however, the empress-dowager decided to move the shrines back to Ch'ang-an again. The reason for this move is given in an edict that admits that Ch'eng-ti's restoration of the Kan-ch'üan and Fen-yin shrines was aimed at procuring the blessings of the deities for an heir, but that the wish was not granted.[51]

When Emperor Ai assumed the throne, more than seven hundred shrines of former times were restored. This was because he was stricken with a grave sickness, and the shrines were intended to procure blessings. The empress-dowager again ordered that the Kan-ch'üan and Fen-yin shrines be restored, although a few years later they were moved back to Ch'ang-an again. When Wang Mang usurped the throne, new shrines for the Yellow Emperor paired with Heaven, and for the Yellow Empress paired with Earth, were founded.[52] In addition to his implementation of a political-theological system that followed the ancient proprieties of the Chou dynasty, although it was in fact imbued with the theory of *yin-yang* and Five Phases,[53] Wang Mang's pious attitude encouraged the proliferation of all sorts of cults and forms of worship. *History of Han (Han-shu)* describes these cults as including:

> Heaven and Earth, the six cult-worships, and others, all the way down to the myriad of minor ghosts and spirits. The total number of these shrines and cult centers exceeded 1700, while the kinds of sacrificial birds and animals numbered more than 300.[54]

In contrast to the Western Han, the official cult of the Eastern Han period experienced less turbulent changes. Emperor Kuang-wu basically followed the ritual procedures and cults prescribed by Wang Mang during Emperor Ai's reign. The deities worshiped included, among a host of minor gods, the Five Emperors, the Five Mountains, the Twenty-eight Constellations, the Lord of Thunder, the Lord of Agriculture, the Lord of Wind, the Lord of Rain, and other deities of the various mountains and seas. The total number was 1514, according to the "Treatise on Rites" in *History of Later Han (Hou-Han-shu)*.[55] It seems that the official cult of the Eastern Han period, with the exception of the establishment of the cult of Lao-tzu by emperor Huan, did not expand beyond that of the end of Western Han.[56]

Personal Factors and Official Religion

We have seen that the establishment of official cults during the Han period was often decided by personal factors. The circumstances that allowed such factors to exert influence on religious policy were related to the nature of the official cults themselves. To be specific, except for basic principles such as worship of Heaven, Earth, the ancestors, and the theories of *yin-yang* and Five Phases, the so-called official religion did not really possess any extensive dogma or theology. A passage from the edict of the empress-dowager of Emperor Ch'eng may be cited as representative of the official theology:

> It is said that the most reverent way for the ruler to serve Heaven and Earth and to communicate with T'ai-i was to make sacrifice. The Emperor Wu, being sagacious and wise, established the shrines for Heaven and Earth and founded the T'ai-ssu at Kan-ch'üan, and the shrine of the Earth at Fen-yin. The deities were satisfied, and the Emperor (Wu) enjoyed a long reign, with numerous descendants. This was followed generation after generation and its benevolence is felt to this day. . . .[57]

Furthermore, the actual form and content of ceremonies were often decided by a politically powerful scholar as a result of his reading traditional texts. There was not a standard answer to any one question surrounding practice. For example, the identities of the important "six worships" (*liu-tsung* 六宗) in the official shrines was a problem even for the Han scholars. They were identified variously as the worship of water, fire, wind, thunder, mountain, sea; as sun, moon, constellations, river, sea, and Mount T'ai; as the Heaven, the Earth, and the four seasons; or even as "what is between the Heaven and the Earth and the four cardinal points." Thus we see a lack of clear theoretical consensus on the official cults.[58] Another example is the identity of the "Nine Heavens" (*chiu-t'ien*). At least two different versions of the names of these nine can be found, one in *Huai-nan-tzu*, the other in *T'ai-hsüan-ching*.[59]

Not only did interpretations differ from one scholar to the other, the emperor himself, who was usually responsible for the final decision, was to a large extent influenced by accidental factors rather than religious convictions or theological considerations.

How far in fact, did the theory of *yin-yang* and Five Phases influence the official religion at this time? Five-Phases thinking was accepted by the Han court from its beginning as the main principle for discussing the succession of dynasties. However, exactly which "power" the Han should be was still a problem during the time of Wen-ti.[60] It was not until Wu-ti that a systematic effort to correlate the sphere of nature with the sphere of human activities, as guided by the principles of *yin-yang* and Five Phases, was formed by Tung Chung-shu.[61] Yet in such official cults as "The Eight Deities," the "Three Ones," or "The Heavenly Spirits and Hundreds of Ghosts," no direct reference to such principles is to be found. Moreover, Wu-ti's obsession with longevity and his consequently credulous attitude toward all sorts of ghosts and spirits propagated by the diviners and shamans created a confusion of mantic cult ideas and was incompatible with Tung Chung-shu's theory.[62] After Wu-ti, Han emperors often issued self-deprecatory edicts when natural disasters occurred.[63] The underlying assumption was the correlation of the emperor's personal behavior with the balance of cosmological forces. When the balance was upset by lack of virtue, the *yin* and *yang* forces would clash and result in natural disasters. On the other hand, rulers also issued self-congratulatory statements when certain auspicious omens appeared.[64] This may be seen as the influence of *yin-yang* and Five-Phases theories on official ideology, yet it still does not mean that such theories prevailed in every aspect of the official cults. One of the reasons for the relatively limited application of Tung's theories is that they did not deal with spirits and ghosts, which were an older fixture of official cults.

A second impediment to the widespread application of Tung's correlative system involved the personal and economic interests of the administrative personnel related to the official cults, who usually would rather participate in the prosperity of a cult than its demise. *History of Han* records that, during the last years of Ch'eng-ti, the emperor took a great interest in the worship of ghosts and spirits. As he was in need of an heir, various types of sacrifice and shamanistic ceremony were suggested. Those who made the proposals were granted access to the court and performed sacrifices in the Shang-lin Park outside of Chang-an, requiring extensive expenditures but without producing any effect.[65] In addition, the back and forth movement of the shrines of T'ai-chih and Hou-t'u, and the abolition and reestablishment of various cults, might have been not only the consequence of struggles over propriety and theory, but also related to the benefits that involved the various administrative personnel. The scale of the state cult operation can be illustrated by the following example. In the various states and commanderies as well as in the capitol, the yearly expenditure of shrines for just the former emperors and empresses during the reign of emperor Hsüan amounted to "food offerings: 24,455 times, guards employed: 45,129, cult officials and musicians 12,147; soldiers for raising sacrificial animals not counted."[66] This practical and economic side of the religious institutions, although well-known with regard to Buddhist temples in the later era,[67] has seldom been noted for the early-imperial period.

Thirdly, as already discussed, the establishment or abolition of a cult was more often than not decided by the personal tastes and beliefs of emperors rather than by theories. On this point, Granet's acute observation may still be relevant:

Under the Empire, the Gods themselves were promoted, demoted, or cashiered; they were merely the officials of a state religion whose true deity was the Emperor. His will alone endowed all the other gods with being.[68]

Of course, *yin-yang* and Five-Phases ideas exerted considerable influence on the ceremonial processes and arrangements of various cults. For example, the ritual of praying for rain, or *ta-yü* 大雩, was originally not related directly to *yin-yang* or Five Phases. However, in Tung Chung-shu's *Ch'un-ch'iu fan-lu*, the ritual was redesigned according to the principle of the balance of the *yang* and *yin* forces. Thus, when drought occurred, the male, or *yang*, element was said to have been concealed, in order to induce *yin*: "Concerning the general principle of praying for rain, the men should be concealed, while the women should be gentle and happy."[69] When too much rainfall, or flooding, occurs and ritual prayers are offered to stop the rain, "the women should be concealed and the men should be gentle and happy."[70] Tung cites his own example of praying for stopping the rain in the year 134 B.C., which shows how the principle of *yin-yang* was actually involved in the religious life of the people through official channels:

> In the twenty-first year, on the *ping-wu* 丙午 day of the eighth month, Chung-shu the chancellor of Chiang-tu informed the *nei-shih* 內史 (administrator) and *chung-wei* 中尉 (commandant): "The excessive rainfall has lasted for too long and one is fearful that it may damage the crops. The rainfall should be stopped immediately. The ceremony for stopping the rainfall is based on the principle of suppressing the *yin* and promoting the *yang* force. Orders are to be issued to the officials of the seventeen counties and eighty individual villages, as well as those in the capital, whose ranks are under one thousand *tan*, and whose wives are living in official accommodations. They should all send their wives back home. No women are allowed to go to the market, and people who live in the market are not allowed to go to the well, which should be covered to prevent the leaking (of the *yin* force). Use meat sacrifice and beat the drum at the Earth shrine. . . ." When the order arrived, the various officials of the county and local shrines, as well as the bailiffs of cities and wards and all the people, went to the Earth shrine and prayed until the afternoon. This lasted three days. It was not yet three days when the sky cleared.[71]

Here, officials are joined by the local people in a cooperative effort, demonstrating the fluid boundary between official and nonofficial religion.

Reassessing Han Official Religion

In light of the above discussion, we see two problems related to the definitions of noncourt, or popular, and official religions during Han. Worshippers in the two categories overlapped, as did the objects of worship.

The most obvious examples of overlapping are the emperors themselves. As the grand priest in the official cults, the emperor had personally to perform major ceremonies, such as the sacrifices to Heaven, Earth, and the Five Emperors. On the other hand, he also adhered to local beliefs. Wu-ti was said to have offered sacrifices to the "stove" after the suggestion of Li Shao-chün, in order to invoke ghosts. He also installed the "Sacred Lord of Shou-kung" so that the spirits of the Sacred Lord and his retinue could travel freely in and out of the palace and pronounce secret plans. *Shih-chi* records that "those secret matters are known to the ordinary people, and are nothing particularly special. Yet the Son of Heaven alone liked it in his heart. The entire affair was conducted in secret and was unknown to the outside world."[72] Wu-ti's attempt at secrecy, however, was useless because it was "known to the ordinary people." His promotion of various ghosts, spirits, and immortals, moreover, actually made him a major patron of popular cults. The case of witchcraft at the end of his reign is an example of the emperor's personal beliefs and those of his subjects in a context of shared concern.

In 91 B.C., a conspiracy of black magic against the emperor was revealed. The culprit was the heir-apparent, Prince Wei. Unsuccessful in gaining the confidence of his aged and sick father and demonstrating his innocence, the prince was forced to start an ill-prepared rebellion. The armed conflict ended with the death of the heir-apparent and many political figures, as well as tens of thousands of citizens of Ch'ang-an. The cause of the numerous deaths of the people was not only armed conflict, but also a series of hysterical false charges, litigations, and hasty executions of sorcerers among the people—in short, an extensive witch hunt.[73]

Although the true cause of this incident far exceeded black magic and was the result of a complex political struggle that involved several factions within the court,[74] the fact that belief in black magic permeated the entire society reveals the nature and extent of this kind of belief. No one questioned the efficacy of the black magic, Wu-ti least of all.

Wu-ti's indulgence in popular beliefs, although extreme, was not unique among emperors. The cases of Wen-ti, Hsüan-ti, and Ch'eng-ti have been noted above. Wang Mang was also known to have believed that he would become an immortal.[75] His practices of divination and black magic, needless to say, did not save his regime.[76]

Objects of worship also overlapped. This is evident in an examination of the various *wu*-shamans summoned to the capital during the reign of Kao-tsu. *Record of History* records:

> The *wu* of Liang sacrificed to the Heaven and the Earth, . . . the *wu* of Chin sacrificed to the Five Emperors, the Lord of the East, and the Lord of the Clouds, . . . the *wu* of Ch'in sacrificed to the Earth Shrine, . . . the *wu* of Ching sacrificed to the T'ang-hsia, . . . the *wu* of the Nine Heavens sacrificed to the Nine Heavens. . . . The *wu* of the River sacrificed to the River at Lin-chin, and the *wu* of the South Mountain sacrificed to the South Mountain at Ch'in-chung. The recipient of the sacrifice at Ch'in-chung was the second emperor of Ch'in.[77]

Among these deities, Heaven, Earth, the Five Emperors, the Nine Skies, and the River were worshipped by official cults before this time. It is reasonable to assume that the *wu*-shamans who performed these sacrifices in the capital performed the same kinds of sacrifice at their home locales. Their moving to the capital did not mean that the original cult was uprooted. One therefore deduces that official and nonofficial objects of worship overlapped. In the time of Wu-ti, the *wu*-shamans of Yüeh were ordered to set up altars in the capital and sacrifice to the heavenly spirits, the Supreme Lord, and myriad ghosts. There is no doubt that other cults worshipped one or more of those deities venerated by the *wu* of Yüeh. Moreover, the Queen Mother of the West received veneration at court during the time of Wang Mang, and her cult was widely celebrated in the countryside.[78]

Here we return to ideas expressed in Chapter 1. The political, social, or economic status of a person did not necessarily reflect his religious practices; members of the "upper class" could still be participants in "popular religion." It is possible for one to have supported "official religion" at court, yet also to have followed "popular religion" at home. Moreover, a cult cannot be labelled as "popular" entirely by its content. Nor can it be labelled based on the existence or not of official status. As the example of the *feng-shan* ceremony shows, even a most grandiose official cult could be used as an instrument of personal needs more in tune with popular religious piety than with the official cults.

Conclusion

To explain the interaction between imperial, court affairs and the development of official cults, we have examined the influence of personal factors on the religious institutions. But how did the personal beliefs of the emperors reflect overall religious feelings or trends?

Our knowledge of religious trends toward the end of the Warring States period cannot be considered sufficient with regard to official cults and the religion of the ordinary people. Nevertheless, discussions in the previous chapters detected three different trends in the development of religion: the state cults, popular beliefs, and elitist views. We have seen extensive worship of various ghosts and spirits among the common people of late Warring States society. We have also seen the similarity between noncourt, local beliefs and the state cults concerning spiritual beings. Divination methods given in daybooks also reveal a mechanical cosmology similar to the correlative mentality expressed in the "Monthly Ordinance" chapter of *Book of Rites*. The elites or intellectuals, who favored a morally based set of principles, opposed the credulity of people inside and outside the court.[79] However, as we shall discuss in Chapter 8, they could not or would not disassociate themselves completely from basic religious tenets shared by all cults: the existence of spiritual beings, and the possibility of communicating with them. They understood well that religious beliefs, given correct direction, could become an important force for establishing a harmonious society.

The official religion of the Ch'in and Han dynasties, being a logical continuation of the state cults of the Warring States period, could not possibly have eradicated the cosmological assumptions that it shared with noncourt cults. The continuous exchange between the local and the official cults further blurred the distinction between official religion and popular beliefs. And when we examine the various cultic or divinational activities of the emperors, we find that some of these activities, which were mainly held for the benefit of the emperor himself, can indeed be viewed as having reflected the characteristics of popular religion of this period. The emperors, in other words, were sometimes simply the most prominent participants in popular cults, a position which nonetheless did not impede their role as the head of the official religion.

One way by which we can actually distinguish noncourt, or popular, religion from that of the ruling center is to examine where the perceived benefits lay. In my understanding, the worshippers of popular cults, and popular beliefs per se, tended to focus on personal welfare, whereas statements about the purpose of the official cult used the pretext of the welfare of the country, or of humanity in general. It may even be said that when a cult possessed both official and popular status, it was only the attitudes and expectations of worshippers that determined the category to which it actually belonged. Of course, the attitudes and expectations of the worshipper are not always unambiguous, which only makes our inquiry more challenging.

Chapter 6

Beliefs and Practices in Everyday Life of the Han Dynasty

And begging priests and soothsayers go to rich men's doors and
make them believe that they by means of sacrifices and incantations
have accumulated a treasure of power from the gods that can expiate
and cure with pleasurable festivals any misdeed of a man or his
ancestors, and that if a man wishes to harm an enemy, at slight cost
he will be enabled to injure just and unjust alike, since they are
masters of spells and enchantments that constrain the gods to serve
their end.[1]

What sacrifices these scoundrels make! They bring their picnic
boxes, their wine-jars, not for the gods, but themselves. The incense
and barley-cake is holy enough. The god gets all that, put there on
the fire; and they put on the tail bone and the bile, because they are
inedible, for the gods—then they gulp down all the rest.[2]

We discussed in the last chapter how political unification under the
Ch'in and Han dynasties brought changes to the official cults. At the
same time, the statuses of both official and popular cults changed. On
the local level, because of the destruction of much of the old clan system
after the prolonged period of war that ended the Warring States and
finally the Ch'in,[3] Chinese society, at least at the rural level, had un-

dergone a more or less thorough reorganization. The basic unit of peasant society in Han times was the *li* 里, or hamlet, which usually consisted of about one hundred families and had its own settlement area. Above the *li*, the administrative unit was the *hsiang* 鄉, or district, which might have included several *li*. At the lowest level of court-appointed officials were those of the *hsien* 縣, county, still one step higher than the *hsiang*.

The world of the non-ruling, local farmers, artisans, and laborers was situated within the *hsiang* and *li*, which the ideology of the central government could only reach in an indirect way.[4] In this world, life was dominated by work in the fields, and work in the fields was tied to the cycle of the seasons.[5] Some old customs related to the natural order persisted even in the new environment. Besides the natural cycle, there was the human life cycle, i.e., birth, marriage, sickness, and death, the basic contours of which remained more or less the same. Here was a fertile ground for the continuous growth of various beliefs, the roots of which stretched back to pre-imperial times.

Religious Activities Related to the Agricultural Cycle

Beliefs related to the cycle of seasons occupied a central position in the religious world of many ancient civilizations, including China. In a primarily agricultural economy, the livelihood of peasants in ancient China depended heavily upon well-balanced seasons. Religious activities related to the agricultural cycle were observed by both ruling and ruled segments of society, both in pre-imperial and imperial times. Unlike the earlier period, however, relatively more Han-era documents exist concerning these activities. The main sources are the "Treatise on Ceremonies" (*li-i chih* 禮儀志) and "Treatise on Sacrifice" (*chi-ssu chih* 祭祀志) sections of *History of Later Han*, which are mostly records of official cult activities. However, although some of the official festivals and ceremonies do not seem to have directly involved the life of the commoners, they were often based on ancient traditions that had deep roots in agricultural life. The rituals and ceremonies relating to the seasons were, on the one hand, signs of the official recognition of the importance of agriculture to society, and, on the other, tools to establish a government-initiated social order. For example, the "plowing ceremony" was performed at the beginning of the first spring month. The emperor led the court officials in the symbolic act of plow-ing a field. It was no doubt a recognition of the importance of agricul-ture, an official act to encourage people to begin field work, as well as a magical act to ensure a good harvest.[6]

Activities related to the season, furthermore, can be corroborated by other sources, such as Ts'ui Shih's *Monthly Ordinances for the Four Classes of People* (*Ssu-min yüeh-ling* 四民月令), or Ying Shao's *A Penetrating Account of Manners and Customs* (*Feng-su t'ung-i* 風俗通義), as belonging to the sphere of religion and belief. Ts'ui Shih (c. A.D. 103–171) came from a family with a long tradition of learning and government service. He was certainly not a "commoner." His *Monthly Ordinances for the Four Classes of People*, however, was written for a self-sufficient manorial estate, which involved the actual workings of peasant life.[7] Ying Shao (c. A.D. 165–204) was a scholar-official living at the end of Eastern Han. His famous work, *A Penetrating Account of Manners and Customs*, was a collection of stories, factual or anec-dotal, about the manners and customs of Chinese society to his time. It is a rich mine of information for social and religious historians of ancient China.[8] Because a study of Han official festivals has already appeared,[9] I shall concentrate on activities celebrated by non-elites outside the court.

The New Year celebration

Derk Bodde has pointed out the different ways of calculating the be-ginning of the new year in Ch'in and Han times.[10] According to the Han calendar, as recorded in *History of Later Han*, the beginning of the official year was set at the first day of the first month.[11] The official celebration consisted of court audiences, amusements, and processions, with little indication of religious practice, unless one considers the congratulations to the emperor, the son of heaven, an expression of piety. According to Ts'ui Shih, the common people celebrated the new year more solemnly:

> The first day of the first month is called the New Year. [The head of the household] personally leads his wife and children reverently to offer sacrifice to ancestors and [deceased] parents. Three days before [the ceremony], the head of the household and those who

have assignments should have observed [a period of] purification. On the day of the ceremony, wine is served to cause the spirits to descend. After the ceremony is over, the whole family, including the old and the young, sit according to seniority in front of the ancestors. The sons, their wives, the grandchildren, and the great-grand-children each presents pepper [blossom] wine to the head of the household, to toast to health and longevity. They do so happily.[12]

Thus, appropriating the blessings of the spirits, gods, and ancestors was the most important act of reverence at the beginning of a new year.

First ting-day (shang-ting 上丁) of the first month

The official calendar mentions this date concerning "the Five Offerings": the Son of Heaven performed offering rituals at the South Suburb, North Suburb, the Hall of Light (*Ming-t'ang* 明堂)[13], and the shrines of Kao-ti and Wu-ti.[14] Thus, basically the ancestors and the ether, or *ch'i*, of south and north were honored. *Monthly Ordinances for the Four Classes of People* gives an explicit explanation for the occasion as celebrated outside the court:

> The hundred kinds of plants sprout. The dormant insects emerge. On the first *ting* day of the month, the guardian deity of travellers is worshipped at the gate side so that the *yang* atmosphere (i.e., aura) is ushered in and the stagnant atmosphere is expelled; [thereby] one prays for blessings and good luck.[15]

The meaning of the offering is clear (with the first sign of the sprouting of the plants, the deity was invoked to ensure the smooth transition between the seasons and the development of the plants, i.e., by guiding the course of the *yang* power to a positive conclusion). The record of the official rituals does not give any such explanation. One may surmise that sacrifices to the south and north suburbs signified piety toward heaven and earth, thus ensuring a good year. In any case, the difference between the official and the non-official cults demonstrates their different orientations.

Similar to the first *ting* day, on the first *hai* 亥 day of the first month, the peasants made offerings to the spirit of farming, First Farmer (*hsien-se* 先穡), and the ancestors, to pray for a successful harvest.[16] The focus of the peasant in their religious life is thus clear: to secure a good harvest and the blessing of the ancestors.

Offering to the t'ai-she, in the second month

On a certain date (not mentioned in our sources) in the second lunar month, people prepared offerings to their ancestors at the *t'ai-she* 太社, the local communal altar.[17] Another offering was placed at the family gravesite the next day. It is interesting that on this occasion people had to consult a "daybook" to determine if it was an auspicious day: the Shui-hu-ti daybook lists various days suitable for making such offerings.[18] Thus, if a certain day was not auspicious for placing offerings on the grave, one had to search for another day.[19]

The offering at the local communal altar is likely to have been part of the supplication offerings that began with the *shang-ting*: farmers first made offering to their ancestors and the spirit of farming at each other's houses, then they gathered at the local community shrine to pray for the welfare of the entire community. The offering of leeks and eggs in this ceremony is symbolic of a good harvest: leeks grow easily and abundantly; and eggs symbolize fertility.

Lustration, or fu-hsi 祓禊, the first ssu-day of the third month

According to the official calendar, on this day,

> All the officials and the people should wash themselves in a river that flows eastward. It is said to clean and purge [evil spirits] and clear old dust and fever. This is the great purification. The reason for the purification is that the *yang*-ether has begun to spread forcefully, and myriad of creatures have begun to appear. Thus [it is necessary] to purify them.[20]

Both Granet and Bodde traced this festival to Chou times, suggesting that there was a connection between it and a poem in *Book of Poetry* where young men and girls were said to play by the river in the spring and send each other love messages.[21] Granet even went so far as to suggest that the poem reflected a mating rite. Bodde, presenting materials concerning *shang-ssu* in Han times, found that the ritual mainly reflected the cleansing of evils and impurities, or funerary rites, such as recalling the soul.[22] Granet's theory about a mating rite, though it has gained support from modern ethnographical data,[23] remains only hypothetical, as is his interpretation of *kao-mei*.[24] The text in the *Book of Poetry* only refers to a joyful outing, without mention of date or ritual activity:

> The Chen and Wei are in full flood,
> The gentleman and the girl are picking
>   *lan*-flowers;
> The girl says: "Have you looked [at the
>   scenery]?"
> The gentleman says: "Yes indeed."
> "Shall we go look?
> "Beyond the river Wei [the field] is wide
>   and joyous."
> Then the gentleman and the girl went
>   cajoling with each other,
> And one gives the other a peony.[25]

Thus, even if there was a lustration ceremony that existed both before and during the Han, as Bodde's study shows, its meaning was understood as having to do with "clearing the old and starting the new" rather than with courtship.[26] In Eastern Han lexicographic sources the word *fu* in the title *fu-hsi* means: "ritual sacrifice to wipe away evil."[27] Lao Kan suggests that the ceremony was held on the particular day because in the system of Chien-ch'u 建除 divination, the *ssu* days are for "ch'u," i.e., for removing things, thus the "removing of evil spirits (i.e., lustration)."[28] Why in the third month? It was held then probably because of the first warmth and the rise in river levels. Yet perhaps the temperature of the water might have precluded bathing, unless we consider the act symbolic. An Eastern Han scholar, Hsüeh Han, commented on the *Book of Poetry* passage thus: "During the time of the third month, when peach blossoms flow on the river, it is the custom of the (young people of the) state of Cheng to go out to the banks of the rivers Chen and Wei. They hold *lan* (in their hands) and recall the spirits and expel the inauspicious."[29] Bathing directly in the water is not mentioned.

The summer solstice

History of Later Han offers an unusually detailed account of activities related to the summer solstice and the midsummer month, i.e., the fifth lunar month. The main activities consisted of using red thread to tie together vegetables with pungent smells and placing five-colored amulet-seals made of peachwood at the doorway to ward off evil on the fifth day of the fifth month. On the day of summer solstice, it was forbidden to make large fires, or to make charcoal, work metals, or smelt minerals.[30] The account does not mention whether these were official activities, yet the use of vegetables and amulets strongly suggests that they refer to the life of the common people. Ying Shao's *A Penetrating Account of Manners and Customs*, for example, mentions that

> On the fifth day of the fifth month, presents are made of "silks of the five colors for prolonging life." It is popularly said that these will increase a man's lifespan.[31]

Another passage from the same work reads:

> The multicolored silks that are bound to the forearm on the fifth day of the fifth month serve to ward off weapons and demons and to save people from epidemics. It is further said that this is done because of Ch'ü Yüan.[32]

Ying Shao's work, to a considerable extent, was devoted to the life of the general populace, thereby corroborating my observation that the text in *History of Later Han* refers to popular belief. The paragraph mentioned above was probably included in the "Treatise on Ceremonies" because the midsummer month had always been agriculturally important, as it was the culmination of the *yang* heat at the beginning point of the new onset of *yin*.[33] Because heat caused spoilage and disease, and since people believed that sickness could be caused by evil spirits, it is only natural that during this time of year apotropaic actions were taken to prevent evil from entering the house. The ban on large fires and metal working might have also been meant to curb the heat) Also, according to Bodde, it was a scholarly device to exemplify *yin-yang* theory,[34] as we have seen in Chapter 5 concerning the rain prayers described by Tung Chung-shu.

In contrast to the detailed account in *History of Later Han, Monthly Ordinances* has only a simple description of the summer solstice:

> Wheat and fish are presented to ancestors and [deceased] parents. When that day dawns, the sacrifice is offered. The day before [the ceremony], [one follows] the procedures for food preparation, purification, and cleansing, all of which are similar to [the ceremony for] presenting leeks and eggs [in the second month].[35]

There is no explanation of the symbolism of the wheat and fish, although one surmises that abundance in farm production was implied in the offering.

The concealment, *fu*, in the sixth month

The day of *fu* 伏, literally "to prostrate," is first mentioned in the Ch'in annals in *Shih-chi*, when the duke of Ch'in sacrificed dogs at the gates of the city to ward off the disease-causing evil spirit or venom (*ku* 蠱).[36] During the Han, the *fu*-day seemed to have been a day for lying down, or staying in the house, presumably to avoid having contact with the evil spirits outside.[37] That the term "three *fu*" refers to a period from the mid-sixth to the mid-seventh lunar month, the hottest period of the summer,[38] indicates that people were encouraged to keep cool at home.[39] Although the official festivals recorded in *History of Later Han* did not mention the *fu*, evidence shows that during the Eastern Han period, the *fu*-day was observed by the government as a day of rest.[40] In western locales, such as Han-chung, Pa, Shu, and Kuang-han, local officials chose the *fu*-day according to local climate.[41] This strongly suggests that the *fu*-day was basically a "summer holiday." The people, nevertheless, developed the custom of offering wheat and melon to the ancestors, similar to the procedures for the summer solstice.[42] The use of dogs or other animals in the exorcistic ritual for driving away evil spirits probably at an earlier point involved the apotropaic power of blood to ward off evil. Ying Shao employed *yin-yang* and Five-Phases theory to explain the use of dogs:

> The dog is the animal of the element of metal, and the act of exorcism (*jang*) was to repel. They repel the element of metal, so that it will not harm what the spring season produces, and allow all creatures to develop according to their own natures.[43]

Kao Yu's commentary to *Lü-shih ch'un-ch'iu*, however, added sheep to the sacrificial animals.[44] Under different circumstances, other animals could be used as sacrifice in exorcistic rituals. Ying Shao mentioned that in his time people used chickens to ward off evil spirits and illnesses,[45] as did Ts'ui Shih in *Monthly Ordinances for the Four Classes of People*.[46] These rituals can be traced back to earlier documents, such as *Classic of Mountains and Seas*, in which are mentioned the use of rooster,[47] dog,[48] sheep,[49] and pig[50] as sacrifices to various deities. These suggest that the use of animals in exorcistic rituals was a deep-rooted tradition that could not be completely replaced by the relatively late *yin-yang* and Five-Phases theories.

Offering to the t'ai-she, in the eighth month

We read in *Monthly Ordinances for the Four Classes of People* that on a selected day in the eighth lunar month, people made offerings (millet and pig) to the ancestors at the communal altar and before the family graves, as they had done six months earlier. The exact date is unspecified, but the text says: "Divine for an auspicious date after the moon festival (*yüeh-chieh*), and make offerings to the revered gods that require worship in the year."[51] We receive no clues as to its significance. Its intention, however, may be a gesture of thanksgiving for the success of the previous prayers for the harvest. The reference to *yüeh-chieh*, which can be read as "moon festival" or "month festival," suggests that a mid-autumn festival was already in existence. Shih Sheng-han suggests that this is the "white dew" (*pai-lu* 白露), one of the twenty-four agricultural "nodes," falling in the eighth month.[52]

Winter solstice, in the eleventh month

The cosmological significance of the winter solstice is found in the return of the *yang* force, represented by the reversal of diminishing daylight. As Ts'ui Shih says: "In this month, the *yin* and the *yang* elements are contending for dominance, and the energy of the blood is dispersed. For five days before and five days after the winter solstice, the husband and the wife should sleep separately."[53] To avoid sexual contact during this period was obviously an application of *yin-yang* theory. It is, however, uncertain whether people would indeed have followed this instruction. Official activities also elaborated on *yin-yang* theory, and produced prognostications for the coming year, weighing of earth and charcoal, and the tuning of the pitch-pipes.[54] For the ordinary people, however, "sacrifices are offered to the water deity at the well, and then to ancestors and [deceased] parents. Purification, food preparation, cleaning, and washing—all are similar to [the procedure for the ceremony of] offering millet and pigs . . . in the first month."[55]

The Great Exorcism, ta-no, in the twelfth month

The *History of Later Han* "Treatise on Ceremonies" describes a display of exorcistic activities called the Great Exorcism, or *ta-no* 大儺, in the twelfth lunar month, one day before the *la* (see below). It involved hundreds of participants, including sons of the ennobled officials, some disguised as demons, some as demon-eaters.[56] The purpose of the exorcism was to expel the evil spirits that had accumulated throughout the year, presumably since the lustration in the third month. Bodde explains the ceremony as an "attempt to depict, in theological terms, this annual drama of death and rebirth, and, through this depiction, to insure the repetition of the natural cycle."[57] Although an official event by this time, the scale of the performance made it a public show, and thus it might be considered as a popular festival. According to other sources, furthermore, the act could have existed earlier, perhaps in the Shang dynasty.[58] Confucius once observed *no*-performance by the rural people.[59] *Rites of Chou* mentions the work of the major character in *no*, Fang-hsiang 方相, as driving away dis-

132

eases from the house, and expelling evil spirits from the tomb chamber during the funeral.[60] It was not until the Han that *no* was performed at the year-end. This is also confirmed by the poet Chang Heng in his "Rhapsody on the Eastern Capital" (*Tung-ching fu* 東京賦).[61] According to Wang Ch'ung, the year-end exorcism was widely imitated,[62] suggesting that it was performed in agricultural locales.[63]

The *la*, in the twelfth month

The last of the annual festivals was the *la* 臘, in the twelfth lunar month. It was held on the third *hsü* 戌 day after winter solstice.[64] Bodde has given a detailed account, and has suggested that it was originally the people's New Year.[65] Its significance is stated in *History of Later Han* in a general fashion: "In the last month of winter, the constellations return and the year ends. As the forces of *yin* and *yang* cross one another, the great celebration of la is performed to soothe the farmers."[66] It was the celebration of the end of the agricultural cycle and the preparation for the coming of a new one, a most important stage for farmers. Already in *Book of Poetry* we find a description of the general sentiment in the Chou period regarding such a festival, in "The Seventh Month (*ch'i-yüeh* 七月)" quoted before:

> In the tenth month, it is cold, with frost;
> The two bottles of spirits are enjoyed,
> And they say, "Let us kill our lambs and sheep,
> And to go to the hall of our lord,
> There raise the cup of rhinoceros horn,
> And wish him long life—that he may live for ever."[67]

The tenth month of the Chou corresponds to the twelfth month of the Han calendar. *Monthly Ordinances for the Four Classes of People* describes the process of celebration, which lasted at least nine days, and in which pigs and sheep were killed for offerings. The spirits honored included ancestors and household gods, as in the new year celebration.[68] In addition, it was believed that in this month a multitude of spirits incessantly moved around; thus, a special ceremony was held to secure their blessings.[69]

133

Supplementary beliefs related to agriculture

The year-round religious activities discussed above are clearly centered on the agricultural life of farmers. Besides these regular activities, other, supplementary, religious activities were important. One of those was the prayer for inducing or stopping rain. We discussed Tung Chung-shu's thoughts on this in Chapter 5. It is worth noting that the extensive preparations described by Tung, although placed in an official context, were in part joined by local people:

> Order the people to close the south gate of fortified towns or farming districts, and place water outside. Open the north gate, prepare a male pig, place it outside the north gate. Prepare another male pig in the market place. When hearing the sound of drums, burn the tails of the pigs, and take the bones of a dead person and bury them. . . .[70]

There is no doubt that prayers for rain were ancient, and were practiced in a variety of ways. The text indicates that the ritual was performed at the local level. The burning of pig's tails and the burying of the bones of the dead, furthermore, may indicate rites of exorcism. The "Treatise on Literature" in *History of Han* lists a work entitled "Praying for Rain and for Stopping Rain" in twenty-six books, which, if extant, would yield more information than what Tung Chung-shu's essays offer.[71] The existence of such works, together with ones in the *shu-shu* (magic and fortune-telling) category, such as *Shen-nung's Instruction for Farming, Soil Inspection, and Cultivation*, or, *Tree Planting, Storing Fruits, and Inspecting Silk Worms*, suggests that a number of cultic or magic treatises related to agricultural life circulated in Han society. Although little of their contents is preserved, one can gain some idea from such sections as "Taboos for the Five Seeds (*wu-chung chi* 五種忌)" or "Horses" in the Shui-hu-ti daybook.[72]

To sum up, the major concern of these rituals and festivals was to secure good harvests and a prosperous life. The idea of *yin-yang* theory was clearly influential in the structure of ritual activities, yet the belief in the efficacy of ancestor spirits and gods was still the underlying element in religious life of the peasantry.

134

Religious Activities Related to the Life Cycle

Similar to the yearly cycles of the changing seasons, social life was made up of the cycle of birth, marriage, old age, sickness, and death. Religious beliefs developed naturally around these subjects. An Eastern Han writer, Wang Ch'ung, hailed as a rare rationalist thinker, left a number of vivid descriptions of, as well as vigorous attacks on, these popular beliefs. Thus, he wrote:

> It is a common belief that evil influences cause our diseases and our deaths, and that in case of continual calamities, penalties, ignominious execution, and derision, there has been some offense. When commencing a building, moving residence, in sacrificing, mourning, burying, and other rites, or in taking up office or marrying, if one does not choose a lucky day, and inauspicious years and months are not avoided, one falls in with demons and meets spirits, which at that ominous time work disaster.[73]

Wang Ch'ung regarded such concepts as false, however, and proceeded to argue against them. Although we do not know whether his voice was heard and heeded, since he was largely unknown to his contemporaries, it should be clear that his argument serves to illustrate that by his time many kinds of religious beliefs concerning people's lives and daily activities permeated society.

Birth

One cannot under normal circumstances choose the date of birth of a child, but there is no logical barrier to divining a child's future based on the day and hour of birth. The Shui-hu-ti daybook already provided us with a section on "childbirth," wherein the future of the child was predicted according to the date of birth in the sexagenary system.[74] Similar beliefs can be found in a Western Han text excavated from a tomb at Yin-ch'üeh-shan, Shantung province.[75] In addition to the daybook predictions, various taboos concerning childbirth also circulated in society. Ying Shao wrote that, "According to a common saying, among those born on the fifth day of the fifth month, the male will harm his father, and the female will harm her mother."[76] Wang Ch'ung also mentioned the belief against bearing a child in the first and the fifth months, for fear of parricide.[77] If what we read in the *History of Later Han* biography of Chang Huan was true, then the taboo may sometimes have been followed to an extreme. According to this account, in the region of Ho-hsi, at the western border, people had the custom of killing children born in the second and fifth months, as well as those who were born in the same month as their parents. It was due to the intervention of Chang Huan that people discontinued this custom.[78] Corroboration of similar taboos for childbirth in the western border regions is found in the bamboo slips from Tun-huang.[79]

Not only did people wish to learn about the future of their children, they also wished to influence the fate of their children by magical measures. One of the methods, known in the medical books as "Yü-tsang 禹藏," (Yü's [placenta] burial method) involved the burial of the placenta according to a certain direction, so that the child would lead a long life.[80] This method was confirmed by a text discovered in the early Western Han Ma-wang-tui tomb, including a diagram of the various possible positions for burying placentas and a special explanatory text.[81] The mother was instructed first to locate the month of the child's birth on the diagram, then to bury the placenta in the direction indicated on the diagram. The idea was that the placenta was believed to be part of the infant's person. When it was buried according to an appropriate direction, it was believed that the life of the child was protected by the related constellation and lengthened life. It was a sympathetic magic based on the principle of correlative cosmology.[82] There were also taboos related to pregnancy and delivery. Several sources held that prohibitions existed with regard to the food that a pregnant woman should eat, one of which was rabbit meat, which caused the child to have deformed lips.[83] Another taboo forbade the eating of ginger, which would cause the appearance of extra fingers on the infant.[84] It is interesting that these medical books make no attempt to distinguish "superstitious" information from material that strikes the modern reader as "scientific." The relatively idealized and rationalized text of *Monthly Ordinance* mentions that,

> During the mid-spring month, . . . three days before the roaring of the thunder, one should sound the bell and advise the people:

"The thunder is about to roar. Anyone who does not attend to his personal hygiene and behavior will not have a healthy child, and bring disaster upon himself."[85]

Although the assertion that personal hygiene could influence the health of the child sounds like modern medical knowledge, it is nevertheless clear that these taboos were mainly based upon the idea of like forces and sympathetic magic. Likenesses were found not only in such concrete things as rabbits or ginger, but in abstract, personal behavior as well. While the *Monthly Ordinance* text is no doubt expounding a type of correlative cosmology, the food taboo can be seen as a materialized version of this cosmology.

Given the state of medical knowledge, many of the measures that people at this time took to influence the sex of the fetus before it was born,[86] as well as some of the food taboos for the mother, must be seen as belonging to the sphere of beliefs rather than empirical medical knowledge, although we cannot assert that people made a clear distinction between the two.[87]

Marriage

Everyday activities were also believed to have had direct correspondence with the auspiciousness of days. Marriage was no exception. Texts such as *Record of History* and *Lun-heng* mentioned the popular custom of divining for the proper day of marriage.[88] The scholar Cheng Chung, when writing his commentary to *Book of Rites*, also remarked that the practice of divining for a marriage day was standard in his day.[89] Archaeologically excavated texts similar to the Shui-hu-ti daybook also provided appropriate days for marriage.[90] The tenacity of such beliefs is shown by an anecdote: during the reign of Wang Mang, Wang wanted to change the taboo days of marriage and adult initiation, but was opposed by the common people.[91]

Sickness and healing

As early as the Shang period, people attributed illness to spirits or ancestors.[92] During the Eastern Chou, however, we first see evidence of arguments denying the role of gods or ghosts in illness. An ancient doctor attributed a certain illness to lascivious behavior;[93] and the earliest medical classic, *Huang-ti nei-ching*, discussed the irregularity of *yin* and *yang*, promoting a mechanistic view of physiology.[94]

But old ways of thinking and healing loomed large in the life of the common people. Toward the end of the Warring States period, the author of *Master Lü's Spring and Autumn Annal* remarked that people were using *wu*-shamans and poisonous drugs to cure sickness.[95] The author tries to invoke the authority of "the ancients," presumably the sages, to disprove contemporary phenomena. This effort, however, only reflects the prevalence of such behaviors among the people, for the author, being a rational intellectual, was certainly among the minority in society. The common people, unused to sophisticated, literate doctors, probably did not distinguish magic from science (both terms, of course, in their modern senses) as divergent activities.

The mixture of empiricism with faith concerning the causes of sickness is also reflected in the daybooks. On the one hand, people could make judgments based on observations, such as the toxicity of spoiled meats. On the other hand, the ancestors, not to mention ghosts and spirits, are still blamed, as in Shang times.[96]

This ambivalence was still seen during the early Han, and is best shown in the medical texts discovered in the Ma-wang-tui tomb number three. In the "Wu-shih-erh ping-fang 五十二病方," or "Prescriptions for Fifty-two Ailments," a number of cases recommended practical treatments and magical spells for the same illness.[97] For example, to stop a simple wound from bleeding, one of the remedies is "to burn hair and press [the ash] on the wound," while another prescribed a magical formula.[98] To use incinerated hair to treat a wound may have had some real effect;[99] incantation, however, was effective only as part of belief.

What kinds of spirits could cause illnesses? Some of the prescriptions indicate that the illnesses themselves are considered forms of evil spirits that could be driven away by exorcism. One prescription for warts says:

> Let the person who has a wart hold a grain stalk, and let someone else shout: "What are you that caused this?" [The sick person should] answer: "I am the wart." Then put away the grain stalk, do not look at it.[100]

Another method:

> On the last day of the month, go to a well on a mound, one that
> has water in it, use a broken broom to brush the wart twice
> seven times, then chant an incantation: "Today is the last day of
> the month, brush the wart to the north." Then drop the broom
> into the well.[101]

Sometimes the "heavenly god" (*t'ien-shen* 天神) was invoked to drive
away the personified sickness:

> On the day of *hsin-ssu*, pronounce the incantation "*Pen!* The day
> is *hsin-ssu*" three times. Recite: "A heavenly god comes down to
> interfere with the illness. The sacred maid (*shen-nü* 神女) leans
> on the wall and listens to the words of the god. This hernia (*hu-
> shan* 狐疝) is at the wrong place. Desist. If you (i.e., the hernia)
> do not desist, [I will use] the axe to kill you." Then you should
> use a piece of cloth to strike [the patient] twice seven times.[102]

The skin disease *ch'i* 漆, which could be caused by coming into contact
with lacquer (*ch'i* 漆), can be treated by pronouncing the following
magic spell:

> "Oh lacquer, the heavenly emperor let you come down to paint
> bows and arrows. Now you have caused people illness, I will smear
> you with pig's excrement." Use the bottom of a shoe to hit it.[103]

As we have seen several times before, the excrement of animals was
considered efficacious for apotropaic actions. Some illnesses were
thought to have been caused by a creature called "*yü* 蜮," which spit
water on people, causing various kinds of illness. Magical spells and
acts were employed either to prevent it from shooting at people, or to
cure those who were infected by it.[104] For illnesses caused by the "child-
ghost" *ch'i* 魃, exorcism was best. One prescription says:

> To treat the child-ghost: Perform the Pace of Yü three times, take
> a twig from the eastern side of a peach tree, split it in middle and
> make [figurines], and hang these on the door, one on each side.[105]

Another paragraph provides the incantation:

Oh you, the father and mother of the child-ghost, do not hide to the north of . . . , the female *wu*-shaman is looking for you and will certainly catch you, and [bind] your limbs, tie up your fingers, and cast you into the water. It is man, it is man, and yet he pretends to be a ghost(?)[106]

The text is difficult to comprehend, but the general meaning is discernible. Clearly, people believed illness to have been connected to gods, or a Heavenly Emperor, since the evil spirits that inflicted illness came under the jurisdiction of the heavenly god. Here, one recalls the Shang Dynasty ruler's frequent inquiries on the identities of the ancestor-spirits who had caused the king's disease. Unlike the daybook, however, the higher gods in our Han text could not be held directly responsible for people's illness. To cure illnesses, people had to perform exorcistic acts to expel the evil spirits. That magical-medical texts were buried with other, more scholarly, medical texts, such as the *Classic of the Eleven Circuits of Foot and Arm* (*Tsu-pei shih-i-mai chiu-ching* 足臂十一脈灸經), *Classic of the Eleven Circuits of Yin and Yang* (*Yin-yang shih-i-mai chiu-ching* 陰陽十一脈灸經), *The Principle of Pulse* (*Mai-fa* 脈法), not to mention the well-known philosophical texts, *The Four Classics of Huang-ti* (*Huang-ti ssu-ching* 黃帝四經) and *Lao-tzu*, poses a problem: what was the relationship between magical and empirical-scholarly medical texts? Since they were discovered in the same tomb, we may assume that the texts were intended for users of the same social status. Yet how much did the owner of these various texts understand the difference between rational and magical medicine? If he did, did he prefer to believe in both methods? Could we, on the other hand, say that the so-called magical-medical texts cannot represent "popular" attitudes at all, since they are "literary" and appeared in the tomb of a noble? Problems such as these appear when corroborating documents on ancient medicine and religion are sparse.

In ancient Greece, concomitant with such "rational" medical treatises as *The Sacred Disease*,[107] there were various kinds of "healers" who, besides empirically based medical knowledge, employed all sorts of magical treatments on their patients. Among these, the evidence provided by the cult of Asclepius at Epidaurus clearly shows that the god sometimes used food or drugs, besides magical touching, for example, to treat the sick.[108] The cult was undoubtedly part of "popular religion," yet the treatments offered by this god (or its ministers) also contained rational elements. On the other hand, many of the so-called rational medical texts, although claiming to have been freed from religion, contained various unsupportable presuppositions and fantasies.[109]

In the case of China, then, I prefer to think that the Ma-wang-tui "Prescriptions for Fifty-two Ailments" text was closer to the inscriptions of the cult of Asclepius than the Hippocratic *On the Sacred Disease*, which is more akin to *Classic of the Eleven Circuits of Foot and Arm* and others. Although we do not know for certain whether "Prescriptions for Fifty-two Ailments" reflected the personal beliefs of its owner, that it was written down in the format of a practical manual suggests that it was intended for everyday use. It was true that in many instances, shamans were the people's choice for exorcism, yet the existence of such manuals as "Prescriptions for Fifty-two Ailments" suggests that people also performed the acts themselves by following textual instructions. I see this as an example of how far everyday religion could penetrate the lives of both non-rulers and the ruling elite.

Death and burial

Among the various beliefs related to death and burial, I will first discuss those related to burial customs and leave the idea of death and the netherworld for a later chapter.

Concerning the time for burial, *Book of Rites* states that the Son of Heaven should be buried seven months after death, the feudal lords five months, and officials, scholars, and commoners three.[110] This was one way to distinguish social classes. In the Han dynasty, however, this rule was not followed at all, and we see various criteria to determine auspicious days for burial sometimes causing delay in burial.[111] According to Wang Ch'ung,

> The calendar for burials prescribes that the nine holes and depressions of the earth, as well as odd and even days, and single and paired months are to be avoided. The day being lucky and innocuous, oddness and evenness agreeing, and singleness and parity tallying, there is luck and good fortune. The non-observance of this calendar, on the other hand, induces to bad luck and disaster.[112]

When no appropriate days could be found, people preferred to wait:

> In cases where several persons die in rapid succession one after the other, so that there are up to ten coffins awaiting burial, they are not concerned about contagion through contaminated air, but only that the day chosen for interment might be un-lucky.[113]

The site for the tomb should also be selected with care, something that may also contribute to delayed burial. A story in *History of Later Han*, however, gives us a different perspective. A young man was very poor when his mother died. He buried her in a simple fashion, without divining for either the tomb site or the date. Local *wu*-shamans predicted that this would cause great disaster for the family, but the young man did not heed their warnings. Later, instead of bad fate, his son and grandson reached high positions in government.[114] Such stories show the extent to which some cultured people abjured superstitions about death and burial. They also revealed what most people, represented by the *wu*-shamans, actually believed in.

In close connection with beliefs about life and death was the worship of the deity Ssu-ming, or the "Lord of Fate," who was in charge of life spans and could revive the dead. He appears as early as the Warring States period.[115] In the T'ien-shui Ch'in tomb text, mentioned in Chapter 3, Ssu-ming effected a resurrection, as controller of lives.[116] *Book of Rites* implies that Ssu-ming was worshipped by the royal family and the feudal lords, but not by the commoners.[117] Yet according to the Eastern Han scholar Cheng Hsüan,

> [Ssu-ming was] a lesser god who lives among the people and examines lesser evils. . . . Ssu-ming was in charge of the three kinds of fate (proper life span, injust life experience, and proper retribution). . . . The common households today often make sacrifice to Ssu-ming in Spring and Autumn.[118]

Thus, at least in the Eastern Han period, Ssu-ming was worshipped by nonelite households. Ying Shao concurs: "Today people only worship Ssu-ming. They carve a wooden human figure, about one foot and two inches long. This is put into the trunk of a traveller or in a small shrine in the house. He is greatly worshipped in the region of Ch'i

(齊, modern Shantung province) and also in many commanderies in Ju-nan (汝南)."[119] A statue discovered some years ago shows a man holding a small child, and the context suggests that it was a cult image of Ssu-ming.[120]

Religious Activities in Everyday Life

Along with beliefs and practices of the agricultural and life cycles, various problems arose in people's daily lives that were often solved through religion.

As already seen in the daybooks, religious beliefs were applied to foods and medicines and correlative ideas were at the root of certain taboos. Drinking on the day of a lunar eclipse (*shih* 蝕), for example, would cause one's mouth to become corrupted (semantically the same as the word "eclipse").[121]

Making new garments was an important event, as evidenced by the existence of special divination books for this purpose, which have turned up as special sections in daybooks.[122] In the Eastern Han period, such handbooks still circulated. Wang Ch'ung mentioned that there were "books for tailors, giving auspicious and inauspicious times. Dresses made on inauspicious days could bring misfortune; made on a lucky day, they attracted happiness."[123] Wang Ch'ung's words are corroborated by documents discovered as far west as Kansu.[124] Related to taboo days concerning manufacture of garments were days for bathing. There was a "Book for baths," as mentioned, once again, by Wang Ch'ung:

> In writings on baths we are informed that if anybody washes his head on a *tzu* 子 day, his appearance is enhanced, whereas if he does so on a *mao* 卯 day, his hair turns white.[125]

Since there were "books" about such taboos, elaborate systems must have been involved in determining auspicious days.

One of the more important issues in daily life concerned living environments. Following the Warring States period, metaphysics of the Five Phases and Four Directions gradually became integrated with geomancy. We have seen geomantic ideas on house building, especially the relative positions of various parts of the house and adjacent structures, given in daybooks.[126] In the Han period, beliefs related to building and siting mainly consisted of the choice of an auspicious day, whether to build or to move, and the choosing of correct positions for houses according to the cardinal directions. In the bamboo texts found in the early-Han tomb at Yin-ch'üeh-shan, we read:

> [On such and such a day one cannot work] on ditches, dikes, or ponds. One cannot work on a city wall of a hundred *chang* or a thousand *chang*, for it will certainly not succeed. One cannot build houses, for there will be disaster.[127]

A story in *Record of History* recounts the words of Meng T'ien, a Ch'in general, before he was forced to commit suicide. Meng T'ien reflected upon his building the Great Wall, and attributed his own misfortune to the disruptive effect of the act of construction upon the earth:

> It [the Great Wall] begins from Lin-yao, and ends at Liao-tung, with more than ten thousand *li* of walls and ditches, could it not have cut through the veins of the earth?[128]

The phrase "veins of earth" is evidence of a belief in the organismic and sacred nature of the earth and its formations. When the "veins of earth" are cut through by artificial means, the area's *ch'i*, or life source, is also extinguished.[129] The belief in the inherent auspiciousness of certain locations is exemplified by the story of Yüan An:

> When An's father died, his mother wanted him to find a burial site. On the road, he met three scholars who asked An's destination. An told them his intention. The scholars then pointed to a spot and said, "Make the burial at this place and your family members will become high officials for generations." After a while, they disappeared. An marveled at this. He then buried his father at that place. This is why his family became prosperous for generations.[130]

That geomancy had become a specialized craft already by Western Han is evidenced by titles in the *History of Han* "Treatise on Literature." *Golden Cabinet for Geomancy (K'an-yü chin-kuei* 堪輿金匱) in fourteen books and *Layout for Houses and Residences* (*Kung-chai ti-hsing* 宮宅地形) in twenty books were obviously handbooks for geomancers.[131] In the Eastern Han period, Wang Ch'ung mentioned other methods for geomancy. For example, "The Principle of Moving" (*I-hsi-fa* 移徙法) employed the positions of the constellations as indications in determining the auspiciousness of a change of domicile.[132] Moreover, "The Art of Charting Houses" (*T'u-chai-shu* 圖宅術) says:

> There are eight schemes, and houses are numbered and classed according to the names of the cycle of the six *chia* 甲. . . . Houses have the Five Sounds, because the surnames (of the owners) are provided with the Five Tones. When the houses do not accord with the surnames, and the latter disagree with the house, people contract virulent diseases and expire, or undergo criminal judgments and meet with adversity.[133]

The art of geomancy went beyond merely observing the positions of buildings and was a system that employed correlative metaphysics in many ways. However, that geomancy was based on *yin-yang*, Five Phases, and correlative cosmology does not mean that supernatural beings were excluded. Wang Ch'ung mentioned *K'an-yü-li* (堪輿曆), a calendar for geomancy: "A great variety of spirits are referred to in the calendars embracing Heaven and Earth (i.e. *K'an-yü-li*), but the sages do not speak of them, the scholars have not mentioned them, and perhaps they are not real."[134] Presumably, these unmentioned spirits were worshipped by common people who had limited access to popular literature like the calendars, but not by the high elite. How such spirits affected people's choice of appropriate days, however, is not clear.

Finally, we deal with travel, about which various beliefs or taboos were already mentioned in connection with daybooks. One imagines that even during the Han period travel in the countryside was rather hazardous.[135] The possibility of encountering monsters, demons, or bandits was always a threat to the traveller. Before setting out, therefore, the Shui-hu-ti daybook advised sacrifice: "When travelling to the east and south, make sacrifice at the left side of the road; when travelling to the west and north, make sacrifice at the right side of the road."[136] The days for setting out as well as coming home also had to be chosen with care. In other texts we see fragmentary passages that deal with auspicious days for travelling.[137] In the "Biographies of the Tortoise and Yarrow Diviners" in *Record of History*, the subject of "divining for travelling" was among the business of the diviners.[138] Although condemned as superstitious by some, diviners nevertheless flourished in marketplaces and were popularly consulted.

A belief in the necessity of choosing auspicious days for travelling existed in all strata of society. The most oft-mentioned taboo days for travelling were the "return of the stem" (*fan-chih* 反支) days, on which any travelling was prohibited, not only for private but also for government business. In the Eastern Han period, as Wang Fu observed, official messengers did not receive and deliver reports to the government offices on *fan-chih* days.[139] Although Wang Fu was criticizing the inefficient aspects of government, the *fan-chih* taboo had a long tradition. *History of Han* mentioned that a prohibition on travelling on *fan-chih* days was observed by some among the elite.[140] The origin of this belief may even go back to the pre-Ch'in era, as seen in daybooks.[141] The taboo for returning home from a journey, since it also concerns travelling, was probably one of the "*fan-chih*" days.[142]

Clearly, most of the beliefs concerning daily activities were built around date-taboos. Thus, various calendars were employed for different purposes: those of burials, sacrifices, taking baths, tailoring, building, or geomancy.[143] The "Biographies of Diviners with Tortoise Shells and Yarrows" provides an impressive list of topics of divination: travelling, fighting bandits, removal from office, success in office, life at home, the harvests, plague, wars, interviews with high officials, chasing fugitives, hunting, rain, etc.[144] Many, of course, appeared in the daybooks. Among the Han documents discovered at the western border fortress of Wu-wei is a "book of date-taboos" for the use of soldiers, and advice is given on such topics as housing, travelling, medicine, garments, having guests, raising cattle, and marriage. The principle for finding auspicious days is based, as expected, on the sexagenary system.[145]

Local Cults

Given the enormous territory of the Han empire, it was natural that differences existed among locales, those remnants of pre-imperial feudal states and their cultures. For example, the Ch'u area culture has often been mentioned as having strong shamanistic elements, although there is no reason to claim that shamanistic activities were solely Ch'u phenomena.[146] Such local customs did not change easily,[147] and it is often difficult to decide whether local religious cults, customs, or taboos originated from a regional difference or from specific situations that had little to do with "regional culture" per se.

Take the custom of "cold foods" in the T'ai-yüan area as an example. Tradition claims that people feared that the spirit of Chieh Tzu-t'ui 介子推, a filial son who let himself be burnt alive together with his mother while hiding in the mountains rather than serve the duke of Chin, did not like to see fire on the anniversary month of his martyrdom; thus, they observed the practice of eating cold meals for an entire month each winter. As a result, we are told, many people died of coldness (in the technical sense defined in Chinese medicine) during this period.[148] In fact, Chieh's story as first told in the *Commentary of Tso* did not contain the scenario of a flaming martyrdom.[149] It was somehow added later, perhaps to give an explanation of the origin of the custom of eating cold food. While it is debatable whether the custom originated from the ancient ritual of "changing the fire,"[150] the basis for the local custom was simply the belief in the involvement of the spirits of the dead with the affairs of the living. There is no way to tell if this belief had any particular affinity with the culture of the old Chin state. The brief description given in the *History of Han*'s "Treatise on Administrative Geography" provides no significant corroboration.[151]

Chieh Tzu-t'ui was perhaps not deified, even though people built a shrine for him after his death. An earlier case concerning general Tu-po, however, is clearly a case of apotheosis, perhaps the earliest recorded one in ancient China. As mentioned in Chapter 5 above, the cult of Tu-po originated from the story of the ghost of Tu-po shooting King Hsüan of Chou. People later worshipped his spirit, and a number of shrines were established in the central Ch'in area. As he was described as "one of the smallest ghosts that are efficacious (i.e., *shen*, having spiritual power),"[152] there presumably were other similar cases. Another example is the deification of the king of Ch'eng-yang, Liu Chang 劉章, who flourished under emperor Wen of Western Han. After his death, the local people of Lang-yeh commandery built shrines to worship him. In time, this cult spread to other regions, and the rituals grew increasingly elaborate.[153] According to Ying Shao,

> From Lang-yeh (the old Ch'i state) to Ch'ing-chou and other commanderies, as far as the towns, villages, and communities of Po-hai, all were erecting shrines for him. They made five carriages for officials of the two-thousand-*tan* rank, supplied by merchants, with official garments and decorations, and staffed with (mock-) officers. People celebrated with feasts and songs for several days. They then spread false rumors, saying that there was a deity who responds quickly to inquiries about one's fortune. This has been going on for many years and no one can correct it.[154]

Ying Shao did not specify the time period covered by his description. During the civil wars at the end of Wang Mang's rule, the king of Ch'eng-yang's cult was popular not only in the countryside, but also in the army of Fan Ch'ung 樊崇, the leader of the "Red Eyebrows (*ch'ih-mei* 赤眉)." It was said that the king of Ch'eng-yang appeared to the shamans in the cult and said: "(You) (i.e., Fan Ch'ung) should be the emperor, why are you acting as a bandit?"[155] This gave Fan Ch'ung a pretense to set up a puppet emperor, Liu P'en-tzu 劉盆子, a descendant of the king of Ch'eng Yang, and establish a new regime.

Another source relates that the king of Ch'eng-yang had descended several times to send messages to his shrine in Lang-yeh, which was attended by officials and people alike, and had caused "disturbances for the palace."[156] We are not told what the "disturbances for the palace" were, but they might have had political implications. Since those who worshipped the king of Ch'eng-yang included officials, the god's messages might have run counter to the interests of the government, thus causing problems when they followed the instructions or messages of the god. From this, we can see that the cult had the potential to be a political force: according to Ying Shao, it was supported by merchants, and assumed symbols of political power, i.e., chariots, official garments, and staff members. This, in fact, prompts one to ponder the possibility that we see here the buds of political uprising disguised under, or in connection with, popular cults, as with the Yellow Turbans at the end of Eastern Han, and numerous cases of sectarian uprising in subsequent dynasties.[157]

Such accounts not only give us an idea of how a local cult spread to other areas, but also some of the details of the actual format of popular cults. In the spread of this cult, however, it is difficult to establish whether the regional culture of Lang-yeh had significant influence. On the other hand, it is a good example of the influence of a popular cult on the non-religious or political affairs of a region, and how a religious cult could involve rich merchants or local forces, whose motives most likely were complex.

In addition, various local officials were worshipped for their benevolent deeds. They had proven themselves able administrators, just and impartial in managing local businesses or in improving livelihoods.[158] However, they were not the only mortals given cults. As we shall see below, others were worshipped by people for their supposedly magical or supernatural powers.

One of the most popular cults was the *she* 社, or local communal altar. The origin of *she* has been traced back to the Shang dynasty, and was explained as the worship of the earth.[159] It was often mentioned together with *chi* 稷, or the worship of grain, in official cult practices. During the Chou period, people with different statuses in the feudal system may have had their own *she*.[160] In Han times, the lowest level of officially established *she* was the county. People thus organized their own *she* through local village and hamlet organizations.[161] According to one source, twenty-five families could establish one communal *she*-altar, and there were cases where five or ten families established a still smaller "private *she*" for the blessing of the fields.[162] During the time of emperor Yüan, the "private *she*" in Yen-chou was banned, although the precise reason is not clear.[163] Local *she*, however, must have developed into various forms of worship that were not confined to the worship of earth. Luan Pu, one of the followers of Han Kao-tsu, for example, was worshipped by the people of Yen and Ch'i after his death. His shrines were called "the *she* of Lord Luan." Thus, in reality the *shes* that were devoted to the worship of individuals were not much different from other personal cults. However, it was during the Han period that an anonymous "Lord of the *she* (*she-kung* 社公)" gradually became the main spirit residing in the *she* shrines and protecting local populations.[164] It was believed that this Lord of the *she* could be manipulated by those possessing shamanic, magical power. Fei Ch'ang-fang 費長房 reportedly "was capable of curing all manner of illnesses. He could exorcise a hundred demons and was master of the deities of the local soil god altars (i.e., *she-kung*)."[165] Sometimes the spirit of a *she* could also be addressed as "the ghost of the *she*."[166] This Lord of the *she* eventually evolved into the "Lord of the Earth" (*t'u-ti-kung* 土地公) in later eras.[167]

Fei Ch'ang-fang was one such shamanic figure who was later accorded the status of an immortal by Ko Hung in *Biographies of Immortals* (*Shen-hsien-chuan*). The immortals, to be sure, were also often the object of worship. A number of shrines known as "shrines of the immortals" (*hsien-jen tz'u* 仙人祠) are known to have existed in the Han period. Some of these were given official status at various times and places, although few details are known.[168] According to Ying Shao, during the time of emperor Ming of the Eastern Han, a certain Wang Ch'iao, who served as the magistrate of Yeh, was known to possess various types of magical power. Local people established a shrine for him after his death. It is said that all who prayed at his shrine were blessed, while those who did not incurred immediate misfortune.[169] Wang Ch'iao is thought to have been the famous immortal Wang Tzu-ch'iao, whose biography is in the *Stories of the Immortals* (*Lieh-hsien-chuan* 列仙傳).[170] Two others, Hsü Yang and Kao Huo, who showed extraordinary magical power, were also worshipped by local people and given shrines,[171] examples perhaps of how "shrines of the immortals" originated.[172]

The personal cult is a chief characteristic of Chinese popular religious piety. The rationale behind such activities was the belief in the spiritual power of the dead. This power came from different sources: Chieh Tzu-t'ui's was from personal moral integrity; Luan Pu's and the king of Ch'eng-yang's were from their social status and benevolent deeds; that of Wang Ch'iao, Hsü Yang, and Kao Huo were from magic. Still others seem to have gained power from human acts like vengeance, as was the case with general Tu-po. On the other hand, the reputation of a personal cult may have had less to do with the worshipped than the worshippers. The "divine lady of Ch'ang-ling," promoted by Wu-ti, for example, was simply an ordinary person whose ghost was supposed to have appeared to her family members.[173]

Compare this with a passage of *Book of Rites*:

According to the institutes of the sage kings about sacrifices, sacrifice should be offered to those who have given (good) laws to the people; those who have labored to the death in the discharge of his duties; who have strengthened the state by laborious toil; boldly and successfully met great calamities; or warded off great evils.[174]

Clearly, official cults emphasized deeds of "political benevolence." It is worth noticing, however, that not all the examples of personal cults are to be interpreted as apotheosis. After all, there is little difference between the Chinese conceptions of ghosts and gods, as discussed before. One man's ghost could be more influential or powerful than another's, and thus be considered "*shen*," which means "having spiritual or godly power." A similar concept is "*ling*," which is the efficacious power of the numinous being—the power to effect tangible results.[175]

Finally, a popular cult may originate not only from the worshipping of certain historical figures, as discussed above, but also from people's misunderstandings, fears, greed, or credulousness. Ying Shao recorded the following story:

A man from Ju-nan caught a deer in a swampy field. He did not take it away (but left it there). Meanwhile, a caravan consisting of more than ten carriages passed by the swamp. The merchants, seeing that the deer was tied, took it with them. Then thinking this improper, they put a salted fish in its place. After a while, the man went back and could not see the deer. Instead, he saw the salted fish. Since the swamp was not the (ordinary) road for people, and yet the deer somehow changed into a salted fish, he thought it was very strange, and believed that there was a certain deity involved. He turned to tell other people, who thereafter came to pray for cures and blessings, and these often were efficacious. So they built a shrine, with tens of shamans performing their craft in the nearby tents. People from several hundred *li* away all came to pray and make offerings. The cult was named God of Mr. Salted Fish. Several years later, the one who left the salted fish passed by the shrine, and asked about the story. He then said: "This was my fish, how could there be any god?" He went up to the shrine and took the fish. The cult was destroyed after this.[176]

This illustrates my discussion perfectly. Local shamans took the opportunity to profit, thus revealing the complex economic aspect of cult activities discussed in Chapter 5. Once a shrine was established, interest groups also began to grow up around the shrine, and tended to perpetuate the cult.[177] In fact, shamans are known to have associated with local shrines or *she* since before the Ch'in.[178] The story about the salted fish may be a typical example of how popular cults formed.[179] They need not have been based on ancient traditions or legends, but simply impromptu developments.

Omens and Portents

Ever since the Eastern Chou period, ample documents have attested the belief in omens, portents, and prodigies as a characteristic of religious piety. As discussed in Chapter 3, the basis of this was often correlative metaphysics. During the Han period, a particular trend of thought developed that made the interpretation of portents and omens an important part of classical, textual exegeses. Tung Chung-shu was the major proponent of this tendency in the Western Han period. In his system, portents and omens were signs that Heaven sent to admonish rulers, to keep them, so to speak, on the right track.[180] Later developments, however, resulted in the rise of "apocryphal texts" (*ch'en-wei* 讖緯), which were mainly used as tools to justify particular political actions under the pretext of heavenly will.[181] The first precedent was set by Wang Mang, who usurped the Han regime (from A.D. 8 to A.D. 23) by claiming to have received the heavenly mandate through political portent texts, which were but one sort of apocrypha. His example was followed by a host of military contenders and passive recipients of thrones (both imperial and local) all the way into the next century.[182]

Our concern is not specifically with the apocryphal texts, nor whether they were used to curb or bolster imperial or personal power. Here, we consider the belief in the efficacy of the omens and portents and the intellectual weight it carried. The texts may have been created for political purposes, and the portents may oftentimes have been fabricated, yet their occasional dramatic political effect suggests that they struck a deep nerve in people's mentality. Emperor Kuang-wu's victory is a good example. He was assisted by the spread of portent texts that favored his imperial mandate. This suggests that both military leaders and their followers believed in the efficacy of the portents.[183]

It has been argued that information concerning portents and prodigies contained in the two major histories of the Han dynasty, the *History of Han* and *History of Later Han*, was reported and furnished solely in order to control court politics, i.e., to warn the emperor or officials about impending disasters, or, if they were good signs, to flatter.[184] Nevertheless, we can use such records to gain an overview of the most common categories of portents.

The "Treatises on the Five Phases" in both *History of Han* and *History of Later Han* list many different kinds of portents. First are unusual meteorological phenomena: eclipses of the sun and the moon, excessive rain, drought, severe cold, hail, thunder in winter, strong winds; then there are natural disasters: avalanches, floods, earthquakes, fire; third, unusual biological phenomena: deformed trees or plants, swarming locusts, rooster-looking hens, man-eating wolves, dogs copulating with pigs, huge fish, cattle plagues, even men transformed into women, or babies with two heads and eight limbs. Finally, certain unusual or unconventional behavior, such as great surges in fashion and unrestrained behavior, could also have been seen as carrying portentous messages. Explanations of portents were made mainly along metaphysical lines, however forced they may have been. Oftentimes the logic of divination was temporal, i.e., explanations assumed that events that happened in a temporal sequence were also causally related. Here, we are not concerned with how persuasive these explanations were, but whether we may call the phenomenon part of the religious mentality of the times.

From the four general categories of portents, we can at least be certain that a fascination with abnormal phenomena, natural or human, prevailed in society. *History of Han* records that during the reign of Emperor P'ing, the governor of Shuo-fang commandery reported a case in which a woman came back to life after being dead lying in the coffin for six days. She claimed to have seen her dead father, who told her that she was "(only) twenty-seven years old, and should not have died (so young)."[185] The event came to be considered as portentous, though the source does not give any associated prophecy.

153

It does not seem to have been fabricated by the governor, since he believed that it was portentous. Yet had the governor not reported it to the court, it might never have become significant. There is no way to know if the people involved in the story also considered it portentous. Yet the scholar who placed it into the official record gave it an explanation according to the *I-ching* exegesis of Ching Fang, an important scholar in the formation of *ch'en-wei* oracle-texts.[186] It was probably not the tale's significance as portent, but rather the news that lifespans were bureaucratically allotted, and subject to revision and restitution on occasion, that had originally raised people's interest in this story. Similar stories of revival are recorded in *History of Later Han*.[187]

Another example shows how portents evolved from news of strange events far from centers of power into court-interpreted metaphysics. During the reign of Emperor Ch'eng, some people heard the screech of owls in the mountains and went to investigate. They saw that the nest in an enormous tree had been burnt and had fallen to the ground, burning three chicks to death. The governor reported the incident to the court. The explanation given was: "The color of the owl is black. It is close to the black-portent, which signifies events of greed and cruelty." The events referred to cryptically were the killing of potential heirs of the emperor Ch'eng by his concubines under the order of the jealous queen Chao Fei-yen and Wang Mang's usurpation.[188] The burning nest incident probably had some basis or other in fact. But this was soon changed into a dangerous political weapon, according to a long tradition of omenology. Could some of the portents be fabricated? The answer is positive. The *History of Later Han* records the following case:

> In the eighth month (of A.D. 167), it was said that a yellow dragon appeared in the commandery of Pa. When the official Fu Chien heard that the office decided to report it to the court, he went to see the governor and said that it was a joke created by a local runner, and should not be taken seriously. The governor did not listen to his advice. Chien told others: "It was a time when the weather was hot and people wanted to bath in the pool. When they saw that the water was muddy, they jokingly told each other, 'there is a dragon in the water.' And so word spread among the people."[189]

[It is very likely that this and possibly many other "auspicious portents" reported to the court started innocently and later turned into super-natural stories, if they were not faked outright for various reasons. Nevertheless, they reflected a widespread belief in the validity of por-tentous events.]

The discrepancy between everyday beliefs and court interpretations can best be illustrated by another example. In the first month of 3 B.C., during the reign of emperor Ai,

It happened that people were disturbed and running around, passing a stalk of grain or flax from one to another, and calling it "the tally for transmitting the edict." More than a thousand people met and passed on the road, some with disheveled hair and bare feet. Some crossed barrier gates (to cities and major roads) during the night; some climbed over the wall to get in; some rode in carriages, and used the courier system to pass on the message. They moved through twenty-six commanderies and kingdoms and reached the capital. That summer, people of the capital and the commanderies gathered in local lanes and fields, made offerings and set up gambling paraphernalia (*po-chü* 博 具).[190] They sang and danced in worship of the Queen Mother of the West. An order was transmitted with the words: "The Mother tells the people that whoever carries this order shall not die. If you do not believe my words, look under the door hinge. There will be white hair." The commotion subsided in the fall.

At that time, the grandmother of the emperor, the dowager queen Fu, was arrogant and controlled court politics. Thus Tu Yeh said (concerning the event): "When the *Ch'un-ch'iu* talked about portents, it used symbolic incidents as language. The tally is used to count numbers. The (nature of) people is *yin*, which belongs to the category of water. Water flows east as its natural course. Now it is flowing west, which is like revolting against the court. This symbolizes the uncontrolled ways and wanton procuring of profits (by the court) against the wishes of the people. The Queen Mother of the West is a name for a woman. Gambling is the business of a man. To gather in lanes and fields signifies leaving the interior and giving over to the outside. To seek fun during worship signifies the surge of the *yang* element.

155

The white hair signifies old age, with a revered body but weak reason; hard to rule but easy to confuse. The door is the passage for the people; the hinge, its pivot. This means presiding over the passage for the people and controlling its pivot. The meaning (of the portent) is quite clear. The families of Ting and Fu are now serving the inner court, and their members occupy important positions. Guilty ones have not received punishment, and those without merit were all accorded offices and titles. Even the examples of Huang-fu and the three Huans, who were mocked by the poet and scorned by the *Ch'un-ch'iu*, do not exceed this. The symbols are amply clear in order to warn the holy court, how could it not have been answered!"

When Emperor Ai died, the mother of Emperor Ch'eng, the Dowager Queen Wang, presided over the court; Wang Mang became the Marshal of State, and the Ting and Fu families were executed. Another explanation says that the evils committed by the Ting and Fu families are small matters. The portent actually refers to the deeds of Dowager Queen Wang and Wang Mang.[191]

The whole event had a significance for noncourt religious participants that was utterly different than for scholars such as Tu Yeh, or the author of *History of Han*. It shows that belief in the Queen Mother of the West was widespread, and that people worshipped her in the hope of gaining immortality. The scholarly interpretation, however, considered only the welfare of the country, the court, or the royal family.

Chapter 7 ———————————

Immortality, Soul, and the Netherworld

He for whom this scroll is recited will prosper, and his children will prosper.
He will be the friend of the king and his courtiers.
He will receive bread, beer, and a big chunk of meat from
the altar of the great god.
He will not be held back at any gate of the west.
He will be ushered in with the kings of Upper and Lower Egypt.
He will be a follower of Osiris.[1]

. . . .

Charidas, what is below?
Great darkness.
What about resurrection?
A lie.
And the God of the Dead?
A myth. We perish utterly.[2]

The Conceptions of Immortality and Soul

The preceding examples of various religious activities and beliefs have shown that, in everyday life outside of the political center, spiritual beings, ghosts, and gods were important factors in beliefs. People's aspirations and hopes were achieved through the help of spiritual beings. This simply continued the development of religious traditions

extant before the Ch'in empire. While it is difficult to claim a fundamental difference between the basic beliefs of pre-Ch'in and post-Ch'in,
several factors seem to have contributed to the growth in beliefs concerning spiritual beings, especially the immortals.

An obvious factor was that the zealous quest for immortality and
spirits displayed by the First Emperor of Ch'in and by Han Wu-ti
encouraged the proliferation of cults and shamanistic activities geared
toward their tastes. As we have discussed in Chapter 5, shamanistic
and cultic activities assumed a place beside other important interests
of the emperors. The official cult of the Ch'in-Han empire gave a
prominent position to Heaven, with *Yin-yang* and Five-Phases ideas
becoming the theoretical basis for court rites and religious activity
after Han Wu-ti. Yet this official theoretical basis did not preclude the
emperors from pursuing their personal needs.[3] The court religion
concentrated on the harmony of heaven and man, and the well-being
of the entire country, but did not provide an adequate answer to the
question of life after death. The reason why the First Emperor of Ch'in,
Han Wu-ti, and even Wang Mang, incessantly sought immortals and
elixirs for longevity was precisely because the official religion could
not provide them with the hope of immortality. The everyday religion
of personal welfare that had developed for millennia in China did, however. Because this religion of personal welfare was not really an organized, consistent doctrine, but a conglomeration of disparate beliefs
and cults, a great variety of practices was available. The various cults,
in one way or another, furnished the hope that immortality was possible,
that ghosts and gods had a real impact on the life of the living. It was
this multiple possibility that allowed such a religion to attract people
to it and keep it vital. Han Wu-ti's efforts to seek immortals and longevity are but the most well-known, most extravagant examples.

One of the most important questions in the study of religion is the
human condition after death.[4] The concept of a soul, or *hun* and *p'o*,
as discussed before, was used by he people of pre-Ch'in China in their
speculations about death. Toward the end of the Warring States period
the abode of the soul, whether the Yellow Spring or the Dark City,
was seen as a terrifying place. For the non-elite, the prospect of death
and the netherworld was not very promising. However, during the
transition to the Ch'in-Han period, ideas of this type developed a new
dimension, that is, the existence of immortals and the possibility for

men to achieve immortality. It was something of a revolt against the old concept of merely having a postmortem soul. People now wished to live forever, and thus avoid bleak conditions after death. A deathless life could certainly solve the problem of inhabiting the generally gruesome world of the dead.

This concept had probably existed in the minds of people long before it appears in documents. Passages in the *Book of Poetry* show that by the western Chou the idea of longevity was circulating.[5] The bronze inscriptions of the western Chou period also contained expressions corresponding to "longevity" (e.g., *mei-shou* 眉壽, *nan-lao* 難老). However, it was only during the Eastern Chou period that the idea of immortality was documented.[6] In a story preserved in *Tso-chuan* and *Yen-tzu ch'un-ch'iu* (*Master Yen's Spring and Autumn Annal*), Duke Ching of Ch'i once exclaimed that it would be a great pleasure if people from ancient times did not die. He of course meant that he also wished to live forever. The witty minister, Yen-tzu, replied to the effect that if the ancients were to live forever, then the ancient rulers would still control the state of Ch'i, and Duke Ching would be toiling in the field as a commoner without the leisure to think of the problems of death.[7] In a *Han-fei-tzu* anecdote, a man claimed to be able to teach the king of Yen "the method for immortality." The king ordered one of his servants to learn the method. Before he began to learn, however, the master suddenly died. The king was infuriated and executed the servant for acting slowly. As *Han-fei-tzu* points out, it is ironic that the master died, but the king of Yen did not realize the fraud.[8] Another story in *Han-fei-tzu* mentions someone's offering the elixir of immortality to the king of Ch'u.[9] The purpose of these stories, to be sure, was to refute the idea of immortality, yet their very existence also indicates how broadly the idea of immortality circulated. Written at the end of the Warring States period, *Master Lü's Spring and Autumn Annal* (*Lü-shih ch'un-ch'iu*) concurred with the above observation: "Nowadays rulers and nobles, no matter if they are competent or inept, all wish to live an eternal life."[10]

Whether this idea of immortality had any relationship with the Taoist philosophy of Lao-tzu and Chuang-tzu, however, is difficult to ascertain. In the *Lao-tzu*, death is part of the cycle of nature, and it is possible to achieve an endless physical existence, although the text never directly mentions the idea of "immortality" (*pu-ssu* 不死).[11] In

Chuang-tzu, though, we see a certain *shen-jen* 神人, or "Divine Man," who rides upon the clouds and drives flying dragons around the world, who survives without food, and is unharmed by flood or fire.[12] The characteristics of this *shen-jen* certainly seem to be the attributes of the immortal, as emphasized in the later era. When the entire thought of Chuang-tzu is taken into consideration, however, there is little doubt that transformation of an individual existence from life to death was seen as part of the eternal Tao. Thus, since death is not a problem in this view, there should be no need to search for a deathless life.[13] It is likely that the description of the fantastic *shen-jen* in *Chuang-tzu* was only a literary, even lyric, celebration of spiritual freedom. On this point, it is worthwhile to note that the *Chuang-tzu* text also mentions *chen-jen* 眞人 (the True Man) and *chih-jen* 至人 (the Ultimate Man), with attributes similar to the *shen-jen*, and in similar contexts.[14] One can argue that the philosophy of *Lao-tzu* and *Chuang-tzu*, and the idea of immortality as represented by the stories in *Han-fei-tzu* and *Yen-tzu*, betray a common mentality that was gradually becoming visible in the literature of the Warring States period.[15] Despite these references, however, the idea of immortality had perhaps not yet assumed a significant position in the belief of the non-elite, since the daybooks make no mention of immortality.

By the beginning of the imperial era the idea of immortality and immortals became popular, due to the persuasions of the "magicians" (*fang-shih* 方士) at court.[16] The land of the immortals, a type of paradise, was first said to be located in the eastern sea, giving rise to recorded references to expeditions in search of this paradise.[17] In time, however, the west was also discussed as the location of the immortals.[18] However, as Yü Ying-shih has pointed out, ideas about the very nature of immortals had undergone a change during this period. In the pre-Ch'in period, especially in the picture derived from *Chuang-tzu*, the immortals were removed from the world; the Ch'in and Han rulers, however, basically aspired to become immortals in this world, in order to continue their pleasures.[19] Later, people accepted two kinds of immortal: the otherworldly, or so-called "heavenly immortals (*t'ien-hsien* 天仙)" (Fig. 7.1), and those who stayed close to the world, or "earthly immortals (*ti-hsien* 地仙)."[20]

There is ample evidence indicating the prevalence of a belief in immortals in the broader society of this time. In fact, even before the

160

Fig. 7.1 Figures of winged immortals. Han.

establishment of the Ch'in, images of bird-headed humans or men with wings appeared on late–Warring States bronze vessels.[21] It has been suggested that these bird-like beings are the earliest representations of immortals.[22] Similar figures, all utilizing elements of the bird-motif, have been found in Han-dynasty tomb paintings and bronze objects.[23] The contexts suggest that they are immortals in their realm, which is usually in the clouds accompanied by fantastic creatures. The pictographic evidence is corroborated by literary evidence. In *Classic of Mountains and Seas*, for example, a "country of feathered-people" with long heads and feathers resembles the world of immortals (*hsien-jen*).[24] The poet Ch'ü Yüan wrote about the land of immortality and described immortals as "the Winged Ones (*yü-jen* 羽人): "I met the Winged Ones on the Hill of Cinnabar; I tarried in the ancient land of Immortality."[25] Also, fraudulent exorcist Luan Ta was said to have been dressed in "clothes of feathers," obviously posing as an immortal, when he received the rank of "General of the Heavenly Way" from Han Wu-ti.[26] When Wang Ch'ung tried to refute the existence of immortals, he described them as feathered and winged: "In representing the bodies of genii (*hsien-jen*, i.e., immortals) one gives them plumage, and their arms are changed into wings with which they poise in the clouds."[27] The paintings of the immortals to which Wang Ch'ung referred are probably similar to those found in tombs, as mentioned above. In this early time, winged flight was a sign of having reached immortality or having been freed from mortal confinement.[28]

The whole notion circulated among the court and the ruling classes.[29] Even highly learned intellectuals, such as Liu Hsiang, collected and transmitted stories about immortals,[30] and Han court lyrics often elaborated on the theme.[31] Bronze mirror inscriptions, furthermore, often bore such phrases as: "The Shang-fang made this mirror and truly it is very fine. Upon it are immortal beings oblivious of old age. When they thirst they drink from the springs of jade; when they hunger they feed on jujubes. They rove at will on the hills of the gods, plucking the Herb of Life. Long life be yours, longer than that of metal, stone, or the Queen Mother of the West."[32]

Can these bits of evidence reflect the attitude of ordinary people in all walks of life? The answer is positive in view of the following considerations. The numerous magicians who claimed to have tried their skills at acquiring immortality,[33] regardless of the outcomes, must have exerted influence on the non-elite throughout China. As mentioned before, a number of "shrines of the immortals" were recorded in the "Treatise on Administrative Geography" in *History of Han*. Many shrines survived the fall of the Han, as observed by the geographer Li Tao-yüan during the Northern Wei.[34] These must have acquired cult support among local populations. A certain T'ang Kung-fang 唐公房, a clerk in the Han-chung local government during Wang Mang's time, was said to have obtained the status of an immortal, and his whole family went up to heaven with him, presumably all becoming immortals.[35] Although T'ang was not strictly a non-elite, his position nevertheless was that of the lowest in the official ladder. That he became an immortal must have been based on a commonly held notion among the populace, since it was recorded on his funerary stele. Furthermore, bronze mirrors are often found in tombs of non-officials and low-level officials,[36] so there is reason to believe that the idea of immortality was not the exclusive concern of the upper classes. Worship of the Queen Mother of the West, moreover, is another example in which the non-ruling, non-elite classes could embrace the idea of immortality,

162

since the Queen Mother was the dispenser of eternal life.[37] Last but not least, the iconographical representations of immortals, whether on mirrors, in tombs, or in shrines, are inevitably the product of artisans who, while creating images, must at the same time have been familiar with the ideas behind them. This observation can be applied to other areas. The physical belongings of the upper class need not have represented only the ideology of the upper classes. The creation of artifacts is a medium for the interaction of ideas and values between different social strata. The direction of the flow of cultural ideas, however, might have been more complicated, because it was a constant and long-term process beginning probably long before the appearance of physical evidence. In the *Biographies of the Immortals (Shen-hsien-chuan* 神仙傳) compiled by Ko Hung in the early fourth century A.D., high social status was not a prominent characteristic of immortals. A number of immortals were actually said to have come from the underclass. The belief in the existence of, or aspiration to, immortals had already become a common phenomenon, and it is difficult to trace specific ideas among different social classes.[38]

Yet it is also quite clear that the majority of people, while perhaps believing in the possibility of immortality, did not really consider themselves candidates. A life beyond death in the form of a soul was probably the most commonly held view. The concept of the soul, as we discussed in Chapter 3, centered on the *hun* and *p'o* in pre-Ch'in times. However, concepts of their exact nature are not easy to identify. The Eastern Han scholar Cheng Hsüan, commenting on a passage in *Book of Rites*, explained it thus:

> *Ch'i* refers to what is breathed in and out, and the function of the ears and eyes are the *p'o*. It is said in *Chiao-t'e-sheng* that, "the *hun* of *ch'i* returns to heaven, the *p'o* of the physique (*t'i*) returns to the earth." As I see it, *hun* and *p'o* are born with a person. The reason for their both having the same written element *kuei* (ghost) is that *hun* and *p'o* cannot leave the physical body, and yet they are not part of the physical body. When the physical body disappears, the *hun* and *p'o* remain. They are the final destination (*kuei* 歸; homophone of *kuei* 鬼, ghost) of man, therefore they (the characters *hun* and *p'o*) have the radical *kuei* (ghost).[39]

According to Cheng Hsüan, then, both *hun* and *p'o* are spiritual entities. Yet he did not really explain the difference between *hun* and *p'o*.
By quoting the passage from *Book of Rites*, he concurred that *hun*
went up to heaven and *p'o* went down into the earth, without discussing whether those are the only destinations. In any case, the ideas of
soul expressed in *Book of Rites* and Cheng Hsüan's commentary represented mainly the Confucian view.[40] It is doubtful that such subtlety
had a great impact. A funerary text written on a bottle for the protection of the dead, dated to the Eastern Han period, has the following
words: "The Yellow-God gave birth to the Five Mountains, and is in
charge of the fortune of the living. He summons the *hun*, summons
the *p'o*, he is in charge of the roster of the dead."[41] Here the destinations of *hun* and *p'o* appear to be the same.

In the medical texts of the Han period, moreover, we can discern
different concepts of life and death, or *hun* and *p'o*. In a text excavated from a tomb of the early Western Han period, entitled *Book of
Pulses* or *Mai-shu* 脈書, the author discussed five different "signs of
death": "if one sweats thinly and (the sweat) does not flow, then the
ch'i is going to die first."[42] Here the term *ch'i* seems to refer to a kind
of physical existence that can also "die." In the famous medical text
attributed to the Yellow Emperor (Huang-ti), the *Ling-shu* 靈樞, another unusual concept of *hun* and *p'o* can be seen: "When one is eighty,
the *ch'i* of the lung declines, the *p'o* then leaves the body, and therefore
one's speech is prone to errors . . . when one reaches one hundred,
the five organs are all empty, the spirit and the *ch'i* both leave, the
body alone remains to the end."[43] Here the *p'o* is thought to be able to
leave the person before death, and even before the spirit and *ch'i* do.
This is different from what the Confucian and Taoist traditions teach.[44]

Elsewhere I have examined the use of the words *hun* and *p'o* during the Han period. *Hun* seems to have become the most commonly
used expression referring to "soul," and *p'o* gradually became synonymous with *hun*.[45] On a tomb brick of the Eastern Han period, we
find the following words: "Alas, the *hun* of the dead returns to the
coffin. Do not fly about randomly. Travel without worry. After ten
thousand years, (we) shall reunite."[46] Here the *hun* of the dead returns
to the coffin, and *p'o* is not even mentioned. These inscriptions must
have represented a widespread conception among the populace.
Whether *hun* and *p'o* are spiritual or physical entities did not seem to

be of concern in mundane, nontextual situations. What was more of concern to the ordinary person was the abode wherein the soul of the dead was to live.]

Further Development of the Idea of the Netherworld

Along with the concept of immortality came the idea of a netherworld. In order to render the terror of death less unacceptable, and assuming that immortality was not in everyone's reach, one could picture the [netherworld, where one's soul was to dwell indefinitely, in a positive light.]

The evolution of burial styles

We return to the idea of the Yellow Spring mentioned in Chapter 3. This was at once a literary metaphor for the tomb and a useful, abstract reference to the residence of the dead. The tomb and the proper rituals of burial had been central concerns of Chinese religion since prehistoric times. Although funerary rituals evolved throughout the centuries, the essential form of the tomb remained the same, i.e., a rectangular, vertical pit with wooden coffins (*kuan* 棺) and caskets (*kuo* 槨). The exact format of the coffins, caskets, and other paraphernalia varied according to the social and political status of the deceased, and may have followed various well-known rules during the Shang and Chou dynasties.[47] Toward the end of the Warring States period, however, this burial system began to change. First, some tombs in the Ch'u area exhibit decorative motifs in the design of coffins and caskets that imitate or symbolize windows, doors, stairs, and upper and lower apartments. In a word, they were clearly intended to serve as models of the houses of the living.[48] Second, in the Central Plain area a new kind of tomb came into style. It used a horizontal cave as the burial chamber, and, instead of wooden caskets as outer coffins, employed rock or clay bricks in the walls and ceilings of the chamber. As the burial chambers expanded from single to multiple, the entire structure came to resemble the houses of the living. This development continued throughout the Han dynasty and by the end of the Eastern Han finally replaced the vertical-pit wooden-casket tomb as the dominant burial style.[49]

165

Fig. 7.2 Banquet scene on a tomb brick from Szechwan.
Eastern Han.

Concurrent with changes in burial style, the funerary paraphernalia also underwent some transformation. Archaeological and textual evidence show that the Chou-era system of paraphernalia represented the socio-political status of the deceased. One example is the layers of coffins and caskets and another is the numbers and sets of bronze vessels: both were in accord with the status of the tomb owner.[50] Beginning in about the middle of Eastern Chou, however, the old burial system began to be violated, as powerful feudal lords sought privileges on a par with those of the Chou royal house. The gradual disintegration of the burial system was in fact symptomatic of the disintegration of the old socio-political order.[51] When Chou society gradually turned into the despotic, bureaucratic, and merit-oriented society of the Warring States period, the burial system began focus on postmortem pleasures. Although old styles of funerary objects were still seen, the orientation of the entire ensemble became geared toward objects of daily use. The most obvious change was the disappearance of ritual bronze vessels, such as *ting* and *kuei*; various everyday pottery items were supplied instead. In addition, all kinds of surrogate objects, representing servants, carriages, mansions, fields, cattle, and the like, became the fashion of Han-era burials.[52]

Furthermore, brick tombs afforded new opportunities for wall and ceiling decoration. These included all kinds of scenes of daily activity in the private estates of the elite and those of public nature, such as battles, banquets and festivities, as well as auspicious omens, animals, and immortals (Fig. 7.2). Although it is possible that such devices distinguished the socio-political status of the tomb owner,[53] their function, since they were intended to be seen by the deceased only, must have been similar to that of funerary objects: for use in the netherworld. The deceased's postmortem life was to be as happy as that depicted in the decorations, just as his movements were enabled by the surrogate carriages.[54]

In sum, the developments in burial style and the material composition of funerary objects reveal a change in the concept of the netherworld that had been in progress since the Warring States period. People began providing the deceased a "living environment" that modelled his quotidian world. The change was gradual enough that it was probably little noticed. Yet through accumulated evidence, we see that it coincided with changes in the conception of the netherworld that are attested elsewhere, as we shall discuss below.

Change in the conception of the netherworld

When Ch'ü Yüan describes the Dark City as the abode of the dead, we are not given details, except that a monstrous "Lord of the Earth" presided. Various Han documents claim that the souls of the dead were destined for Mount T'ai, or Kao-li and Liang-fu, two small mountains in the vicinity of Mount T'ai. However, very little can be known about this world of the dead, except for the name of the ruler: "Lord of T'ai-shan."[55] Parallel with this idea was the simple phrase "underneath the ground." Here, more evidence is at our disposal. On bamboo slips that record funerary objects found in early–Western Han tombs, there are various official titles, such as "Lord of Underworld (*ti-hsia-chu* 地下主)":

> In the fourth year, the ninth month, day of *hsin-hai*, the *wu-fu* (伍夫) of Ping-li, Chang Yen dares to tell the Lord of the Underworld: the garments and objects of Yen, each are dispatched according to the laws and ordinances.[56]

or "Assistant Magistrate of the Underworld (*ti-hsia-ch'eng* 地下丞),"

> On the thirteenth year, the fifth month, day of *keng-ch'en*, the Assistant Magistrate of Chiang-ling dares to tell the Assistant Magistrate of the Underworld that the *wu-fu* 伍夫 of Shih-yang, Sui Shao-yen, and the slave Liang and others, a total of twenty-eight persons . . . and four riding-horses, can be used to serve. (I) hereby dare to report to the Lord.[57]

The "Lord of the Underworld" and "Assistant Magistrate of the Underworld" are probably the same personage, i.e., local administrators in the netherworld, whose earthly counterpart is "the Assistant Magistrate of Chiang-ling (Chiang-ling-ch'eng)." There are also officials in charge of the funerary objects, similar to the treasurer of the government. A text accompanying a list of funerary objects reads:

> In the twelfth year [c. 168 B.C.], the second month, day of *wu-ch'en*, the Assistant of the House (*chia-ch'eng* 家丞) dispatches to the Assistant of the Dead (*chu-tsang lang-chung* 主藏郎中) a list of funerary objects, the list is written to present to the Lord of the Grave (*chu-tsang-chün* 主藏君).[58]

In some of the so-called "tomb-quelling texts" (*chen-mu-wen* 鎮墓文) of the Eastern Han period, more elaborate titles are mentioned. One such text reads:

> The Messenger of Heaven and Earth informs the house of Chang, (with regard to) the two mounds and five graves, to the Left (Retinue) and Right (Retinue) of the graves, the grave-owner in

the center, the Minister and Magistrate of Grave Mounds, the Commander of Ordinance for the Mounds, the Neighborhood Head (*t'ing-chang* 亭長) of the gate of the souls, the Police of the Mounds, etc. (I) hereby inform the Minister of the Grave Mounds, the Count of Graves, the 2,000-*tan* of Underneath (*ti-hsia erh-ch'ien-tan* 地下二千石), the Marquis of the Eastern Mound, the Count of the Western Mound, the Official of Underneath, the Head of Five (*wu-chang* 伍長) of Kao-li, etc. . . .[59]

A similar texts reads:

The Yellow Emperor informs the Minister of the Mounds, the Count of the Graves, the 2,000-*tan* of Underneath, the Left and Right (Retinues) of the grave, the Warden in charge of the grave, the Neighborhood Head in charge of the gate of the grave . . .[60]

[It is obvious that the bureaucratic structure of the netherworld was modelled on the real-world political structure, especially that of local administration. There is, consequently, less information about "high-level" officials in the netherworld] The highest official, the 2,000-*tan* official of the Underworld, is probably the equivalent of the Governor of a commandery, the highest office in the local administration.[6][Pre-siding over such local officials were the Yellow Emperor, the Heavenly Emperor (*t'ien-ti* 天帝), and the Yellow God (*huang-shen* 黃神).[62] All seem to be different names for the sovereign of the netherworld.]They (or He) made their wills known to the inhabitants of the netherworld through the Messengers of the Heavenly Emperor (*t'ien-ti shih-che* 天帝使者), or the Messenger of the Emperor (*huang-ti shih-che* 皇帝使者).[63] It is unclear, however, whether the Yellow Emperor or Heavenly Emperor lived in the heaven above earth, or in a "heaven" in the netherworld. Moreover, it is uncertain whether the terms Yellow Emperor, Yellow God, or Heavenly Emperor are identifiable with those worshipped in the official cults.[64]

The textual and archaeological evidence presented above clearly suggests that, by the Eastern Han period, a netherworld similar to the mundane world had become a commonplace idea.[65] The Han-tomb "land purchase contract" explains how this worked. Originally such contracts only imitated the real land-purchase contract in order to serve as evidence of the legality of the tomb site. Later, the content of the contract became greatly exaggerated and included texts similar to "tomb-quelling texts," thus taking on the function of a funerary text, and giving evidence of general conceptions of life after death.[66] The netherworld was so modelled on this world, in fact, that the deceased paid taxes to the underworld government. By making one's abode after death practically identical to the normal abode, the dead (or the dying) perhaps were thought to be relieved of the dread of uncertainty.

Life in the netherworld

What did Han-era people imagine life in this netherworld to be? The skeptic Wang Ch'ung gave a vivid description:

> Thus ordinary people, on the one side, have these very doubtful arguments, and on the other they hear of Earl Tu and the like, and note that the dead in their tombs arise and have intercourse with sick people whose end is near. They then believe in this, and imagine that the dead are like the living. They commiserate with them, [thinking] that in their graves they are lonely, that their souls are solitary and without companions, that their tombs and mounds are closed and devoid of grain and other things. Therefore they make dummies to serve the corpses in their coffins, and fill the latter with eatables, to gratify the spirits. This custom has become so inveterate, and has gone to such lengths, that very often people will ruin their families and use up all their property for the coffins of the dead.[67]

Archaeological finds have amply testified to Wang Ch'ung's observation: funerary objects containing real or surrogate food, utensils, cattle, mansions, fields, clay money, figurines of servants, all intended for the deceased's happy life after death. Many wall paintings and reliefs in tombs, furthermore, portray daily activities that may be seen as also representing future activities in the netherworld.[68] Similar sentiment was expressed in the inscriptions found stamped on tomb bricks, such as "Longevity, as Mount T'ai," "Eternal life and old age," "Fortune and Prestige,"[69] and inscriptions on funerary bronze mirrors, such as:

There is happiness daily, and fortune monthly. There is joy without (bad) events, fit for having wine and food. Live leisurely, free from anxiety. Accompanied by flute and zither, with contentment of heart. Years of happiness are secure and lasting.[70]

Some even aspired to life as an immortal:

If you climb Mount T'ai, you may see immortal beings. They feed on the purest jade, they drink from the springs of elixir. They yoke the scaly dragons to their carriage, they mount floating clouds. The white tiger leads them straight to heaven. May you receive a never-ending span, long life that lasts for ten thousand years, with a fit place in office and safety for your children and grandchildren.[71]

Such material and textual evidence presents a happy cross-section of the ideal life after death. Yet this is not the whole story. Concurrent with this optimistic mentality was one of anxiety and fear, an apprehension over the plight of the dead and the fate of the living.

Because Han-era people believed that life after death basically resembled life on earth, for the ordinary, relatively poor families, this meant that the deceased would continue to encounter problems. An obvious problem for non-ruling subjects of empire was the tax and corvée burdens and the incessant harassment of associated officials. One tomb-quelling text (*chen-mu-wen*) has the following words:

Today is an auspicious day. It is for no other reason but the deceased Chang Shu-ching, who unfortunately died prematurely, is scheduled to descend into the grave. The Yellow God, who produced the Five Mountains, is in charge of the roster of the deceased, recalling the *hun* and *p'o*, and in charge of the list of the dead. The living may build a high tower; the dead returns and is buried deeply underneath. Eyebrows and beards having fallen, they drop and became dirt and dust. Now therefore I (the Messenger of Heavenly Emperor) present the medicine for removing poll-tax and corvée conscription, so that the descendants will not die. Nine pieces of *jen-shen* 人蔘 from Shang-tang substitute for the living. The lead-man is intended to substitute for the dead. The soybeans and mellon-seeds are for the dead to pay

for the taxation underneath. Hereby I establish a decree to re-
move the earthly evil, so that no disaster will occur. When this
decree arrives, restrict the officer of the Underworld (*ti-li* 地吏),
and do not disturb the Chang family again. Doubly urgent as
prescribed by the laws and ordinances.[72]

In some of the so-called "tomb-quelling bottles" (*chen-mu-p'ing* 鎮墓
瓶) on which the tomb-quelling texts were written, we see small lead
figurines (*ch'ien-jen* 鉛人). These figurines were, presumably after
proper magical spells had been cast on them, able to substitute for
the deceased in netherworld corvée. Another text describes the function of the lead-man:

Use the lead-man to substitute for oneself. The lead-man is ver-
satile, he can grind grain and cook, he can drive a carriage and
write letters.[73]

The function of lead figurines, contrary to the surrogate servants (*yüng*
俑) usually found among funerary objects, was not to serve the deceased in the netherworld, but to substitute at hard labor. It is no
wonder that they are usually found in poorer tombs, for the under-
privileged naturally would worry about such impositions by the state.[74]
This is a remarkable way by which to deduce the social status of the
deceased.

From a comparative perspective, however, the custom of using surrogate servants and lead-men was not unique in the ancient world.
Ancient Egyptians, for example, provided two kinds of funerary figurine in their tombs. The first was a wooden replica of various household servants in action: in the kitchen, in the fields, catching fish, or
spinning and weaving.[75] These figurines were usually placed in the
tombs of persons with considerable social and political status. Their
function, as with other funerary objects, was to be of service to the
dead in the netherworld. Another kind of figurine, however, serves a
different function. The so-called "ushabti" figures are of a standard
form, a standing mummy. On the figurine was written a standardized
spell:

Ye ushabtiu, if N. is counted off, (if N. is assigned) to any work
that is wont to be done yonder in the god's domain (lo, obstacles

have been set up for him yonder—) as a man to his duties, to cultivate the fields, to irrigate the shores, to transport sand of the east to the west, "I will do (it); here am I," shall ye say.[76]

The ushabti, therefore, were substitutes for the dead for the forced labor in the netherworld, just as the lead-men in the Han tombs were. Unlike the lead-men, however, the ushabtis are found not only in tombs of commoners, but also in those of nobles, while (the lead-men so far are found only in poorer tombs) In the imagination of the ancient Egyptians, it seems, even people with high status could be asked to do hard labor in the netherworld.[77]

In China, besides taxes and forced labor, the entombed dead needed protection against disasters and malfeasance. (One of the major functions of the tomb-quelling texts was to provide this security, thus the phrase, quoted earlier, "to release the culpability, so that no disaster will occur.") Similar expressions are found in other texts:

The Messenger of the Heavenly Emperor hereby reverently establishes safety and security for the tombs of the Yang family. It is reverently done, using lead-men and gold and jade, to release culpability for the dead, and dismiss wrong doings for the living. After this bottle reaches (the tomb), it is decreed that the people should be relieved. The deceased should enjoy his own rent-income underneath, which amounts to twenty million per year. It is decreed that generations of sons and grandsons shall serve in offices and be promoted to the ranks of duke and marquis, with fortune and prestige as marshals and ministers without end. (This decree) is to be dispatched to the Minister of Grave Mound and the Governor of the Grave, to be employed accordingly, as decreed by the law and ordinance.[78]

Another text reads:

May the deceased in the tomb not be disturbed or have fear, and stay tranquil as before. It is decreed that the descendants shall increase in wealth and number, without misfortunes for thousands of years. He is hereby reverently provided with a thousand *chin* of gold, to fill the gate of the grave mound, and to eliminate the names (of the descendants?) on the roster of the dead underneath, without other calamity, and with harmony among the people (?), and to use this essence of the five kinds of stone to secure the grave, to benefit posterity. Thus the sacred bottle is used to guard the gate of the grave, as decreed by the law and ordinance.[79]

The stones were a surrogate funerary object, often in the form of clay ingots or cakes, which represented gold. It is worth noting that the tomb-quelling texts were written not only for the dead, but also for the survivors. These included preventing premature death,[80] or to ward off evil spirits that haunted the living. By protecting the dead, the descendants were expected to lead prosperous lives.

Thus, burial and funerary equipment, no matter how shabby, was not exclusively for the benefit of the dead. In many of the documents mentioned, such as daybooks and geomantic manuals for choosing burial sites, the principle was whether the site would be auspicious for descendants.

On the whole, except for literary evidence with special views of life and death,[81] the impression one gains from *in situ* funerary texts is that of fear and revulsion toward the dead. One text reads:

How hurting and sad, concerning Hsü Ah-ch'ü, who was just five years old, and yet left the world of glory, to join the long night, without seeing the sun and stars. His soul dwells by itself, returned down to the darkness, separated forever from his family, with no hope of seeing his (?) face.[82]

Yet, although the living mourned the dead, they preferred to have no more contact with the dead, except through sacrifices and offerings. A tomb-quelling text reads: "The living and the dead go different ways; they should not become obstacles to each other."[83] Death as a long, dark journey of no return is seen in such expressions: "The *hun* of the dead returns to the coffin. . . . After ten thousand years, (we) shall reunite."[84] On a wooden tomb slip, a spell for expelling ghosts read as follows:

He who died on the *i-ssu* day has the ghost-name "heavenly light" (*t'ien-kuang* 天光). The Heavenly Emperor and Sacred Teacher already know your name. Quickly go away 3,000 miles. If you do not go immediately, the (monster ?) of the South Mountain is ordered to eat you. Hurry, as prescribed by the law and ordinance.[85]

There is no hint that this ghost is malicious to the living, yet he was obviously unwelcome. On the other hand, although the living did not want to be close to the dead, they nevertheless wished that the dead, their ancestors, could somehow bring them good fortune, as some of the tomb-quelling texts make clear. An inscription found on a stone tomb-brick from Shantung gives us a revealing perspective:

The scholar shall be promoted to high offices and decorated with seals and cordons. The one managing business shall earn ten thousand times profit daily. He who is forever to stay in the darkness shall be separated. The grave pit shall be closed and not to be opened again.[86]

How, then, could a mentality of fear of death and revulsion of the dead be reconciled with the optimism toward postmortem life, as mentioned above? That our evidence is from tombs of different social strata is certainly worth considering. Rich tombs, with abundant funerary equipment and colorful decoration, may give the impression that life in the netherworld was considered a happy one, but the tomb-quelling texts from poorer tombs present another perspective. However, one should perhaps not try to reconcile or to separate these attitudes, for it is perfectly possible that the two could coexist even in the same social stratum; there is no restriction prohibiting the ancient mentalities, or even modern ones, from operating along mutually contradictory lines. If we may take a further step in speculating, it can also be argued that, paradoxically, the reason that rich tombs presented an optimistic attitude was exactly because people fundamentally held a pessimistic or skeptical view of life after death. Abundant equipment for the deceased allowed a happy and comfortable postmortem existence; but it could also be explained as the result of a fear of hardship. Seen in this perspective, then, the rich funerary equipment may have originated from the same mentality that produced tomb-quelling texts, wherein the poorer dead were equipped with soybeans to pay tax in the netherworld.

Social Change, the Development of Burial Styles, and the Idea of the Netherworld

The above discussion has shown that, corresponding to the development of burial styles, there was a development in the conception of the netherworld from the Warring States period down through the Han dynasty. What caused these changes? What was the relationship between the change in burial style and the conception of the netherworld? We mentioned that the disintegration of Chou social and political structures contributed to the change in burial styles among different social strata. Yet this change, mostly during the Eastern Chou period, was mainly within the old burial system. The difference was that the *li*, or rites, in the old system were destroyed by those political upstarts who, assuming that the *li* were reserved for those of higher status, attempted to flaunt their newly acquired wealth and power. When, during the Warring States period, society began to focus on the rule of central government and the achievement of individuals based mainly on merit rather than blood and family ties,[87] a more aggressive attitude was encouraged. To gain prestige and wealth, therefore, depended more on one's own effort than on family background. The most obvious example of this new society was the state of Ch'in, where the government ranked its people into twenty degrees, based only on merit gained in combat. This, of course, was not a democratic or even an egalitarian society. Yet since men were encouraged to achieve better status and accumulate more wealth, we see this reflected in funerary and postmortem outlays. Supposedly, the netherworld also encouraged personal merit. One therefore prepared all necessary equipment to assist the deceased to gain a better living. Commoners would include more "treasures" in a tomb than the owner actually possessed while alive, and, as one text has it, "to enjoy his own rent-income underneath, which amounts to twenty million per year." If the imagination of man concerning the netherworld was determined by his value system, a netherworld that encouraged personal advancement could only have appeared after such a real world had already existed.

The new society of the Warring States period fostered the formation of a new idea of the netherworld, which in turn motivated a series of changes related to burial style and funerary paraphernalia. In other words, theses changes were the material and mental manifestations of the changes in socio-political structure. When the structure of society changed, the material symbols that were used to differentiate various social classes also changed.[88]

We should be aware, however, of the fact that, in most ancient civilizations, with the notable exception of Egypt,[89] the netherworld was never a clearly conceived place. Thus says S. C. Humphreys: "It is difficult in most cultures to locate the dead unambiguously in one place."[90] The Mycenaean Greeks seem to have believed that their dead had needs similar to those of the living,[91] but a clear concept of the netherworld did not emerge even in classical Greece.[92] The ancient Mesopotamians as well as the early Israelites, similarly, possessed no clear and positive concept of the netherworld.[93] Thus, the example furnished by the ancient Chinese is worth investigating not only for its intrinsic meaning in the development of Chinese religion, but also for its significance from a comparative point of view.

Chapter 8

Popular Religiosity and Its Critics

Superstitiousness, I need hardly say, would seem to be a sort of cowardice with respect to the divine.[1]

And herein is a proof that God has given the art of divination not to the wisdom, but to the foolishness of man. No man, when in his wits, attains prophetic truth and inspiration, but when he receives the inspired word, either his intelligence is enthralled in sleep or he is demented by some distemper or possession.[2]

Literacy and the Commoners

So far, we have seen that a major characteristic of everyday religious activity was a preoccupation with personal well-being. This was true for ruling and nonruling classes, elite and lowly. Much of our evidence, however, comes from the lower social echelon—common people, who constituted the broad population base of the peasant society of ancient China. Many elements of their beliefs were transmitted from one generation to the next without ever being recorded in written form. When recorded, these ideas and activities inevitably show the imprint of the ideas of the literate, elite class. Such is the case with most pre-Ch'in documents.

Following the disintegration of Chou society, reading and writing ceased to be the exclusive prerogative of the ruling classes. People with various degrees of literacy were dispersed in society and served as transmitters of cultural values. Moreover, many commoners rose to high positions at local and national courts, bringing with them a variety of values and beliefs.[3] This trend culminated with the founding of the Han dynasty. Han court culture was mixed in nature. The first emperor, Liu Pang, came from a humble background, and many in his entourage were of similar origins.[4] A number of important members in the imperial court, on the other hand, were from the pre-Ch'in aristocracy of the Six Kingdoms.[5] When the Han government, after passing through initial crises involving the remnant kingdoms,[6] began to form a relatively meritocratic bureaucracy,[7] literacy became a universally desirable skill.

The popularization of literacy coincided with the emergence of the *shih* 士. Originally, in the Chou dynasty, they were the lowest of the ruling types, performing civil and military service for feudal lords. With the disintegration of the Chou system, the *shih* increased in number because they occupied an intermediate level among shifting social groups. Because they possessed literary skills, they became, so to speak, freelance advisers and educators, released from their former obligations and seeking employment at various political levels. In Chapter 3, I referred to them as "intellectuals."[8] During the Han period, the term *shih* became almost synonymous with "scholar" or "learned person." In a study on Han social structure, Ch'ü T'ung-tsu categorized the *shih*-scholars as commoners, particularly when they did not hold official posts.[9] Thus, everyone outside officialdom (excluding, of course, the relatives of various royal and noble families) can be considered as a commoner. As a criterion of social status, this is unambiguous, but not as useful in delineating a person's religious inclination. For even within the *shih*-scholar "class," religious attitudes varied: some may have identified with ruling ideology; others may have gone along with the practices of peasants or artisans; still others may have criticized both. Whether officials or not, the attitudes of *shih*-scholars toward things religious were complex, as I will discuss later. Ch'ü's findings also related to the complicated nature of literacy in Han society. According to his categorization, the "commoners" include such groups as scholars, farmers, artisans, merchants, and other occupations such as physician, diviner, butcher, and runner. Given the various levels of status within each group,[10] it is obvious that the "commoner class" was a mixture of people with various degrees of literacy, although it should be clear that the highly literate would always be the minority.]

Although so far no comprehensive investigation has been done concerning literacy in the Han period, and perhaps the question will never be satisfactorily answered,[there is little doubt that literacy, that is, the ability at least to read and write simple communications and keep account books, was widespread.[11]Even during the Ch'in dynasty there existed various primers for the purpose of teaching young students basic literary skills. [The development from *chuan* 篆 to *li* 隸 calligraphic styles during this time, moreover, testifies to the increasing need for writing and associated materials.[12]These primers no doubt circulated broadly in society. According to *History of Han*, during the early-Han, "local book-teachers (*lü-li shu-shih* 閭里書師)" combined the earlier primers into a single text with the title *Ts'ang-chieh* 倉頡, the name of the legendary inventor of Chinese script, which included fifty-five chapters, each with sixty words. A number of primers were produced during the subsequent era.[13] Judging from the mention of "local teachers," from the Ch'in and early-Han onward[there were continuous and conscious efforts, both official and private, to initiate the common people into basic literacy.[14]During the Eastern Han, according to Wang Ch'ung, children could graduate from the local schools (*shu-kuan* 書館) when they were eight, and study the classics. Wang Ch'ung himself began his studies with *Lun-yü* 論語 and *Shang-shu* 尚書.[15] We may surmise that the material he used in the local school included such primers as *Ts'ang-chieh*.

The spread of literacy in Han society comes through in the following examples. It is known that artisans often inscribed their names, the names of their workshops, dates of manufacture, and the contents of funerary objects on their products, especially lacquer ware.[16] Archaeologists have also discovered tomb bricks bearing notes about the order of bricks or the names of the workers who carved the rock or molded the clay bricks.[17] The well-known bronze mirrors, furthermore, often include auspicious phrases and characters as part of the decoration,[18] and the errors contained therein suggest that the artisans had a limited command of writing. On the other hand,[the large amount of simplified characters for daily and speedy use by artisans indicates that writing was widespread at the lower stratum of society.[19]Artisans

Fig. 8.1 A talisman.
Eastern Han.

were certainly not considered "intellectuals," yet it is obvious that they possessed a certain degree of literacy. To borrow a term from W. V. Harris's discussion of Greek and Roman literacy, this could be called "craftsman's literacy."[20] Scribes who wrote the lists of funerary objects and soldiers who kept daily journals in border fortresses, furthermore, were probably men of significant literacy, although they should still be categorized as commoners. In fact, the frontier military might have afforded more learning opportunity to common soldiers than to farmers and artisans, since reading was essential for many aspects of effective military operations.[21] Although literacy was widespread in Han society, the literacy "rate" was probably not high. In any event, there is no way to estimate such rates, nor do we have comparative data. One can only say that literacy was widespread among various sectors in society.

Regarding spells and talismans written on "tomb-quelling bottles" (discussed in Chapter 7), it is possible that people of relatively high literary ability were involved, whether considered intellectuals or not. In view of the systems of symbols used on some of the talismans, it is possible that they were the creation of learned persons. A number of talismans of the Eastern Han period were combinations of words and astral graphs. Meanings were based on the combined symbolic value of the various elements in the talisman. In one example (Fig. 8.1), the talisman was composed of such characters as *shih* 時 (period, or moment, of time), *jih* 日 (sun), *yüeh* 月 (moon), *wei* 尾 (constellation), and *kuei* 鬼 (constellation). The entire talisman can thus be interpreted as the following: "The life and death of everything was controlled by time. The living belong to the world of the sun (*yang*), while the dead belong to the world of the moon (*yin*). The *wei*-constellation was the protector of the family of the deceased; the *kuei*-constellation was in charge of the dead."[22] The purpose of the talisman, if we accept the above interpretation, was to proclaim the divine verdict of the gods and to set the tomb and the deceased in a correct cosmological position. In another example, the talisman was composed of a rope, an astral configuration, and a sentence declaring "the gods of Tai-i and T'ien-i are in charge of expelling evil demons with the rope."[23] Clearly the person who composed the talisman must have possessed a considerable degree of knowledge to be able to employ the language in this way. This skill area, furthermore, must have gradually become a branch of learning in local, noncourt religious traditions. The *History of Han* "Treatise on Literature" mentioned a book *"Chih-pu-hsiang he-kuei-wu* 執不祥劾鬼物," translated roughly "To seizing inauspicious (demons) and to indict ghosts and goblins,"[24] which most likely contained apotropaic talismans that the magicians made use of. *History of Later Han* describes Chü Sheng-ch'ing's "skill at writing vermilion amulets to control and allay ghosts and spirits, and to make them do his bidding."[25] We also learn that a certain Fei Ch'ang-fang was given an apotropaic talisman in the market by an old healer. From this old man—an immortal, in fact—he later learned demonifugic arts, including the writing of talismans.[26] Such persons later practiced as Taoist priests, writing spells and talismans for people of all sorts.[27] For example, *The Scripture of Supreme Peace* (*T'ai-p'ing-ching* 太平經), one of the earliest Taoist texts, preserves a large number of talismans presumably used by such priests,[28] as does Ko Hung's *Pao-p'u-tzu*.[29]

Thus, the transmission of these specific elements of religious expression relied on the input of people with literary skills. It is imprecise, in sum, to speak of "the elite class" and "the commoners" of the Han period as different social groups in terms of their religious beliefs.

[Further, the term "elites" should not mean "intellectuals," as many intellectuals were commoners. On the other hand, the term "commoners" should not mean "illiterate people," but ordinary people who did not have any political positions, who may or may not have formal intellectual or scholarly training] These people, in any case, were not cut off completely from literacy and therefore received various degrees of influence from the "great tradition." This may have occurred through the gradual adoption of ideas involving correlative cosmology, the Confucian mandate of heaven, and the like. As Schwartz pointed out,

> [In] the course of time, like the bureaucratic image of the divine world, the categories of correlative cosmology are gradually absorbed into the fabric of popular culture . . . particularly as they affect the life of the family and the individual in such matters as geomancy, medicine, fortunetelling, horoscope reading, and other concerns of daily life.[30]

Conversely, the non-elite—the great bulk of the population—also injected their own ideas and local customs into the relatively more sophisticated and literary traditions of the elite. Thus, one cannot assume the existence of a "religion of the intellectuals" and a "religion of the commoners" without seriously oversimplifying the situation.

A story contained in *The Record of History* reveals the complexity of the situation. Sun Chung and Chia I, disappointed with the mediocre quality of their court colleagues, went to the market in search of "sages of ancient times, who were [to be found] at court or among the diviners and doctors [in the market]." They had some contentious words with a certain Ssu-ma Chi-chu, who disagreed with their comment that people despised the diviners as exaggerators and deceivers. Su-ma denounced instead hypocritical scholar-officials and extolled the diviners's profession.[31] The author of *The Record of History*, while making his point about petty court politics and the intellectual atmosphere, also shows us that learned persons, for one reason or another, were to be found among artisans and merchants. They were transmitters of cultural values and religious ideas between both the worlds of the elite and the non-elite.[32]

History of Later Han describes a certain Kao Feng, a self-taught young man from a peasant family who became a scholar famous for refusing official positions. When pressed by a local governor, he claimed that his family used to practise *wu*-shamanism, thus official service was unsuitable.[33] Analytically, his family background categorizes him as a commoner, yet he was also a learned scholar of high repute. The family's history as *wu*-shamans, however, places him in the world of everyday, popular religion. This defies simple categorization.

With this understanding of literacy and the meaning of "commoners" in Han society, clearly the "common religion" at this time was a complex social phenomenon. One cannot assume that it had nothing to do with the intellectuals or the ruling elite. Moreover, we need to reconsider the idea that evidence concerning the religious beliefs of the common people, especially texts from Han tombs, necessarily bears the bias or misrepresentation of the elites. It is undeniable that the literary vehicles may carry certain ideological assumptions of the elite. Yet it is also possible that they might have represented the commoners' beliefs expressed through less sophisticated words. We must explore further the roles of intellectuals to comprehend the world of everyday, popular religion in the Han period.

Intellectuals as Critics of Popular Religion and Local Cults

We might define a Han-era intellectual as someone trained in classical texts and, at least in the majority of cases, holding a career in the state bureaucracy. By their service and through their knowledge, intellectuals supplied the conduit between the literary, scholarly tradition and the culture of everyday, noncourt life. The most significant examples are those "good officials" (*hsün-li* 循吏) who brought the ideals of classical Confucianism to the people in ways that they could understand.[34] In the process of teaching, however, intellectuals often became critics of local, everyday beliefs.

A term often employed by Han intellectuals in criticizing popular religion was "excessive cult" (*yin-ssu* 淫祠).[35] According to the official view:

(The Son of Heaven) sacrifices to Hou-chi in the suburb to accompany the heaven, and makes ancestral sacrifice in the Ming-t'ang to accompany Shang-ti. All the people within the four seas come to offer sacrifice according to their offices. The Son of Heaven makes sacrifice to the famous mountains and great rivers under heaven, to appease the hundred deities. . . . The feudal lords make sacrifice to the famous mountains and great rivers within their own domain; the officials make sacrifice to the gate, the door, the well, the hearth, and the impluvium (*chung-liu* 中霤). The literati and commoners (make sacrifice to) ancestors only. Each according to their ceremonies; and excessive cults (*yin-ssu*) are prohibited.[36]

What, then, were excessive cults? These may simply have been any cults not mentioned in the text, perhaps including some that were supported by the government. Emperor Ch'eng once accepted a suggestion to abolish various cults established since the dynasty's beginning.[37] The later historical record referred to this as "abolishing various excessive cults."[38] Thus, it seems that [cults originally part of the official establishment could suddenly be considered excessive.]

The term not only refers to those cults that were not under government sponsorship, but also carries derogatory connotations, and was used as a weapon to attack virtually any cult viewed as undesirable by the speaker or writer. For example, Pan Ku described Wang Mang's indulgence in cult activities as "worshipping ghosts, spirits, and excessive cults."[39] Wang Mang, however, worshipped spirits and sought immortality no more "excessively" than Wu-ti did. Pan Ku's use of "*yin-ssu*" to describe Wang Mang's activities had mostly to do with Wang Mang's reputation as usurper. In other words, the term "*yin-ssu*," although definable in a technical sense, was often used subjectively and prone to controversy. For example, during the Wei and Chin dynasties, when Taoist movements and practices were developing and beginning to compete with local cults, Taoist adepts referred to activities not congruent with their own rites and tenets as "excessive cults."[40]

[When applied to local cults, "excessive cults" also could mean cults considered by critics as immoral or abusive] Ying Shao states the following in *A Penetrating Account*:

By custom, [people of] Kuei-chi favored excessive cults and preferred divination. Everyone used cattle to make sacrifices. Shamans collected money and gifts (from the people), but the people did not dare to refuse for fear that they be cursed by the shamans. Thus people's wealth was spent on ghosts and spirits, and their properties were consumed by sacrifices. Some poor families who were unable to make timely sacrifice did not even dare to eat beef. [It is said that] a person about to die from illness would make the mooing sound of cattle. That is how they fear (the shamans).[41]

This is a typical description of an "excessive cult." Several characteristics would have been deemed unacceptable by critics: shamans abused their exorcistic functions and extracted wealth; second, the people were timid and superstitious. Because cattle were an important asset,[42] it is easy to accept Ying Shao's description of the destitution of households by their using cattle for sacrifices. The economic consequences of the excessive cults therefore could be serious. To make things more complicated, local officials were probably among those supported cult operations. When Ti Wu-lun 第五倫 was sent to be governor of Kuei-chi, his initial order to abolish the excessive cults was opposed by local officials. It was only after he introduced heavy punishment for noncompliance that his order began to take effect.[43] This suggests that local officials had a personal interest in the cults. The story of Hsi-men Pao 西門豹, below, illustrates this, as do the official cults discussed in Chapter 5. Ying Shao comments at one place on the above two points:

(I) heard that the local custom here favors excessive cults; wealth was wasted and farming hindered, while disturbances increased and apprehensions accumulated. The people's extravagance is despicable, their foolishness pitiful.[44]

Among excessive cult abuses was divination, an activity criticized by intellectuals since the end of the Warring States period.[45] A typical criticism is found in "Biographies of the Day-diviners" in *Record of History*:

(Chia I claimed that) The diviners are despised by people in society. People say that diviners usually spoke with exaggeration to gain sympathy; falsely proclaiming the good fortune and fate of people to please their minds; recklessly predicting misfortune to hurt people's hearts; deceitfully speaking through ghosts and spirits to drain people's wealth; and asking dearly for payments for their own use.[46]

This passage, posed as part of a debate, represents the viewpoint of intellectuals who loathed the work of diviners in society. Wang Ch'ung concurred in *Lun Heng*:

The world believes in divination with shells and stalks. The first class of diviners questions Heaven; the second, Earth. The milfoil has something spiritual; tortoises are divine; and omens and signs respond, when asked. Therefore they disregard the advice of their friends, and take to divination; they neglect what is right and wrong, and trust solely to lucky and unlucky portents. In their belief, Heaven and Earth really make their wishes known, and stalks and tortoises verily possess spiritual powers.[47]

Wang Ch'ung then demonstrated that since heaven and earth do not have ears and mouths, they cannot have heard or replied to the questions of men. Yet, typically, Wang Ch'ung upholds the idea of a mysterious fate, and simply criticizes diviners' lack of true knowledge:

Omens and signs are true by any means. If good and bad fortunes do not happen as predicted, it is the fault of the diviners who do not understand their business.[48]

This attitude is found among many Confucian intellectuals who, while criticizing extravagant customs, nevertheless did not logically deny the fundamental rationale behind them. The Eastern Han scholar Wang Fu 王符, for example, attacked shamanistic divination and cult activities:

Nowadays many people abandon their housework and silk weaving, and instead embark on the ways of the shaman: drumming and dancing, paying homage to the deities, cheating commoners and deceiving the people. . . . Those who were cheated by the mischievous and injured by the bandits, who were harmed by disasters and divine retributions and became seriously ill, their numbers are numerous. Some even abandoned medicine and went to serve the deities, and thus finally died. They did not realize that they were deceived by the shamans, but regretted that they were too late to learn from the shamans. This is the most extreme case of (the shamans') deceiving the commoners.[49]

Wang Fu did not repudiate, however, the efficacy of divination,[50] nor did he deny the existence of ghosts and spirits:

> That evil does not prevail over virtue, and that the wicked do not conquer the just are the norms of heaven. Although sometimes it is not entirely straight, the wise abide in the right way, and do not approach lascivious ghosts (*yin-kuei* 淫鬼). The so-called lascivious ghosts are those wandering evil spirits, they are not true deities and spirits who have their proper duties.[51]

By such warnings, Wang Fu actually concedes that the beliefs were popular:

> As for secret spells of the *wu*-shamans and shamanesses, feared by the commoners, the seven spirits of the Earth Lord, the Flying Corpse, the Evil Ghost, the Northern Lord, Hsien-chu the Way Blocker, the Straight Talisman, as well as the various taboos concerning building activities and some trivial matters, these should not be the concern of the Heavenly King.[52]

The "seven spirits" were obviously those evil spirits that Wang Ch'ung once mentioned as fearful of the "twelve just deities" in the house, including the Blue Dragon and the White Tiger.[53] As these "should not be the concern of the Heavenly King (*t'ien-wang* 天王)," they were undoubtedly feared by the commoners.

Chung-ch'ang T'ung 仲長統, a contemporary of Wang Fu, also criticized popular cults, without fundamentally denying the tradition of ancestor worship, sacrifice to heaven and earth, or divination. He states the following in an essay on abolishing excessive cults and taboos:

> Be scrupulous about rituals and composure. To live by the middle way; to uphold morality and virtue; to perform benevolence and righteousness; to pay homage to heaven and earth; and to make sacrifice to the ancestral shrine: these are auspicious practices.

189

If, unfortunately, disaster happens, then one should control one-self and criticize one's own behavior. Afterwards, one performs the ritual of praying, and have shamans make divinations according to the middle way and offer sincerity and piety as much as possible. In the degenerate world, people forget righteousness and become the stepping-stone for evil things (to move forward). Subsequently we get the lascivious and grotesque rituals, extra-ordinary and bizarre stories, and talismans and apotropaic objects. Taboos observed by the ordinary people and fashions current in society are deeply distressful to the learned.[54]

Thus, "irrational" elements in popular belief that did not conform to Wang's subjective view of piety and justice are seen as "excessive" or "lascivious" cults.

Besides criticism of this type, there was skepticism about the fundamental ideas in Han popular beliefs, such as the existence of immortals. Yang Hsiung 揚雄, for example, took a naturalistic stand:

Someone asked: "Are there immortals as people say?" Alas, I heard that Mi-hsi, Shen-nung had died; Huang-ti, Yao, and Shun had also passed away. . . . Someone says: "The sages did not learn to be immortals, for their ways were different. The sages worried that there should be one thing in the world that they did not know; while the immortals worried that there should be one day that they did not live." (I) say: "Alive! Alive! (The immortals are) alive in name, but dead in fact. . . . The living are destined to die, and those having a beginning must also have an end. This is the way of nature."[55]

Yang further pointed out fraudulent elements in popular beliefs:

Someone asked about [the authenticity of] *The Beginning and End of Huang-ti (Huang-ti chung-shih* 黃帝終始)." I said: "It is a fake. In the ancient times, Ssu-shih (i.e., king Yü) was said to have contained the flood, therefore *wu*-shamans performed the pace of Yü [to claim that they possessed the magical power of Yü]. Pien Ch'üeh was from the Lu state, therefore most doctors claimed that they also were from Lu. Those that intended to cheat are bound to imitate the genuine."[56]

Here Yang Hsiung had in effect denied some of the fundamental elements of popular religion: the authenticity of the sacred books and the efficacy of the shamanistic rituals and medicine. Another early Eastern Han scholar, Huan T'an 桓譚, also refused to ascribe efficacy to longevity techniques, as practiced by *fang-shih*, or men of magical arts. According to him in *Hsin Lun* 新論, or *New Treatise*:

> There was no such thing as the Way of the Immortals but that it had been invented by those who liked strange things. The Marquis of Ch'ü-yang accepted the service of Hsi-men Chün-hui, a gentleman versed in the arts of magic, to teach him the art of driving old age away. I saw the Marquis and said: "The sages did not learn the way of immortals yet an ordinary person now wants to learn. There is nothing so deceiving than this." Ch'ün-hui said: "The tortoise is said to be able to live for three thousand years, and the crane for one thousand years. Considering the qualities of man, why is he not the equal of insects and birds?" I replied, "Who could live long enough to learn how old a tortoise or a crane is?"[57]

Neither did Huan T'an believe in portents. Another passage in the same work states:

> Cranes are eaten throughout the empire's commanderies and kingdoms. But in the three capital districts no one dares to catch one because of the [omenology that associates] thunder with the captive of a crane. Could it be that Heaven originally favored only this bird? [No], the killing of the bird merely coincides with thunder.[58]

Huan T'an's rational attitude also prevented him from believing in the apocryphal texts that were current in his day. This almost caused his execution, and he was dismissed from government by the emperor Kuang Wu.[59]

The Eastern Han was an age of religious movements, such as that of the Yellow Turbans. Yet Hsün Yüeh 荀悅 expressed serious doubts about the truth of immortality:

> Someone inquired about the art of [becoming] immortal. I said: "How pretentious [are those who talk about the art of becoming

immortal]! The less one is concerned with it [the better]. [The Sage does not study it. This is not because he despises life. [It is because] the beginning and the end [of all things] are [the result of] cosmic cycles. Long or short life is determined by fate. [The workings of nature and fate are not affected by human effort."]

Someone said: "Is it true that there are some human beings who [are able to] transform themselves and become immortal?" I said: "I have never heard of this before. Even if [such a metamorphosis] did occur, [the result would be] a monster, not an immortal. There have been cases of a man being changed into a woman, and a dead person regaining his life. But is this the nature of human beings? It has nothing to do with the cosmic numbers [common fate]."[60]

On the whole, critics of excessive cults and popular beliefs accepted the fundamental ideas of Chinese religions, but opposed cult abuses for the harm they caused. In a similar vein, some Han intellectuals criticized contemporary excesses in funerals and burials. Some of their criticism was based on a naturalistic view of life and death. By denying the afterlife, they also denied the meaning of funerary equipment. Most, however, did not refute the idea of souls and spirits. Criticism of lavish burial was mainly based on a utilitarian point of view: that extravagance, whether in burials or for such occasions as marriage and cult worship, induced moral corruption and thus should be curbed.[61]

Intellectuals as Reformers of Popular Religion

Wang Ch'ung's essays contain a wealth of information about the world of popular religion in the Han period. It is doubtful, however, that men like him ever brought about changes in the contemporary society; in fact, as mentioned before, *Lun Heng* remained unknown during Wang's lifetime.[62] Some other writers, however, did set out to reform the practices of popular cults when they were in the position to do so.

One of the more famous stories about the confrontations between scholar-officials and excessive cults features Hsi-men Pao 西門豹 and the River Lord (*Ho-po* 河伯). In the prefecture of Yeh, where Hsi-men Pao was appointed magistrate, a young girl was annually sent, by custom, into the river to be the bride of the River Lord. The shamans and shamanesses who mediated between the River Lord and the people naturally profited from performing these services. The people, however, were distressed over the fate of their daughters and the loss of wealth, but were held back for fear of the Lord's retributions. When Hsi-men Pao learned of this, he pretended to be lenient toward the shamans and attended the "wedding" ceremony. Before the girl was to be thrown into the river, Hsi-men Pao claimed that she was not pretty enough and forced a shamaness into the river to convey an appropriate message to the River Lord. When, after a while, the shamaness did not come back to report, he threw her disciples into the river one after another. This straightforward method crushed the influence of the shamans.[63]

Hsi-men Pao lived in the Warring States period. His story, however, may be considered typical of later confrontations between intellectuals and cult activities. In the Eastern Han period, for example, shamans in Chiu-chiang commandery made the local people comply with the purported directives of the gods of the mountains of T'ang and Chu concerning annual delivery of brides and bridegrooms. They were also required to supply abundant dowries and gifts. After serving a one-year term, furthermore, the consorts were forbidden to marry for the rest of their lives. A governor of the region by the name of Sung Chün 宋均 ordered that, since the shamans were close to the mountain gods, it was appropriate to use members of their families as consorts of the gods. This made the shamans concede their deceitfulness, and they were executed.[64]

As mentioned above, Ti Wu-lun forcefully banned the cult of cattle slaughtering in Kuei-chi.[65] However, such actions could not wipe out tenacious local customs. The cult of the king of Ch'eng-yang, thriving in eastern areas, was said to have been banned by Ts'ao Ts'ao when he was governor there.[66] When Ying Shao himself became the magistrate of Ying-ling, near Chi-nan, however, he found that the cult was still practiced. Ying could only persuade the people not to slaughter cattle, and he had to allow them to provide other offerings for their cult.[67]

When acting as reformers of popular cults, scholar-officials often based their judgment on material or practical aspects of cults that they considered excessive. In other words, their actions were civic and secular in nature, with little theoretical discussion.[68] This is shown in the following stories. A certain Chao Ping 趙炳, famous for magical arts, developed a host of followers. He was executed by the local magistrate under the charge of "deluding the people."[69] One Liu Ken 劉根 was accused of practicing witchcraft and misleading the people.[70] In both cases the concern was about deluding and misleading the people, thus potentially creating a situation of unrest. Officeholders were much concerned with keeping a peaceful social atmosphere. The kind of large-scale social movements such as the one associated with the worship of the Queen Mother of the West, mentioned in Chapter 6, must have caused tremendous uneasiness for local officials.

Thus, the demarcation between official and popular, between "normal" and "excessive" cults, often accorded less with theory than with circumstantial conditions, such as political positions and personal judgments. The criticisms expressed by those Han intellectuals against popular cults, as presented above, were unsystematic and piecemeal. In any case, their voices could not have reached the wide populace, given the condition of commucations and their own social positions at the time. Many intellectuals themselves, moreover, often participated in popular cults.

Intellectuals as Participants in Popular Religion

Hsi-men Pao and Sung Chün provide us with examples of intellectuals' efforts to reform popular religion. We are not told, however, about the attitudes of such intellectuals toward the spiritual. Their edicts to destroy cults did not necessarily imply that they were agnostics. It is more likely that they believed in the existence of gods, ghosts, and spiritual beings.

Luan Pa offers an example of this. He was a learned official at the court of Emperor Shun, and was later promoted to be governor of Yü-chang, a district brimming with demons and goblins of the mountains and rivers. People often spent fortunes to propitiate them. It is said that Luan Pa possessed exorcistic arts (*tao-shu* 道術), and was able to control ghosts and spirits. So he destroyed the shrines and removed the treacherous *wu*-shamans. Then the demons and monsters disappeared on their own accord.[71] Thus, although Luan Pa acted as a reformer of local "excessive cults," he himself still relied upon the art of exorcism, which presupposed the existence of ghosts and spirits. In this sense, therefore, he should be seen as an active participant in popular religion.]

Chia I, as we recall, expressed doubts on the efficacy of divination when he met Ssu-ma Chi-chu. In other writing, however, he once commented:

> People think that ghosts and gods can bestow fortune and bring disaster, therefore they prepare sacrifice and sacrificial vessels, fast, and make offerings to the ghosts and spirits to gain happiness. Thus it is said: It is for this blessing that sacrifices are offered to the ghosts and spirits.[72]

Was he contradicting himself? Because we cannot be sure about the veracity of such speeches, there is no way to tell for sure. Nevertheless, we are reminded that the attitude of intellectuals toward popular religion was complex: some criticized popular cults; some were participants; still others held seemingly contradictory ideas.\

The participation of intellectuals in popular religion thus should be considered from two different angles. On the one hand were followers of common practice who were unaware or uncritical. On the other were those who participated actively in popular cults. Tung Chung-shu's scholarly stature would ordinarily lead us to assume that he had had no relations with popular beliefs and practices. His rain prayer, however, shows that he had adopted certain popular cultic practices, such as burying human bones and burning pigs' tails.[73] Thus, he accepted, at least partially, such beliefs. "Treatise on Literature" in *History of Han* lists a work called *"Praying for Rain and for Cessation of Rain"* in twenty-six *chüan*; it must have contained magical methods used in rain prayers. Besides, Huan T'an also mentioned in his work that the great scholar Liu Hsin employed clay dragons and various exorcistic methods in praying for rain.[74] Thus, Tung Chung-shu's methods were not unusual.

Ts'ui Shih 崔寔 provides another type of intellectual. As we have seen in Chapter 6, Ts'ui was from a prominent official family and had received a thorough training in the classics.[75] *Monthly Ordinances for the Four Classes of People*, a record of his own estate, describes seasonal religious activities reflecting the general situation of local society. Thus, we may infer that his own participation in religious activities is also beyond reasonable doubt. According to his biography, Ts'ui followed the contemporary custom of "lavish burial" when his father died.[76] In his famous work, "Cheng-lun 政論," or "On Statecraft," however, he is an enthusiastic reformer of contemporary vices, including lavish burials.[77] How should one explain this contradiction? I would argue that, as a member of the scholar-official community, his more self-conscious work, "On Statecraft," expressed a view that fulfilled the expectation of that community, while his private work (*Monthly Ordinances for the Four Classes of People*) and his family activities (such as the lavish burial of his father) uncritically followed contemporary customs.

The examples of Tung Chung-shu and Ts'ui Shih show that popular culture and religion penetrated the lives of individuals in an imperceptible way, affecting even the elite. A more complicated case is found in the life and views of Chang Huan 張奐, who flourished in the time of Emperor Huan of the Eastern Han (2nd c. A.D.).

In Wu-wei 武威 Commandery on the western frontier, where Chang Huan once served as governor, people by custom killed children born in the second and fifth months, or in the same month as the parents' birthdays. Chang Huan forcefully prohibited this custom, and the people established a shrine for him in his lifetime. It is interesting that, on the one hand he was a reformer of certain improper practices, while on the other hand he accepted such practices as a "living shrine" (*sheng-ssu* 生祠) that gave him the status of local demigod.[78] In a sense, therefore, he was a participant in popular religion. Chang Huan's will, however, seems to imply disbelief in the hereafter:

> It is just darkness below ground, and time there is long and without a moment of light. It is not pleasant, then, to be re-wrapped in fine cloth and sealed tightly in the coffin with nails. Should I be fortunate enough to have a grave, if I die in the morning, you should bury me the same afternoon. Put my body on the bier; use only one piece of cloth. I would not follow the extravagant example of the Duke of Chin, neither would I be so stringent as Yang Wang-sun.[79]

Considering Chang's active military and civilian life, it is difficult to understand his rejection of worldly success and glory. His instructions, therefore, may be sober reflections on worldly vanity at the approach of death. Thus, for many, ideas concerning what constituted a proper worship were probably not fixed, just as their ideas concerning life and death did not necessarily conform to the spirit of their actual deeds.

There were, of course, intellectuals actively involved in religious activities. Yen Chün-p'ing 嚴君平 was a famous scholar known for his explanations of *Lao-tzu* and *Chuang-tzu*. Yet he made his living by divination in the market place of Ch'eng-tu. When asked, he explained his philosophy:

> Divination is a lowly profession. Yet it can benefit the people. When people ask about goodness and evil, I then explain the distinction between good and bad by means of the yarrows and turtle shells. When speaking to a son, I explain according to the way of filial piety (*hsiao* 孝). When speaking to a brother, I explain according to obedience (*shun* 順). When speaking to a subject, I explain according to the way of loyalty (*chung* 忠). Each is guided toward goodness according to his situation.[80]

Thus, his participation in popular religion might have been based on educating people toward social harmony. In his view, the object of education, it is particularly worth noticing, was to propagate teachings such as filial piety and loyalty instead of his favorite Taoist philosophy. We again confirm the "syncretic" and "political" nature of Han intellectuals. For many of them, whether Taoist or not, maintaining a peaceful society was the main goal.

The magicians (*fang-shih*) present another aspect of the intellectuals' participation in religions. The term *fang-shih* literally means "scholar (*shih* 士) with arts and recipes (*fang* 方)."[81] They were often learned in such subjects as *Yin-yang* and Five-Phases theory, divination, and exorcistic methods. Some of the early *fang-shih* were also called *sheng* 生, which usually refers to a learned scholar.[82] Many were familiar with the classics, in addition to exorcistic methods. Thus, they can be considered intellectuals.

Kung-sha Mu 公沙穆 is a typical case. He lived in the first half of the second century A.D., and came from a humble background. He studied the *Han Commentary of Book of Poetry* (*Han-shih* 韓詩) and *Kung-yang Commentary of the Spring and Autumn Annals* (*Kung-yang Ch'un-ch'iu* 公羊春秋), in addition to the numerology of *River*

197

Chart (*Ho-tu* 河圖) and *Lo Writing* (*Lo-shu* 洛書). He eventually became a member of the scholar-official class:

> Mu was transferred, becoming prefect of Hung-nung. In the outlying districts crops were being devoured by moths and the local populace was alarmed. Mu thereupon built an altar and appealed to heaven: "The people have transgressed, but their crimes originate with me! I myself am the offering for this prayer." Immediately there was a violent cloudburst, and as soon as the clouds cleared, the pests vanished of their own accord. All the people called Mu a god (*shen*).[83]

This act of praying for rain by symbolic human sacrifice was of course based on ancient tradition. The example of King T'ang 湯 offering himself as sacrifice for rain no doubt resonated in the back of Kung-sha Mu's mind.[84] At this time, such practices were obviously still accepted as effective ritual.[85] Once again, scholar-officials were participants in religious activities. For them, there were probably no clear distinctions between civil and religious responsibilities.

Kung-sha Mu was one of many *fang-shih* presented in the "Biographies of Magicians" in *History of Later Han*. His other art, shared by many other magicians, was calendric divination. When we examine the background of those mentioned in the "Biographies of Magicians," clearly most may be considered learned, whether in the Confucian classics or other divinational, astrological, calendric, exorcist, or medicinal arts.[86] In other words, these magicians had a wide range of interests. For example, Li Ho 李郃 was not only versed in the Five Classics, but also in *River Chart* and *Lo Writing* arts.[87] T'ang T'an 唐檀 once studied in the imperial academy, and was versed in the *Book of Change* (*I-ching*), *Book of Poetry*, and *The Spring and Autumn Annals*. His main interest, however, was divination involving portents and astrology.[88] Even some of those who were not listed literally as "*fang-shih*" had a similar learning background.[89] This syncretism was part of a Later Han trend among intellectuals.[90]

When we examine the ideological background of popular religious concepts, we see that intellectuals were involved. For example, it is improbable that the idea of an underworld with a bureaucratic organization similar to that of the living world could have emerged without the involvement of at least literate subofficials. The producing of spells and talismans, furthermore, also betrays the hand of some learned persons.

The "Treatise on Literature" in the *History of Han*, moreover, lists a rather large number of contemporary works devoted to divination, geomancy, and exorcist methods that were also the concerns of popular religion. Works such as *Huang-ti's Divination of Dreams by Long Willows (Huang-ti ch'ang-liu chan-meng* 黃帝長柳占夢), *Various Divinations on Sneezes and Ear-Buzzings (T'i erh-ming tsa-chan* 嚏耳鳴 雜占), *Monstrous Mutations of Man and Animals (Jen-kuei ching-wu liu-ch'u pien-kuai* 人鬼 精物六畜變怪), *Seizing the Inauspicious Demons and Indicting the Ghosts and Goblins (Chih-pu-hsiang he-kuei-wu* 執不祥劾鬼物), *Imploring (Celestial) Officials to Expel the Monstrous and Portentous (Ch'ing-kuan ch'u-yao-hsiang* 請官除妖 祥), or *Praying for Rain and Stopping Rain (Ch'ing-yü chih-yü* 請雨 止雨), to cite but a few examples, were all closely related to people's daily life. A comparable listing in the *History of Sui (Sui-shu* 隋書), half a millennium after the *History of Han*, has similar works.[91] Although most of them are now lost, we can assume that they were produced by intellectuals, for only intellectuals could write and organize the originally disparate source materials into a whole. The various versions of daybooks of the Ch'in and Han period are also examples of such works.

As participants in popular religion, most of these literate persons followed contemporary customs or contributed to the literature in a tradtional manner. However, a few of them participated actively and even creatively. The most famous case involved the rise of Taoist movements at the end of Eastern Han. I cite the paragraph in the *History of the Three Kingdoms (San-kuo-chih* 三國志) concerning the Five Pecks of Rice Taoists under Chang Ling 張陵:

(Chang Ling) studied Tao in the mountain of Ku-ming. He produced Taoist books to deceive the people. Those who accepted his teaching were obliged to contribute five pecks of rice. Thus they were called "the rice bandits." When Ling died, his son Heng continued his teaching. When Heng died, Lu again continued his teaching. . . . Lu thus occupied Han-chung, and taught people the demon's art (*kuei-tao* 鬼道), calling himself "Master Lord (*shih-chun* 師君)." Those who came to learn the art were first called "demon soldiers (*kuei-tsu* 鬼卒)." When they had accepted the art and become adepts, they were called "Libationers (*chi-chiu* 祭酒)." Each Libationer led his own congregation. Those whose congregations were large were called "Great Libationers." All taught honesty and trustworthiness, and to refrain from cheating. The sick were made to repent their misdeeds, mostly similar to that of the Yellow Turbans. Each Libationer built free roadside inns (*i-she* 義舍), similar to the station (*t'ing* 亭) and post stop (*ch'uan* 傳) of nowadays. Then they provided free rice and meat, hanging in the inns. The travellers were to take only what they needed. If they took more than that, the demon's way would make them sick. Those who committed a crime were pardoned three times before they were punished. There were no officials, and the Libationers were the administrators. The people and the barbarians alike were happy to comply. The government could not defeat them, so Lu was made the Commander of Palace Gentlemen (*chung-lang chiang* 中郎將) . . . [92]

This passage shows the degree to which the rise of Taoist religion was a mixture of intellectuals and commoners. According to Ko Hung's *Biographies of the Immortals*, Chang Ling was once a student in the Imperial Academy, and was learned in the classics.

When he became old, he sighed and said: "This (classical learning) has no use for prolonging life." He then began to learn the way of immortality. . . . and acquired secret books and cryptic literature and the art of controlling the myriad spirits of mountains.[93]

It is uncertain if he was indeed a student in the Imperial Academy. Nevertheless, there was a strong idealistic sense in his rules that the adepts were supposedly to follow. The moralistic way of teaching the followers, the manufacturing of talismans, and the organization of the followers all suggest that Chang Ling, Chang Lu, and the nuclear group around them were literate men familiar with government and scholarship.

According to another source, Chang Lu adopted various methods of a certain Chang Hsiu (not a relative) who also practiced the Way of Five Pecks of Rice in Han-chung. Hsiu's method of curing the sick was to put them in a quiet room and have them repent their faults. He further required the Libationers to learn the text of *Lao-tzu*. There were also the demon-officials (*kuei-li* 鬼吏) whose work was to pray for the sick. The manner of praying was to write down the name of the sick persons, and state that they had admitted their wrongdoings. Then, three communications were issued: one for heaven, which was placed on high mountains; one buried underground; and one sunk in the river.[94] Chang Lu's mother, for example, served as shamanic priestess for the household of Liu Yen, then governor of Yi-chou (Szechwan) province.[95] All these were impossible without the involvement of people with skills in writing and organization. It is no surprise, therefore, that many families of officials in the Chin Dynasty were followers of the Five Pecks of Rice Taoists.[96]

Just prior to Chang Lu's ascendancy in Szechwan, a much larger religious rebellion broke out in the eastern part of the empire. This was the Yellow Turban movement led by Chang Chüeh 張角. It is generally assumed that Chang Chüeh based his religious teachings on *T'ai-p'ing ch'ing-ling-shu*, or *The Book of Supreme Peace with Black Margins*, the exact content of which is still the subject of scholarly debate.[97] According to the *History of Later Han*, it "was based on the theories of *yin-yang* and Five Phases, and was mixed with various unorthodox sayings of *wu*-shamanism."[98] This work was attributed to a certain Kan Chi 干吉 (or 于吉), who was versed in Five Phases theory, *wu*-shamanism and medicine. Kan's disciple presented it to the court of Emperor Shun and claimed that it was meant for the sovereign to save the world. Thus, the original audience was not that of the non-elite, local people, but court officials, who rejected it as fraudulent and unorthodox.[99] The point here is that the Yellow Turban movement was oriented towards textual revelation and textual exegesis. Earlier, Chang Chüeh had sent out missionaries to central and east China to spread his message.[100] His teachings included worship of Huang-ti and Lao-tzu, and healing through spells and talismans, much like the Five Pecks of Rice Taoists in the west.[101] After the uprising, he divided his followers into thirty-six divisions, requiring educated advisers. Finally, there is some evidence that the Yellow Turbans were supported by local elites. According to Ch'en Ch'i-yun, the Eastern Han gentry, including their political networks, were primary co-conspirators of the Yellow Turbans. When the gentry withdrew, the insurrection folded.[102] This sort of scenario would be basically repeated by the Five Pecks of Rice Taoists a generation later.

From the Early Han period onward, intellectuals had acted ambivalently concerning local and personal religion. Some tried to influence and reform unorthodox and so-called excessive cults. But most actually participated in such religious practices. Through contact with the everyday world of work and trade, Han intellectuals, especially those known as *fang-shih*, exerted their influence. As a result, popular religion was permanently imprinted with divine courts and postmortem imperial bureaucracies. The aim of religious activities paralleled that of the secular government: the achievement of social peace and prosperity. This is why some intellectuals endorsed popular cults. For them, religious activities, private or public, popular or official, were part of the political process.

The influence of popular religion in the other direction is also apparent. From the beginning of the Ch'in and Han empires, as has been pointed out, the court elites are known to have participated in popular cults. Even the performance of witchcraft, so popular among the people that Wu-ti forbade it,[103] enjoyed popularity amongst grievance-filled courtiers.[104]

That the elite were influenced by religious concepts can also be shown in their funerary equipment. The famous silk painting from Ma-wang-tui shows religious motifs from both official and popular religion.[105] Tomb reliefs and paintings juxtaposed scenes depicting Confucian ethics and official life, on the one hand, and images of phantasms not mentioned in the official religion—like the images of the Queen Mother of the West (Fig. 8.2)—on the other. Such juxtaposition revealed not only "a thoroughly Confucianized paradise."[106] It can also be seen as a sign of the acceptance of popular beliefs by the Confucian elites.

A Penetrating Account contains an anecdote in which Emperor Wu expresses belief in the efficacy of *wu*-shamans from Yüeh and Tung Chung-shu then remonstrates. Emperor Wu subsequently wanted to test Tung's own theories and ordered a *wu*-shaman to curse him. During the duel, the shaman cast spells on Tung, while the latter sat calmly and recited the Confucian classics. The result was that the shaman died suddenly.[107] At the least, this shows that during the Eastern Han some intellectuals perceived the Confucian classics, or their

Fig. 8.2 The Queen Mother of the West. Eastern Han.

main advocate Tung Chung-shu, as maintaining magical power on a par with that of witchcraft and shamans. In fact, in other anecdotes of this period, such classics such as "*Hsiao-ching* 孝經" (*Classic of Filial Piety*) were considered powerful enough to fend off evil spirits.[108]

These stories, and the ones given above, can be thought of as indications of a competition between the official religion and non-official, local religions. The actions by scholar-officials to close "excessive" cults and expel *wu*-shamans, in a sense, can be considered as a pattern of religious persecution—the orthodox religion, represented by officials, persecuted the unorthodox local cults, represented by *wu*-shamans. The motivation was mainly political and ethical, rather than religious.[109] A similar situation pertained in the Roman Empire. For

203

example, the Roman government often prohibited the cult of Isis, which began to gain popularity during the first century B.C.[110] Charges against it mainly concerned the secret rituals of the cult and the fanatic behavior of worshippers, including "loose morality"—a term quite similar to Han scholar-officials' use of *yin-ssu*. Moreover, the gathering of worshippers in secret, in such frantic emotional conditions, was potentially threatening to public security.[111] The early Christians were charged with similar crimes. In fact, of course, official prohibitions could not really expunge them. When Christianity became the official religion of Rome, however, it turned its attentions toward the persecution of the pagans.[112] In the fourth and fifth centuries A.D., when Taoist cults and Buddhist orders began to vie for official status, we perceive again patterns similar to those of early Europe. In both civilizations, we see a need on the part of the official religion to curb the non-official, although what was official might have originated from non-official sources.

Chapter 9 _____

Conclusion

> The gods have not revealed all things to men from the beginning,
> but by seeking they (men) find in time what is worthwhile.[1]

This book tries to fill a gap in the history of Chinese religions. Its purported task is that of describing the main features of an ancient religious mentality at a personal and local level. I have not offered the reader a comprehensive account of all religious phenomena in ancient China. Instead, I have chosen to discuss salient aspects of belief that I think are indispensable for our understanding of the religious life of the ancient Chinese people. At the same time, the reader has had the chance to ponder the main problems involved in such an endeavor.

I have defined the scope of this study as the religious expressions of both the common people (non-ruling, toiling people with varying degrees of literacy and various relations with and means of access to ruling officialdom) and ruling types (hereditary nobles and government officials). I have also tried to define religion as man's understanding and expressions of his relationship with the extra-human powers. My investigation has suggested that three different levels of religious expression unfolded in ancient China. Beginning from perhaps the late Neolithic period, and definitely by the Shang, religious expressions become divided based on the richness of ritual acts and paraphernalia, a distinction that developed as the result of a stratified society. The religious expression of the ruling class was to develop into the traditional official religion, with ancestor and nature worship as its main features. These were, however, also the basic constituents of local, non-elite cults and practices.

With the establishment of the Chou dynasty, the idea of a moral heaven developed, first among the ruling elite, then the intellectuals, who formed a third line of religious expression. Toward the Eastern Chou and the Warring States period, these three lines of religious expression, i.e., the official, the intellectual, and the popular, each developed distinctive features. The chief difference among the three, besides the outward ritual paraphernalia, was in their different expectations. As evidence from Chou and later eras shows, the purpose of official religion was mainly to benefit the ruler and, by extension, the entire state. The ruler's subjects—farmers, artisans, soldiers, merchants, even officials—on the other hand, expected to gain personal or familial well-being from their worship of extra-human powers and ancestors. Intellectuals, though not necessarily opposing the official line of thinking, placed their emphasis on personal piety toward a supreme being, with less stress on gaining material welfare.

I have also tried to show that, despite these threefold developments, there was a basal religious mentality that reached from the court to all local levels. It was typified by its emphasis on personal protection from demons and evil spirits and establishing liaison with benevolent deities. Suppliants were individuals and families acting on their own behalf or that of their ancestors. They employed magic (spells and talismans), mantic techniques, shamanic rituals, or simply prayers to effect their wish. It was, thus, a religion of personal welfare and sought control of extra-human powers. My discussion, of necessity, has concentrated on the beliefs of the peasants or common people.

To sum up, I shall concentrate on the following points: the nature of extra-human powers; man's relationship with these powers, and the correlative cosmic order; the concept of the netherworld; apotheosis; and the relationship between piety and happiness. Finally, I introduce some materials from early Buddhism and religious Taoism, to show the continuity of the religious mentality in the post-Han era.

The Nature of Extra-Human Powers

The responsibility of a historian of religion, no doubt, is to reveal the world view of the people he studies. This must of necessity apply to their gods and spirits, a major segment of the extra-human powers to which they subscribed. Extra-human powers varied in type; not every one of the powers can be said to have had exactly the same nature, and not everyone in ancient China had the same conception about the nature of the powers. My study has mentioned beliefs in the neolithic and Shang eras regarding anthropomorphic gods, or powers. This is only to say that their particular actions were conceived in terms of human activities, not that they possessed a personality. For people outside the ruling court, however, it was only the practical abilities of the extra-human powers that were noticed and appreciated. Their understanding of gods and spirits concentrated on things that concerned people's welfare, injury, or peril. In other words, the central concern of a cult was whether a given deity was efficacious.[2] People rarely troubled themselves with the *raison d'être* of extra-human powers. The important matter was propitiation, not where or how the powers came from, or why the powers existed at all.

Thus, while the official religion postulated a supreme Heaven as the guarantor of universal justice, the deities worshipped in households and cults throughout the empire were mainly responsible for the immediate welfare of the worshippers. On the moral level, people were bound to think on various occasions that the powers could equally choose to do harm or effect justice. The choice made, furthermore, depended less on the personal behavior of supplicants than on their propitiation or apotropaic arts. In other words, people regarded spiritual beings in the context of techniques. As exemplified by the daybooks, what mattered was external ritual conduct, not the propriety of moral behavior. Further, when the extra-human world was conceived with a point of view typical of secular government, such as occurred during the Han dynasty, the relationship between men and spirits tended to conform to a formalistic, bureaucratic style. It was only in the teaching of the early-Taoist Five Pecks of Rice movement that moral behavior was explicitly raised to the level of a prerequisite for joining the sect. Unethical acts brought down demonic illness, according to the teaching of Chang Lu. However, as I have suggested elsewhere, there was a sense of utilitarianism in the moral teachings of early Taoism, and goodness was literally to be calculated in numbers.[3]

An intriguing aspect of the nature of ghosts and spirits, however, deserves to be discussed. This, as I have already pointed out but did not elaborate in Chapter 4, is the idea that a ghost or spirit can be "killed." If the basic rationale of witchcraft is that man can actively control or threaten ghosts and spirits, then the idea of "killing the spirits and ghosts" could be seen as one step further in this direction. Yet what kind of ghost or spirit was it if it could be "killed?" It seems that such an idea implies that ghosts and spirits are limited beings. They are limited by their existence and forms, and they have beginnings and ends. Their power may be stronger than that of ordinary human beings, but man can still control them through magical or ritual acts. This is to say, there exist in the world other powers that can be utilized by man against ghosts and spirits. Moreover, this also reveals that man's conception of the nature of ghosts and spirits was based on his own existence. This concept considerably differs from the idea expressed in the *Book of Rites* that gods and ghosts lead a spiritual or transcendental existence. In ancient Greece, the gods were also conceived as having physical bodies and such human needs as appetite and thirst. Yet since gods were immortals, why did they have such needs? According to the interpretation of Vernant, the Greek vocabulary of the corporeal, the descriptions and concepts concerning body and its ability, desire, and character, did not acknowledge a distinction between body and soul, nor did it establish a radical break between the natural and the supernatural. The human body was composed of imperfect qualities, while the god's body was the flawless combination of those elements in their perfect condition. It was not that man created god according to his own image; on the contrary, "in all its active aspects, in all the components of its physical and psychological dynamism, the human body reflects the divine model as the inexhaustible source of a vital energy when, for instance, the brilliance of divinity happens to fall on a mortal creature."[4] Thus, the seemingly contradictory situation that gods also needed food and drink has its deep semantic and psychological background. The Greek example, as explained by Vernant, urges us to be cautious: there might have been some unexplored background to seemingly illogical beliefs. The idea that ghosts and spirits are "mortal" suggests that, although man imagines that ghosts and spirits existed in a purely spiritual state that could break all the material and physical restraints imposed on human beings by nature, he could not but use his own state of existence as a reference to construct the world of ghosts and spirits. Because human beings are mortal, ghosts and spirits can be killed. The various apotropaic methods described in the daybooks show that people believed that ghosts and spirits would respond to the physical acts of man. Thus, [the world of man is accessible to the "divine beings," and vice versa]

Belief in a Correlative Cosmological Order

A special feature of Chinese religion was a deep-rooted belief in a mechanical, correlative, cosmic order. This belief was much earlier than the theory of *yin-yang* and Five Phases. In fact, *yin-yang* theory as very early professed by Tsou Yen was probably a distillation of beliefs that had long been developed and transmitted amongst people in eastern China during the Warring States period, and with roots into deep antiquity.[5]

The central theme of this correlative cosmology, as explored in Chapter 4, was that man's fate has a one-to-one correspondence with such natural systems as time and direction. This reflects an understanding that time and space constituted the frame of reference for man's life and activities; and the same factors were also the axis of the progression of the world. The correspondence between man's actions and natural systems was built on this basic correlation. Exactly which systems of nature corresponded to human life, however, may not be constant, or consistent. Thus, new systems may be created, and mutually contradictory systems existed side by side, as we see in the daybooks. (Time and direction, with *yin-yang* and the Five Phases added later, therefore constituted the basic ingredients in almost all the divinatory methods as well as cult rituals in Chinese religion]

What, then, was the relationship between the actions of the spirits and gods and the cosmic order? As there was no concept of divine creation,[6] the spirits and gods were conceived as existing within, not outside, the cosmos. Did the gods have to conform to the cosmic order? In the intellectualized version of cosmology, such as that in *Monthly Ordinance*, the gods of every direction and time seem to have been bound to specific positions and were assigned specific functions. There was no sign of their having any initiative. They were, like everything else in the universe, part of the order.[7] In personal and household practices, as well as in cults, however, many gods and spirits were more freely involved in people's lives. Benjamin Schwartz has suggested that in the popular religious consciousness, there was "a sense of the divine world as a world of unaccountable forces and spirits not easily contained by any prescribed system of order, either divine or human."[8] Indeed, the forces and spirits were not easily contained, yet the situation was not hopeless. People employed all sorts of divinatory and exorcistic methods to deal with them.

Unlike the religions of the Greeks and Romans, therefore, one hardly finds a sense of mystery in the everyday religion of personal welfare in ancient China.[9] Neither was there divine revelation concerning the fate of man such as that found in Judeo-Christian traditions. In addition, there was also the idea that, although the cosmic order was impersonal, a man's fated events corresponding to that order were changeable. Since the cosmic events operated through dates and directions, as revealed in various daybook-type systems, and since these systems were known, a person could change his fate either by choosing to follow systems favorable to his particular needs, or by propitiating the spirits and employing mantic tools to ward off the evil ghosts. Such an idea was fundamentally based on a belief in magic.[10] In its developed form, such as Tung Chung-shu's theory of cosmic resonance, however, literary language often obscured this aspect. The act of "changing one's fate," one might add, is still a popular subject in the fortune-telling business in contemporary China. In other words, there was seldom total despair. Every problem elicited a solution: prayer, offering, divination, or exorcistic ritual. This reflected a confidence in the ability of man to deal with the powers successfully, that is to say, before one's death. It also reflected man's conception of his own position, as opposed to that of the spirits and gods: he was inferior only in respect to his power to battle demons or to affect the cosmos. But he could choose to employ whatever forces he could muster to suppress, to overcome, or to evade the powers of the ghosts and spirits. His inferiority with respects to the gods was not a moral problem but a physical one.

Death and the Netherworld

In ancient China, through the Han, the living propitiated the spirits or gods, hoping to continue their living world, or even do better, at death. My discussion in Chapter 7 indicates that the dead faced similar issues in the netherworld as on earth. What they could hope for in the afterlife was to solve such practical problems as paying taxes, serving corvée conscriptions, facing criminal charges, etc. What the messenger of the heavenly emperor could do was to solve these problems for man. No deity, however, was the recipient of a living person's prayer for a blessed afterlife. The living always aspired to a happy life in this world, rather than in the afterlife. Can this mean that people did not aspire to a blessed afterlife? If so, how shall we explain the bronze mirror inscriptions that abound with ideas of immortality? Is the existence of the immortals a form of afterlife? A common understanding is that immortality was realized in a deathless life. Thus, one cannot say that immortality came after death. Yet it is also a common idea that one could become an immortal after death. In people's minds, therefore, the meaning of the word "immortal-*hsien*" was rather hazy. Were the immortals merely "deathless?" Or were they "resurrected" after death?[11] These two possibilities oscillated in people's minds, so that the world of the immortals could exist simultaneously out of this world as well as in it, e.g., in a remote mountain.

In any case, our evidence indicates that the dead were supposed to have gone to a permanent home in the netherworld, never to return. When a person died, his family members provided him with an environment, not identical, but similar, to his living one. The dead became *hun* and *p'o*, which were "souls" without bodily substance, yet which could appear to the living under certain conditions. The conception of the netherworld, when it became recognizable, was modelled on the structure of Han imperial society. This is not unique among ancient cultures, although one cannot say that it was a prevailing phenomenon. The ancient Egyptians also had a clear idea of the netherworld, a world with earthly hardships and the notion of undergoing taxes and conscription labor, ruled by the just king Osiris and his entourage. Yet this court was not exclusively a netherworld phenomenon, since Osiris was not only the sovereign of the dead, but also the guarantor of agricultural abundance.[12]

It is important to note that we cannot assume a uniform conception and attitude toward death, but must admit that it was possible to have varieties of expressions. As pointed out in Chapter 7, we may overlook a subtle side of Chinese death and afterlife if we think that it was either optimistic or pessimistic about a human being's ability to achieve a blessed afterlife. Even in the seemingly universal Egyptian conception of a happy land of the dead there is evidence showing that death was not welcome and that the netherworld was a gloomy and uncertain place.[13]

Apotheosis

A prominent feature of Chinese religion was that humans could be apotheosized. The royal ancestors of the Shang, seen as abiding by the side of Ti and dispensing fortune or misfortune to descendants, can be considered as a form of apotheosis. More important, a person could be apotheosized not only after death, but sometimes even when alive. The existence of living shrines is a clear indication of this feature, as witnessed through the cult of Chang Huan.[14]

Thus, it was believed that certain people possessed extra-human powers both when alive and dead. Yet where did the powers come from? There is little evidence about this. The Greek hero-cults also assumed that the soul of a prominent dead person could somehow protect his relatives or countrymen. The heroes' power basically had to do with their might as warriors when alive, and their efficacy was shown by their appearing with the rank and file to fight together with their people.[15] In China, certain individuals were considered to have possessed divine power because of an extraordinary act. The avenging spirit of Tu-po is an example. However, the power was not always clearly defined, nor did it have any direct relationship with the nature of the act. Moreover, unlike the official apotheosis of the founding heroes of the Greek cities or the Roman emperors, in China apotheosis could be initiated by people outside of the official court.

It is also worth mentioning that there was no guarantee that deified persons would be benevolent. The cult of Chiang Tzu-wen 蔣子文 can be singled out as an example. He was a military commander at the end of the Eastern Han dynasty, and was killed by local bandits in an action. People later believed that his ghost had great power. Before he was officially canonized by the Chin government, people already regarded him as a *de facto* god and worshipped him at various cult places.[16] From the stories collected in Kan Pao's *Records of an Inquest into the Spirit-Realm (Sou-shen chi)*, we see that his power was not connected with his role as a military commander. In fact, the stories reveal that he was not really an upright person. He was said to have inflicted plague and calamities on the people for not worshipping him soon enough. He also killed people irrationally, or for very petty matters, while he himself seduced young girls. Kan Pao described him as "alcoholic and lascivious, acting irreverently and with no discretion" when he was alive.[17] It seems that his cult arose out of people's fear of his wrath and malice rather than benevolence. When he was officially apotheosized and worshipped by the rulers of the southern dynasties, however, his role as a helpful warrior god became more prominent.[18] This is also an example that shows that the origin of a cult does not have to be consistent with its later significance, and the meaning and function of a cult could change over time.[19]

If our observations on the confidence of man to deal with the spirits and ghosts is not far from the truth, there was really little obstacle to a person's taking the further step of becoming transcendent. Indeed, according to the Taoist theory, one could gain spiritual powers by proper training and eventually became an immortal. Judging from the existence of a number of shrines of the immortals, they were somehow worshipped by the people as divine figures. Thus, in a sense, the immortals were also apotheosized human beings. The differences among a man with supernatural power, an immortal, and an apotheosized person were probably not very clear in the popular conception.

Piety and Happiness

As the title of this book suggests, the central theme of the religious beliefs of the ancient Chinese was the search for personal welfare, or, to use a common saying, to seek for happiness and to avoid misfortune. The previous chapters have shown how this happiness was found. The remaining questions are, what was happiness and what was misfortune? It seems clear that ordinary people had similar ideas about what constituted a happy life: to keep away from sickness, fear, and hunger. This is reflected in the common saying: "Happiness is to have no misfortunes and illnesses." (*wu-tsai wu-ping pien-shih fu* 無災無病

便是福).” Happiness was the condition of life that one finds acceptable, while misfortune was the unacceptable. In this sense, to seek
for happiness is to avoid misfortune. There is of course more to happiness than merely avoiding misfortune: for the dead in the nether
world, happiness meant a life abundant with all the necessities of life;
for the living descendants, [longevity, wealth, and high social positions.]

All these considerations, it should be clear, are centered around
the human self. There was no divine commandment for the people to
follow, but they put forth hopes of happiness and expected the deities
to help them. Except for perhaps a few, happiness was expected to be
found not in heaven but on earth. As we have seen in Chapter 7, life
after death was not really an ideal option; people held proper burials
for their dead not only for the welfare of the dead, but even more for
the benefit of the living. Here we recall for the reader a most revealing
paragraph from a tomb-quelling text quoted before: “May the deceased
in the tomb not be disturbed or have fear, and stay tranquil as before.
It is decreed that the descendants shall increase in wealth and number,
without misfortunes for thousands of years.”

We have not dealt with the view of the elite, since our attention
was on the religious mentality of the wider populace. However, some
observations can be offered to compliment the impression conveyed
above. As expected, the intellectuals, especially those with Confucian
inclination, proclaimed that one’s happiness or misfortune rested on
one’s virtue, behavior, and fate, but not on material offerings toward
the supernatural beings. Thus says the Eastern Han scholar Wang Fu:

> Concerning one’s happiness or misfortune, it mainly depends on
> his conduct, but eventually decided by fate. Behavior is the mani-
> festation of one’s own character, fate is what heaven controls.
> One can certainly improve on what lies in himself, he can not
> know what lies in heaven. The prayers of *wu*-shamans could also
> help a person, yet not without his having virtue. . . . Thus only
> when one’s virtue and justice are installed, would ghosts and
> gods accept his offering. When ghosts and gods accept the offer-
> ing, one’s happiness and fortune would then become abundant.[21]

Similar opinions could be multiplied easily.[22] Even the Eastern Chin
scholar Ko Hung, who propagated the art of immortality in *Pao-p’u-*

(handwritten margin note: Virtue above all else)

tzu, expressed a disdain toward the "superstitious" worship of demons and insisted that virtue was as important as physical nurturing:

> As for those commoners, deficient in virtue, and unnurtured in body, wished to seek a prolongation of years through the sacrifice of three animals and wine and food, and imprecations directed toward the ghosts and gods, what misconception could be greater than this![23]

Thus, we see that the means propagated by the elite to achieve happiness differs from that upheld by the common populace. Yet the nature of hope itself seems to have been the same in both cases. Excepting hopes related to the grandiose idea of promoting the welfare of society and state, the personal benefit that an intellectual hoped to gain from religious activities differed little from the common people. The Eastern Han scholar Ts'ui Shih was a good example. In his *Ssu-ming yüeh-ling*, the *Monthly Ordinance for the Four Classes of People*, he listed various religious activities around the seasons, to be participated by elite and farmers alike.[24]

From texts such as these, it seems that the hopes of the ancient Chinese in religious activities were fundamentally this-world oriented. The question is, was there unconditional devotion in such beliefs? By this, I mean did the devotee have complete trust in the divine efficacy and benevolence of his/her god, and as a believer was he/she not in a state of mind to bargain for personal welfare? This involves the devotee's conceptions about the relationship between religious piety and happiness. It is clear that not everyone who made sacrifices and offered prayers could be blessed by the deities. How did they explain the "injustice" they suffered, given the fact that they had performed the proper rituals and maintained honorable conduct? Before the introduction of the Buddhist idea of *karma*, or the peculiar idea of *ch'eng-fu* (承負, inherited evil) in the *Scripture of Supreme Peace*,[25] various ideas relating to theodicy might have solved some of the problems, but perhaps not entirely.[26] In sum, complete devotion may not have been difficult to achieve, but devotion without underlying *do ut des* relationship between the human and the divine was something that has yet to be discovered.

Epilogue

In the sixth century, the monk Hui-chiao 慧皎 (A.D. 496–554) compiled the biographies of eminent monks who lived before his time.[27] When describing the deeds of An Shih-kao 安世高, a Parthian monk who made his career in China as a translator of Buddhist texts, he stated:

> He was known for his filial piety when he was young, and was diligent and intelligent in learning. He was versed not only in foreign texts, but also in the "Seven Stars," the "Five Phases," medical recipes, exotic magic, as well as the languages of birds and beasts. Once when walking he saw a flock of swallows, he suddenly told his companions: "The swallows say: Someone shall send food (to us)." After a while it indeed happened. Everyone was amazed.[28]

It may seem somewhat surprising that Hui-chiao should have attributed to An Shih-kao those mantic abilities that were not directly related to his career as a Buddhist scholar. When we look at the *Biographies of the Eminent Monks*, however, many are said to have possessed various supernatural abilities: flying, transforming themselves into multiple persons, taming wild beasts, moving hundreds of miles in an instant, crossing a river without a boat, prophecy, magical healing, and controlling ghosts and spirits. In fact, Hui-chiao established a special category titled *shen-i* 神異, or thaumaturgy, although many monks in the other categories possessed similar abilities.[29]

Why Hui-chiao included such information in a biography of an eminent monk is related to another more extensive problem: the origin and function of supernatural abilities of monks not just in the *Biographies of the Eminent Monks* but throughout early Chinese Buddhist literature. As has been pointed out, many supernatural abilities can also be found in the Indian Buddhist tradition, and themes of immortality may have been due to the influence of the Taoist religion.[30] However, even though some of these supernatural abilities may have come from the Indian tradition, their function in the biographies should be explained in terms of the Chinese people who were the audience and target of Buddhist proselytization.

Ko Hung's *Biographies of the Immortals* reveals, however, that the supernatural powers of eminent monks were essentially the same as those possessed by immortals.[31] This reflects not only how such monks and Taoist seekers presented themselves, or how the compilers presented them, but, more important, what their images were in the eyes of the people. Undoubtedly, both *Biographies of the Immortals* and *Biographies of the Eminent Monks* were written for a literary audience. They not only preserved fantastic stories, but also propagated respective religious tenets through the help of literary adepts. In this regard, they are similar to the Western hagiographies of the Middle Ages.[32] In the European case, it has been pointed out that the works of the clergy, since they were produced in order to persuade, were made attractive by design and can be studied as sources of popular mentality.[33] In the same way, one may assume that the biographies of immortals and eminent monks could reflect the religious mentality of the non-elite to a certain extent.

After relating the stories of theurgists, Hui-chiao defended supernatural powers: "The use of divine methods was to subdue the powerful, to destroy the uncouth, to curb the fierce, and to solve disputes."[34] He did not deny the existence of ghosts and spirits,[35] nor the magical powers of Taoists, but only refuted the appropriateness of their art.[36] Such a rebuke of Taoist magic only strengthens the view that descriptions of eminent monks and immortals were products of their time and reflections of a common religious mentality. This mentality could be detected in many other contemporary documents.[37] The situation of early Christianity was similar. Pagans and Christians both believed in the effectiveness of miracles and prophecies. The problem then was not which was false, but which group, or system, had greater power. Thus, Porphyry, a pagan philosopher and student of religion of the third century, says in the same spirit as Hui-chiao, that Christians "have performed some wonders by their magic arts," but adds that "to perform wonders is no great thing," for Apollonius and Apuleius and many others have done as much.[38]

If we return to An Shih-kao, we see that, besides possessing supernatural abilities, he was also a filial son and was diligent in learning, which is a typical description of a good Confucian scholar. His knowledge of the "Seven Stars" and "Five Phases," on the other hand, places him in the category of *fang-shih* magicians. Thus, what is presented is a composite image: a monk with some of the admirable Confucian and Taoist attributes, as well as traces from the ancient everyday, personal beliefs. This could not have been accidental. It reflects how traditions from different sources were blended in the mind of the author, or in the conception of the contemporary Buddhist circle. This composite image foreshadows the syncretistic development of Buddhist, Taoist, and Confucian teachings in the later era.[39]

In ancient Greece, it has been argued, common people, or peasants, did not really believe in the truth of their myths, but kept faith in the numerous local cults of heroes and nymphs, even after the collapse of the classical city-states. These local cults were the true religious life of the common people. Christianity changed the upper stratum of the official religion by replacing the pagan gods with a monotheistic God, yet the substratum, the ubiquitous mode of religious expression, changed only very slowly.[40] For religion has always been the most conservative social force binding society across political and social disruptions. In the centuries after the Han, Buddhism and Taoism formed the new religious horizon of China. However, the soil on which they grew was something that scholars of Chinese religion had rarely described in its own right. This soil was the religious mentality of the people, the basis on which Buddhist and Taoist institutions thrived. The recognition and articulation of this basal religious mentality, which I have attempted in this book, is vital in our understanding of the development of Chinese religions in subsequent eras. The development of Buddhism and Taoism should be seen not only as the triumph of doctrines, but also in the light of the continuous development of this religious base.

I did not engage in a comprehensive comparison between Chinese popular religion and Greek or Near Eastern religions. It is not my intention, nor is it compatible with the scope of the present study. I have, however, included in my discussions some comparative material, in the hope that they might provoke further discussions by scholars interested in the wider significance of the phenomenon of religion. I submit that the similarities between some aspects of Chinese religion and the non-Chinese demonstrate that human religiosity prescribes elements that are fundamental to every society. The differences, on the other hand, clearly delineate the peculiar environment and problems of each society. This study is only a small contribution toward our understanding. If it arouses the attention of the scholarly community so that more work is undertaken, it will have served its purpose.

Notes

Introduction

1. See F. C. Grant ed. 1953: 20–39; A. D. Nock 1933: 1–16; F. E. Peters 1970: 446–479.

2. Yü Ying-shih 余英時 1980: 205–329; E. Balazs 1964: 226–254.

3. See the classic study by T'ang Yung-t'ung 湯用彤 1962: 188 ff.; also Jen Chi-yü 任繼愈 ed. 1981: 106–121; A. F. Wright 1959: 21 ff.

4. For example, see E. Zürcher 1972: 2; K. Ch'en 1964: 48 ff.; P. Demieville 1956: 19–38.

5. Jen Chi-yü 1990: 17–18; Miyakawa Hisayuki 宮川尙志 1974: 143–147.

6. M. P. Nilsson 1941–50: 682; quoted in E. R. Dodds 1965: 1–2.

7. P. Byrne 1988: 3–28.

8. The term "religious mentality" refers partly to the psychological factors, partly to the unnoticed customs or traditions that influence the development of belief. For a discussion of this term, see A. Gurevich 1988: 12–20.

9. On popular religious expression in the Han period, see A. Seidel 1987. See also M. Loewe 1982, for a general introduction to the ideas of the elite. Two short surveys of Chinese religions with emphasis on the modern popular religions are D. L. Overmyer 1986 and C. Jochim 1986. For an overview of the state of the field, see D. L. Overmyer et al. 1995.

10. For example, the tomb paintings and reliefs of the Han period often

include images of demons and monstrous animals as well as gods and immortals. See K. Finsterbusch 1966: 287–288; 1972: 294–296 for some monstrous beasts. See also Hayashi Minao 1974: 223–306; 1989: 127–218. For a study of Han tombs, see Mu-chou Poo 1993a.

11. For a discussion of Han ideas on thrifty versus rich burial, see Mu-chou Poo 1990. See also Chapter 8 below.

12. On the methodology of the study of popular culture, see P. Burke 1978: 23 ff. A collection of important papers on popular culture in Europe is that of Steven L. Kaplan ed. 1984. On the Chinese side, see C. Bell 1989; C. Jochim 1988; Steven Sangren 1984. I return to this problem later in this chapter.

13. For a preliminary effort, see Mu-chou Poo 1993. See also Chapter 4 below.

14. See Byrne 1988: 3–28. The state of the field is given in W. Lessa and E. Z. Vogt eds. 1979. A historical overview of definitions is in Eric J. Sharpe 1986, see also M. B. Hamilton 1995: 1–20.

15. As suggested by A. Bharati ed. 1976.

16. M. E. Spiro 1963: 96.

17. R. Horton 1960: 211.

18. J. Goody 1961: 157.

19. See the discussion on the problem of "commoners" and literacy in Chapter 7 below.

20. For examples, Li Yih-Yuan 李亦園 1992: 64–94; Sung Kuang-yü 宋光宇 1995; Stephan Feuchtwang 1992. Also of interest are: Robert P. Weller 1987; Jordan and Overmyer 1986; S. Teiser 1995.

21. Valerie Hansen 1990.

22. Teiser 1988.

23. Feuchtwang 1992: 7.

24. See the collection of essays in P. H. Vrijhof and J. Waardenburg eds. 1979. For the use of the term "popular religion" in the European setting, see Natalie Z. Davis 1982: 321–343, in Steven Ozment ed. 1982: 321–343; Mary R. O'Neil 1986: 222–226.

25. R. Redfield 1956.

26. See the works of Sangren, Jochim, and Bell, cited above.

27. As discussed by C. K. Yang 1976: 3–6. Yang proposes two characteristics, the "diffused" and the "institutional."

28. C. K. Yang 1976. A recent example of this view is Cheng Chih-ming 鄭志明 1986: 1–3.

29. Marcel Granet 1932, 1975.

30. Freedman 1979: 1–29.

31. For chronology, see E. L. Shaughnessy 1991: 217–235.

32. See Chang Ssu-ch'ing 張素卿 1991: 95–109; 152–159.

33. J. J. M. de Groot 1892–1910.

34. For a critical view of de Groot's work, see M. Freedman 1979: 351–369.

35. Freedman 1979: 351–369.

36. Benjamin Schwartz 1985: 408.

37. Schwartz 1985: 410.

38. David Johnson 1985: 34–72, esp. 56; Johnson recently stated that elite and popular mentalities in traditional China differed sharply in the realm of religion, but were not isolated from each other and were in constant dialogue. See Johnson 1995: 8.

39. One might ask, for example, why Johnson divides the grid into three degrees instead of four or more? See Jochim 1988: 18–24. The European side of the problem is discussed ably by Burke 1978: 23–64.

40. Jordan and Overmyer 1986: 7–12; 276–280.

41. Teiser 1988.

42. Weller 1987.

43. Max Weber 1951.

44. Weller 1987: 11.

45. Yang 1976: 20–21; 294–340. See also Jochim 1986: 157–162.

46. P. Steven Sangren 1987: 4.

47. A relevant, though not parallel, situation was that of Greco-Roman Egypt, where most people, rich or poor, were part of the popular religious cults, and only the temple priests were the keepers of the official tradition. See F. Dunand 1984.

48. In our period, it is impossible to define "official" and "popular" religion as precisely as Romeyn Taylor did for the Ming dynasty: "By 'official religion' I mean that comprehensive body of religious practice that was defined and prescribed in legal documents for all levels of society. By 'popular religion' I mean the loosely systematized array of cults that developed outside the official religion without either the sanction of the law or the authority of the officially registered and regulated Buddhist and Taoist clergies." See Taylor 1990: 128.

49. This view is inspired by R. Chartier 1984: 233.

50. E. Zürcher 1990: 158–182.

51. Basic introductions are Chung-kuo she-hui k'o-hsüeh-yüan k'ao-ku yen-chiu-so 中國社會科學院考古研究所 1984; K. C. Chang 1980; 1986; Cho-yun Hsu and Katheryn M. Linduff 1988; Li Xueqin 李學勤 (Li Hsüeh-ch'in) 1985; Wang Zhongshu 1982.

52. Poo 1993a: Chapter 7; also see Chapter 7 below.

53. For early Chinese texts, see M. Loewe ed. 1993. Interested readers should refer to this basic work in the following chapters whenever a traditional text is mentioned.

54. For two recent summaries of the newly discovered texts of the Warring States and Ch'in-Han period, see Li Hsüeh-ch'in 1994; M. Loewe 1994.

Roots of a Religion of Personal Welfare

1. Sextus Empiricus, *Outlines of Pyrrhonism* III. 218–238; quoted in F. C. Grant ed.1953: 100.

2. William C. Hayes 1965: 119–120; Michael A. Hoffman 1979: 110, 196.

3. An important work on the Egyptian concept of the western land of the dead is that of Hermann Kees 1956: 59ff.

4. For example, Hoffman 1979: 199.

5. The eastern sky was one possibility, cf. Henri Frankfort 1961: 105–123; Kees 1956: 59–66; Assmann 1995.

6. On the Yang-shao culture, see Kwang-chih Chang 1986: 108 ff.

7. Chung-kuo k'o-hsüeh-yüan k'ao-ku yen-chiu-so and Shan-hsi-sheng

Hsi-an Pan-p'o po-wu-kuan eds. 中國科學院考古研究所、陝西省西安半坡博物館編 1963: 219.

8. See Chin Tse-kung 金則恭 1981. For a summary, see Mu-chou Poo 1989.

9. *Li-chi chu-shu* 禮記注疏 9/16.

10. Chung-kuo k'o-hsüeh-yüan k'ao-ku yen-chiu-so and Shan-hsi-sheng Hsi-an Pan-p'o po-wu-kuan eds. 中國科學院考古研究所、陝西省西安半坡博物館編 1963: 220.

11. For discussion, Lei Chung-ch'ing 雷中慶 1982. This practice is actually a world-wide phenomenon, see M. Eliade 1984: 9-10; Seton Lloyd 1984: 46–47.

12. Chung-kuo k'o-hsüeh-yüan k'ao-ku yen-chiu-so and Shan-hsi-sheng Hsi-an Pan-p'o po-wu-kuan eds. 中國科學院考古研究所、陝西省西安半坡博物館編 1963: 181–185; Shih Hsing-pang 石興邦 1962.

13. Shih Hsing-pang 石興邦 1962: 326. The assertion that there was a stage in Chinese history dominated by totemism, however, must remain a hypothesis.

14. See Wen I-to 聞一多 1975: 117–138. For a review of the fish-style decorations on neolithic pottery, see Liu Yün-hui 劉雲輝 1990.

15. See, for example, Jordan Paper 1986. For discussions from the mythological point of view, see Sun Tso-yün 孫作雲 1943; 1945; 1946.

16. See Louisa G. F. Huber 1981.

17. Wu Hung 1985. For a comprehensive study of these signs, see Teng Shu-p'ing 鄧淑蘋 1993. Salviati 1994 suggests a possibile iconographic connection between the bird motive and the "feathered man—immortal" of the Han era, which is plausible but impossible to substantiate. See also Wu Hung 1995: 37–43.

18. Liao-ning-sheng wen-wu k'ao-ku yen-chiu-so 遼寧省文物考古研究所 1986: 1–17. For a summary of the recent discussions, see Elizabeth Childs-Johnson 1992; also see Jordan Paper 1978: 28–30.

19. For a discussion of dragon worship, see M. Loewe 1987.

20. Sun Shou-tao and Kuo Ta-shun 孫守道、郭大順 1986; T'ang Ch'ih 湯池 1994. For other prehistorical "altars," see Ch'ang-wei ti-ch'ü i-shu-kuan 昌濰地區藝術館 1977; Chung-kuo k'o-hsüeh-yüan k'ao-ku yen-chiu-so Kan-su kung-tso-tui 1974.

21. Wang Chen-chung 王震中 1988.

22. P'u-yang-shih wen-wu kuan-li wei-yüan-hui 濮陽市文物管理委員會 1988. See a critique of this report, Yen Ming 言明 1988.

23. Chang Kwang-chih 張光直 1990c.

24. K. C. Chang 1990d, calls attention to the theory of pan-Asia-American shamanism that might have existed from the paleolithic era, as proposed by Peter T. Furst 1972: 261–278. See also K. C. Chang 1993. For shamanism in general, see M. Eliade 1951; I. M. Lewis 1971.

25. Ch'ing-hai-sheng wen-wu kuan-li-ch'u k'ao-ku-tui and Chung-kuo she-hui k'o-hsüeh-yüan k'ao-ku yen-chiu-so eds. 青海省文物管理處考古隊 and 中國社會科學院考古研究所編 1984: 116.

26. J. G. Andersson 1943: 241.

27. Li Yang-sung 李仰松 1986.

28. K. C. Chang 1993.

29. Yeh Mao-lin 葉茂林 1992.

30. K. C. Chang 1990b; *idem*. 1989.

31. K. C. Chang 1980: 339.

32. For example, out of 109 burials at the site of Tao-shih, only seventeen are equipped with funerary objects; and at the cemetery of Liu-wan, twenty per cent of the 564 graves can be considered as "rich burials." See Shan-tung ta-hsüeh li-shih-hsi k'ao-ku chuan-yeh 山東大學歷史系考古專業 1980: 13 ff; Ch'ing-hai sheng wen-wu kuan-li-ch'u k'ao-ku tui and Chung-kuo k'o-hsüeh yüan k'ao-ku yen-chiu-suo Ch'ing-hai tui 青海省文物管理處考古隊、中國科學院考古研究所青海隊 1976: 365 ff. See also Shan-tung-sheng wen-wu kuan-li-ch'u and Chi-nan-shih po-wu-kuan 1974: 8–9.

33. K. C. Chang 1986: 107 ff.

34. K. C. Chang 1990b; *idem*. 1989. For the rise of political authority, see K. C. Chang 1983d: 107–129.

35. See K. C. Chang 1980.

36. For an introduction, see David N. Keightley 1978; also Chang 1980: 1–65; Tsung-Tung Chang 1970.

37. Ch'en Meng-chia 陳夢家 1956: 561–604; Hu Hou-hsüan 胡厚宣 1959; Chang Tsung-tung 1970; Itō Michiharu 伊藤道治 1956; Ikeda Suetoshi

池田末利 1981: 25–63. Itō marks five developmental stages of the Shang idea of ancestor spirit, corresponding to the five periods of the oracle bone inscriptions discovered at An-yang: from emphasis on the importance of natural spirits in the first stage to the final establishment of the absolute power of the ancestor spirits, corresponding to the growth of a strong patriarchal royal authority. But the entire corpus of oracle bone inscriptions found at An-yang represents only the later years of Shang history, which does not warrant such complicated "development." Robert Eno 1990 questions the existence of an omnipotent "god on high" in Shang religion. See also a recent general account, Julia Ching 1993: 15–50.

38. Keightley 1978: 211–225.

39. See K. C. Chang 1990a; 1990b; 1993a.

40. This idea was inspired by the theory of M. Eliade that emphasized the separation of man from the divine world as the reason for the rise of shamans, for they alone possessed the abilities to communicate with the divine beings. Ch'en Meng-chia also thinks that "although the king himself was the political leader, he was at the same time the head of the *wu*-shamans." See Ch'en Meng-chia 1936: 535.

41. K. C. Chang 1983c; 1990a; 1983d: 56 ff. For a similar view that sees the king as a *wu*-shaman, see Eichhorn 1973: 25–28.

42. K. C. Chang 1990c.

43. K. C. Chang 1990c: 93–94.

44. This assumes the definition of "shaman" according to Eliade's model. David Keightley, "Royal Shamanism in the Shang: Archaic Vestige or Central Reality?" paper presented at the Workshop on Divination and Portent Interpretation in Ancient China, Berkeley, June 20–July 1, 1983. K. C. Chang 1970: 263–264, maintains that the *wu*-shamans were not the determining personnel in the Shang ancestor cult.

45. See Chiang Hsiao-yüan 江曉原 1991, Chapter 3.

46. Jordan Paper 1978. On shamanic masks, see M. Eliade 1951: 167–168.

47. Paper 1978: 36; *idem*. 1995: 82 restates his position. However, see Powers 1995 for an in-depth discussion of the meaning of decorative patterns on bronzes.

48. Liu Shih-o 劉士莪 and Huang Shang-ming 黃尚明 1993.

49. Li Xueqin 1992.

50. Wang Tao 1992. A radical view is that of Minao Hayashi 1990, who holds that *t'ao-t'ieh* was the image of Ti (帝).

51. See Sarah Allan 1991: 124–170. As a balance to Allan's argument, see Robert Bagley 1992.

52. Virginia C. Kane 1974–75; K. C. Chang 1980: 39–60; Robert W. Bagley 1988; *idem.* 1990.

53. Shan-tung-sheng po-wu-kuan 山東省博物館 1972.

54. Max Loehr 1968:13: " . . . the ornaments on Shang bronzes . . . cannot have had any ascertainable meaning—religious, cosmological, or mythological—meanings, at any rate, of an established literary kind." A recent conference rekindled the debate between those who consider the primary importance of the *t'ao-t'ieh* as a decorative motif (Robert W. Bagley, Jessica Rawson) and those who consider that the *t'ao-t'ieh* was the key to the religion of Shang religion (Sarah Allen). See Whitefield 1992. See also L. Kesner 1991; M. Powers 1995.

55. For examples, see M. Alliot 1949–54; D. Arnold 1962; A. R. David 1973.

56. For example, on temple-relief themes, see J. Osing 1977: 65 ff. Also Mu-chou Poo 1995a: Chapter 3.

57. Ho-nan-sheng wen-hua-chü wen-wu kung-tso-tui and Chung-kuo k'o-hsüeh-yüan k'ao-ku yen-chiu-so eds. 河南省文化局文物工作隊、中國科學院考古研究所編 1959: 25; Chung-kuo k'o-hsüeh-yüan k'ao-ku yen-chiu-so 中國社會科學院考古研究所 1987: 128.

58. See, for example, W. Hochstadter 1952: 88–90. For a crude *t'ao-t'ieh* on a clay bowl, see William Watson 1966: 56, Ill. 38.

59. Kesner 1991.

60. Ch'en Meng-chia 1956: 20 ff.; Chang Ping-ch'üan 1988: 31 ff. Recent archaeology has discovered what may be oracle bones at a Yang-shao site at Hsi-ch'uan Hsia-wang-kang in Ho-nan, see Ho-nan-sheng wen-wu yen-chiu-so and Ch'ang-chiang liu-yü kuei-hua pan-kung-shih k'ao-ku-tui Ho-nan fen-tui eds. 河南省文物研究所、長江流域規劃辦公室考古隊河南分隊 1989: 200; the earliest bones come from the Fu-ho 富河 culture, Inner Mongolia. See Li Ling 李零 1992: 52–59.

61. Ch'en Meng-chia 1956.

62. K. C. Chang 1988: 168.

63. For oracle bones in other cultures, see A. L. Kroeber 1948: 476–478; Li Heng-ch'iu 李亨求 1982.

64. Ho-nan wen-wu kung-tso i-tui 河南文物工作一隊 1957: 70.

65. The so-called "non-royal oracle inscriptions" found at the Shang capital are still a subject of unresolved debate; see Li Chin 李瑾 1984.

66. See Cho-yun Hsu and Katheryn M. Linduff 1988: 63–64. A more detailed description is Ch'en Ch'üan-fang 陳全芳 1988: 101–157. Although the Chou predynastic rulers were not "commoners," they at least did not belong to the Shang royal family.

67. Ch'en Meng-chia 1956: 573–577. It is not clear, however, whether these "nature deities" themselves were considered animate or whether human or other spirits inhabited them. See Sarah Allan 1979: 1–21.

68. K. C. Chang 1983b: 346.

69. The mingling of the human and the divine world was not unique to the Shang. The ancient Greeks, for example, believed that the Olympian gods lived "on earth," i.e., Mount Olympus, and that they could rescue or punish mortals at will when prayers were pronounced. This is the traditional view of Homer and the tragedians, and is an important aspect of Greek religion. The ancient Mesopotamians saw their world as full of spirits closely related to daily life. The world itself was the stage of the deities, and men were only part of the divine drama. See H. Frankfort *et al.* 1977: 125–184; Thorkild Jacobsen 1976. The word "supernatural" is inapplicable in both the Greek and the Mesopotamian cases.

70. Ch'en Meng-chia 1956. The "pragmatic" nature of Chinese ancestor worship has often been mentioned, e.g., S. Allan 1979: 19.

71. Ch'en Meng-chia 1956: 523–529; 552–557.

72. Keightley 1978: 132, 135.

73. B. Karlgren 1936; *idem*. 1937. See a recent assessment by Jessica Rawson 1990: 32–38.

74. K. C. Chang 1976b.

75. K. C. Chang 1976b; Hsü Fu-kuan 徐復觀 1969: 15–35.

76. Ch'en Meng-chia 1956: 580; Ch'ao Fu-lin 晁福林 1990; Eno 1990.

77. For example, see the inscription of Ta Yü ting: "The honorable king Wen had received the mandate from Heaven." See Kuo Mo-jo 郭沫若 1957: 5.

78. Hsu and Linduff 1988; H. G. Creel 1970: 81 ff.; D. Howard Smith 1970: 12–31; Schwartz 1985: 50–52. For the identification of Shang-ti with *t'ien*, as well as the changing importance of the concept of these two terms in the Chou documents, see Hsü Fu-kuan 1969: 36–41; Creel 1970: 493–506, thinks that *t'ien* was a concept referring to the Chou ancestors collectively. Also see Fu Ssu-nien 傅斯年 1952: 1–201. For a recent historical and philosophical discussion of *ti*, *shang-ti*, *t'ien*, and *ming*, particularly in the thought of Confucius, see David L. Hall and Roger T. Ames 1987: 195–216. Hall and Ames emphasize that "although there is an unmistakable anthropomorphic interpretation of deity in this period, neither *ti* nor *t'ien* is ever presented as a transcendent deity." (p. 204)

79. Ch'en Meng-chia 1956: 101–157. See also L. Vandermeersch 1980: 1–15, esp. p. 10; Wang Yü-hsin 王宇信 1986.

80. "Shih Ch'iang *p'an* 史墙盤," quoted and translated in Edward L. Shaughnessy 1991: 185.

81. Fu Ssu-nien 1952: 92–99; Hsu and Linduff 1988.

82. See Creel 1970: 94–100; Hsü Fu-kuan 1969: 20–35. Hsü emphasizes the idea of *ching* 敬, or reverence, toward one's own behavior, as the central concept for a responsible person with humanistic spirit. However, his examples of "humanistic spirit" are basically political proclamations.

83. For the official religion of western Chou, see L. J. Bilsky 1975: 32–58.

84. Granet 1932; Shirakawa Shizuka 白川靜 1979, both depend upon the material in *Shih-ching* to reconstruct the life of the Chou people.

85. Legge 1985 IV: 232–233. My translation follows that of Legge unless otherwise noted.

86. Granet 1932: 155–166; 198–202. For the text, see *Lü-shih ch'un-ch'iu* 呂氏春秋 2/1a or *Li-chi chu-shu* 禮記注疏 14–17; *Chou-li chu-shu* 周禮注疏 15–16.

87. Granet 1932: 126–133; 200–206; 221. Ch'en Meng-chia 1937, also argues along the line of fertility cult, and emphasizes *kao-mei* as worship, as in ancestor shrines.

88. *Chou-li* 14/15–16.

89. *Han-shu* 漢書 99b/4106. See Granet 1932: 155–166.

90. *Lü-shih ch'un-ch'iu* 2/1a; *Li-chi chu-shu* 15/4–5; The two words *kung-shih* 弓矢, which Derk Bodde 1975: 244–261 explained as bows and

arrows, should simply be read as "arrows," which makes perfect sense to-gether with the previous clause, "given bows and cases." The character 媒 is interchangeable with 禖.

91. As Derk Bodde 1975: 260 argues .

92. Bodde 1975: 257. See Chapter 6 below.

93. *Lü-shih ch'un-ch'iu* 10/2a. Another version appears in *Li-chi* 禮記 17/13. Legge 1885: 299–300.

94. Granet 1932: 166–180, esp. 169, 179, claims that the tenth-month festival was also a sexual orgy celebrating the completion of the farming cycle.

95. Legge 1985 IV: 305–306. Legge translates *"p'i"* 羆, a kind of bear, as "grisly (grizzly)."

96. Legge 1985 IV: 309, translation mine.

97. On dream interpretation in ancient China, see Roberto K. Ong 1985; also see Rudolf G. Wagner 1988.

98. *Chou-li chu-shu* 24/13; 25/1. See Fu Cheng-ku 傅正谷 1988.

99. Legge 1985 IV: 98.

100. Chung-kuo k'o-hsüeh-yüan k'au-ku yen-chiu-so 中國科學院考古研究所 ed. 1962: 111.

101. On the relationship between divination and numbers in Ancient China, see Hsü Hsi-t'ai 徐錫台 1982.

102. See Jao Tsung-i 饒宗頤 1982; Li Ling 李零 1992: 218–255.

103. See Ch'ü Wan-li 屈萬里 1956. Ch'ü's idea that *I* originated from the oracle bone divination, however, needs to be discarded. Li Ching-ch'ih 李鏡池 maintains that proto-*Chou-i* divination statements only appeared during the latter half of the Western Chou. See Li Ching-ch'ih 1978: 130–150. Li Hsüeh-ch'in 1992: 1–14, concludes that the divination statements were very probably formed in early Chou, and no later than mid-Chou.

104. For a summary of the subjects divined in *I-ching*, see Kao Heng 高亨 1984: 59–109.

105. See Kao Heng 1984: 60, 61, 65, 66, 74.

106. See Chapter 4 below for divination subjects and methods presented in the *jih-shu*.

107. Legge 1985 IV: 321.

108. Ch'en 1956: 237–249.

109. Legge 1985 IV: 25 translation mine.

110. Legge 1985 IV: 205; The key term is "*wang* 望," which I translate as "to perform sacrifice." *Wang* is a term for ritual performance in general. See Ma Ch'ih-ying 馬持盈 1971: 190.

111. *Shih-ching* 7/4–5; Legge 1985 IV: 206.

112. *Han-shu* 28/1653.

113. Legge 1985 IV: 380–381. Translation mine.

114. Chung-kuo k'o-hsüeh-yüan k'ao-ku yen-chiu-so 中國科學院考古研究所 ed. 1962: 111.

115. Ling Ch'un-sheng 凌純聲 1959; B. Karlgren 1930. Both scholars argue that the worship of sexual organs represented the earliest form of ancestor worship with the graph for "ancestor" (*tsu* 且) having represented the phallus. See also Li Ling 李零 1992: 403–424.

116. Legge 1985 IV: 346. Translation slightly altered.

117. Legge 1985 IV: 255. Translation mine.

118. Legge 1985 IV: 312. More of similar tone, see Legge 1985 IV: 325–326.

119. Legge 1985 IV: 198–199, with minor changes.

120. *Tso-chuan* 左傳 19a/7; Legge 1985 V: 244.

121. For the problem of human sacrifice in China, see Huang Chan-yüeh 黃展岳 1974; 1990: 154–225. Other examples in *Tso-chuan* are discussed by Ku Te-jung 顧德融 1982.

Personal Welfare in the Context of Mantic Technique

1. Xenophanes on the true god; quoted in W. H. Auden ed. 1971: 68–69.

2. See a summary of the problem of the Chou dating in Fan Yü-chou 范宇周 1986. Also see David Nivison 1983. I follow Shaughnessy 1991: 217 ff.

3. See Hsu and Linduff 1988.

4. See Li Xueqin 1985: 16–17; Li Hsüeh-ch'in 1991a: 14–18.

5. Cho-yun Hsü 1965; T'ung Shu-yeh 童書業 1946; Yang K'uan 楊寬 1980. For material culture of this period, see Li Xueqin 1985.

6. See Bilsky 1975 vol. 1: 103–124.

7. *Tso-chuan* 6/11–15; Legge 1985 V: 46. I follow Legge's translation except for the last sentence.

8. *Li-chi* 46/4. See Legge 1885 v. 2: 202–203.

9. *Chou-li* 25–26.

10. The exact date of the composition of the three *"Books of Rites"*, i.e., *Chou-li*, *I-li*, and *Li-chi* is much debated. Scholars generally agree that part of the material may be dated to as early as the Eastern Chou. The date of the composition of *Li-chi* is held to be Han-dynasty, although one can hardly deny that, as with *Chou-li* and *I-li*, it may contain pre-Ch'in material; e.g., *Yüeh-ling* in *Li-chi*. My choice of textual passages tries merely to sketch a general sense of the situation.

11. On the content, style, and authenticity of *Tso-chuan* and other pre-Ch'in texts, see Hsu Cho-yun 1965: 183–192; B. Watson 1962: 19 ff.; M. Loewe ed. 1993.

12. *Tso-chuan* 9/8; Watson 1989: 207–208.

13. Another example of snake-omen is found in the sixteenth year of the Duke of Wen; see Legge 1985 V: 274.

14. *Tso-chuan* 48/10; Legge 1985 V: 668; with minor changes.

15. *Tso-chuan* 52/11–12; Legge 1985 V: 718, with minor changes.

16. For example, *Tso-chuan* 58/3 ; see Watson 1989: 213.

17. *Kuo-yü* 國語 1/10, . The same story also appears in *Tso-chuan* (Chao 23) see Legge 1985 V: 699.

18. There are numerous discussions on this subject. The following works are basic references: Feng Yu-lan 1952–53 vol. 2: 7ff.; Joseph Needham 1956 vol. 2: 232 ff.; Schwartz 1985: 350–382. See also Chapter 5 below.

19. *Tso-chuan* 51/15; Legge 1985 V: 709.

20. See Tu Wen-lan 杜文瀾 1986: 27, 29, 49, 56, 66, 74, 79; J. Riegel 1983.

21. *Tso-chuan* 14/15–16; Legge 1985 V: 171. Translation of the last two sentences mine.

22. It can be questioned, of course, how far one should go in defending

the "authenticity" of the children's rhymes. Problems such as the reason why these rhymes were preserved, and for what purpose, need to be studied. See Riegel 1983.

23. *Tso-chuan* 48/25; Legge 1985 V: 675.

24. Tzu Ch'an apparently made an apotropaic sacrifice to avert fire calamity. See *Tso-chuan* 48/17; Legge 1985 V: 671.

25. See Chapters 6 and 8 below.

26. There are at least thirty-six cases in *Tso-chuan* where bones or yarrow stalks are used in divination, see Liang Chao-t'ao 梁釗滔 1989: 128–133.

27. *Tso-chuan* 9/23; Legge 1985 V: 103.

28. See Chapter 4 below.

29. *Tso-chuan* 41/24; Legge 1985 V: 580.

30. The major finds are those from T'ien-hsing-kuan tomb no. 1, and Pao-shan tomb no. 2. See Hu-pei-sheng Ching-chou ti-ch'ü po-wu-kuan 湖北省荊州地區博物館 1982; Hu-pei-sheng Ching-sha-t'ieh-lu k'ao-ku-tui 湖北省荊沙鐵路考古隊 1991. For a study of the Pao-shan text, see P'eng Hao 彭浩 1991.

31. P'eng Hao 1991. See also Michael Loewe 1988b.

32. Wang Hsien-ch'ien 1971 11/211; B. Watson 1963: 85.

33. Wang Hsien-shen 1962 5/78.

34. Wang Hsien-shen 1962 19/356; Watson 1967: 127.

35. *Lü-shih ch'un-ch'iu* 3/5a.

36. Wang Hsien-ch'ien 1971 5/107–108; Watson 1963: 49.

37. *Li-chi* 3/15a–16b; Legge 1885 vol. 1: 94.

38. *Chou-li* 17/ 14a–b.

39. See Ch'en Meng-chia 1937; P'eng Chung-t'o 彭仲鐸 1935; Chan Ping-leung 1972: 107–156. For a different view of Ch'ü Yüan's status as a shaman, see Heather A. Peters 1985: 125–133, who suggests that Ch'ü Yüan was more a "ritual specialist" than a "shaman." For an analysis of the shamanistic element in *Ch'u-tz'u* from the perspective of literary forms and textual transmissions, see David Hawkes 1967; Fujino Iwatomo 藤野岩友 1969.

40. *Tso-chuan* 4/24; Legge, 1985 V: 33.

41. The famous story about the king of Sung's magical acts of shooting the effigy of heaven and slashing the earth is another example of the use of black magic. See *Chan-kuo ts'e* 戰國策 30/9b; 23/7b. For a discussion of target magic, see Riegel 1982. On black magic, see Li Hui 李卉 1960; H. Y. Feng and J. K. Shryock 1935.

42. *Tso-chuan* 39/3–4. On peachwood, see Bodde 1975: 84, 127.

43. The figure has been explained variously as the mountain god (Wang Jui-ming 王瑞明 1979); the god of the underworld (Ch'en Yao-chün 陳躍鈞 and Juan Wen-ch'ing 阮文清 1983); the dragon (P'eng Hao 彭浩 1988); an exorcist-demon (Chiang Wei-tung 蔣衛東 1991); and a shaman (Ch'iu Tung-lien 邱東聯 1994). See also Colin Mackenzie 1992.

44. *Tso-chuan* 47/22; Legge 1985 V: 665.

45. *Tso-chuan* 48/18; Legge 1985 V: 671.

46. *Tso-chuan* 14/26; Legge 1985 V: 180. A similar incident is found in *Li-chi chu-shu* 10/23.

47. Ch'en Meng-chia, 1956: 602–603; *idem*. 1936.

48. *Lü-shih ch'un-chiu* "Shun-min," 9/3. See S. Allen 1984; Edward H. Shafer 1951.

49. *Li-chi* 52/12; Legge 1885 vol.2: 307–308.

50. Sun I-jang 1974 12/276.

51. Sun I-jang 1974 8/139; Watson 1963: 95.

52. *Lun-yü chu-shu* 論語注疏 6/8; Legge 1985 I: 191.

53. *Tso-chuan* 21/21; Legge 1985 V: 296–297. Translation mine.

54. *Tso-chuan* 10/21–22; Legge 1985 V: 120, with minor changes.

55. *Kuo-yü* 國語 1/11–12. In some texts, Tan-chu is the son of Yao. See Sun Tso-yün 1946; Yüan K'o 袁珂 1987: 34.

56. Sun I-jang 1974 8/153 ; B. Watson 1967: 107.

57. Tu-po was killed unjustly by King Hsuan of Chou. His ghost appeared three years later and shot and killed the king as revenge. See *Kuo-yü* 1/11.

58. *Tso-chuan* 8/17; Legge 1972: 82.

59. *Ch'u-tz'u* "Ta-chao 大招"; See David Hawkes 1959: 110.

60. Sun I-jang 1974 8/141; Yüan K'o 1987: 69; J. Riegel 1989–90.

61. *Kuo-yü* 8/4b–5. *Shan-hai-ching* describes a snake in his left ear. See Yüan K'o 1981: 227; Regiel 1989–1990: 55–83.

62. *Tso-chuan* 26/29; Legge 1985 V: 374.

63. *Kuo-yü* 14/11b.

64. Wang Hsien-shen 1962 11/202. A similar idea is in *Huai-nan-tzu* 淮南子 13/6a: "Nowadays painters like to draw ghosts and demons and dislike drawing dogs and horses. Why? This is because ghosts and demons never appeared on earth, while dogs and horses can be seen daily."

65. Wang Hsien-shen 1962 10/182–183; W. K. Liao 1959: 7–8.

66. Wang Hsien-ch'ien 1971 15/270; Watson 1963: 134–135.

67. Hu-pei-sheng po-wu-kuan 湖北省博物館 1989 vol. 1: 28–45. For a discussion of *chen-mu-shou* and other Ch'u motifs, see Colin Mackenzie 1992.

68. See Jao Tsung-i 饒宗頤 and Tseng Hsien-t'ung 曾憲通 1985: pls. 1–7; Li Ling 1992: 167–185; N. Barnard 1972.

69. For a review, see Jao Tsung-i and Tseng Hsien-t'ung 1985: 152–210; see also Hayashi Minao 林巳奈夫 1971; *idem.* 1972.

70. *Tso-chuan* 26/8; Legge 1985 V: 357. Translation mine.

71. Similarly, *Tso-chuan* 12/23, the Duke of Chin says: "My sacrificial offerings have been abundant and pure; the spirits will not forsake but will sustain me." His minister replied: "I have heard that spirits do not favor personal intimacy, but that it is virtue to which they cleave." Legge 1985 V: 146.

72. *Tso-chuan* 14/22; Legge 1985 V: 177.

73. *Tso-chuan* 10/22; Legge 1985 V: 120, translation mine.

74. *Tso-chuan* 16/26–27.

75. *Lun-yü* 7/12; Legge 1985 I: 206.

76. Sun I-jang 1974 3/50.

77. Schwartz 1985: 135–172.

78. Ikeda Suetoshi 1981 vol.1: 199–215.

79. Wang Kuo-wei 王國維 1959 vol. 1: 19–26.

80. Ying-shih Yü 1987c: 370; *idem.* 1981.

81. *Tso-chuan* 44/13–14; Legge 1985 V: 618, translation mine.

82. Wang Hsien-shen 1962 6/104.

83. *Li-chi* 26/21.

84. I borrow Karlgren's idea of the "free" and "systematizing" texts, in Karlgren 1946: 201.

85. *Ch'u-t'zu chi-chu* 楚辭集注 136; Hawkes 1959: 104–105. I translate the term "yu-tu 幽都" as "dark city," rather than Hawkes's "Land of Darkness." The word *tu* usually means a "city," not a "land."

86. *Li-chi* 10/19.

87. Sun I-jang 1974 9/178; Watson 1967: 125.

88. On the ritual of recalling souls, see Yü Ying-shih 1987c; Li Ping-hai 李炳海 1989: 107ff.

89. Chang Cheng-lang 張政烺 1981: vol. 5, pp. 27–33.

90. Loewe 1982: 25–37; Yü Ying-shih 1087c.

91. *Tso-chuan* 2/20; Legge V: 6.

92. *Meng-tzu chu-shu* 孟子注疏 6b/8. Other occurrences include a passage in *Chuang-tzu*: "the earth worm has no sharp claws or teeth, no strong bones and sinews, yet it can eat the dirt above and drink the yellow spring below." (*Chuang-tzu chi-shih* 莊子集釋 601); and in *Kuan-tzu* 管子 8/5b: " . . . even if I were killed under the yellow spring, (my) death would be immortal."

93. See a detailed discussion by Egashira Hiroshi 江頭廣 1980. Another study, Nakahachi Masakazu 1979, unconvincingly argues that the Yellow Spring is related to the Yellow River and water, thus symbolizing a paradise.

94. Ho Shuang-ch'üan 何雙全 1989; Li Hsüeh-ch'in 李學勤 1990; D. Harper 1994.

95. For the tales of anomaly affairs, see Karl S. Y. Kao ed. 1985; Anthony C. Yu 1987. For a most recent and comprehensive study in English, see R. F. Campany 1996.

96. See Laurence G. Thompson 1989.

97. Hsu Cho-yun 1982: 423–452 ; Kuo Mo-jo 1951: 1–65.

98. Yü Ying-shih 1980: 1–108.

99. See Robert Eno 1990: 79 ff.

Newly Discovered Daybooks and Everyday Religion

1. *Job* 1: 6.

2. The main publication is Yün-meng Shui-hu-ti Ch'in-mu pien-hsieh tsu 雲夢睡虎地秦墓編寫組 1981. The slip numbers quoted are from this work, henceforth abbreviated as *SHT*. A new transcription of all the texts with commentary is Shui-hu-ti ch'in-mu chu-chien cheng-li hsiao-tsu 1990. For bibliography, see Hori Tsuyoshi 堀毅 1988: 438–442; Kan-su wen-wu k'ao-ku yen-chiu-so 甘肅省文物考古研究所 ed. 1989: 314–330.

3. For a recent study, with bibliography and corrections of published transcriptions, see Poo Mu-chou 1992. See also Li Ling 1993: 186–217; Liu Lo-hsien 1994. The material presented in this chapter is based on Poo 1992, 1993.

4. M. Loewe 1988; Li Ling 李零 1992: 39–43.

5. For general introductions to the structure of these divinational methods, see Kudō Motoo 工藤元男 1986; M. Kalinowski 1986; and Loewe 1988. Also an introduction to divination in ancient China, in M. Loewe and C. Blacker eds. 1981: 38–62.

6. *SHT*, no. 731.

7. *SHT*, nos. 884, 895 ver.

8. *SHT*, nos. 803, 809, 797, 801.

9. *SHT*, nos. 807, 823, 894 ver., 891 ver., 893 ver., 895 ver., 886 ver.

10. *SHT*, no. 818.

11. *SHT*, no. 887 ver.

12. *SHT*, nos. 799, 993.

13. *SHT*, no. 894 ver.

14. *SHT*, no. 892 ver.

15. *SHT*, nos. 806=1000, 817=983, 820=986, 822=988.

16. *SHT*, no. 811.

17. *SHT*, nos 812=978.

18. *SHT*, no. 890 ver.

19. *SHT*, nos. 869–878.

20. *SHT*, nos. 800, 870, 876, 802, 874.

21. *SHT*, nos. 870, 871.

22. *SHT*, nos. 797, 811, 991.

23. *SHT*, nos. 805, 809.

24. *SHT*, no. 813.

25. *SHT*, nos. 798, 992.

26. *SHT*, no. 873.

27. *SHT*, nos. 791, 869, 874.

28. *SHT*, nos. 743, 745, 763, 765, 771, 752 ver. The tomb owner of the Shui-hu-ti daybook had held some low-level local offices.

29. *SHT*, nos. 869, 870, 871, 877.

30. *SHT*, nos. 872, 873, 875.

31. *SHT*, nos. 741, 744, 761, 767, 771, 773, 856, 1027.

32. *SHT*, nos. 814, 815, 820, 829, 980.

33. *SHT*, nos. 733, 745, 753–754, 762, 767, 809, 813, 821, 826–838, 1005–1009.

34. *SHT*, nos. 856–68.

35. *SHT*, nos. 742, 755, 761, 824, 783 ver.–774 ver.

36. *SHT*, nos. 737, 741, 744, 756, 761, 767, 769, 771, 773, 820.

37. For details, see Poo 1992.

38. *SHT*, no. 781 ver. Similarly, no. 755.

39. Wang Ch'ung attests a "Book for Making Garments" in his time; Liu P'an-sui 1957: 477.

40. *SHT*, no. 829.

41. *SHT*, nos. 882 ver.–873 ver. Poo 1992.

42. For the origin of geomancy in China, see Yin Hung-chi 尹弘基 1989; Stephan Feuchtwang 1974; Richard J. Smith 1991: 131–171.

43. *SHT*, nos. 808 ver.–804 ver.

44. *SHT*, nos. 1039–1041.

45. *SHT*, no. 785 ver.

46. Ma-wang-tui Han-mu po-shu cheng-li-hsiao-tsu 馬王堆漢墓帛書 整理小組 1985 vol. 4: 49, "Wu-shih-erh ping-fang 五十二病方," *SHT* no. 210.

47. See Jao Tsung-i and Tseng Hsien-t'ung 1982: 20–23; Kudō Motoo 1990.

48. See Chapter 3.

49. *SHT*, nos. 741, 744, 767.

50. *SHT*, no. 797–798.

51. *Tso-chuan* 41/26.

52. *Huang-ti nei-ching* 黃帝內經 dated perhaps to the Warring States period or a little later, is the earliest extent medical treatise. The ideas in it, however, may be even older. See Chao P'u-shan 趙僕珊 1983: 31–34; Fan Hsing-chun 范行準 1989: 273–274; Unschuld 1985: 56, 106–108.

53. *SHT*, nos. 761, 938, 773, 804, 769.

54. *SHT*, nos. 762–775; 949–958.

55. For the military system of the Warring States period, see Li Chün-ming 李均明 and Yü Hao-liang 于豪亮 1981; Tu Cheng-sheng 杜正勝 1990: 49–96. A study of war in this period is Mark E. Lewis 1990.

56. See Yang K'uan 楊寬 1980, appen. "Chan-kuo ta-shih nien-piao 戰國大事年表."

57. *SHT*, no. 738.

58. *SHT*, nos. 827 ver.–814 ver.; 1148–1154 ver.

59. *SHT*, nos. 371–420.

60. *SHT*, nos. 380, 383, 395.

61. *SHT*, nos. 737, 744, 765, 769.

62. *SHT*, nos. 1044–1047.

63. Sun I-jang 1974: 17/316; W. K. Liao 1959 vol. 2: 233, with minor changes.

64. The full implication of this phenomenon must be considered in light of the socio-political situation of the late Warring States period, which warrants a sparate study. See Wu Shu-ping 吳樹平 1981.

65. Li Hsüeh-ch'in 李學勤 1985.

66. Donald Harper 1985. Some of the exorcistic methods mentioned in daybooks are rather similar to those found in the European demonology. See Ioan P. Couliano 1987: 144–173.

67. *SHT*, nos. 848 ver.–847 ver.

68. *SHT*, no. 862 ver.

69. *SHT*, nos. 859 ver.–858 ver.

70. For example, the *Tso-chuan* (Chao 4) states that "a bow of peach wood and arrows of thorn were employed to put away calamitous influences." Legge 1985 V: 596. Even in the *chieh* section itself, we can find the use of peach wood (nos. 872 ver., 869 ver.), mulberry wood (nos. 864–863 ver., 848 ver.), as well as *mu-chi* (a kind of wood) (nos. 871 ver., 868 ver., 845 ver., 830 ver.) as materials for making exorcist weapons. See Bodde 1975: 127–138.

71. *SHT*, no. 885 ver.

72. *SHT*, nos. 854 ver., 852 ver., 838 ver., 839 ver.

73. *SHT*, no. 834 ver.

74. *SHT*, no. 846 ver.

75. *SHT*, no. 862 ver.

76. *SHT*, nos. 819, 732.

77. *SHT*, nos. 869 ver.–868 ver.

78. *SHT*, nos. 865 ver.–863 ver.

79. Harper 1985; also see Chu T'ien-shun 朱天順 1982. The reader, however, should take note of the author's lack of historical perspectives.

80. *Li-chi* 46/4; Legge 1885 vol. 2: 203.

81. Sun I-jang 1974: 6/104–105, translation mine. See Liao 1959 vol. 1: 185–186.

82. *Chou-li* 37/7.

83. *Kuo-yü* 18/1a–2a. See K. C. Chang 1983a; 1976a: 162–163.

84. *SHT*, nos. 869 ver., 864 ver., 862 ver., 848 ver.

85. *SHT*, nos. 833 ver., 842 ver., 840 ver., 852 ver.

86. *SHT*, nos. 859 ver., 856 ver., 852 ver.

87. *SHT*, no. 764 ver.

88. See Tou Lien-jung 竇連榮 and Wang Kuei-jün 王桂鈞 1989.

89. *Shih-chi*, 28. For the worshipping of the White Emperor, p. 1358, the Azure Emperor, p.1360, the Yellow Emperor, p.1364. In Han times, the "Black" Emperor was added to the list. For a short introduction, see M. Granet 1975: 110 ff. Also see M. Loewe 1974: 166–168.

90. *SHT*, no. 734.

91. *SHT*, nos. 869 ver.–868 ver.

92. *Li-chi* 14; originally contained in the *Lü-shih ch'un-ch'iu* 1–12; another version is found in *Huai-nan-tzu* 4. See Loewe 1988.

93. For the employment of the Five-Phases theory in the *Jih-shu*, see nos. 974–978; 813 rev.–804 rev. See Liu Lo-hsien 1994: 431–440.

94. Schwartz 1985: 412, observes that "*Yin, yang* and the five elements . . . provided the 'theory' of many shared elite and popular beliefs. Yet they never seem to have totally displaced the role of spirits which resist incorporation into abstract schemes . . . one can thus find themes of correlative cosmology intricately interwoven with the active intervention of spirits . . ." I would suggest that, in the *JS* at least, the active intervention of spirits was still controllable and controlled.

95. Ho Shuang-ch'üan 何雙全 1989a. For some "Daybooks" of the Han period, see Kan-su-sheng po-wu-kuan and Chung-kuo K'o-hsüeh-yüan k'ao-ku yen-chiu-so 甘肅省博物館 and 中國科學院考古研究所 1964: 136–139; Kuo-chia wen-wu-chü ku-wen-hsien yen-chiu-shih, Ho-pei sheng po-wu-kuan and Ho-pei-sheng wen-wu yen-chiu-so Ting-hsien Han-mu chu-chien cheng-li-tsu 國家文物局古文獻研究室、河北省博物館、河北省文物研究所定縣漢墓竹簡整理組. 1981: 11–19; Ho-nan-sheng wen-wu yen-chiu-so Chou-k'ou ti-ch'ü wen-hua-chü wen-wu-k'o 河南省文物研究所周口地區文化局文物科. 1983: 21; Chang-chia-shan Han-mu chu-chien cheng-li hsiao-tsu 張家山漢墓竹簡整理小組. 1985.

96. For discussion, see Poo Mu-chou 1992: 259.

97. For example, Chang Ming-ch'ia 張銘洽 1988, identified sources that came from six different schools of divination in the various sections of the *jih-shu*.

98. *Shih-chi* 127/3222. Among these divination systems, the *Chien-ch'u, Ts'ung-ch'en*, and *Li* are found in the Shui-hu-ti daybooks, while others

are not explicitly mentioned. This may indicate that a number of the divination systems contained in the daybook later became independent, if they were not so from the beginning.

99. *SHT*, nos. 858–859.

100. H. Frankfort 1961: 1–29; Th. Jacobsen 1976: 11–17; J. Bottéro 1992: 211–231.

101. See Chapter 2 above.

102. For a discussion of this organismic cosmology, see F. W. Mote 1970: 17 ff.

103. *Han-shu* 30.

104. A convenient subject index of the contents of the Shui-hu-ti daybook is provided in Jao Tzung-i and Tseng Hsien-tung 1982. Most of the scholars agree that the daybook represents the lifestyle of the common people. A different view, however, is expressed by Okushi Atsuhiro 大節敦弘 1986, in which he maintains that the daybook reflects the daily life of the manorial aristocracy. For discussion, see Poo 1992.

105. *SHT*, no. 735.

106. *SHT*, no. 736.

107. *SHT*, nos. 761–762.

108. Kudō Motoo 1990. Also see Chang Wen-yü 張聞玉 1987.

109. See a detailed study and useful bibilography of this manuscript by Jao Tzung-i and Tseng Hsien-t'ung 1985: 71–85 for this brief section. See also Li Ling 1993: 167–185.

110. Jao and Tseng 1982: 97.

111. Lin Chien-ming 林劍鳴 1987: 71; Wang Kuei-chün 王桂鈞 1988: 66; Li Hsaio-tung 李曉東 and Huang Hsiao-fen 黃曉芬 1987. See the famous essay by Chia I 賈誼, *Kuo Ch'in Lun* 過秦論, in *Shih-chi* 6/276 ff. Although it is not easy to discredit all the accounts, one may suspect that the formation of this negative image of Ch'in culture may have been due to the animosity of the people of the Central Plain states, who were proud of their own cultural traditions, but who, ever since the Eastern Chou period, had been unable to curb the rapid growth of the "barbarian" Ch'in influence. For a reevaluation of the traditional conception of the Legalist tradition in the Ch'in state and empire, see L. B. Fields 1983.

112. Ho 1989; Kan-su-sheng wen-wu k'ao-ku yen-chiu-so ed. 甘肅省文物考古研究所編 1989: 7–28.

113. Representing this view is Lin Chien-ming 1993. It will be interesting to see, when the "*I 乙* " version of T'ien-shui Daybook is published, whether more gods and spirits are to be found.

114. Li Hsiao-tung and Huang Hsiao-fen 1987.

115. *SHT*, no. 858.

116. *SHT*, no. 808.

117. *SHT*, no. 932.

118. *SHT*, no. 1039. See Kudō Motoo 1988. An earlier study is Chiang Shao-yüan 江紹原 1937.

119. Sun I-jang 1974 12/270.

120. *Shih-chi* 127/3318.

121. See Yoshinami Takashi 1988. Also see Loewe 1988.

122. *Hsieh-chi pien-fang shu* 協紀辨方書 811.

123. One such "Daybook" published in 1991 in Taiwan, for example, still lists under each day various activities and their auspiciousness in a language almost the same as that found in the *jih-shu*. Its utilitarian nature, albeit modernized, is amply illustrated by a section that "predicts" the rise and fall of the stock market in a sexagenary cycle. (*Chung-kuo min-li*, distributed by the Farmers Association of Taipei County) For a study of divination in the late-impreial period, see R. J. Smith 1991.

124. Lin Chien-ming 1991.

125. See Kao Min 高敏 1979; also see Yü Ying-shih 1987b: 212–215.

126. This raises the question of why the tomb owner Hsi possessed such a text. Some scholars suggest that the purpose of his collecting the Daybooks (since there are two versions of *jih-shu* in his tomb) was to help him better understand and therefore control the local population. (See Kudō Motoo 1988; Lin Chien-ming 1991.) This is possible since, as a local official, he bore the responsibility to "teach" the people, as was made clear by the text *Wei-li chih-tao*.

127. *SHC* is probably the most controversial document in the study of ancient Chinese history and religion. Not only the date and the authorship

are uncertain; the unity and nature of the text itself is also problematic. From the *Han-shu I-wen-chih* 漢書藝文志 onward until the *Ssu-k'u ch'üan-shu* 四庫全書, it has been categorized by traditional scholars as a book about divination, ancient geography, or one of the earliest "novels." Modern scholars give it fashionable names such as "encyclopedia," "ethnography," or even "history of sciences." See Chung-kuo Shan-hai-ching hsüeh-shu t'ao-lun-hui 中國山海經學術討論會 ed. 1986: 7, 156, 241. It is generally assumed, however, that the earliest possible date of the composition of the text itself, or at least part of it (which is still in debate), cannot go beyond the Warring States period. See a recent review by Kominami Ichirō 1986.

128. Yüan K'o 1988: 17–20; for a bibliography and a useful introduction to the problems concerning the date of the text, see Riccardo Fracasso 1983. A translation and study of this text is R. Mathieu 1983.

129. For a series of studies on the forms of the monsters or demons in the *Shan-hai-ching*, see Itō Seiji 伊藤清司 1968–1969. A collection of the monsters and spiritual beings is found in John Wm. Schiffeler 1978.

130. Yüan K'o 袁珂 1980: 8, 15, 38, 47, 58, 136.

131. For a recent discussion of the changing images of Hsi Wang-mu, see Riccardo Fracasso 1988.

132. Yüan K'o 1980: 8.

133. Yüan K'o 1980: 82.

134. Yüan K'o 1980: 89.

135. Yüan K'o 1980: 227.

136. Sun I-jang 1974 1/141–142.

137. See Jao Tsung-i and Tseng Hsien-t'ung 1985: 152–210. For the images of the twelve gods, which Jao identifies with the gods of the twelve months, see pp. 204–210. Hayashi Minao 1971, thinks that the twelve "gods" are actually the gods of twelve shaman groups of Ch'u, which have nothing to do with the spirits in *Shan-hai-ching*. His view of the identity of the twelve gods is untenable given the argument provided by Jao and Tseng, but the identification of these gods with any of the spirits in *Shan-hai-ching* is by no means certain. Hayashi's idea that the images of the twelve gods on the Ch'u silk, instead of representing only the idea of the Ch'u artist, reflect the iconographical ideas of a wider area, seems to be a sound one. See also Hayashi Minao 1972.

138. Hu-pei-sheng po-wu-kuan 1988 vol. 1: 28–45. The tomb-protecting spirit/monster, as represented by a kind of statue found in a number of Ch'u tombs of the Warring States, is also shown as a kind of hybrid monster. See Ch'iu Tung-lien 1994; C. Mackenzie 1992.

139. See Hawkes 1959. For the image of Ho-po in particular, see W. Lai 1990.

140. Hu-nan-sheng po-wu-kuan and Chung-kuo k'o-hsüeh-yüan k'ao-ku yen-chiu-so ed. 湖南省博物館、中國科學院考古研究所編 1973.

141. Chou Shih-jung 周世榮 1990: 10.

142. Tseng Chao-yü 曾昭燏 1956. For discussion, see Hayashi Minao 1989: 127–218; esp. 129–131.

143. For a discussion of the iconographic evidence for this argument, see A. Thote 1992.

144. For example, see Cheng Te-k'un 1959: 237 ff.; K. C. Chang 1983d: 56 ff.

145. Yüan K'o 1980: 47, 77, 85, 110, 124.

146. Hsiao Ping 蕭兵 1986, esp. 127.

147. The two occurrences are "ghost grass" *kuei-ts'ao* and "ghost country" *kuei-kuo*.

148. Yüan K'o 1988:17–55.

149. Yüan K'o 1980: 256.

150. Yüan K'o 1980: 329.

151. Yüan K'o 1980: 45.

152. Yüan K'o 1980: 43.

153. Yüan K'o 1980: 113.

154. See Hsü Chung-shu 徐中舒 and T'ang Chia-hung 唐嘉弘 1986: 93–101.

155. Yüan K'o 1980: 456.

156. See Fracasso 1983.

157. Yüan K'o 1980: 42.

158. In the stories about ghosts and monstrous beings of the Six

Dynasties period, ghosts and "gods" are often "killed" by people in various ways. This might be a continuation of the mentality shown in *jih-shu* and *Shan-hai-ching*. See Lu Hsün 魯迅 1990: 200, 265, 293, 300.

159. See an early study on this point by Chiang Shao-yüan 1937. Also see the summary of different views on the original purpose of the text in Fracasso 1983: 659–669.

160. The original story is in *Tso-chuan*, year 3 of Duke Hsüan. See Legge 1985 V: 293. The meaning of this passage is somewhat controversial, mainly because of the interpretation of the character *wu* 物. K. C. Chang 1983d: 64 ff., thinks that it should refer to the sacrificial animal or animal with power that the shamans used in their communications with heaven and spirits. Powers 1995:226 sees the meaning of *wu* as allusive designs for socio-political status, while Wu Hung 1995:5 sees it as "symbols" or "emblems" of different regions. I have taken it to mean "monstrous animal." The passage in *Tso-chuan* refers to the "people (*min* 民)" who went out to the rivers, marshes, hills, and forests. Unless we can prove with certainty that the word *min* should be translated as "the shaman" and not the more usual meaning of "people," and that their going to the countryside was an act of shamanism, a more general reading of *wu* as monstrous animals or supernatural beings is preferable.

161. One should keep in mind that there are different styles in the text of *Shan-hai-ching* and not all of them can be considered as belonging to a "handbook." It has also been suggested that *Shan-hai-ching* was originally only a kind of explanation appended to a collection of drawings of the various spirits and monsters, although no conclusion can be reached unless some new evidence comes to light. See Fracasso 1983.

162. See Kudō Motoo 1988.

Emperors, Courtiers, and the Development of Official Cults

1. From a Sumerian hymn to Enlil, the air-god. See S. N. Kramer 1963: 120.

2. On Akhenaten, see D. B. Redford 1984.

3. J. B. Pritchard 1955: 365–368; M. Lichtheim 1976–80 vol. 2: 86–89.

4. For a recent discussion on this point as well as on other not-so-

revolutionary aspects of Akhenaten's reforms, see Nicolas Grimal 1988: 274–275. See also Jan Assman 1995, who demonstrates forcefully that the Amarna period is but one particular aspect of the phenomenon of solar cult in the New Kingdom.

5. *Shih-chi* 28/1355.

6. *Li-chi* 46/797.

7. Eichhorn 1973: 110–114; Howard J. Wechsler 1985: 170–176.

8. See D. Twitchett and M. Loewe eds. 1986: 52–64. The origins of many of the changes, of course, were much earlier.

9. For the origin and application of the *yin-yang* and Five-Phases theories, see Needham 1956: 232–252; Schwartz 1985: 350–382; Henderson 1984: 1–58, Graham 1986.

10. *Shih-chi* 28/1366. For a consideration of the problem of the Five Phases in the context of dynastic legitimacy, see Hok-lam Chan 1984: 19–30.

11. According to *Shih-chi*: "During the time of king Wei and king Hsüan of Ch'i, the disciples of Tsou-tzu wrote about circular destiny according to the five powers. When the Ch'in empire was established, people from Ch'i presented this theory. That is why the First Emperor adopted it." (*SC* 28/1368–1369.) It has also been argued, based on another passage in *Shih-chi* 28/1366, which originated from *Lü-shih ch'un-ch'iu* (13/127), that it was introduced by scholars of the *Lü-shih ch'un-ch'iu* school. See Hu Shih 胡適 1971: 500–502; Hsü Fu-kuan 1976: 5–8. In fact, the two stories could both be true, since one referred to the circumstance when the theory was first presented to the emperor, while the other represented the final version as the theory was put down in writing.

12. Bilsky 1975: vol. 2, 240–250; Eichhorn 1973: 95–97.

13. *Shih-chi* 28/1371–1377.

14. *Shih-chi* 8/1377; *Han-shu* 25/1209.

15. *Shih-chi* 28/1375; *Han-shu* 25/1207.

16. *Shih-chi* 28/1374; *Han-shu* 1206.

17. This aspect of the Chinese religion has often been pointed out by scholars on modern Chinese society. For example, see Wolf 1974; Philip C. Baity 1977: 75–84; Cohen 1988: 180–202. For a structuralist explanation of the religious symbolism of the social relations, see Sangren 1987: 127–131, esp. p. 128. For similar phenomenon in Mesopotamia, see Bottéro 1992: 212–215.

18. *Shih-chi* 28/1375; *Han-shu* 25A/1207.

19. The story is mentioned as being a well-known one in *Kuo-yü* "Chou-yü" 1A/11–12.

20. *Shih-chi* 28/1377.

21. *Shih-chi* 6/247, 252.

22. *Shih-chi* 6/257.

23. *Shih-chi* 6/258. This very fact, of course, says something of the identity of the "scholars": they were certainly not all "Confucian."

24. *Shih-chi* 6/263; 28/1377.

25. *Shih-chi* 28/1367.

26. *Shih-chi* 28/1377.

27. *Shih-chi* 28/1378.

28. *Shih-chi* 8/347.

29. *Shih-chi* 28/1378.

30. *Shih-chi* 28/1378–1379.

31. Hu Shih 1971: 524.

32. *Shih-chi* 28/1380.

33. *Shih-chi* 28/1382–1383. For the art of watching for the ether, see Peng-yoke Ho 1985: 146–149; Derk Bodde 1981: 351–372; Michael Loewe 1988a: 500–520.

34. *Shih-chi* 28/1382.

35. *Shih-chi* 28/1383.

36. *Shih-chi* 12/ 456; 28/1386. See M. Loewe 1974: 169–170; Eichhorn 1973: 114–115.

37. It has been pointed out that the Three Ones might have been the Three Emperors (Heavenly Emperor, Earthly Emperor, and Grand Emperor) mentioned in *Shih-chi* in connection with the First Emperor of Ch'in. But there is no evidence of their being worshipped officially. See Ku Chieh-kang 顧頡剛 1952: 24–25; Wang Pao-hsüan 王葆玹 1992.

38. *Shih-chi* 12/ 452–453; 28/1384; *Han-shu* 2/1216.

39. *Shih-chi*: 12/478; 28/1399–1400; *Han-shu* 25/1241.

40. See a classical study by Edouard Chavannes 1910; Wechsler 1985: 170–176; Eichhorn 1973: 110–114.

41. *Shih-chi* 28/1366–1367.

42. *Shih-chi* 28/1397.

43. *Shih-chi* 28/1389.

44. Wu-ti's various activities in this regard are vividly portrayed in *Shih-chi* 28. His credulous attitude toward the supernatural beings was probably deeply influenced by his maternal grandmother P'ing-yüan-chün. See Hu Shih 1971: 534–539.

45. *Shih-chi* 28/1397. For the relationship between *feng-shan* and immortality, see Fukunaga Mitsuji 福永光司 1981: 207–264.

46. *Han-shu* 64B/2828–2830.

47. *Han-shu* 25/1249–1250.

48. For details, see M. Loewe 1974: 154–192.

49. *Han-shu* 25/1257–1258. For details, see Loewe 1974: 170 ff.

50. *Han-shu* 25/1259.

51. *Han-shu* 25/1263.

52. *Han-shu* 99B/4106.

53. *Han-shu* 25/1265–69; 99B/4103–4104.

54. *Han-shu* 25/1270.

55. *Hou-Han-shu* 3157–1360.

56. It should be noted that the sacrificial temple of the imperial family of the Eastern Han was arranged differently from that of the Western Han, mainly as the result of an effort to solve the problem prompted by the fact that Emperor Kuang-wu, being in the same generation as Emperor Ch'eng, was not a legitimate successor of the Former Han dynasty. See Wu Hung 1989: 31–44; esp.31–34. The worship of Lao-tzu by Emperor Huan, in addition, was no more than a personal act. See *Hou-Han-shu* 3188; A. Seidel 1978.

57. *Han-shu* 25/1259.

58. For details of the opinions of the Han scholars, see *Li-chi* 46/6a–b; *Hou-Han-shu* 3184–3187.

59. *Huai-nan-tzu* 3/2b; *T'ai-hsüan-ching* 太玄經 93.

60. *Shih-chi* 10/429; *Han-shu* 25/1212.

61. See an in-depth discussion of Tung Chung-shu's thought by Hsü Fu-kuan1976 vol. 2: 295 ff.; Schwartz 1985: 350–382; Henderson 1984: 1–58; Queen 1991; Arbuckle 1991. The last two recent works cast doubts on the authorship of the work (*Ch'un-ch'iu fan-lu* 春秋繁露) traditionally attributed to Tung.

62. Schwartz 1985: 374–375.

63. For examples, *Han-shu* 8/245, 249. Two important studies on Han portents are H. Bielenstein 1950; W. Eberhard 1957: 33–70. An explanation from the iconographical point of view is Martin Powers 1983.

64. For examples, *Han-shu* 8/253, 258; 9/262, 263.

65. *Han-shu* 25/1260.

66. *Han-shu* 73/3116.

67. See Huang Min-chih 黃敏枝 1971; Ho Tzu-ch'üan 何茲全 1986; Hsieh Ch'ung-kuang 謝重光 1990. Jacques Gernet 1956. For an example of the modern period, see Sung Kuang-yü 1995: 103–163.

68. Granet 1975: 111.

69. *Ch'un-ch'iu fan-lu* 春秋繁露 16/2a–7a.

70. *Ch'un-ch'iu fan-lu* 16/7a–8b.

71. *Ch'un-ch'iu fan-lu* 16/7a–8b. For rain ritual, see Michael Loewe 1987: 195–213.

72. *Shih-chi* 28/1388–89.

73. See Loewe 1974: 37–90.

74. Poo 1986.

75. *Han-shu* 99/4169.

76. *Han-shu* 99/4186.

77. *Shih-chi* 28/1378–1379.

78. *Han-shu* 12/342; 84/3432. See Twitchett and Loewe 1986: 669; Chapter 6 below.

79. For example, see Poo 1990.

Beliefs and Practices
in Everyday Life of the Han Dynasty

1. Plato, *Republic* II, 364b–c. Quoted from E. Hamilton and H. Cairns eds. 1963: 611.

2. Menander, *Dyskolos*, 447–453. Quoted from D. G. Rice and J. E. Stambaugh eds. 1979: 109.

3. Tu Cheng-sheng 1990: 398–413; Yang K'uan 1980: Chapters 7 and 8.

4. See Loewe, M., and D. Twitchett eds. 1986 vol. 1: 551–59.

5. For a study of Han agricultural life, see Hsü Cho-yun 1980.

6. *Hou-Han-shu* 3106; Bodde 1975: 223–241.

7. For his life and work, see Shih Sheng-han 1965: 79–108.

8. Michael Nylan 1982.

9. Derk Bodde 1975. See a review of this work by W. Boltz 1979.

10. Bodde 1975: 45–74.

11. *Hou-Han-shu* 3130; Bodde 1975: 139–163.

12. Shih Sheng-han 1965:1; translation follows Hsu Cho-yun1980: 215.

13. See a comprehensive study of Ming-t'ang by Ming-chorng Hwang 1996.

14. *Hou-Han-shu* 3102.

15. Shih Sheng-han 1965: 7; Hsu Cho-yun 1980: 215–216.

16. Shih Sheng-han 1965: 7; Hsu Cho-yun 1980: 215–216.

17. On the problem of *she*, see the discussion below.

18. *SHT*, nos.731, 732, 735, 736, 739.

19. Shih Sheng-han 1965: 19.

20. *Hou-Han-shu* 3111.

21. Granet 1932: 147 ff.; Bodde 1975: 273 ff.

22. Bodde 1975: 276–280.

23. W. Eberhard 1968: 33–43, also associates the Lustration rite with the modern minority people in the south-west China, specifically the Yao people.

24. See discussion in Chapter 2 above. It is even more improbable to see the existence of two "mating rituals," the *kao-mei* and the Lustration, in Chou times. Neither was explicitly mentioned in the *Shih-ching*.

25. *Shih-ching*, "*chen-wei* 溱洧"; Legge 1985 IV: 148; see Bodde 1975: 274 ff. for discussion of the symbolic meaning of the peony and *lan*-flower. Despite their being symbols of love, the entire poem still cannot be said to represent a mating "rite."

26. Bodde's study basically conforms to the exegeses of Wang Hsien-ch'ien, *Hou-Han-shu chi-chieh* 後漢書集解 9b–10b, where most of the basic Han dynasty material concerning this ceremony is listed.

27. Hsu Shen 許慎, *Shuo-wen chieh-tzu* 說文解字, see Wang Yün 王筠 1988: 1/8a. The word *hsi* is not listed in *Shuo-wen*. According to another Eastern Han scholar, Ying Shao, the word *hsi* is the same as *chieh* 潔, to clean. See Wang Hsien-ch'ien, *Hou-Han-shu chi-chieh* 9b.

28. Lao Kan1970: 243–262, esp. 248–249 on the *ssu* days.

29. *I-wen lei-chü* 藝文類聚 4, as quoted in Chuang Shen 莊申 1991.

30. *Hou-Han-shu* 3122.

31. Bodde 1975: 308; Wang Li-ch'i 1982: 605.

32. Wang Li-ch'i 1982: 605.

33. See the detailed discussion in Bodde 1975: 289–316.

34. Bodde 1975: 311.

35. Shih Sheng-han 1965: 41; Hsu 1980: 221–222. See Bodde 1975: 294.

36. *Shih-chi* 5/184.

37. For detailed discussion, Bodde 1975: 317–325.

38. Bodde 1975: 318.

39. T'ang scholars who commented on the significance of *fu* drew heavily on the *Yin-yang* and the Five-Phases theory, which were obviously *post facto* explanations. See Bodde 1975: 320.

40. Bodde 1975: 320, 323. Reference are from *Han-kuan-i* 漢官儀 2/9a; and *Han-shu* 65/2846.

41. Wang Li-ch'i 1982: 604.

42. Shih Sheng-han 1965:43; Bodde 1975: 294.

43. Wang Li-ch'i 1982: 377.

44. *Lü-shih ch'un-ch'iu* 3/3b.

45. Wang Li-ch'i 1982: 375–376.

46. Shih Sheng-han 1965: 77; Hsü Cho-yun 1980: 228, a chicken's head was to be chopped off at the eastern gate during the *la* sacrifice in the twelfth month.

47. Yüan K'o 1981: 79, 84, 129, 136, 163.

48. Yüan K'o 1981: 19, 105.

49. Yüan K'o 1981: 32, 113.

50. Yüan K'o 1981: 79, 84.

51. Shih Sheng-han 1965: 60.

52. Shih Sheng-han 1965: 60; Hsu 1980: 224.

53. Shih Sheng-han 1965: 71; Hsu 1980: 226.

54. Bodde 1975: 165–188.

55. Shih Sheng-han 1965: 71; Hsu 1980: 226.

56. *Hou-Han-shu* 3127–3128. For a discussion, see Bodde 1975: 75–138; Boltz 1979.

57. Bodde 1975: 117.

58. Ch'en Meng-chia 1936.

59. *Lun-yü chu-shu* 10/9.

60. *Chou-li* 31/12.

61. *Ch'üan shang-ku san-tai Ch'in-Han liu-ch'ao-wen* 全上古三代秦漢六朝文 53/5.

62. Liu P'an-sui 1957 25/505; Forke 1962 I: 534..

63. Bodde 1975: 117–127.

64. This is according to Hsü Shen, *Shuo-wen chieh-tzu*, see *Shuo-wen chieh-tzu chu-tu* 8/19b.

65. Bodde 1975: 49–74.

66. *Hou-Han-shu* 3127. Bodde's translation is different from mine in the rendering of the character *chiao*. He translates it as "make contact with

one another" (p. 50), while I render it as "cross one another."

67. Legge 1985 IV: 233. See discussion in Chapter 2.

68. Shih Sheng-han 1965: 74; Hsu 1980: 226.

69. Shih Sheng-han 1965: 74; Hsu 1980: 226.

70. *Ch'un-ch'iu fan-lu* 16/7a.

71. *Han-shu* 30/1772.

72. Shui-hu-ti Ch'in-mu chu-chien cheng-li hsiao-tsu 1990: 227.

73. Liu P'an-sui 1957:24/487; see Forke 1962 I: 525. Translation follows Forke with one minor change.

74. See Chapter 4.

75. Wu Chiu-lung 1985: 22, no. 0273. The fragmentary text reads: " . . . no birth, even if birth comes about, [there will be] no son . . ."

76. Wang Li-ch'i 1982: 561.

77. *Lun-heng* 23; see Liu P'an-sui 1957: 470.

78. *Hou-Han-shu* 65/2138–2144.

79. Lo Chen-yü 羅振玉 1969 vol. 7: 2812.

80. Examples can be seen in an early collection of prescriptions (ninth century) perserved in Japan, *I-hsin fang* 醫心方 (*Ishimpō*) 23/374–376.

81. Ma-wang-tui Han-mu po-shu cheng-li-hsiao-tsu 1985 vol. 4: 126, 134–139.

82. Li Chien-min 李建民 1994.

83. Liu P'an-sui 1957: 27; *Chin-kuei yao-lueh* 金匱要略 2/12a, 14b; *Po-wu-chih* 博物志 10/1b. The text of "t'ai-ch'an-shu" from Ma-wang-tui also mentions the prohibition of eating rabbit soup. See Ma-wang-tui Han-mu po-shu cheng-li-hsiao-tsu 1985 vol. 4: 136.

84. *Ibid.*

85. *Lü-shih ch'un-ch'iu* 2/1a.

86. See Ma-wang-tui Han-mu po-shu cheng-li-hsiao-tsu 1985 vol. 4: 136–138.

87. For a general introduction to the medical knowledge of this period, see Unschuld 1985: 51–100.

88. *Shih-chi* 127/3219; Liu P'an-sui 1957 24/487; Forke 1962 I: 525.

89. *Li-chi* 13/9b, Cheng's commentary.

90. Wu Chiu-lung 1985: 20, 24, 25; nos. 0244, 0296, 0306. Kan-su-sheng po-wu-kuan and Chung-kuo k'o-hsüeh-yüan k'ao-ku yen-chiu-so 甘肅省博物館、中國科學院考古研究所 1964: 138.

91. *Han-shu* 99B/4138. The custom, of course, persisted until modern times. See R. J. Smith 1992: 62.

92. Hu Hou-hsüan 1944.

93. *Tso-chuan*, Duke Chao, year one; Legge 1985 V: 581.

94. It is generally agreed that the earliest portion of *Huang-ti nei-ching* took form during the Warring States period. See Lu Gwei-djen and Joseph Needham 1980: 88–90. The discovery of such texts as *Tsu-pei shih-i-mai chiu-ching* 足臂十一脈灸經, *Yin-yang shih-i-mai chiu-ching* 陰陽十一脈灸經, *Mai-fa* 脈法, etc. in the early Han Wa-wang-tui tomb no. 3 suggest a long process of development in the preceding era. See Ma-wang-tui Han-mu po-shu cheng-li-hsiao-tsu 馬王堆漢墓帛書整理小組 1985 vol. 4: 1ff. For an introduction to *Huang-ti nei-ching*, see Ilza Veith 1949.

95. *Lü-shih ch'un-ch'iu* 3/5a.

96. See Chapter 4.

97. See Donald Harper 1984: 67–106.

98. Ma-wang-tui Han-mu po-shu cheng-li-hsiao-tsu 馬王堆漢墓帛書整理小組 1985 vol. 4: 27.

99. As mentioned in *Pen-ts'ao kang-mu* 本草綱目 vol. 4: 52/2927–2933, incinerated human hair can be used to treat wounds.

100. Ma-wang-tui Han-mu po-shu cheng-li-hsiao-tsu 1985 vol. 4: 39.

101. Ma-wang-tui Han-mu po-shu cheng-li-hsiao-tsu 1985 vol. 4: 39.

102. Ma-wang-tui Han-mu po-shu cheng-li-hsiao-tsu 1985 vol. 4: 50.

103. Ma-wang-tui Han-mu po-shu cheng-li-hsiao-tsu 1985 vol. 4: 68.

104. Ma-wang-tui Han-mu po-shu cheng-li-hsiao-tsu 1985 vol.4: 127–129. We have seen this *yü* 蜮, or "short fox" in the *Shih-ching*. See Chapter 2. A description of it can be found in *Pao-p'u-tzu* 17/80.

105. *Pao-p'u-tze* 17/74. For the Pace of Yü, see Chapter 4.

106. *Pao-p'u-tze* 17/74.

107. J. Chadwick and W. N. Mann tr. 1987: 237–251.

108. G.E.R Lloyd 1979: 40–41; James Longrigg 1993: 24–25.

109. Lloyd 1979: 20–25; 56–57.

110. *Li-chi* 12/10b.

111. See a collection of the examples of late burial in Yang Shu-ta 楊樹達 1989: 132–147. The burial dates vary from seven days to more than a year after death.

112. Liu P'an-sui 1957: 24/467, 477; A. Forke 1962 II: 393–394.

113. Liu P'an-sui 1957: 24/489; Forke 1962 I: 529.

114. *Hou-Han-shu* 46/1546.

115. Kuo Ch'ing-fan 1978: 619. E. Erkes 1940: 185–210, argues that Ssu-ming was the god of death.

116. Ho Shuang-ch'üan 何雙全 1989; Li Hsüeh-ch'in 李學勤 1990.

117. *Li-chi chu-shu* 46/12.

118. *Li-chi chu-shu* 46/12–13.

119. Wang Li-ch'i 1982: 384.

120. Sun Tso-yün 孫作雲 1963.

121. Wang Li-ch'i 1982: 563.

122. *SHT*, no. 755.

123. Liu P'an-sui 1957 24/480; Forke 1962 II: 398.

124. Kan-su-sheng po-wu-kuan and Chung-kuo k'o-hsüeh-yüan k'ao-ku yen-chiu-so 甘肅省博物館、中國科學院考古研究所 1964: 138.

125. Liu P'an-sui 1957 24/479; Forke 1962 II: 397.

126. Chapter 4.

127. Wu Chiu-lung 1985: 23. *Chang* 丈 is a unit of length equal to ten "*ch'ih* (feet)."

128. *Shih-chi* 88/2570. In fact, as is common knowledge now, the Great Wall was not the result of a single act, but was a combination of several sections of walls built over a long period of time by different states since the late Warring States era.

129. See Richard J. Smith 1991: 131 ff.

130. *Hou-Han-shu* 45/1522.

131. *Han-shu* 30/1768, 1774.

132. Liu P'an-sui 1957 24/492; Forke 1962 II: 402.

133. Liu P'an-sui 1957 25/499; Forke 1962 II: 410.

134. Liu P'an-sui 1957 24/481; Forke 1962 II: 401.

135. Chiang Shao-yüan 1937.

136. *SHT*, no. 1040. See Kudō Motoo 1988.

137. Wu Chiu-lung 1985: 114, no. 1951; 226, no. 4881.

138. *Shih-chi* 128/43.

139. *Ch'ien-fu Lun* 潛夫論 18/92. For the explanation of "fan-chih," see *Hou-Han-shu Chi-chieh* 49/8.

140. *Han-shu* 92/3714, commentary by Li Ch'i.

141. Jao Tsung-i and Tseng Hsien-t'ung 1982: 17–18.

142. For examples: *Hou-Han-shu* 46/1546; Liu P'an-sui 1957 24/490.

143. Such as mentioned in Wang Ch'ung's essay "chi-jih." Forke 1962 II: 393–401.

144. *Shih-chi* 127/3241–3242. For the practice of divination in the Han period in general, see M. Loewe 1988b: 81–118.

145. Ch'en Meng-chia 1980.

146. See Wen Ch'ung-i 文崇一 1990: 173–234.

147. Writing in the eastern Han period, Pan Ku still remarked about the Ch'u people as believing in shamans and spirits, and making proliferate sacrifices. (*Han-shu* 28/1666.)

148. *Hou-Han-shu* 61/2024.

149. Legge 1985 V: 191–92.

150. W. Eberhard 1942 vol. 1: 36–51, argues that this cult of cold meal had to do with the custom of "changing the fire," and was later related to the Ch'ing-ming festival. Ch'iu Hsi-kui 1992 concurs with this view. Donald Holzman disagrees with this explanation and concludes that we can only assume, according to the earliest evidence, that the reason Chieh Tzu-t'ui was worshiped by the people was because of his personal moral integrity. See Donald Holzman 1986.

151. *Han-shu* 28/1656.

152. *Shih-chi* 28/1375.

153. *Hou-Han-shu* 11/479; 42/1451.

154. W ng Li-ch'i 1982: 394.

155. *HHS* 11/479–480.

156. *HHS* 42/1451.

157. For example, see Miyakawa Hisayuki 1979: 83–101. Also see discussions in Chapter 8 below.

158. For examples: Shih Ch'ing 石慶, *HS* 46/2197; Hu Chien 胡建, *HS* 67/2912; 段會宗 *HS* 70/3130; Wen Weng 文翁, *HS* 89/3627; Chu I 朱邑, *HS* 89/3637; Chao Hsin-ch'en 召信臣, *HS* 89/3642; Teng Hsün 鄧訓, *HHS* 16/612; Ts'en P'eng 岑彭, *HHS* 17/661–662; Chi T'ung 祭彤, *HHS* 30/746; Hsün Shu 荀淑, *HHS* 62/2049; Wang Huan 王渙, *HHS* 76/2470; Hsü Ching 許荊, *HHS* 76/2472; Chou Chia 周嘉, *HHS* 81/2676; Chiang Shih 姜詩, *HHS* 84/2784.

159. For discussions of the problem of *she*, see E. Chavannes, *Le T'ai Chan* 1910; Mori Mikisaburo 1940; Lao Kan 1943; and Ch'en Meng-chia 1956: 382–384; Kominami Ichirō 1988, thinks that different types of *she* might have different origins.

160. *Li-chi* 46/11–12.

161. *Han-shu* 25/1212.

162. The commentary by Ch'en Tsan, in *Han-shu* 27/1413.

163. *Han-shu* 27/1413.

164. See Lao Kan 1943.

165. *Hou-Han-shu* 2744; DeWoskin 1983: 80. DeWoskin translates "*she-kung*," literally "Lord of *she*," as "deities of the local soil god altars."

166. *Han-shu*, 99C/4190.

167. Lao Kan 1943.

168. *Han-shu* 25b/1250, 1258; 28a/1585.

169. Wang Li-ch'i 1982: 82. This story was utilized by Fan Yeh in *Hou-Han-shu* 82a/2712. For translation of the *Hou-Han-shu* text, see DeWoskin 1983: 52–53.

170. *Lieh-hsien-chuan*, in *Tao Tsang* 道藏 5/68.

171. *Hou-Han-shu* 82a/2710, 2711; DeWoskin 1983: 49–52.

172. Such as the one in *Han-shu* 28/1555. For the idea of immortality, see Chapter 7 below.

173. See Chapter 5.

174. *Li-chi* 46/13; Legge 1885: 207–208.

175. For the modern manifestation of this concept, see Sangren 1987: 141–165.

176. Wang Li-ch'i 1982: 403. I translate the term "*pao-yü* 鮑魚" as "salted fish" rather than "abalone," as it suits the context of the story better. My translation differs considerably from that of Nylan 1982: 532–533.

177. See further discussions in Chapter 7 below.

178. For example, *Mo-tzu* mentions that it was customary for the shamans to dwell close to the communal *she*-altars. See Sun I-jang 1974: 15/340. For the activities of the *wu*-shamans in the Han period, see Lin Fu-shih 1988.

179. See a similar story about the formation of a cult of plum tree in Wang Li-ch'i 1982: 405.

180. For a general introduction on this subject, see Michael Loewe 1982: 80–90. See Hsü Fu-kuan 1976 vol. 2: 295–438, for a detailed study of Tung's thought. For Tung's position in the tradition of the apocryphal texts, see Jack L. Dull 1966: 26–42; for Tung's system as a check on the emperor's power, also see Schwartz 1985: 372, 378–379; Eichhorn 1976: 113–115.

181. In addition to works cited in the last note, see further Ch'en P'an 1991; Yasui Kōzan 1984; Yasui Kōzan and Nakamura Shōhachi 1987.

182. Dull 1966: 152 ff.

183. Dull 1966: 186 ff.

184. H. Bielenstein 1950; 1984; W. Eberhard 1957: 33–70; see also Rafe de Crespigny 1976; Martin Powers 1991: 224–278. M. Beck 1990, thinks that the *History of Han* "Treatise on the Five Phases" was an interpretation of the Spring and Autumn Annals and that the Han portents were not the center of the author's attention. Nevertheless, it cannot be denied that this interpretation of the Spring and Autumn Annals was still aimed at criticizing the court politics.

185. *Han-shu* 27/473.

186. Dull 1966: 77–96.

187. *Hou-Han-shu* 3348. One of these stories (Li O 李娥) was later elaborated in Kan Pao's *Sou-shen-chi* 15/180–182.

188. *Han-shu* 27/1416.

189. *Hou-Han-shu* 3344.

190. The design on the gambling board has cosmological meanings and was related to the *shih* 式-divination board and the so-called TLV mirrors. See Loewe 1979: 60–85; Li Ling 1993: 82–166.

191. *Han-shu* 27/1476–77. The event is also recorded in the "Treatise on Astronomy" (*t'ien-wen-chih*) in *Han-shu* 26/1312. For the cult of the Queen Mother of the West in the Han period, see Dubs 1942; M. Loewe 1979. *Han-shu* 27/1476–1477. The event is also recorded in the "Treatise on Astronomy" (*t'ien-wen-chih*) in *Han-shu* 26/1312. For a study of the origin and development of this cult, see Fracasso 1988; Wu Hung 1989: 108–141; S. Cahill 1993: 11–32.

Immortality, Soul, and the Netherworld

1. From Egyptian *Book of the Dead*, see M. Lichtheim 1976 vol.2: 132.

2. Callimachus. Conversation between a living man and a dead man. Quoted in A. Sinclair 1967: 13–14.

3. See Chapter 5.

4. For a general introduction, see S. G. F. Brandon 1967; Jean Yoyotte *et al.* 1961; J. Gwyn Griffiths 1991.

5. Uchino Kumaichirō 內野熊一郎 1984.

6. The term "deathless (*pu-ssu* 不死)" was found only in the eastern Chou bronzes inscriptions. See Hsü Chung-shu 徐中舒 1936; Tu Cheng-sheng 1995.

7. *Tso-chuan* 49/19; Legge 1985 V: 684. *Yen-tzu ch'un-ch'iu chiao-chu* 晏子春秋校注 1/25; 7/180.

8. *Han Fei-tzu chi-chieh* 11/201.

9. *Han Fei-tzu chi-chieh* 7/130.

10. *Lü-shih ch'un-ch'iu* 1/7b.

11. Ellen Marie Chen 1972.

12. *Chuang-tzu chi-shih* 28–31; see B. Watson 1964: 27–28.

13. Ellen M. Chen 1972; Mu-chou Poo 1990.

14. See Kuo Ch'ing-fan 1978: 226 (*chen-jen* 眞人); 96 (*chih-jen* 至人).

15. The *Shan-hai-ching* mentioned a country of deathless people, ("Ta-huang nan-ching") and a "deathless drug" ("Hai-nei hsi-ching"). See Yüan K'o 袁珂 1980: 197, 370. Although it is difficult to pinpoint the date of these accounts, they serve as indicators of the belief or imagination in immortals in late–Warring States and early imperial eras.

16. For a general introduction, see DeWoskin 1983; also see Ngo, Van Xuyet 1976; Ch'en P'an 陳槃 1948 has given a comprehensive treatment of the origin of *fang-shih* and their various careers and functions in the Ch'in-Han period. See also Ku Chieh-kang 顧頡剛 1955.

17. *Shih-chi* 28/1369 (king Wei, Hsuan of Ch'i, and king Chao of Yen); 1370 (First Emperor of Ch'in); 1385, 1397, 1398, 1399, 1401 (Han Wu-ti).For the land of the immortals, see W. Bauer 1976: 153 ff.

18. See Bauer 1976; also see Ying-shih Yü 1964–65.

19. Yü Ying-shih 1964–65.

20. It is impossible to enumerate all the important works on the origin and development of the idea of immortality in China. Besides the works of Bauer, Yü Ying-shih, and Ku Chieh-kang, also see Fu Ch'in-chia 傅勤家 1975; Tsuda Sokichi 津田左右吉 1939; Murakami Yoshimi 村上嘉賓 1956; Wen I-to 聞一多 1975: 153–180; H. Maspero 1981: 310 ff.; Ch'ing Hsi-t'ai 卿希泰 ed. 1988 vol 1.

21. Jung Keng 容庚 1929: 88; Sun Tso-yün 1947: 30–31.

22. Sun Tso-yün 1947.

23. Sun Tso-yün 1947. Also see the winged-figure in the tomb painting of Pu Ch'ien-ch'iu, Sun 1977; Kate Finsterbusch 1966–1971,nos. 16, 104, 118, 132, 143;see vol. 1, p.213 index under "Geflugeltes menschliches Wesen." For such figures on bronze objects, see Hayashi Minao 1989: 146–152.

24. Yüan K'o 1980:187.

25. *Ch'u Tz'u*, "Yüan Yu 遠遊"; D. Hawkes 1959: 81.The country of the feathered people is also mentioned in *Huai-nan-tzu* 4/8b.

26. *Shih-chi* 28/1391.

27. Liu P'an-sui 1957 2/32; Forke 1962 vol. 1: 330.

28. In ancient Egypt, the *Ba*-soul is usually depicted as a bird with a human head, and is said to be able to fly in and out of the tomb. The ancient Greeks also imagined that the souls of the deceased were equipped with wings. See E. Vermeule 1979: 7–32. For further discussion of the image of plumaged immortals, see Patricia A. Berger 1980: 158–167.

29. See Chapters 5 and 8.

30. *Lieh-hsien-chuan*, attributed to Liu Hsiang. For a translation, see M. Kaltenmark 1953. For a discussion of Liu Hsiang's connection with the idea of immortality, see Fukunaga Mitsuji 福永光司 1981:299–318.

31. For a study on the idea of immortality in the court lyrics, see Sawaguchi Takeo 澤口剛雄 1966; Anne Birrell 1988: 64–77.

32. See K'un Hsiang-hsing 孔祥星 and Liu I-man 劉一曼 1984: 75; M. Loewe 1979: 200–201. For a translation of many mirror inscriptions, see B. Karlgren 1934.

33. *Shih-chi* 6/1397: "People from Ch'i reported prodigious things and secret recipes (for immortality), they number in the ten thousands."

34. See Miyakawa Hisayuki 宮川尚志 1964: 380–386.

35. *Ch'üan Hou-Han-wen* 全後漢文 106/1–2.

36. See Kuang-chou-shih po-wu-kuan and Kuang-chou-shih wen-wu kuan-li wei-yüan-hui 1981 v. 1: 149–154; Chung-kuo she-hui k'o-hsüeh-yüan k'ao-ku yen-chiu-so ed. 1959: 165–176.

37. Loewe 1979: 86–126.

38. Poo 1990a; 1995.

39. *Li-chi* 47/14.

40. For discussion, see Yü Ying-shih 1987c; Poo 1993c.

41. Ikeda On 1981: 273, no.6.

42. Chiang-ling Chang-chia-shan Han-chien chcng-li-hsiao-tsu 1989: 74.

43. *Ling-shu ching* 靈樞經 8/91.

44. For a general discussion of the idea of *ch'i*, *hun*, *p'o*, and *ching*, see Tu Cheng-sheng 1991.

45. For detailed discussion and further examples, see Poo 1993a: 216–217.

46. *Wen-po chien-hsün* 文博簡訊 1977, 9: 93.

47. Poo 1993a: ChapterII.

48. Poo 1993a: Chapter III.

49. Poo 1993a: Chapter V; also Wang Zhongshu 1982: 175–183.

50. Ch'en Kung-jou 陳公柔 1956; Yü Wei-ch'ao 俞偉超 1985; Wang Fei 王飛 1986: 29–33; Tu Cheng-sheng 1989; Poo 1993a: Chapter II.

51. See Cho-yun Hsu 1965: 78–106.

52. Wang Zhongshu 1982: 175 ff.; Poo 1993a: Chapter VI.

53. See Powers 1991; Wu Hung 1989a. For a discussion of the relationship between Han wall painting and tomb painting, see Hsing I-t'ien 邢義田 1986.

54. See Poo 1993a: Chapter VII.

55. For discussion, see Yü Ying-shih 1981; 1987a: 123–143; 1987c. Earlier studies include E. Chavannes 1910; and Sakai Tadao 酒井忠夫 1937.

56. Ch'iu Hsi-kui 裘錫圭. 1974: 49.

57. Chi-nan-ch'eng Feng-huang-shan no. 168 Han-mu fa-chüeh cheng-li tsu 1975: 4.

58. Hu-nan sheng po-wu-kuan and Chung-kuo she-hui k'o-hsüeh-yüan k'ao-ku yen-chiu-so 1974: 43. For discussion of this text, see Yü Ying-shih 1987c: 384–385.

59. Kuo Mo-jo 郭沫若 1965: 22; Ikeda 1981: 273, no. 6.

60. Lo Chen-yü 1870: 15; Ikeda 1981: 215, no. 7.

61. One text mentions The Ruler of Ts'ang-lin and the King of Wu-wei (Ikeda 1981: 272, no. 5), whose functions are not clear to us.

62. Ikeda 1981: p. 273, no. 6.

63. Ikeda 1981: p. 274, nos. 8–12.

64. Some scholars suggest that, since all the extent Han texts mentioning Yellow God appeared at the time when the Yellow Turbans were active, they reflect the works of the followers of the Yellow Turbans. (Ch'en Chih 陳直 1988: 390–392.) However, the term Yellow God appeared in similar funerary texts even after the fall of Han when the Yellow Turbans had long since disappeared. Thus, the connection between the two cannot be substantiated. See an example quoted in Harada Masami 原田正巳 1967: 17–35, esp. 22.

65. Also see Anna Seidel 1987: 28–30.

66. Ikeda 1981 *passim*.; Fang Shih-ming 方詩銘 1973; Terry F. Kleeman 1984. A most useful discussion is 吳天穎 1982.

67. Liu P'an-sui 1957 23/461; Forke 1962 II: 369.

68. See Poo 1993a: Chapter VII.

69. K'ao-ku t'ung-hsün pian-chi wei-yüan-hui 考古通訊編輯委員會 1956: 58; Hu-nan wen-kuan-hui 湖南文管會. 1958: 1–4; Kuang-chou-shih po-wu-kuan and Kuang-chou-shih wen-wu kuan-li wei-yüan-hui 廣州市博物館及廣州市文物管理委員會 1981: no. 5015, 5041.

70. P'ing-shuo k'ao-ku tui 平朔考古隊 1987: 44.Similar mirror inscriptions, Lin-i-shih po-wu-kuan 臨沂市博物館 1989: 42; K'ung Hsiang-hsing 孔祥星 and Liu I-man 劉一曼 1984:70; Karlgren 1934: nos. 79–82.

71. See Loewe 1979: nos. 92–96.

72. Ikeda 1981: p. 273, no.6.

73. Ikeda 1981: p. 270, no.2.

74. See Chüeh Chen-hsi 禚振西 1980: 48.

75. For examples, see M. Saleh and H. Sourouzian 1987: no. 74–78.

76. T. G. Allen 1974: 150i. For specimens of ushabti, see Saleh and Sourouzian 1987: nos. 150, 151, 172, 182.

77. For an overview of the problem of ushabti, see "Uschebti" in W. Helck ed. 1986 vol. 6: 896–899.

78. Ikeda 19891: p.275, no. 12.

79. Ikeda 1981: p. 273, no. 8.

80. Ikeda 1981: 270, no.2; 271, no.3.

81. See Poo 1990.

82. Nan-yang shih po-wu-kuan 1974.

83. Ikeda 1981: p. 222, no. 17 = Ho-pei sheng wen-hua-chü wen-wu kung-tso-tui 1959: 13. Similar phrases, Ikeda 1981: 223, no. 21; 224, no. 22; 270, no. 1.

84. *Wen-po chien-hsün* 文博簡訊 1977: 93.

85. Chiang-su-sheng wen-wu kuan-li wei-yüan-hui 1960: 18.

86. Ikeda 1981: 214, no. 5.

87. Cho-yun Hsu 1965: 24–52; Tu Cheng-sheng 1990: 43.

88. For a theoretical discussion, see Morris 1987: 16, 42.

89. The Egyptians had quite detailed images of the netherworld. They also conceived the concept that a person might have three soul-like entities, the *ba, ka,* and *akh.* See H. Frankfort 1961: 92–102; also H. Kees 1926, 1956: 33–58.

90. Humphreys, 1993: 161.

91. A. Schnaufer 1970: 1–33.

92. E. Vermeule 1979: 33–41; J. Bremmer 1983: 70 ff.; R. Garland 1985: 48–76; W. Burkert 1985: 194–99; N. J. Richardson 1985.

93. M. Hutter 1985: 161–163; K. Spronk 1986: 66–69.This does not, however, necessarily contradict the fact that the idea of judgment after death is a widespread one. See Yoyotte *et al.* 1961; J. Le Goff 1981: 17–51; J. Gwyn Griffiths 1991.

Popular Religiosity and Its Critics

1. Theophrastus on superstition, quoted in W. H. Auden ed. 1971: 516.

2. Hamilton and H. Cairns eds. 1963: 1194.

3. See Cho-yun Hsu 1965, for a general picture of this change before the unification.

4. For example, Fan K'uai was a butcher (*SC* 95/2651); Kuan Ying was a cloth peddler (*SC* 95/2667); Li I-chi was a gate keeper (*SC* 97/2691).

5. King Hsin of Han was the descendent of the old King Hsiang of the State of Han (*SC* 93/631); T'ien Chan was related to the old royal house of Ch'i (*SC* 94/2643); Shu-sun T'ung was an erudite (*po-shih*) at the Ch'in court (*SC* 99/2720).

6. See Michael Loewe 1986 vol. I: 139–144; Kuan Tung-kuei 管東貴 1989.

7. See, in general, Wang Yü-ch'üan 1949: 134–187; Hans Bielenstein 1980; Michael Loewe 1986 vol. 1: 463–490.

8. The origin and function of the *shih* had been a subject for debate

among scholars, some held that they were warriors originally; others held that they were both warriors and ritual performers. For discussion, see Yü Ying-shih 1980: 1–108; esp. p. 22.

9. T'ung-tsu Ch'ü 1972: 101–107.

10. Not only did the scholars differ by their degree of learning and literacy, the farmers and merchants also differed greatly among themselves, as some of them were landowners and entrepreneurs, while others were merely tenants and peddlers. See Ch'ü T'ung-tsu 1972: 109.

11. For an introduction into the practice of writing and various materials for writing in ancient China, see Ch'un-hsün Tsien 1962. Also see the Chinese and revised version of the same work, *Chung-kuo ku-tai shu-shih* 中 國古代書史. For the difficulty of defining "literacy," as well as methodological problems involved in studying literacy in an ancient society, see William V. Harris 1989: 1–24.

12. *HS* 30/1721.

13. *HS* 30/1721.

14. See Shen Yüan 沈元 1962.

15. Liu P'an-sui 1957 30/580.

16. E.g., for artisan's names: Yang-chou po-wu-kuan 揚州博物館 1987: 5; Nan-ching po-wu-yüan 南京博物院 1987: 490; for workshop location: Nan-ching po-wu-yüan I-cheng po-wu-kuan ch'ou-pei pan-kung-shih 1992: 505; for dates: P'ing-shuo k'ao-ku tui 平朔考古隊 1987: 46.

17. E.g., I-ch'ang ti-ch'ü po-wu-kuan and I-tu-hsien wen-hua-kuan 宜 昌地區博物館、宜都縣文化館 1987: 882; Ho-tse ti-ch'ü po-wu-kuan and Liang-shan-hsien wen-hua-kuan 荷澤地區博物館、梁山縣文化館 1988: 979; Sun Te-jun 孫德潤 and He Ya-i 賀雅宜 1987; Tai T'ung-hsin 戴彤心 and Chia Mai-ming 賈麥明 1988: 9.

18. See B. Karlgren 1934; see also M. Loewe 1979: 60–85, 158–203.

19. See Lin Su-ch'ing 林素清 1993.

20. As opposed to the "scribal literacy" prevailing in the ancient Near Eastern societies. Harris 1989: 7–8. Harris refers to "craftsman's literacy" not as the literacy of an individual craftsman, but the condition in which the majority, or near majority, of skilled craftemen are literate. Scribal literacy, on the other hand, refers to the sort of literacy restricted to a specialized social group that used it for such purposes as maintaining palace records or religious texts.

21. Documents discovered at Yü-men, Kansu province, also included fragments of *Ts'ang-chieh*. The writing of these documents, which may be excercises, reveal many examples of erroneous inscribed characters. See Kan-su-sheng wen-wu kung-tso-tui and Kan-su-sheng po-wu-kuan 1984. For education in the military settlements, see Hsing I-tien 邢義田 1993.

22. Wang Yü-ch'eng 王育成 1991: 46–48 for the example quoted.

23. Wang Yü-ch'eng 1991.

24. *HS* 30/1772.

25. *HHS* 82B/2749; DeWoskin 1983: 87.

26. *HHS* 82B/2743–44; DeWoskin 1983: 77–81.

27. Wu Jung-tseng 吳榮曾 1981.

28. Wang Ming 1960: 473–509. These are given the designation of "*fu-wen*," 複文, i.e., "composite characters," as each of the signs is composed of several characters. They are not quite the same as the talismans discovered on the tomb-quelling bottles or in *Pao-p'u-tzu*, but the principle of composition is similar.

29. *Pao-p'u-tzu* 17/82–92.

30. Schwartz 1985: 412. See also D. Johnson 1985, for a discussion of the situation of literacy and cultural transmission in late Imperial period.

31. *SC* 127/3215–3220.

32. For examples, Lang K'ai (*HHS* 30B/1053), Chiang Hung (*HHS* 53/1750), Li Hsieh (*HHS* 63/2089–90), and Fan Jan (*HHS* 81/2689) all once worked, for various reasons, as diviners in the markets.

33. *HHS* 83/2769. The claim that people with *wu* background should not serve in the government does not seem to have been an established law in the Han period. For discussion, see Lin Fu-shih 1988: 40–43.

34. See Yü Ying-shih 1987: 167–258, for a discussion of the mutual influence of the Great and Little traditions through the "good officials" during the Han period.

35. The word *yin*, which I translate as "excessive," carries the connotation of "licentious" in many instances. The term *yin-ssu*, therefore, means not only "excessive cult," but also "morally debased cult." For a discussion of this subject in the Taoist and later traditions, see T. F. Kleeman 1994a.

36. *HS* 25A/1193–1194. Similarly, *Po-hu t'ung-i* A/16–17.

37. See Chapter 5.

38. *HS* 81/3344; also see *HS* 25B/1257–1258; see Chapter 5.

39. *HS* 25B/1270.

40. See Rolf A. Stein 1979.

41. Wang Li-ch'i 1981 9/401–402; also see *HHS* 41/1413.

42. Han Fu-chih 韓復智 1980.

43. *HHS* 41/1397.

44. Wang Li-ch'i 1981 9/395.

45. See Chapter 3.

46. *SC* 117/3216.

47. Liu P'an-sui 1957 24/482; Forke 1962 I: 182.

48. Liu P'an-sui 1957 24/486; Forke 1962 I: 190.

49. *Ch'ien-fu lun* 潛夫論 3/9b–10b.

50. *Ch'ien-fu lun* 6/1b–5a.

51. *Ch'ien-fu lun* 6/7b.

52. *Ch'ien-fu lun* 6/8a. The meaning of the name of Hsien-chu, literally "pick and collect," is obscure.

53. Liu P'an-sui 1957 25/505 ; Forke 1962 I: 534.

54. *Ch'ang-yen* 昌言 89/11–12.

55. *Fa-yen* 12/4–5.

56. *Fa-yen* 10/1–2.

57. *Hsin Lun*, 13. Translation follows Timotheus Pokora 1975: 149–150. Since Huan's work only came down in fragments, some of the paragraphs may seem contradictory to each other. See the discussion in Yü Ying-shih 1964–65:109–110.

58. *Hsin Lun* 11, see Pokora 1975: 122.

59. See discussion in Jack Dull 1966: 235–237.

60. Hsün Yüeh, *Shen Chien* 申鑒 16–17; translation follows Ch'en Ch'i-yun 1980: 155 (3.8), 157 (3.11).

61. See Mu-chou Poo 1990, for a detailed discussion.

62. See a discussion of Wang Ch'ung's life and work in Forke 1962 I: 4–44.

63. For the story of Hsi-men Pao, see *SC* 127/3211–3213. See a recent discussion on the symbolic meaning of this story by W. Lai 1990: 335–350.

64. *HHS* 41/1413; Wang Li-ch'i 1981 9/400.

65. *HHS* 41/1397.

66. *SKC* 1/4; quoting from *Wei-shu*.

67. Wang Li-ch'i 1981 9/395.

68. David Johnson has similar observation regarding the later imperial period: "The fundamental concern of educated reformers was with ethics, not theology, that is to say, behavior, not doctrine." See Johnson, 1995: 14.

69. *HHS* 82b/2742.

70. *HHS* 82b/2746.

71. *HHS* 57/1841.

72. *Hsin Shu* 新書 8/10a.

73. *Ch'un-ch'iu fan-lu* 16/3.

74. *Hsin Lun* 11.

75. See Shih Sheng-han 1965: 79–88.

76. *HHS* 52/1731.

77. See *Ch'üan hou-Han-wen* 46/5.

78. Other cases of people who enjoyed a "living shrine" are: Yü Kung (*HS* 71/3041); Ch'en Chung (*HHS* 12/501); Wang T'ang (*HHS* 31/1105); Jen Yen (*HHS* 76/2462).

79. *HHS* 65/2143. Yang Wang-sun was famous for his idea of extremism in thrifty burial—to bury himself naked. See Mu-chou Poo 1990: 56–57.

80. *HS* 72/3056.

81. See Ch'en P'an 陳槃 1948; DeWoskin 1983: 1–42; Li Ling 1992.

82. For examples, there were Shih Sheng, Lu Sheng during the reign of the First Emperor of Ch'in, *SC* 6/252.

83. *HHS* 82/2730–2731; translation follows DeWoskin 1983: 70.

84. For the custom of using human sacrifice in praying for rain, see

Ch'en Meng-chia 1936; H. Schafer 1951:130–84; Sarah Allen 1984.

85. Other cases of self-sacrifice for rain-ritual include Tai Feng (*HHS* 81/2684), Liang Fu (*HHS* 81/2694).

86. DeWoskin proposes three areas as the background of the thought and technology of the *fang-shih*: astrology and calendrics; the practices of *wu* mediums and conjury; and pharmaceutical and hygienic medicine. See DeWoskin 1983: 6–29.

87. *HHS* 82A/2717. Similarly, Fan Yin 樊英 and Han Yüeh 韓說, *HHS* 82A/2721; 82B/2733.

88. *HHS* 82B/2729.

89. *HHS* 30/1053 (Lang Tsung 郎宗); 36/1243 (Chang K'ai 張楷).

90. See Mu-chou Poo 1990: 60–62.

91. *Sui-shu* 34/1026–1039, under the category of "Five Phases."

92. *SKC* 8/263; also see *HHS* 75/2435–2436. See also Henri Maspero 1981: 309–430; H. Welch 1965: 113–123. For general introductions to Taoism in China, see K. Schipper 1993; J. Lagerwey 1987; Fukui Kōjun 1983. For the early history of Taoism, see Jen Chi-yü 1990: 6–41; Ōfuchi Ninji 1964: 3–9; Miyakawa Hisayuki 1983: 93–113. For an introduction to the study of Taoism in the West, see Seidel 1990.

93. *Shen-hsien chuan* 5/8.

94. *SKC* 8/264, excerpt from *Tien-lueh*, quoted in P'ei Sung-chih's commentary.

95. *HHS* 75/2432.

96. See Ch'en Yin-k'o 陳寅恪 1933: 439–466; Jen Chi-yü 1990: 113–122.

97. There has been a long series of discussions on the content of this *T'ai-p'ing ch'ing-ling-shu* 太平清領書 and its relationship with an earlier *Pao-yüan t'ai-p'ing-ching* 包元太平經, and the *T'ai-p'ing-ching*. See T'ang Yung-t'ung 湯用彤 1983; Max Kaltenmark 1979; Mansvelt Beck 1980; J. O. Peterson 1989; 1990; T'ang I-chieh 湯一介 1988: 19–76. A bibliography of *T'ai P'ing-ching* studies can be found in Lin Fu-shih 1992.

98. *HHS* 30B/1084.

99. Another Kan Chi, also from Lang-yeh, appeared at the court of Sun Ts'e about half a century later. He "built a 'pure house' (*ching-she*),

burnt incense and recited books on the Way, and produced mantic water (*fu-shui*) to cure the sick. Many people from Wu followed him." (*SKC* 46/1110, P'ei Sung-chih's commentary, quoting from the Biography of Chiang Piao.) There is no reference of any book by this Kan Chi. Thus, some scholars do not consider the two Kan Chis to have been the same person.

100. *HHS* 71/2299.

101. For a comparison of the two sects, see Fu Ch'in-chia 傅勤家 1975: 72–74. Fu listed several aspects: 1) Forbidding the drinking of wine; 2) Following one's nature; 3) Free shelter; 4) Moralistic teachings; 5) Repentance as cure of sickness; 6) The reverence of Lao-tzu. The text of *Lao-tzu* that the Way of Five Pecks of Rice used has been identified as the *Lao-tzu hsiang-erh-chu* 老子想爾注, which was attributed to the hand of Chang Ling. See Jao Tsung-i 1991: 1–5; 115–133. T'ang I-chieh, however, held that it was Chang Lu who wrote *Hsiang-erh chu*. See T'ang I-chieh 1988:96–100. Jen Chi-yü 1990: 37–38, agrees with T'ang on Chang Lu's authorship.

102. See Ch'en Chi-yun 1988: 57–68; esp. p. 66.

103. *HS* 6/203.

104. See, for example, Mu-chou Poo 1986: 511–538.

105. See a detailed discussion by Michael Loewe 1979: 17–59 ; also see a recent discussion by Wu Hung 1992.

106. For a discussion on the juxtaposition of the different scenes and their explanation, see Martin J. Powers 1991: 277–278.

107. Wang Li-ch'i 1981 9/423.

108. *HHS* 81/2694; Wang Li-ch'i 1981 9/428.

109. Jean Levi 1989: 266. David Johnson has a similar idea concerning popular religion in the late Imperial period: "The fundamental concern of educated reformers was with ethics, not theology, that is to say, with behavior, not doctrine." See D. Johnson ed. 1995: 14.

110. See F. Solmsen 1979.

111. See Franz Cumont 1956: 80–85; R. M. Ogilvie 1969: 2–3; E. R. Dodds 1965: 111–112. For the mystery cults of the Greco-Roman period, see Walter Burkert: 1987.

112. This is a familiar theme, cf. J. B. Bury 1958 II: 366–372; Harold Mattingly 1967: 70–74.

Conclusion

1. Xenonphanes, quoted from W. H. Auden ed. 1971: 69.

2. For a discussion of the idea of efficacy (*ling*) in modern Chinese religion, see S. Sangren 1987.

3. See Poo 1990a; 1995.

4. Jean-Pierre Vernant 1991: 27–49, esp. 35–36.

5. Schwartz has pointed out (1985: 351) that this correlative thought is a common mode of thought in most "primitive" societies, as Lévi-Strauss expounded in his *The Savage Mind*.

6. The only creation story in ancient China was the one on Nu Wa's fashioning of man with yellow dirt and rope, first recorded in Ying Shao's *Feng-su t'ung-i*, see Wang Li-chi 1981: 601; Derk Bodde 1961: 369–408; esp. 386–389. As for the creation of the world, the myth of P'an-ku was even later and might be of foreign origin. See Derk Bodde 1961: 382–386. For a discussion of the methodological problems in the study of Chinese myths, see N. J. Girardot 1976: 289–318.

7. Schwartz 1985: 372; Chapter 4.

8. Schwartz 1985: 411.

9. For discussions of the meaning of mystery in Greco-Roman religions, see W. Burkert 1987: 1–11; and C. Kerényi 1978: 32–42. It has to do with festivals and initiations, but is not necessarily connected with "mysticism"—a term used to designate those beliefs that cultivate a nonrational, extraordinary experience of the transcendental reality. "Mysticism" is sometimes used to refer to a strand of Taoist thought that concentrated on the cultivation of inner vitality. See Livia Kohn 1992: 3–16.

10. Schwartz at one point also considers the effort of the rulers and his officials to align themselves with the cosmic rhythms as a magical act. See Schwartz 1985: 367.

11. See Miyakawa Hisayushi 1983: 439–458.

12. For an introduction to Osiris and his cult, see J. Gwyn Griffiths 1980. One should take notice of the fact that Egyptian religion itself was not really a coherent logical structure, and that many contradictory concepts appeared side by side. See Frankfort 1961: 3–29; John Baines 1991.

13. See the tomb inscription of Thothrekh, son of Petosiris: "I was rich in friends, all the men of my town, not one of them could protect me! All the town's people, men and women, lamented very greatly, because they saw what happened to me, for they esteemed me much. All my friends mourned for me, father and mother implored death; my brothers, they were head-on-knee, since I reached this land of deprivation." (M. Lichtheim 1976–80 v.3: 53); or the funerary stela of Taimhotep: "The West, it is a land of sleep, darkness weighs on the dwelling-place, those who are there sleep in their mummy-forms. They wake not to see their brothers, they see not their fathers, their mothers, their hearts forgot their wives, their children. . . . As for death, 'Come!' is his name, all those that he calls to him come to him immediately, their hearts afraid through dread of him." (M. Lichtheim 1976–80 v.3: 63.) See J. Zandee 1960.

14. For some examples in the later era, see the apotheosis of Pao-sheng Ta-ti 保生大帝: Kristofer M. Schipper 1990; the apotheosis of the Hsu brothers: Edward L. Davis 1985.

15. M. P. Nilsson 1948: 9–10; K. Kerényi 1959: 1–22; W. Burkert 1985: 203–208. See also E. Rohde 1925; L. G. Farnell 1921; A. D. Nock 1944: 141–174.

16. The earliest record is Kan Pao, *Sou-shen chi* 搜神記 5/57–61; see Miyakawa Hisayushi, 1974: 213–231; Liang Man-ts'ang 梁滿倉 1991.

17. *Sou-shen chi* 5/57.

18. Ibid.; *Chin-shu* 64/1738; *Sung-shu* 99/2433; *Nan-shih* 55/1356; *Nan-ch'i shu* 7/105. Liang Man-ts'ang suggests that it was because of his supposed loyalty to the Han government that the rulers of the Southern dynasties considered him a worthwhile character and promoted his cult.

19. A later example is the god Wen-ch'ang, see Kleeman 1994.

20. *Han-shu* 28a/1545, 1555, 1585.

21. Wang Fu, *Ch'ien-fu-lun* 潛夫論, "Wu-lieh 巫列" 6/6a–b.

22. For example, *Shih Chi* 24/1235: "Therefore heaven grants happiness to those who did benevolent deeds, and inflicts misfortune on those who did evil deeds."

23. Wang Ming 1985: 256; cf. James R. Ware 1966: 234.

24. For his life and work, see Shih Sheng-han 1965: 79–108.

25. B. Hendrischke 1991.

26. Ning Chen 1994.

27. See A. F. Wright 1954: 383–432.

28. *Kao-seng-chuan* 1/3.

29. As many as 86, or one-third, out of 257 monks in the *Kao-seng-chuan*, possessed such supernatural powers. Thus, the supernatural abilities of the monks were important elements in their biographies. For the meaning of theurgy, see G. Luck 1985: 20–23.

30. Murakami Yoshimi 村上嘉實 1961: 1–17. See John Kieschnick 1995.

31. See Mu-chou Poo 1990a; 1995.

32. See R. and Ch. Brooke 1984: 31–45; Gurevich 1992: 39 ff.

33. See discussion in Gurevich 1992: 50–52.

34. *Kao-seng-chuan* 284.

35. The following biographies all contain descriptions concerning ghosts and spirits: Book 2, T'an Wu-ch'an; Book 5, Shih T'an-i; Chu-fa-k'uang; Book 6, Huei-yung; Shih T'an-yung; Book 12, Po Seng-kwang; Chu T'an-yu; Book 14, Hui-kuo; Hui-ching. See Poo 1995.

36. *Kao-seng-chuan* 285.

37. For an overview, see Wang Kuo-liang 王國良 1984; Campany 1995.

38. See E.R. Dodds 1965: 125.

39. For example, see Judith Berling 1980. Berling's emphasis is on the philosophical and theoretical aspects of the Three Teachings. For a contrast, on the inadequacy of the use of "syncretism" in the Chinese situation, see Anna Seide 1989–90: 246.

40. See Frank R. Trombley 1994 vol. 1: 331–332; vol. 2: 380–386; Timothy E. Gregory 1986: 229–242.

Bibliography

Primary Documents

Chan-kuo ts'e 戰國策. SPPY ed. Taipei: Chung-hua, 1965.

Ch'ang-yen 昌言. By Chung-ch'ang T'ung 仲長統. In *Ch'üan shang-ku san-tai Ch'in-Han Liu-ch'ao-wen* 全上古三代秦漢三國六朝文 vol. 2, *Ch'üan hou-Han wen* 全後漢文, 89. Ed. by Yen K'o-jün 嚴可均, Taipei: Shih-chieh, 1982 reprint.

Ch'ien-fu lun 潛夫論. By Wang Fu 王符. *SPPY* ed. Taipei: Chung-hua, 1972.

Chin-kuei yao-lüeh 金匱要略, in *Chang Chung-ching ch'üan-shu* 張仲景全書 vol. 5. By Chang Chung-ching 張仲景. Shanghai: Chung-i ku-chi ch'u-pan-she, 1929.

Chin-shu 晉書. By Fang Huan-ling 房玄齡. Peking: Chung-hua, 1971.

Chou-li chu-shu 周禮注疏. *SSCCS* ed. Taipei: I-wen ch'u-pan-she, 1976.

Chuang-tzu chi-shih 莊子集釋. By Kuo Ch'ing-fan 郭慶藩. Peking: Chung-hua, 1978.

Ch'u-t'zu chi-chu 楚辭集注. By Chu Hsi 朱熹. Shanghai: Hsin-hua, 1979.

Ch'üan shang-ku san-tai Ch'in-Han Liu-ch'ao-wen 全上古三代秦漢三國六朝文, Ed. by Yen K'o-jün 嚴可均. Taipei: Shih-chieh, 1982 reprint.

Ch'un-ch'iu fan-lu 春秋繁露. *SKCS*, vol. 181. By Tung Chung-shu 董仲舒. Taipei: Shang-wu.

Fan-yen 法言. By Yang Hsiung 揚雄. *SPPY* ed. Taipei: Chung-hua, 1968.

Feng-su t'ung-i chiao-chu 風俗通義校注. Ed. by Wang Li-ch'i 王利器. Peking: Chung-hua, 1981.

Han-fei-tzu chi-chieh 韓非子集解. By Wang Hsien-shen 王先慎. Taipei: Shih-chieh, 1962.

Han-kuan-i 漢官儀. By Ying Shao 應劭.In *P'ing-chin-kuan ts'ung-shu* 平津館叢書, vol. 5.

Han-shu 漢書. By Pan Ku 班固. Peking: Chung-hua, 1971.

Hou-Han-shu chi-chieh 後漢書集解. By Wang Hsien-ch'ien 王先謙. Peking: Chung-hua, 1981.

Hou-Han-shu 後漢書. By Fan Yeh 范曄. Peking: Chung-hua, 1971.

Hsün-tzu chi-chieh 荀子集解. By Wang Hsien-ch'ien 王先謙. Taipei: Shih-chieh, 1971.

Hsieh-chi pien-fang shu 協紀辨方書, in *SKCS*, no. 811. Taipei: Shang-wu.

Hsin Lun 新論. By Huan T'an 桓譚. *SPPY* ed. vol. 1435. Taipei: Shang-wu.

Hsin Shu 新書. By Chia I 賈誼. *SPPY* ed. Taipei: Chung-hua,1965.

Huai-nan-tzu 淮南子. *SPPY* ed. Taipei: Chung-hua, 1971.

Huang-ti nei-ching su-wen 黃帝內經素問. *SPCKCP* ed. Taipei: Shang-wu.

I-hisn-fang 醫心方. By Tamba Yasuyori 丹波康賴. Peking: Hua-hsia ch'u-pan-she, 1993.

Kao-seng chuan 高僧傳. By Hui-chiao 慧皎. Taipei: Taiwan Yin-ching ch'u, 1973.

Kuan-tzu 管子. *SPPY* ed. Taipei: Chung-hua, 1972.

Kuo-yü 國語. *SPPY* ed. Taipei: Chung-hua, 1971.

Lü-shih ch'un-ch'iu 呂氏春秋. *SPPY* ed. Taipei: Chung-hua, 1972.

Li-chi chu-shu 禮記注疏. *SSCCS* ed. Taipei: I-wen ch'u-pan-she, 1976.

Lieh-hsien-chuan 列仙傳, in *Tao Tsang* 道藏 5: 68. Peking: Wen-wu, 1988.

Ling-shu ching 靈樞經. *SPCKCP* ed. Shanghai: Shang-wu yin-shu-kuan.

Lun-heng 論衡. By Wang ch'ung 王充. Ed. by Liu P'an-sui 劉盼遂. *Lun-heng chi-chieh* 論衡集解. Shanghai: Ku-chi ch'u-pan-she, 1957.

Mo-tzu hsien-ku 墨子閒詁. By Sun I-jang 孫貽讓. Taipei: Shih-chieh, 1974.

Nan-Ch'i-shu 南齊書. By Hsiao Tzu-hsien 蕭子顯. Peking: Chung-hua, 1971.

Nan-shi 南史. By Li Yen-shou 李延壽. Peking: Chung-hua, 1971.

Pao-p'u-tzu 抱朴子. By Ko Hung 葛洪. Ed. by Sun Hsing-yen 孫星衍. Taipei: Shih-chieh, 1969.

Pen-ts'ao kang-mu 本草綱目. By Li Shih-chen 李時珍. Peking: Jen-min wei-sheng, punctuated ed. 1975.

Po-hu t'ung-i 白虎通義. *SKCS*, vol. 850. Taipei: Shang-wu.

Po-wu-chih 博物志. By Chang Hua 張華. *Kuang Han-Wei ts'ung-shu* 廣漢魏叢書, vol. 97.

San-kuo-chih 三國志. By Ch'en Shou 陳壽. Peking: Chung-hua, 1971.

Shan-hai-ching chiao-chu 山海經校注. By Yüan K'o 袁珂.Shanghai: Ku-chi ch'u-pan-she, 1980.

Shen Chien 申鑒. By Hsün Yüeh 荀悅. *SPPY* ed. Taipei: Shang-wu, v. 1436.

Shen-hsien chuan 神仙傳. *SKCS*, vol. 1059. Taipei: Shang-wu.

Shih-chi 史記. By Ssu-ma Ch'ien 司馬遷. Peking: Chung-hua, 1971.

Shih-san-ching chu-shu 十三經注疏. Ed. by Juan Yüan 阮元. Taipei: I-wen ch'u-pan-she, 1976.

Shuo-wen chieh-tzu 說文解字. By Hsü Shen 許慎. Tuan Yü-ts'ai 段玉裁, *Shuo-wen chieh-tzu-chu* 說文解字注. Taipei: I-wen ch'u-pan-she, 1988.

Sou-shen chi 搜神記. By Kan Pao 干寶. Shanghai: Ku-chi ch'u-pan-she, 1982.

Ssu-min yüeh-ling chiao-chu 四民月令校注. By Ts'ui Shih 崔寔. Ed. by Shih Sheng-han 石聲漢. Peking: Chung-hua, 1965.

Sung-shu 宋書. By Shen Yüeh 沈約. Peking: Chung-hua, 1971.

T'ai-hsüan-ching 太玄經. By Yang Hsiung 揚雄. Shanghai: Ku-chi ch'u-pan-she, 1990.

T'ai-p'ing-ching ho-chiao 太平經合校. By Wang Ming 王明. Peking: Chung-hua, 1960.

Yen-tzu ch'un-ch'iu chiao-chu 晏子春秋校注. By Chang Ch'un-i 張純一. Taipei: Shih-chieh, 1971.

Secondary Sources

Akitsuki Kan'ei 秋月觀暎 ed. 1987. *Dōkyō to shūkyō bunka* 道敎と宗敎文化. Tokyo: Hirakawa.

Allan, Sarah. 1979. "Shang Foundation of Modern Chinese Folk Religion." In *Legend, Lore and Religion in China*, ed. by S. Allan and A. P. Cohen, 1–21. San Francesco: Chinese Materials Center.

———. 1984. "Drought, Human Sacrifice and the Mandate of Heaven in a Lost Text from the Shang Shu." *BSOAS* XLVII, part 3: 523–539.

———. 1991. *The Shape of the Turtle: Myth, Art, and Cosmos in Early China*. New York: State University of New York Press.

Allen, T. G. 1974. *The Book of the Dead, or Going Forth by Day*. Chicago: University of Chicago Press.

Alliot, M. 1949–54. *Le Cult d'Horus à Edfou*, 2 vols. Cairo: Institut Français d'Archeologie Orientale.

Andersson, J. G. 1943. "Researches into the prehistory of the Chinese." *BMFEA* 15.

Arbuckle, Gary. 1991. "Restoring Dong Zhongshu (B.C.E. 195–115): An Experiment in Historical and Philosophical Reconstruction." Ph.D. dissertation, University of British Columbia.

Arnold, D. 1962. *Wandrelief und Raumfunktion in Ägyptischen Tempeln des Neuen Reiches*. Munich: Akademie Verlag.

Assmann, Jan. 1995. *Egyptian Solar Religion in the New Kingdom*. London: Kegan Paul International.

Auden, W. H. ed. 1971. *The Portable Greek Reader*. New York: The Viking Press.

Bagley, Robert W. 1988. "Sacrificial pits of the Shang period at Sanxingdui in Guanghan county, Sichuan Province." *Arts Asiatiques* 43: 78 ff.

———. 1990. "A Shang City in Sichuan Province." *Orientations* 21: 52–67.

———. 1992. "Meaning and Explanation." In *The Problem of Meaning in Early Chinese Ritual Bronzes*, ed. by Roderick Whitfield, 34–54. London: University of London.

Baines, John . 1991. "Society, Morality, and Religious Practice." In *Religion in Ancient Egypt*, ed. by B. E. Shafer, 123–200. Ithaca: Cornell University Press.

Baity, Philip C. 1977. "The Ranking of the Gods in Chinese Folk Religion." *Asian Folklore Studies* 35: 75–84.

Balazs, E. 1964. "Nihilistic Revolt or Mystical Escapism."In *Chinese Civilization and Bureaucracy*, 226–254. New Haven: Yale University Press.

Barnard, N., and D. Fraser eds. 1972. *Early Chinese Art and Its Possible Influence in the Pacific Basin*, vol. I: *Ch'u and the Silk Manuscript*. New York: Intercultural Arts Press.

———. 1972. *Scientific Examination of an Ancient Chinese Document as a Prelude to Decipherment, Translation, and Historical Assessment: The Ch'u Silk Manuscript*, Revised and Enlarged. Canberra: Australian National University.

Bauer, Wolfgang. 1976. *China and the Search for Happiness*. New York: Seabury.

Beck, Mansvelt. 1980. "The Date of the Taiping jing." *T'oung Pao* 66, nos. 4 and 5: 149–182.

———. 1990. *The Treatises of Later Han: Their Author, Sources, Contents and Place in Chinese Historiography*. Leiden: E. J. Brill.

Bell, C. 1989. "Religion and Chinese Culture: Toward an Assessment of Popular Religion." *History of Religions* 28: 33–57.

Bendann, E. 1930. *Death Customs*. New York: Knopf.

Berger, Patricia A. 1980. "Rites and Festivities in the Art of Eastern Han China: Shantung and Kiangsu Provinces." Ph. D. dissertation, University of California, Berkeley.

Berling, Judith. 1980. *The Syncretic Religion of Lin Chao-en*. New York: Columbia University Press.

Bharati, A. ed. 1976. *The Realm of the Extra-Human: Agents and Audiences*. The Hague: Mouton.

Bielenstein, Hans. 1950. "An Interpretation of the Portents in the Ts'ien-Han-shu." *BMFEA* 22: 127–143.

———. 1980. *The Bureaucracy of Han Times*. Cambridge.

———. 1984. "Han Portents and Prognostications." *BMFEA* 56: 97–112.

Bilsky, L. J. 1975. *The State Religion of Ancient China*, 2 vols. Taipei: The Orient Cultural service.

Birrell, Anne. 1988. *Popular Songs and Ballads of Han China*. London: Unwin Hyman.

Bodde, Derk. 1961. "Myths of China." In *Mythologies of the Ancient World*, ed. by S. N. Kramer, 369–408. New York: Anchor Books.

———. 1975. *Festivals in Classical China*. Princeton: Princeton University Press.

———. 1981. "The Chinese Cosmic Magic Known as Watching for the Ethers." In *Essays on Chinese Civilization*, ed. by Charles Le Blanc and D. Borei, 351–372. Princeton: Princeton University Press.

Boltz, William G. 1979. "Review Article: Philological Footnotes to the Han New Year Rites." *JAOS* 99, 3: 423–440.

———. 1990. "Notes on the Textual Relation Between the *Kuo Yü* and the *Tso Chuan*." *BSOAS* 53, 3: 491–502.

Bottéro, Jean. 1992. *Mesopotamia: Writing, Reasoning, and the Gods*. Chicago: University of Chicago Press.

Brandon, S. G. F. 1967. *The Judgment of the Dead: the Idea of Life After Death in the Major Religions*. New York: Scribner.

Bremmer, J. 1983. *The Early Greek Concept of Soul*. Princeton: Princeton University Press.

Brooke, R. and Ch. 1984. *Popular Religion in the Middle Ages*. London: Thames and Hudson.

Burke, Peter. 1978. *Popular Culture in Early Modern Europe*. New York: Harper and Row.

Burkert, Walter. 1985. *Greek Religion*. Cambridge: Harvard University Press.

———. 1987. *Ancient Mystery Cults*. Cambridge: Harvard University Press.

Bury, J. B. 1958. *History of the Later Roman Empire*, 2 vols. New York: Dover.

Byrne, P. 1988. "Religion and the Religions." In *The World's Religions*, ed. by S. Southerland et al., 3–28. London: Routledge.

Cahill, Suzanne E. 1993. *Transcendence and Divine Passion: The Queen Mother of the West in Medieval China*. Stanford: Stanford University Press.

Campany, Robert F. 1995. *Strange Writing, Anomaly Accounts in Early Medieval China*. Albany: State University of New York Press.

Chadwick, J., and W. N. Mann tr., 1987. *Hippocratic Writings*. Harmondsworth: Penguin Books.

Chan, Hok-lam. 1984. *Legitimation in Imperial China*. Seattle: University of Washington Press.

Chan, Ping-leung. 1972. "Ch'u Tz'u and Shamanism in Ancient China." Ann Arbor: University Microfilms.

Chang, Cheng-lang 張政烺.1981. "Ai-ch'eng-shu ting shih-wen 哀成叔鼎釋文." *Ku-wen-tzu yen-chiu* 古文字研究 5, 27–33.

Chang, Ch'un-i 張純一. 1971. *Yen-tzu ch'un-ch'iu chiao-chu* 晏子春秋校注. Taipei: Shih-chieh.

Chang, Kwang-chih 張光直. 1976. *Early Chinese Civilization: Anthropological Perspectives*. Cambridge: Harvard University Press.

———. 1976a. "A Classification of Shang and Chou Myths." In *Early Chinese Civilization: Anthropological Perspectives*, 149–173.

———. 1976b. "Changing Relationships of Man and Animal in Shang and Chou Myths and Art." In *Early Chinese Civilization: Anthropological Perspectives*, 174–198.

———. 1980. *Shang Civilization*. New Haven: Yale University Press.

———. 1983. *Chung-kuo ch'ing-t'ung shih-tai* 中國青銅時代. Taipei: Lien-ching.

———. 1983a. "Shang-chou shen-hua chih fen-lei 商周神話之分類." In *Chung-kuo ch'ing-t'ung shih-tai*, 285–325. Taipei: Lien-ching.

———. 1983b. "Shang-Chou shen-hua yü mei-shu chung shuo-chian jen yü tung-wu kuan-hsi chih yien-pien, 商周神話與美術中所見人與動物關係之演變." In *Chung-kuo ch'ing-t'ung shih-tai*, 327–354.

———. 1983c. "Shang-chou ch'ing-t'ung-ch'i shang ti tung-wu wen-yang 商周青銅器上的動物紋樣." In *Chung-kuo ch'ing-t'ung shih-tai*, 355–383.

———. 1983d. *Art, Myth, and Ritual*. Cambridge: Harvard University Press.

———. 1986. *The Archaeology of Ancient China*, 4th ed. New Haven: Yale University Press.

———. 1989. "An Essay on Cong." *Orientations* 20, 6: 37–43.

———. 1990. *Chung-kuo ch'ing-t'ung shih-tai (erh-chi)* 中國青銅時代 (二集). Peking: San-lien.

———. 1990a. "Shang-tai te wu yü wu-shu 商代的巫與巫術." In *Chung-kuo ch'ing-t'ung shih-tai (erh-chi)*, 39–66.

———. 1990b. "T'an ts'ung chi ch'i tsai Chung-kuo ku-shih shang te i-i 談琮及其在中國古代史上的意義." In *Chung-kuo ch'ing-t'ung shih-tai (erh-chi)*, 67–80.

———. 1990c. "P'u-yang san-chiao yü Chung-kuo ku-tai mei-shu shang te jen-shou mu-t'i 濮陽三蹻與中國古代美術上的人獸母題." In *Chung-kuo ch'ing-t'ung shih-tai (erh-chi)*, 95–101.

———. 1990d. "Lien-hsü yü p'o-lieh: i-ko wen-ming ch'i-yüan hsin-shuo ti ts'ao-kao 連續與破裂：一個文明起源新說的草稿." In *Chung-kuo ch'ing-t'ung shih-tai (erh-chi)*, 131–143.

———. 1993. "Yang-shao wen-hua te wu-hsi tzu-liao 仰韶文化的巫覡資料." *BIHP* 64, 3: 611–625.

———. 1993a. "Shang Shamans." In *Power of Culture*, ed. by Willard Peterson, 10–36. Princeton, Princeton University Press.

Chang, Ming-ch'ia 張銘洽. 1988. "Yün-meng Ch'in-chien jih-shu chan-pu-shu ch'u-t'an 雲夢秦簡日書占卜術初探." *Wen-po*, 3: 68–74.

Chang, Ping-ch'üan 張秉權. 1988. *Chia-ku-wen yü chia-ku-hsüeh* 甲骨文與甲骨學. Taipei: Kuo-li Pien-i-Kuan.

Chang, Ssu-ch'ing 張素卿. 1991. *Tso-chuan ch'eng-shih yien-chiu* 左傳稱詩研究. Taipei: National Taiwan University.

Chang, Tsung-Tung. 1970. *Der Kult der Shang-Dynastie im Spiegel der Orakelinschriften: Eine palaeographische Studie zur Religion im archaischen China*. Wiesbaden: Otto Harrasowitz.

Chang, Wen-yü 張聞玉. 1987. "Yün-meng Ch'in-chien jih-shu ch'u-t'an 雲夢秦簡日書初探." *Chiang-han lun-t'an* 1987, 4: 68–73.

Chang, Yün 張蘊 and Yeh, Yen-jui 葉延瑞. 1987. "Hsien-yang t'a-erh-p'o han-mu ch'ing-li chien-chi 咸陽塔爾坡漢墓清理簡記." *Kao-ku yü wen-wu* 1987, 1: 10–13.

Chang-chia-shan Han-mu chu-chien cheng-li hsiao-tsu 張家山漢墓竹簡整理小組. 1985. "Chinag-ling Chang-chia-shan Han-chien kai-shu 江陵張家山漢簡概述." *WW1*: 9–15.

Ch'ang-wei ti-ch'ü i-shu-kuan 昌濰地區藝術館. 1977. "San-tung chiao-hsien san-li-ho i-chih fa-chüeh chien-pao 山東膠縣三里河遺址發掘簡報." *KK* 1977, 4: 262–267

Chao, P'u-shan 趙璞珊. 1983. *Chung-kuo ku-tai i-hsüeh* 中國古代醫學. Peking: Chung-hua.

Ch'ao, Fu-lin 晁福林. 1990. "Lun yin-tai shen-ch'üan 論殷代神權." *Chung-kuo she-hui k'o-hsüeh* 中國社會科學 1990, 1: 99–112.

Chartier, R. 1984. "Culture as Appropriation: Popular Culture Uses in Early Modern France." In *Understanding Popular Culture: Europe from the Middle Ages to the Nineteenth Century*, ed. by L. Kaplan, 229–253. Berlin: Mouton.

Chavannes, Edouard. 1910. *Le T'ai Chan*. Paris: Ernest Leroux.

Chen, Ellen Marie. 1972. "Is there a Doctrine of Physical Immortality in the Tao Te Ching?" *History of Religions* 12, 2: 231–247.

Chen, Ning. 1994. "The Problem of Theodicy in Ancient China." *Journal of Chinese Religions* 22:51–73.

Ch'en, Ch'i-yun. 1980. *Hsün Yüeh and the Mind of Late Han China: A Translation of the Shen-chien with introduction and annotations*. Princeton: Princeton University Press.

―――. 1988. "Who Were the Yellow Turbans?" *Cina* 21: 57–68.

Ch'en, Chih 陳直. 1988. "Han Chang Shu-ching chu-shu t'ao-p'ing yü Chang Chüeh huang-chin-chiao te kuan-hsi 漢張叔敬朱書陶瓶與張角黃巾教的關係." In *Wen-shih k'ao-ku lun-ts'ung* 文史考古論叢, by Ch'en Chih, 390–392. T'ientsin: Ku-chi ch'u-pan-she.

Ch'en, Ch'üan-fang 陳全芳. 1988. *Chou-yüan yü Chou wen-hua* 周原與周文化. Shanghai: Jen-min publishing Co.

Ch'en, Kenneth. 1964. *Buddhism in China*. Princeton: Princeton University Press.

Ch'en, Kung-jou 陳公柔. 1956. "Shih-sang-li chi-hsi-li chung so chi-tsai te sang-tsang chih-tu 士喪禮既夕禮中所記載的喪葬制度." *KKHP* 1956, 4: 67–84.

Ch'en, Meng-chia 陳夢家. 1937. "Kao-mei chiao-she tsu-miao t'ung-k'ao 高媒郊社祖廟通考." *Ch'ing-hua hsüeh-pao* 清華學報 12, 3: 445–472.

―――. 1956. *Yin-hsü pu-tz'u tsung-shu* 殷墟卜辭綜述. Peking: Science Press.

―――. 1936. "Shang-tai te shen-hua yü wu-shu 商代的神話與巫術." *Yen-ching hsüeh-pao* 燕京學報 20: 485–576.

―――. 1980. "Wu-wei Han-chien pu-shu 武威漢簡補述." In *Han-chien chuei-shu* 漢簡綴述, 285–86. Peking: Chung-hua.

Ch'en, P'an 陳槃. 1948. "Chan-kuo Ch'in-Han chien fang-shih lun-k'ao 戰國秦漢間方士論考." *BIHP* 17 : 7–57.

———. 1991. *Ku-ch'en-wei yen-t'ao chi ch'i shu-lu chieh-t'i* 古讖緯研討及其書錄解題. Taipei: Kuo-li pien-i-kuan.

Ch'en, Yao-chün 陳躍鈞 and Juan Wen-ch'ing 阮文清. 1983. "Chen-mu-shou lüeh-k'ao 鎮墓獸略考." *Chiang-han k'ao-ku* 江漢考古 1983, 3: 63–67.

Ch'en, Yin-k'o 陳寅恪. 1933. "T'ien-shih-tao yü pin-hai ti-yü chih kuan-hsi 天師道與濱海地域之關係." *BIHP* 3: 439–466.

Cheng, Chih-ming 鄭志明. 1986. *Chung-kuo she-hui yü tsung-chiao* 中國社會與宗敎. Taipei: Student Book Co.

Cheng, Te-k'un 鄭德坤. 1959. *Shang China*. Cambridge: W. Heffer and Sons.

Chi-nan-ch'eng Feng-huang-shan no. 168 Han-mu fa-chüeh cheng-li tsu 紀南城鳳凰山一六八號漢墓發掘整理組. 1975. "Hu-pei Chiang-ling Feng-huang-shan no. 168 Han-mu fa-chüeh chien-pao 湖北江陵鳳凰山一六八號漢墓發掘簡報." *WW* 1975, 9: 1–8.

Chiang, Hsiao-yüan 江曉原. 1991. *T'ien-hsüeh chen-yüan* 天學眞原. Liao-ning chiao-yü ch'u-pan-she.

Chiang, Shao-yüan 江紹原. 1937. *Chung-kuo ku-tai lü-hsing chih yen-chiu* 中國古代旅行之研究. Shanghai: Shang-wu.

Chiang, Wei-tung 蔣衛東. 1991. "Chen-mu-shou i-i pien 鎮墓獸意義辨." *Chiang-han k'ao-ku* 1991, 2: 40–44.

Chiang-ling Chang-chia-shan Han-chien cheng-li-hsiao-tsu 江陵張家山漢簡整理小組. 1989. "Chiang-ling Chang-chia-shan Han-chien 'Mai-shu' shih-wen 江陵張家山漢簡脈書釋文." *WW* 1989, 7: 74.

Chiang-su-sheng wen-wu kuan-li wei-yüan-hui 江蘇省文物管理委員會. 1960. "Chiang-su Kao-yu Shao-chia-kou Han-tai i-chih te ch'ing-li 江蘇高郵邵家溝漢代遺址的清理." *KK* 1960, 10: 18–23.

Childs-Johnson, Elizabeth. 1992. "Jades of the Hongshan Culture: the dragon and fertility cult worship." *Arts Asiatiques* XLVI: 82–95.

Chin, Tse-kung 金則恭. 1981. "Yang-shao wen-hua te mai-tsang chih-tu 仰韶文化的埋葬制度." *K'ao-ku-hsüeh chi-k'an* 考古學集刊 1981, 4: 248–251.

Ching, Julia. 1993. *Chinese Religions*. London: Macmillan Press.

Ch'ing, Hsi-t'ai 卿希泰 ed. 1988. *Chung-kuo Tao-chiao-shih* 中國道教史 vol. I. Ch'eng-tu: Ssu-ch'uan jen-min.

Ch'ing-hai-sheng wen-wu kuan-li-ch'u k'ao-ku-tui and Chung-kuo k'o-hsüeh-yüan k'ao-ku yen-chiu-so Ch'ing-hai-tui 青海文物管理處考古隊、中國科學院考古研究所青海隊. 1976. "Ch'ing-hai Lo-tu Liu-wan yüan-shih she-hui mu-ti fan-ying ch'u te chu-yao wen-t'i 青海樂都柳灣原始社會墓地反映出的主要問題." *KK* 1976, 6: 365 ff.

Ch'ing-hai-sheng wen-wu kuan-li-ch'u k'ao-ku-tui and Chung-kuo she-hui k'o-hsüeh-yüan k'ao-ku yen-chiu-so eds. 青海省文物管理處考古隊 and 中國社會科學院考古研究所編. 1984. *Ch'ing-hai Liu-wan* 青海柳灣. Peking: Wen-wu.

Ch'iu, Tung-lien 邱東聯. 1994. "Chen-mu-shou pien-k'ao 鎮墓獸辨考." *Chiang-han k'ao-ku* 1994, 2: 54–59.

Ch'iu, Hsi-kui 裘錫圭. 1974. "Hu-pei Chiang-ling Feng-huang-shan shih-hao Han-mu ch'u-t'u chien-tu k'ao-shih 湖北江陵鳳凰山十號漢墓出土簡牘考釋." *WW* 1974, 7: 49–63.

———. 1992. "Han-shih yü kai-huo 寒食與改火." In *Ku-tai wen-shih yen-chiu hsin-t'an* 古代文史研究新探, 524–554. Nanking: Chiang-ssu ku-chi.

Chou, Shih-jung 周世榮. 1956. "Ch'ang-sha Pai-ni-t'ang fa-hsien Tung-Han chuan-mu 長沙白泥塘發現東漢磚墓." *K'ao-ku t'ung-hsün* 1956, 3: 58.

———. 1990. "Ma-wang-tui Han-mu te shen-ch'i-t'u po-hua 馬王堆漢墓的神祇圖帛畫." *KK* 1990, 10.

Chu, Hsi 朱熹. 1979. *Ch'u-t'zu chi-chu* 楚辭集注. Shanghai: Hsin-hua.

Chu, T'ien-shun 朱天順. 1982. *Chung-kuo ku-tai tsung-chiao ch'u-t'an* 中國古代宗教初探. Shanghai: Jen-min.

Ch'u, T'ung-tsu. 1972. *Han Social Structure*. Seattle: University of Washington Press.

Ch'ü, Wan-li 屈萬里. 1956. "I-kua yüan-yü kuei-pu k'ao 易卦源於龜卜考." *BIHP* 27 :117–133.

Chuang Shen 莊申. 1991. "Hsi-su te yen-pien 禊俗的演變," in *K'ao-ku yü li-shih wen-hua* 考古與歷史文化, ed. by Sung Wen-hsün 宋文薫 *et al.*, 113–144.

Chung-kuo k'o-hsüeh-yüan k'ao-ku yen-chiu-so and Shan-hsi-sheng Hsi-an

Pan-p'o po-wu-kuan eds. 中國科學院考古研究所、陝西省西安半坡博物館編. 1963. *Hsi-an Pan-p'o* 西安半坡. Peking: Wen-wu.

Chung-kuo k'o-hsüeh-yüan k'ao-ku yen-chiu-so 中國科學院考古研究所 ed. 1962. *Feng-hsi fa-chüeh pao-kao* 灃西發掘報告. Peking: Wen-wu.

Chung-kuo k'o-hsüeh-yüan k'ao-ku yen-chiu-so Kan-su kung-tso-tui 中國科學院考古研究所甘肅工作隊. 1974. "Kan-su Yüng-ching Ta-ho-chuang i-chih fa-chüeh pao-kao 甘肅永靖大何庄遺址發掘報告." *KKHP* 1974, 2: 38.

Chung-kuo Shan-hai-ching hsüeh-shu t'ao-lun-hui 中國山海經學術討論會 ed. 1986. *Shan-hai-ching hsin-t'an* 山海經新探. Ch'eng-tu: Ssu-ch'uan She-hui k'o-hsüeh-yüan.

Chung-kuo she-hui k'o-hsüeh-yüan k'ao-ku yen-chiu-so ed. 中國社會科學院考古研究所編. 1959. *Lo-yang Shao-kou Han-mu*. Peking: K'o-hsüeh.

———ed. 1984. *Hsin-Chung-kuo te k'ao-ku fa-hsien ho yen-chiu* 新中國的考古發現和研究. Peking: Wen-wu.

———ed. 1987. *Yin-hsü fa-chüeh pao-kao* 殷墟發掘報告. Peking: Wen-wu.

Chüeh, Chen-hsi 禤振西. 1980. "Shan-hsi Hu-hsien te liang-tsuo Han-mu 陝西戶縣的兩座漢墓." *K'ao-ku yü wen-wu* 考古與文物 1980, 1: 44–48.

Cohen, Myron L. 1988. "Souls and Salvation: Conflicting Themes in Chinese Popular Religion." In *Death Ritual in Later Imperial and Modern China*, ed. by James L. Watson and Evelyn S. Rawski, 180–202. Berkeley: University of California Press.

Couliano, Ioan P. 1987. *Eros and Magic in the Renaissance*. Chicago: University of Chicago Press.

Couvreur, S. 1896. *Cheu King*. Hou Kien fou: Impriemerie de la Mission Catholique.

Creel, H. G. 1970. *The Origins of Statecraft in China*. Chicago: University of Chicago Press.

Cumont, Franz. 1956. *Oriental Religions in Roman Paganism*. New York: Dover.

David, A. R. 1973. *Religious Rituals at Abydos*. Warminster: Aris and Phillips.

Davis, Edward L. 1985. "Arms and the Tao: Hero Cult and Empire in Traditional China." *Sōdai no shakai to shūkyō* 宋代の社會と宗教 (Sōdai-shi kenkyūkai kenkyū hōkoku 宋代史研究會研究報告) 1985, 2: 1–56.

Davis, Natalie Z. 1982. "From 'Popular Religion' to Religious Cultures." In *Reformation Europe: A Guide to Research*, ed. by Steven Ozmen, 321–343. St. Louis: Center for Reformation Research.

de Crespigny, Rafe. 1976. *Portents of Protest in the Later Han Dynasty: The Memorials of Hsiang K'ai to Emperor Huan*. Canberra: Australia National University Press.

de Groot, J. J. M. 1892–1910. *The Religious Systems of China*, 6 vols. Leiden.

Demieville, P. 1956. "La Pénétration du Bouddhisme dans la tradition philosophique chinoise." *Cahiers d'histoire mondiale* III: 19–38.

DeWoskin, K. J. 1983. *Doctors, Diviners and Magicians of Ancient China: Biographies of Fang-shih*. New York: Columbia University Press.

Dien, Albert E. 1987. "Chinese Beliefs in the Afterworld." In *The Quest for Eternity: Chinese Ceramic Sculptures from the People's Republic of China*, ed. by Susan L. Caroselli, 1–16. Los Angeles: Los Angeles County Museum of Art.

Dodds, E. R. 1965. *Pagan and Christian in an Age of Anxiety*. New York: Norton.

Dubs, Homer H. 1942. "An Ancient Chinese Mystery Cult." *Harvard Theological Review* 35: 221–240.

Dull, Jack L. 1966. "A Historical Introduction to the Apocryphal (Ch'an-wei) Texts of the Han Dynasty." Ph.D. dissertation, University of Washington.

Dunand, F. 1984. "Religion Populaire et Iconographie en Égypte Hellenistique et Romaine." In *Visible Religion* v. III, *Popular Religion*, ed. by K. G. Kippenberg *et al.*, 18–23. Leiden: E. J. Brill.

Eberhard, W. 1957. "The Political Function of Astronomy and Astronomers in Han China." In *Chinese Thought and Institutions*, ed. by J. King Fairbank, 33–70. Chicago: University of Chicago Press.

———. 1968. *The Local Cultures of South and East China*. Leiden: E. J. Brill.

———. 1942. *Lokalkulturen im alten China*. vol. 1. Leiden: E. J. Brill.

Ebrey, Patricia. "Estate and Family Management in the Later Han as seen in the Monthly Instructions for the Four Classes of People." *Journal of Economic and Social History of the Orient* 17, 2: 173–205.

Egashira Hiroshi 江頭廣. 1980. "Kōsen ni tsuite 黃泉について," In *Ikeda Suetoshi hakushi koki kinen tōyōgaku ronshu* 池田末利博士古稀紀念東洋學論集, 109–126. Hiroshima.

Eichhorn, W. 1973. *Die Religionen Chinas*. Stuttgart: Kohlhammer.

———. 1976. *Die Alte Chinesische Religion und das Staatskultwesen*. Leiden: E. J. Brill.

Eliade, M. 1984. *A History of Religious Ideas*, 3 vols. Chicago: University of Chicago Press.

———. 1951. *Shamanism: Archaic Techniques of Ecstasy*. New York: Pantheon.

Eno, Robert. 1990. "Was there a High God Ti in Shang Religion?" *Early China* 15: 1–26.

———. 1990a. *The Confucian Creation of Heaven*. Albany: State University of New York.

Erkes, E. 1940. "The God of Death in Ancient China." *T'oung Pao* 35 : 185–210

Fan, Hsing-chun 范行準. 1989. *Chung-kuo ping-shih hsin-i* 中國病史新義. Peking: Chung-i ku-chi.

Fan, Yü-chou 范宇周. 1986. "Chia-ku-wen yüeh-shih chi-shih k'o-t'zu k'ao-pien 甲骨文月蝕記事刻辭考辨." In *Chia-ku-wen yü Yin-Shang-shih*, vol. 2, ed. by Hu Hou-hsüan, 310–337. Shanghai: Ku-chi ch'u-pan-she.

Fang, Shih-ming 方詩銘. 1973. "Ts'ung Hsü Sheng ti-ch'üan lun Han-tai ti-ch'üan chih chien-pieh 從徐勝地券論漢代地券之鑑別." *WW* 1973, 5: 52–55.

Farnell, L. G. 1921. *Greek Hero-Cults and Ideas of Immortality*. Oxford: Clarendon Press.

Feng, H. Y., and J. K. Shryock. 1935. "The Black Magic in China known as ku." *JAOS* 55: 1–30.

Feng, Yu-lan. 1952–53. *A History of Chinese Philosophy*, 2 vols. Tr. by Derk Bodde. Princeton: Princeton University Press.

288

Feuchtwang, Stephan. 1974. *An Anthropological Analysis of Chinese Geomancy*. Vientiane and Paris: Vithagna.

———. 1992. *The Imperial Metaphor: Popular Religion in China*. New York: Routledge.

Fields, L. B. 1983. "The Legalists and the Fall of Ch'in: Humanism and Tyranny." *Journal of Asian History* 17: 1–39.

Finsterbusch, K. 1966, 1972. *Verzeichnis und Motivindex der Han Darstellungen*, 2 vols. Wiesbaden: Otto Harrassowitz.

Forke, A. 1962. *Lun Heng*, 2 vols. New York: Paragon Book Gallery.

Fracasso, Riccardo. 1983. "Teratoscopy or Divination by Monsters: Being a Study of the Wu-tsang shan-ching." *Han-hsüeh yen-chiu* 1, 2: 657–700.

———. 1988. "Holy Mothers of Ancient China: A New Approach to the Hsi-wang-mu Problem." *T'oung-Pao* 74: 1–46.

Frankfort, Henri. 1961. *Ancient Egyptian Religion*. New York: Harper and Row.

Frankfort, H. et al. 1977. *The Intellectual Adventure of Ancient Man*. Chicago: University of Chicago Press.

Freedman, M. 1979. "On the Sociological Study of Chinese Religion." *The Study of Chinese Society: Essays by Maurice Freedman*, 351–369. Stanford: Stanford Univeristy Press.

Fu, Cheng-ku 傅正谷. 1988. "Lun shih-ching chung te chan-meng-shih yü ku-tai chan-meng chih-tu 論詩經中的占夢詩與古代占夢制度." *Chung-chou hsüeh-k'an* 1988, 1: 94–97.

Fu, Ch'in-chia 傅勤家. 1975. *Chung-kuo Tao-chiao-shih* 中國道教史. Taipei: Shang-wu reprint.

Fu, Ssu-nien 傅斯年. 1952. "Hsing-ming ku-hsün pien-cheng 性命古訓辨正." *Fu Meng-chen hsien-sheng chi* 傅孟眞先生集 vol. 3, 1–201. Taipei.

Fujino, Iwatomo 藤野岩友. 1969. *Fukei bungaku ron* 巫系文學論. Tokyo: Daigaku shobo.

Fukui, Kōjun 福井康順 *et al*. eds. 1983. *Dōkyō* 道教. Tokyo: Hirakawa.

Fukunaga, Mitsuji 福永光司. 1981. *Dōkyō shisōshi kenkyū* 道教思想史研究. Tokyo: Iwanami.

Furst, Peter T. 1972. "Hallucinogens and the Shamanic Origins of Religions." In *Flesh of the Gods*, ed. by P. T. Furst, 261–278. New York: Praeger.

Garland, R. 1985. *The Greek Way of Death*. Ithaca: Cornell University Press.

Gernet, Jacques. 1956. *Les aspects économiques du bouddhisme dans la societé chinoise du Ve au Xe siecle*. Saigon: École Française d'Extrême-Orient) = *Buddhism in Chinese Society: An Economic History* (Fifth to Tenth Century). Tr. by C. Franciscus Verellen. New York: Columbia University Press, 1994.

Girardot, N. J. 1976. "The Problem of Creation Mythology in the Study of Chinese Religion." *History of Religions* 15, 4: 289–318.

Goody, J. 1961. "Religion and Ritual: The Definitional Problem." *British Journal of Sociology* 12: 157.

Graham, A. C. 1986. *Yin-Yang and the Nature of Correlative Thinking*. Singapore: Institute of East Asian Philosophies.

Granet, Marcel. 1932. *Fêtes et Chansons anciennes de la Chine*. (Paris, 1919, 1922). = *Festivals and Songs in Ancient China*. Tr. by E. D. Edward. London: George Routledge and Sons.

———. 1975. *La religion des Chinois* (Paris, 1922)=*The Religion of the Chinese People*. Tr. by M. Freedman. New York: Harper and Row.

Grant, F. C. ed. 1953. *Hellenistic Religions*. New York: Bobbs-Merrill.

Gregory, Timothy E. 1986. "The Survival of Paganism in Christian Greece: A Critical Essay." *American Journal of Philology* 107: 229–42.

Griffiths, J. Gwyn. 1980. *The Origins of Osiris and His Cult*. Leiden: E. J. Brill.

———. 1991. *The Divine Verdict*. Leiden: E. J. Brill.

Grimal, Nicolas. 1988. *Histoire de l'Égypte Ancienne*. Paris: Fayard.

Gurevich, A. 1988. *Medieval Popular Culture: Problems of Belief and Perception*. Cambridge: Cambridge University Press.

———. 1992. *Historical Anthropology of the Middle Ages*. Cambridge: Polity Press.

Hall, David L., and Ames, Roger T. 1987. *Thinking Through Confucius*. Albany: State University of New York Press.

Hamilton, E., and Cairns, H. eds. 1963. *The Collected Dialogues of Plato*. Princeton: Princeton University Press.

Hamilton, M. B. 1995. *The Sociology of Religion*. London: Routledge.

Han, Fu-chih 韓復智. 1980. "Hsi-Han wu-chia ti pien-tung yü ching-chi cheng-ts'e chih kuan-hsi 西漢物價的變動與經濟政策之關係." In Han, Fu-chih, *Han-shih lun-chi* 漢史論集. Taipei: Wen-shih-che.

Hansen, Valerie. 1990. *Changing Gods in Medieval China*. Princeton: Princeton University Press.

Harada, Masami 原田正巳. 1967. "Bokenbun ni mirareru meikai no kami to sono sekai 墓券文に見れる冥界の神とその世界." *Tōhō shūkyō* 29: 17–35.

Harper, Donald. 1984. "The 'Wu Shih Erh Ping Fang': Translation and Prolegomena." Ann Arbor: University Microfilms International.

———. 1985. "A Chinese Demonography of the Third Century B.C." *HJAS* 45: 459–498.

———. 1994. "Resurrection in Warring States Popular Religion." *Taoist Resources* 5,2: 13–28.

Harris, William V. 1989. *Ancient Literacy*. Cambridge: Harvard University Press.

Hawkes, David. 1959. *Ch'u Tz'u: The Song of the South*. Oxford: Clarendon Press.

———. 1967. "The Quest of the Goddess." *Asia Major* n.s. 13, 1/2.

Hayashi, Minao 林巳奈夫. 1971. "Chōsha shutsudo So hakusho no junishin no yūrai 長沙出土楚帛書の十二神の由來." *Tōhō gakuhō* 42: 1–63.

———. 1972. "The Twelve gods of the Chan-kuo period silk manuscript excavated at Ch'ang-sha." In *Early Chinese Art and Its Possible Influence in the Pacific Basin* vol. I: *Ch'u and the Silk Manuscript*, ed. by N. Barnard and D. Fraser, 123–186. New York: Intercultural Arts Press.

———. 1974. "Kandai kishin no sekai 漢代鬼神の世界," *Tōhō gakuhō* 46: 223–306 =*Kandai no kamigami* 漢代の神神, 127–218.

———. 1989. *Kandai no kamigami* 漢代の神神. Kyoto: Rinkawa shoten, 1989.

———. 1990. "So-wei t'ao-t'ieh wen piao-hsian te shih shen-mo 所謂饕餮紋表現的是什麼." In *Jih-pen k'ao-ku-hsüeh yen-chiu-che Chung-kuo k'ao-ku-hsüeh yen-chiu lun-wen-chi* 日本考古學研究者中國考古學研究論文集, ed. by Higuchi Takayasu 桶口隆康, 133–201. Hong Kong: Tung-fang.

Hayes, William C. 1965. *Most Ancient Egypt*. Chicago: University of Chicago Press.

Helck, W. ed. 1975–1986. *Lexikon der Aegyptologie* 6 vols. Wiesbaden: Otto Harrassowitz.

Henderson, John B. 1984. *The Development and Decline of Chinese Cosmology*. New York: Columbia University Press.

Hendrischke, Barbara. 1991. "The Concept of Inherited Evil in the Taiping Jing." *East Asian History* 2: 1–30.

Higuchi, Takayasu 桶口隆康 ed. 1990. *Jih-pen k'ao-ku-hsüeh yen-chiu-che Chung-kuo k'ao-ku-hsüeh yen-chiu lun-wen-chi* 日本考古學研究者中國考古學研究論文集. Hong Kong: Tung-fang.

Ho, Peng-yoke. 1985. *Li, Qi and Shu: An Introduction to Science and Civilization in China*. Hong Kong: Hong Kong University Press.

Ho, Shuang-ch'üan 何雙全. 1989. "T'ien-shui fang-ma-t'an Ch'in-chien tsung-shu 天水放馬灘秦簡綜述." *WW* 1989, 2: 23–31.

———. 1989a. "T'ien-shui fang-ma-t'an Ch'in-chien chia-chung jih-shu k'ao-shu 天水放馬灘秦簡甲種日書考述." In Kan-su-sheng wen-wu k'ao-ku yen-chiu-so ed. *Ch'in-Han chien-tu lun-wen-chi*, 7–28.

Ho, Tzu-ch'üan 何茲全. 1986. *Wu-shih nien-lai Han T'ang fo-chiao ssu-yüan ching-chi yen-chiu* 五十年來漢唐佛教寺院經濟研究. Peking: Shih-fan ta-hsüeh.

Ho-nan-sheng wen-hua-chü wen-wu kung-tso-tui and Chung-kuo k'o-hsüeh-yüan k'ao-ku yen-chiu-so eds. 河南省文化局文物工作隊、中國科學院考古研究所. 1959. *Cheng-chou erh-li-kang* 鄭州二里岡. Peking: K'o-hsüeh.

Ho-nan-sheng wen-wu yen-chiu-so and Ch'ang-chiang liu-yü kuei-hua pan-kung-shih k'ao-ku-tui Ho-nan fen-tui eds. 河南省文物研究所、長江流域規劃辦公室考古隊河南分隊. 1989. *Hsi-ch'uan Hsia-wang-kang* 淅川下王崗. Peking: Wen-wu.

Ho-nan-sheng wen-wu yen-chiu-so Chou-k'ou ti-ch'ü wen-hua-chü wen-wu-k'o 河南省文物研究所周口地區文化局文物科. 1983. "Ho-nan Huai-yang P'ing-liang-t'ai Lung-shan wen-hua ch'eng-chih shih-chüeh chien-pao 河南淮陽平糧台龍山文化城址試掘簡報." *WW* 1983, 3: 21–36.

Ho-nan wen-wu kung-tso i-tui 河南文物工作一隊. 1957. "Cheng-chou Shang-tai i-chih te fa-chüeh 鄭州商代遺址的發掘." *KKHP* 1: 53–70.

Ho-pei-sheng wen-hua-chü wen-wu kung-tso-tui ed. 河北省文化局文物工作隊. 1959. *Wang-tu erh-hao Han-mu* 望都二號漢墓. Peking: Wen-wu.

Ho-tse ti-ch'ü po-wu-kuan and Liang-shan hsien wen-hua-kuan 荷澤地區博物館、梁山縣文化館. 1988. "Shan-tung Liang-shan tung-Han chi-nien mu 山東梁山東漢紀年墓." *KK* 11: 975–982.

Hochstadter, W. 1952. "Pottery and Stoneware of Shang, Chou and Han." *BMFEA* 24: 81–108.

Hoffman, Michael A. 1979. *Egypt Before the Pharaohs*. New York: Dorset.

Holzman, Donald. 1986. "The Cold Food Festival in Early Medieval China." *HJAS* 46, 1: 51–79.

Hori, Tsuyoshi 堀毅. 1988. "Yu-kuan yün-meng Ch'in-chien te tzu-liao ho chu-shu mu-lu 有關雲夢秦簡的資料和著述目錄." In *Ch'in-Han fa-chih-shih lun-k'ao* 秦漢法制史論考, 438–442. Peking: Fa-lü.

Horton, R. 1960. "A Definition of Religion." *Journal of Royal Anthropological Institute* 90, 2: 211.

Hsu, Cho-yun. 1965. *Ancient China in Transition*. Stanford: Stanford University Press.

———. 1980. *Han Agriculture*. Seattle: University of Washington Press.

Hsu, Cho-yun 許倬雲. 1982. "Hsien-ch'in chu-tzu tui t'ien te kuan-nien 先秦諸子對天的觀念." In *Ch'iu-ku pien* 求古編, 423–452. Taipei: Lien-ching.

Hsu, Cho-yun, and Katheryn M. Linduff. 1988. *Western Chou Civilization*. New Haven: Yale University Press.

Hsü, Chung-shu 徐中舒. 1936. "Chin-wen ku-t'zu shih-li 金文嘏辭釋例." *BIHP* 6, 1: 1–44.

Hsü, Chung-shu 徐中舒 and T'ang Chia-hung 唐嘉弘. 1986. "Shan-hai-ching ho Huang-ti 山海經和黃帝." In *Shan-hai-ching hsin-t'an*, ed. by Chung-kuo Shan-hai-ching hsüeh-shu t'ao-lun-hui, 93–101.

Hsü, Fu-kuan 徐復觀. 1969. *Chung-kuo jen-hsing-lun shih hsien-Ch'in p'ien* 中國人性論史先秦篇. Taipei: Shang-wu.

———. 1976. *Liang-Han ssu-hsiang-shih* 兩漢思想史, vol. 2. Taipei: Hsüeh-sheng.

Hsü, Hsi-t'ai 徐錫台. 1982. "Shu yü Chou-I kuan-hsi te t'an-t'ao 數與周易關係的探討." In *Chou-I tsung-heng-lu* 周易縱橫錄, 197–222. Hu-pei jen-min ch'u-pan-she.

Hsiao, Ping 蕭兵. 1986. "Shan-hai-ching—ssu-fang min-su wen-hua te chiao-hui 山海經——四方民俗文化的交匯." In *Shan-hai-ching hsin-t'an*, 125–137.

Hsieh, Ch'ung-kuang 謝重光. 1990. *Han-T'ang fo-chiao she-hui shih-lun* 漢唐佛教社會史論. Taipei: Kuo-chih wen-hua.

Hsing, I-tien 邢義田. 1986. "Han-tai pi-hua te fa-chan ho pi-hua-mu 漢代壁畫的發展和壁畫墓." *BIHP* 57, 1: 139–70.

———. 1993. "Han-tai pien-sai li-tsu ti chün-chung chiao-yü 漢代邊塞吏卒的軍中教育." *Ta-lu tsa-chih* 大陸雜誌 87, 3: 97–99.

Hu, Hou-hsüan 胡厚宣. 1944. "Yin-jen chi-ping k'ao 殷人疾病考." In *Chia-ku-hsüeh Shang-shih lun-ts'ung ch'u-chi* 甲骨學商史論叢初集.

———. 1959. "Yin pu-tz'u chung te shang-ti ho wang-ti 殷卜辭中的上帝和王帝." *Li-shih yen-chiu* 歷史研究 1959,9: 23–50; 1959,10: 89–110.

Hu, Shih 胡適. 1971. *Chung-kuo chung-ku ssu-hsiang-shih ch'ang-pien* 中國中古思想史長編. Taipei: Hu-shih chi-nien-kuan.

Hu-nan-sheng po-wu-kuan and Chung-kuo k'o-hsüeh-yüan k'ao-ku yen-chiu-so ed. 湖南省博物館、中國科學院考古研究所編. 1973. *Ch'ang-sha Ma-wang-tui i-hao Han-mu* 長沙馬王堆一號漢墓. Peking: Wen-wu.

Hu-nan-sheng po-wu-kuan and Chung-kuo she-hui k'o-hsüeh-yüan k'ao-ku yen-chiu-so 湖南省博物館、中國社會科學院考古研究所. 1974. "Ch'ang-sha Ma-wang-tui erh-san-hao Han-mu fa-chüeh chien-pao 長沙馬王堆二、三號漢墓發掘簡報." *WW* 1974, 7: 39–48.

Hu-nan wen-kuan-hui 湖南文管會. 1958. "Hu-nan Ch'ang-sha Nan-t'ang-ch'ung ku-mu ch'ing-li chien-pao 湖南長沙南塘沖古墓清理簡報." *K'ao-ku t'ung-hsün* 1958, 3: 1–4.

Hu-pei-sheng Ching-chou ti-ch'ü po-wu-kuan 湖北省荆州地區博物館. 1982. "Chiang-ling T'ien-hsing-kuan i-hao Ch'u-mu 江陵天星觀一號楚墓." *KKHP* 1982, 1: 71–116.

Hu-pei-sheng Ching-sha-t'ieh-lu k'ao-ku-tui 湖北省荆沙鐵路考古隊. 1991. *Pao-shan Ch'u-chien* 包山楚簡. Peking: Wen-wu.

Hu-pei-sheng po-wu-kuan 湖北省博物館. 1989. *Tseng-hou I mu* 曾侯乙墓 2 vols. Peking: Wen-wu.

Huang, Chan-yüeh 黃展岳. 1974. "Wo-kuo ku-tai te jen-hsün ho jen-sheng 我國古代的人殉和人牲." *KK* 1974, 3: 153–163.

————. 1990. *Chung-kuo ku-tai te jen-sheng jen-hsün* 中國古代的人牲人殉. Peking: Wen-wu.

Huang, Min-chih 黃敏枝. 1971. *T'ang-tai ssu-yüan ching-chi te yen-chiu* 唐代寺院經濟的研究. Taipei: National Taiwan University.

Huang-ho shui-k'u k'ao-ku tui Hua-hsien-tui 黃河水庫考古隊華縣隊. 1959. "Shan-hsi Hua-hsien Liu-tzu-chen ti-erh-tz'u fa-chüeh te chu-yao shou-huo 陝西華縣柳子鎮第二次發掘的主要收穫." *KK* 1959, 11: 585–587.

Huber, Louisa G. F. 1981. "The tradition of Chinese Neolithic pottery." *BMFEA* 53: 1–150.

Humphreys, S. C. 1993. *The Family, Women and Death*. Ann Arbor: The University of Michigan Press.

Hutter, M. 1985. *Altorientalische Vorstellungen von der Unterwelt: Literar- und Religionsgeschichtliche Überlegungen zu "Nergal" und "Ereski- gal."* Freiburg: Universitäts Verlag.

Hwang, Ming-chorng. 1996. "Ming-tang: Cosmology, Political Order and Monuments in Early China." Ph. D. dissertation, Harvard University.

I-ch'ang ti-ch'ü po-wu-kuan and I-tu-hsien wen-hua-kuan 宜昌地區博物館、宜都縣文化館. 1987. "Hu-pei I-tu-hsien Liu-chia wu-ch'ang tung-Han mu 湖北宜都縣劉家屋場東漢墓." *KK* 1987, 10: 882–888.

Ikeda, On 池田溫. 1981. "Chūgoku rekidai boken ryakkō 中國歷代墓券略考." *Tōyōbunka kenkyūjo kiyō* 東洋文化研究所紀要 86, no.6: 193–278.

Ikeda, Suetoshi 池田末利. 1981. *Chūgoku kodai shūkyōshi kenkyū* 中國古代宗教史研究. Tokyo: Tokai Daigaku.

Itō, Seiji 伊藤清司. 1968–1969. "Yamagawa no kamigami—Sangaikyo no kenkyū 山川の神神: 山海經の研究." *Shigaku* 史學 41,4: 31–61; 42,1: 29–78, 42,2: 73–106.

Itō, Michiharu 伊藤道治. 1956. "Bokuji ni mieru sorei kannen ni tsuite 卜辭に見える祖靈觀念について." *Tōhō gakuhō* 東方學報 (Kyoto) 26: 1–35.

Jacobsen, Thorkild. 1976. *The Treasure of Darkness*. New Haven: Yale University Press.

Jao, Tsung-i 饒宗頤, and Tseng Hsien-t'ung 曾憲通. 1985. *Ch'u po-shu* 楚帛書. Hong Kong: Chung-hua.

————. 1982. *Yün-meng Ch'in-chien jih-shu yen-chiu* 雲夢秦簡日書研究. Hong Kong: Chinese University.

Jao, Tsung-i 饒宗頤. 1982. "Yin-tai i-kua chi yu-kuan chan-pu chu wen-t'i 殷代易卦及有關占卜諸問題." *Wen Shih* 文史 20: 1–13

————. 1991. *Lao-tzu Hsiang-erh-chu chiao-cheng* 老子想爾注校正. Shanghai: Ku-chi.

Jen, Chi-yü 任繼愈 ed. 1981. *Chung-kuo fo-chiao shih* 中國佛教史 vol. 1. Peking: Hsin Hua.

————. 1990. *Chung-kuo tao-chiao-shih* 中國道教史. Shanghai: Jen-min.

Jochim, C. 1986. *Chinese Religions*. Englewood Cliffs: Prentice-Hall.

————. 1988. "Great and Little, Grid and Group: Defining the Poles of the Elite-Popular Continuum in Chinese Religion." *Journal of Chinese Religions* 16: 18–24.

Johnson, David. 1985."Communication, Class, and Consciousness in Late Imperial China." In *Popular Culture in Late Imperial China*, ed. by D. Johnson, A. J. Nathan, E. S. Rawski, 34–72. Berkeley: University of California Press.

————ed. 1995. *Ritual and Scripture in Chinese Popular Religion*. Berkeley: Chinese Popular Culture Project.

Jordan, David K., and Overmyer, Daniel L. 1986. *The Flying Phoenix, Aspects of Chinese Sectarianism in Taiwan*. Princeton: Princeton University Press.

Juan, Yüan 阮元 ed. 1976. *Shih-san-ching chu-shu* 十三經注疏. Taipei: I-wen ch'u-pan-she reprint.

Jung, Keng 容庚. 1929. *Pao-yün-lou i-ch'i t'u-lu* 寶蘊樓彞器圖錄. Peking: Ku-wu ch'en-lieh-so.

Kalinowski, M. 1986. "Les Traités de Shuihudi et l'Hemerologie Chinoise à la Fin des Royaumes-Combattants." *T'oung Pao* 72: 175–228.

Kaltenmark, Max. 1953. *Le Lie-sien tchouan*. Peking.

————. 1979."The Ideology of T'ai-p'ing ching." In *Facets of Taoism*, ed. by H. Welch and A. Seidel, 19–52. New Haven and London: Yale University Press.

Kan-su-sheng po-wu-kuan and Chung-kuo k'o-hsüeh-yüan k'ao-ku yen-chiu-so 甘肅省博物館、中國科學院考古研究所. 1964. *Wu-wei Han-chien* 武威漢簡. Peking: Wen-wu.

Kan-su-sheng wen-wu k'ao-ku yen-chiu-so ed. 甘肅省文物考古研究所編. 1989. *Ch'in-Han chien-tu lun-wen-chi* 秦漢簡牘論文集. Kansu jen-ming.

Kan-su-sheng wen-wu kung-tso-tui and Kan-su-sheng po-wu-kuan 甘肅省文物工作隊、甘肅省博物館. 1984. "Yü-men Hua-hai Han-tai feng-sui i-chih ch'u-t'u te chien-tu 玉門花海漢代烽燧遺址出土的簡牘." *Han-chien yen-chiu wen-chi* 漢簡研究文集, 15–33. Kansu Jen-min.

Kane, Virginia C. 1974–75. "The Independent Bronze Industries in the South of China Contemporary with the Shang and Western Chou Dynasties." *Archives of Asian Art* 28: 77–107.

Kao, Heng 高亨. 1984. *Chou-I ku-ching chin-chu* 周易古經今注. Peking: Chung-hua.

Kao, Karl S.Y. ed. 1985. *Classical Chinese Tales of the Supernatural and the Fantastic*. Bloomington: Indiana University Press.

Kao, Min 高敏. 1979. "Ch'in-chien Wei-li chih-tao so fan-ying te Ju-Fa jung-ho ch'ing-hsiang 秦簡爲吏之道所反映的儒法融合傾向." In *Yün-meng Ch'in-chien ch'u-t'an* 雲夢秦簡初探, 224–240. Honan Jen-min.

Kao, Ta-lun 高大倫. 1992. *Chang-chia-shan Han-chien mai-shu chiao-shih* 張家山漢簡脈書校釋. Ch'eng-tu: Ch'eng-tu ch'u-pan-she.

K'ao-ku t'ung-hsün pian-chi wei-yüan-hui 考古通訊編輯委員會. 1956. "K'ao-ku chien-hsün 考古簡訊." *K'ao-ku t'ung-hsün* 1956, 3: 58.

Kaplan, Steven L. ed. 1984. *Understanding Popular Culture: Europe from the Middle Ages to the Nineteenth Century*. Berlin: Mouton.

Karlgren, Bernard. 1930. "Some Fecundity Symbols in Ancient China." *BMFEA* 2: 1–66.

———. 1934. "Early Chinese Mirror Inscriptions." *BMFEA* 6: 9–79 .

———. 1936. "Yin and Chou in Chinese Bronzes." *BMFEA* 8: 9–156.

———. 1937. "New Studies of Chinese Bronzes." *BMFEA* 9: 1–168

———. 1946. "Legends and Cults in Ancient China." *BMFEA* 18: 201.

Kees, Hermann. 1956. *Totenglauben und Jenseitsvorstellungen der alten Ägypter*. Leipzig: C.J. Hinrichs Verlag.

Keightley, David N. 1978. *Sources of Shang History: The Oracle-Bone Inscriptions of Bronze-Age China*. Berkeley: University of California Press.

———. 1978a. "The Religious Commitment: Shang Theology and the Genesis of Chinese Political Culture." *History of Religions* 18: 211–225.

———. 1983. "Royal Shamanism in the Shang: Archaic Vestige or Central Reality?" paper presented at the Workshop on *Divination and Portent Interpretation in Ancient China*, Berkeley, June 20–July 1, 1983.

Kerényi, C. 1978. "The Mysteries of the Kabeiroi." In *The Mysterie*, ed. by Joseph Campbell, 32–42. Princeton: Princeton University Press.

———. 1959. *The Heroes of the Greeks*. London: Thames and Hudson.

Kesner, L. 1991. "The *Taotie* Reconsidered: Meaning and Functions of Shang Theriomorphic Imagery." *Artibus Asiae* 51, 1/2: 29–53.

Kieschnick, John. 1995. "The Idea of the Monk in Medieval China: Asceticism, Thaumaturgy and Scholarship in the *Biographies of the Eminent Monks*." Ph.D. dissertation, Stanford University.

Kleeman, Terry F. 1984. "Land Contracts and Related Documents." In *Chūgoku no shūkyō shiso to kagaku* 中國の宗教思想と科學. *Makio Ryokai Festschrift*, 1–34. Tokyo: Kokusho Kankōkai.

———. 1994. *A God's Own Tale*. Albany: State University of New York Press.

———. 1994a. "Licentious Cults and Bloody Victuals: Sacrifice, Reciprocity, and Violence in Traditional China." *Asia Major* 3rd. Series. 7. 1: 185–211.

Kohn, Livia. 1992. *Early Chinese Mysticism: Philosophy and Soteriology in the Taoist Tradition*. Princeton: Princeton University Press.

Kominami, Ichirō 小南一郎. 1988. "Sha no saishi no sho keitai to sono kigen 社の祭祀の諸形態とその起源." *Koshi shunjū* 古史春秋 4: 17–37.

———. 1986. "Sangaikyo kenkyū no genkyō to gadai 「山海經」研究の現況と課題." *Chūgoku—shakai to bunka* 2: 220–226.

Kramer, S. N. 1963. *The Sumerians*. Chicago: University of Chicago Press.

Kroeber, A. L. 1948. *Anthropology: Race, Language, Culture, Psychology, Prehistory*. New York: Harcourt Brace and Co.

Ku, Chieh-kang 顧頡剛. 1955. *Ch'in Han te fang-shih yü ju-sheng* 秦漢的方士與儒生. Shanghai: Ch'un-lien.

Ku, Te-jung 顧德融. 1982. "Chung-kuo ku-tai jen-hsün jen-sheng-che te shen-fen t'an-hsi 中國古代人殉人牲者的身份探析." *Chung-kuo-shih yen-chiu* 中國史研究 1982, 2: 112–123.

Kuan, Tung-kuei 管東貴. 1989. "Feng-chien-chih yü Han-ch'u tsung-fan wen-ti 封建制與漢初宗藩問題." *Ti-erh-chieh kuo-chi Han-hsüeh hui-i lun-wen-chi* 第二屆國際漢學會議論文集. Taipei: Academia Sinica.

Kuang-chou-shih po-wu-kuan and Kuang-chou-shih wen-wu kuan-li wei-yüan-hui 廣州市博物館及廣州市文物管理委員會. 1981. *Kuang-chou Han-mu* 廣州漢墓. Peking: Wen-wu.

Kudō, Motoo 工藤元男. 1986. "Suikochi Shinbō chikukan Nissho ni tsuite 睡虎地秦墓竹簡日書について." *Shiteki* 史滴 7: 15–39.

———. 1988. "Suikochi Shinbō chikukan *Nissho* yori mieta hō to shūzoku 睡虎地秦墓竹簡日書より見えた法と習俗." *Mokkan kenkyū* 木簡研究 10: 113–129.

———. 1990. "Unbo-Suikochi Shinkan *Nissho* to Dōkyō no shūzoku 雲夢睡虎地秦簡日書と道教の習俗." *Tōhō shūkyō* 東方宗教 76: 43–61.

———. 1988. "Umorete ita kōshin—Shutoshite Shinkan Nissho ni yoru 埋もれていた行神——主として秦簡日書による." *Tōyōbunka Kenkyūjo Kiyō* 東洋文化研究所紀要 106: 163–207.

———. 1990."The Ch'in Bamboo Strip Book of Divination (Jih-shu) and Ch'in Legalism." *Acta Asiatica* 58: 24–37.

Kuo, Ch'ing-fan 郭慶藩. 1978. *Chuang-tzu chi-shih* 莊子集釋. Peking: Chung-hua.

Kuo, Mo-jo 郭沫若. 1951. "Hsien-Ch'in t'ien-tao-kuan chih chin-chan 先秦天道觀之進展." In *Ch'ing-t'ung shih-tai* 青銅時代. Shanghai: Hsin-wen-i, 1–65.

———. 1957. *Liang-Chou chin-wen-tz'u ta-hsi k'ao-shih* 兩周金文辭大系考釋. Peking: K'o-hsüeh.

———. 1965. "Yu Wang Hsieh mu-chih te ch'u-t'u lun-tao lan-t'ing-hsü te chen-wei 由王謝墓志的出土論到蘭亭序的眞僞." *WW*, 6: 1–22.

Kuo-chia wen-wu-chü ku-wen-hsien yen-chiu-shih, and Ho-pei-sheng po-wu-kuan, and Ho-pei-sheng wen-wu yen-chiu-so Ting-hsien Han-mu chu-chien cheng-li-tsu 國家文物局古文獻研究室、河北省博物館、河北省文物研究所定縣漢墓竹簡整理組. 1981. "Ting-hsien ssu-shih-hao Han-mu ch'u-t'u chu-chien chien-hsün 定縣 40 號漢墓出土竹簡簡訊." *WW* 1981, 8: 11–19.

K'ung, Hsiang-hsing 孔祥星 and Liu I-man 劉一曼. 1984. *Chung-kuo ku-tai t'ung-ching* 中國古代銅鏡. Peking: Wen-wu.

Lagerwey, John. 1987. *Taoist Ritual in Chinese Society and History*. New York: Macmillan.

Lai, W. 1990. "Looking for Mr. Ho Po." *History of Religions* 29, 4: 335–350.

Lao, Kan 勞榦. 1943. "Han-tai she-ssu te yüan-liu 漢代社祀的源流." *BIHP* 11: 49–60.

———. 1970. "Shang-ssu k'ao 上巳考." *Bulletin of the Institute of Ethnology* 29: 243–262.

Le Goff, J. 1981. *The Birth of Purgatory*. Tr. by A. Goldhammer. Chicago: University of Chicago Press.

Legge, J. 1985. *The Chinese Classics*, 5 vols., I *Confucian Analects*; II *The works of Mencius*; III *The shoo king, or the book of historical documents*; IV *The She King, or the book of poetry*; V *The Ch'un Ts'ew, with the Tso chuen*. Taipei: Southern Materials Center reprint.

———. 1885. *Li Ki*. In *Sacred Books of the East* vol. 27, ed. by Max Müller. Oxford: Claredon Press.

Lei, Chung-ch'ing 雷中慶. 1982. "Shih-ch'ien tsang-su te t'e-cheng yü ling-hun hsin-yang te yen-pien 史前葬俗的特徵與靈魂信仰的演變." *Shih-chieh tsung-chiao yen-chiu* 世界宗教研究 1982, 3: 133–142.

Lessa, W., and E. Z. Vogt eds. 1979. *Reader in Comparative Religion: An Anthropological Approach*, 4th ed. New York: Harper and Row.

Levi, Jean. 1989. *Les Fonctionnaires Divins*. Paris: Seuil.

Lewis, I. M. 1971. *Ecstatic Religion*. Harmondsworth: Penguin.

Lewis, Mark E. 1990. *Sanctioned Violence in Early China*. Albany: State University of New York Press.

Li, Chi. 李濟. 1970. *Yin-hsü ch'u-t'u ch'ing-t'ung ting-hsing-ch'i chih yen-chiu* 殷墟出土青銅鼎形器之研究. Taipei: Academia Sinica.

Li, Chien-min 李建民.1994. "Ma-wang-tui Han-mu po-shu Yü-tsang mai-pao-t'u ch'ien-cheng 馬王堆漢墓帛書「禹藏埋胞圖」箋證." *BIHP* 65, 4: 725–832.

Li, Chin 李瑾. 1984. "Lun fei-wang pu-tz'u yü Chung-kuo ku-tai she-hui chih ch'a-i 論非王卜辭與中國古代社會之差異." *Hua-chung shih-yüan hsüeh-pao* 華中師院學報 1984, 6: 57–68.

Li, Ching-ch'ih 李鏡池. 1978. *Chou-I t'an yüan* 周易探源, 130–150. Peking: Chung-hua.

Li, Chün-ming 李均明 and Yü Hao-liang 于豪亮. 1981. "Ch'in-chien so fan-ying te chün-shih chih-tu 秦簡所反映的軍事制度." *Yün-meng Ch'in-chien yen-chiu*, 152–170. Peking: Chung-hua.

Li, Heng-ch'iu 李亨求. 1982. "Po-hai yen-an tsao-ch'i wu-tzu pu-ku chih yen-chiu—chien-lun ku-tai tung-pei-ya chu-min-tsu chih pu-ku wen-hua 渤海沿岸早期無字卜骨之研究——兼論古代東北亞諸民族之卜骨文化." *Ku-kung chi-k'an* 故宮季刊 16, 1: 41–56; 16, 2: 41–64; 16, 3: 55–81.

Li, Hsaio-tung 李曉東, and Huang Hsiao-fen 黃曉芬. 1987. "Ts'ung Jih-shu k'an Ch'in-jen kuei-shen-kuan chi Ch'in-wen-hua t'e-cheng 從日書看秦人鬼神觀及秦文化特徵." *Li-shih yen-chiu* 歷史研究 1987, 4: 56–63.

Li, Hsüeh-ch'in 李學勤. 1985. "Shui-hu-ti Ch'in-chien Jih-shu yü Ch'u Ch'in she-hui 睡虎地秦簡日帛書與楚秦社會." *Chiang-han k'ao-ku* 1985, 4: 60–64.

———. 1990. "Fang-ma-t'an chien chung te chih-kuai ku-shih 放馬灘簡中的志怪故事." *WW* 1990, 4: 43–47.

———. 1991. "Chia-ku chan-pu te pi-chiao yen-chiu 甲骨占卜的比較研究." In *Pi-chiao k'ao-ku-hsüeh sui-pi* 比較考古學隨筆, 139–150. Hong Kong: Chung-hua.

———. 1991a. *Tung-Chou yü Ch'in wen-ming* 東周與秦文明. Peking: Wen-wu.

———. 1992. *Chou-i ching-chuan suo-yüan* 周易經傳溯源. Ch'ang-ch'un: Ch'ang-ch'un ch'u-pan-she.

———. 1994. "Ch'u-t'u chien-po i-chi yü ku-tai hsüeh-shu wen-hua te yen-pien 出土簡帛佚籍與古代學術文化的演變." Paper presented at the International Symposium on the Integration of Chinese Archaeology and History, Taipei, Academia Sinica, Jan. 18–19, 1994.

Li, Xueqin (Li Hsüeh-ch'in). 1985. *Eastern Zhou and Qin Civilization*. New Haven: Yale University Press.

———. 1992. "Liangzhu Culture and the Shang Dynasty Taotie Motif." In *The Problem of Meaning in Early Chinese Ritual Bronzes*, ed. by R. Whitfield, 56–66. London: University of London.

Li, Hui 李卉. 1960. "Shuo ku-tu yü wu-shu 說蠱毒與巫術." *Bulletin of the Institute of Ethnology* 9: 271–284.

Li, Ling 李零. 1991. "Shih-t'u yü Chung-kuo ku-tai te yü-chou mo-shih 式圖與中國古代的宇宙模式." *Chiu-chou hsüeh-k'an* 九州學刊 4, 1: 5–52; 4,2: 49–76.

———. 1993. *Chung-kuo fang-shu-k'ao* 中國方術考. Peking: Jen-min Chung-kuo ch'u-pan-she.

Li, Ping-hai 李炳海. 1989. "Chung-kuo shang-ku shih-chi te chao-hun i-shih 中國上古史籍的招魂儀式." *Shih-chieh tsung-chiao yen-chiu* 1989, 2: 107ff.

Li, Shih-chen 李時珍. 1975. *Pen-ts'ao kang-mu* 本草綱目. Peking: Jen-min wei-sheng, punctuated ed.

Li, Yang-sung 李仰松. 1986. "Ch'in-an Ta-ti-wan i-chih Yang-shao wan-ch'i ti-hua yen-chiu 秦安大地灣遺址仰韶晚期地畫研究." *KK* 1986, 11: 1000–1004.

Liang, Chao-t'ao 梁釗滔. 1989. *Chung-kuo ku-tai wu-shu tsung-chiao te ch'i-yüan ho fa-chan* 中國古代巫術宗教的起源和發展. Chung-shan University Press.

Liang, Man-ts'ang 梁滿倉. 1991. "Lun Chiang-shen tsai liu-ch'ao ti-wei te kung-ku yü t'i-kao 論蔣神在六朝地位的鞏固與提高." *Shih-chieh tsung-chiao yen-chiu* 1991, 3: 58–68.

Liao, W. K. 1959. *The Complete Works of Han Fei Tzu*, 2 vols. London: Arthur Probsthain.

Liao-ning-sheng wen-wu k'ao-ku yen-chiu-so 遼寧省文物考古研究所. 1986. "Liao-ning Niu-ho-liang Hung-shan wen-hua nü-shen-miao yü chi-shih chung-ch'ün fa-chüeh chien-pao 遼寧牛河梁紅山文化女神廟與積石冢群發掘簡報." *WW* 1986, 8: 1–17.

Lichtheim, M. 1976–80. *Ancient Egyptian Literature*, 3 vols. Berkeley: University of California Press.

Lin, Chien-ming 林劍鳴. 1987. "Ts'ung Ch'in-jen chia-chih-kuan k'an Ch'in wen-hua te t'e-tien 從秦人價值觀看秦文化的特點." *Li-shih yen-chiu* 1987, 3: 71.

———. 1991. "Jih-shu yü Ch'in-Han shih-tai te li-chih 日書與秦漢時代的吏治." *Hsin-shih-hsüeh* 新史學 2, 2 (1991): 31–51.

———. 1993. "Shui-chien yü Fang-chien jih-shu pi-chiao yen-chiu 睡簡與放簡日書比較研究." *Wen-po* 1993, 5: 15–20.

Lin, Fu-shih 林富士. 1988. *Han-tai te wu-che* 漢代的巫者. Taipei: Tao-hsiang.

———. 1992. "Shih-lun T'ai p'ing-ching te chi-ping kuan-nien 試論太平經的疾病觀念." *BIHP* 62, 2: 225–263.

Lin, Su-ch'ing 林素清. 1993. "Liang-Han ching-ming ch'u-t'an 兩漢鏡銘初探." *BIHP* 63, 2: 325–370.

Lin-i-shih po-wu-kuan 臨沂市博物館. 1989. "Shan-tung Lin-i Chin-ch'üeh-shan chiu-tso Han-tai mu-tsang 山東臨沂金雀山九座漢代墓葬." *WW* 1: 21–47.

Ling, Ch'un-sheng 凌純聲. 1959. "Chung-kuo ku-tai shen-chu yü yin-yang hsing-ch'i ts'ung-pai 中國古代神主與陰陽性器崇拜." *Bulletin of the Institute of Ethnology* 8: 1–46.

Liu, Kwang-Ching ed. 1990. *Orthodoxy in Late Imperial China*. Berkeley: University of California.

Liu, Lo-hsien 劉樂賢.1994. *Shui-hu-ti Ch'in-chien jih-shu yen-chiu* 睡虎地秦簡日書研究. Taipei: Wen-chin ch'u-pan-she.

Liu P'an-sui 劉盼遂. 1957. *Lun-heng chi-chieh* 論衡集解. Shanghai: Ku-chi ch'u-pan-she.

Liu, Shih-o 劉士莪, and Huang Shang-ming 黃尚明. 1993. "Shang-Chou mien-chü ch'u-t'an 商周面具初探." *Kao-ku yü Wen-wu* 1993, 6: 70–74.

Liu, Yün-hui 劉雲輝. 1990. "Yang-shao wen-hua 'yü-wen' 'jen-mien yü-wen' nei-han erh-shih-shuo p'ing-shu 仰韶文化魚紋人面魚紋內涵二十說述評." *Wen-po* 1990, 4: 64–75.

Lloyd, G.E.R. 1979. *Magic, Reason and Experience*. Cambridge: Cambridge University Press.

Lloyd, Seton. 1984. *The Archaeology of Mesopotamia*. London: Thames and Hudson.

Lo, Chen-yü 羅振玉. 1969. *Liu-sha chui-chien* 流沙墜簡. In *Lo Hsüeh-t'ang hsien-sheng ch'üan-chi hsü-pien* 羅雪堂先生全集續編, v.7.

———. 1870. *Chen-sung-t'ang chi-ku i-wen* 貞松堂集古遺文.

Loehr, Max. 1968. *Ritual Vessels of Bronze Age China*. New York: The Asia Society.

Loewe, M. 1974. *Crisis and Conflict in Han China*. London: Allen and Unwin.

———. 1979. *Ways to Paradise: The Chinese Quest for Immortality*. London: George Allen and Unwin.

———. 1982. *Chinese Ideas of Life and Death*. London: Allen and Unwin.

———. 1987. "The Cult of the Dragon and the Invocation for Rain." In *Chinese Ideas about Nature and Society*, ed. by C. Le Blanc and S. Blader, 195–213. Hong Kong: Hong Kong University Press.

———. 1988. "The Almanacs (*jih-shu*) from Shui-hu-ti." *Asia Major* 3rd series. vol. I, pt. II: 1–28.

———. 1988a. "The Oracles of the Clouds and the Winds." *BSOAS* LI: 500–520.

———. 1988b. "Divination by Shells, Bones, and Stalks during the Han Period." *T'oung Pao* 74: 81–118.

——— ed., 1993. *Early Chinese Texts: a Bibliographical Guide*. Berkeley: Society for the Study of Early China.

———. 1994. "Recent Archaeological Discoveries and the History of the Ch'in and Han Periods." Paper presented at the International Symposium on the Integration of Chinese Archaeology and History, Taipei, Academia Sinica, Jan. 4–8, 1994.

Loewe, M. and C. Blacker eds. 1981. *Oracles and Divination*. Boulder: Shambhala Pub. Inc.

Loewe, M. and D. Twitchett eds. 1986. *Cambridge History of China*, vol. I. Cambridge: Cambridge University Press.

Longrigg, James. 1993. *Greek Rational Medicine*. London and New York: Routledge.

Lu, Gwei-djen, and Joseph Needham. 1980. *Celestial Lancets: A History and Rationale of Acupuncture and moxa*. Cambridge: Cambridge University Press.

Lu, Hsün 魯迅. 1990. *Ku-hsaio-shuo kou-ch'en* 古小說鉤沉. Taipei: T'ang-shan reprint.

Luck, G. 1985. *Arcana Mundi*. Baltimore: The Johns Hopkins University Press.

Ma, Ch'ih-ying 馬持盈. 1971. *Shih-ching chin-chu chin-i* 詩經今註今譯. Taipei: Shang-wu.

Ma-wang-tui Han-mu po-shu cheng-li-hsiao-tsu 馬王堆漢墓帛書整理小組. 1985. *Ma-wang-tui Han-mu po-shu* 馬王堆漢墓帛書. Peking: Wen-wu.

Mackenzie, Colin. 1992. "Meaning and Style in the Art of Chu." In *The Problem of Meaning in Early Chinese Ritual Bronzes*, ed. by R. Whitfield, 119–149. London: University of London.

Major, John S. 1993. *Heaven and Earth in Early Han Thought*. Albany: State University of New York Press.

Maspero, H. 1981. *Taoism and Chinese Religion*. Tr. by F. A. Kierman. Amherst: University of Massachusetts.

Mathieu, R. 1983. *Étude sur la Mythologie et l'Ethnologie de la Chine Ancienne*, Trad. annotée du Shanhaijing. Paris: College de France-Institut des Hautes Études Chinoise, *Mem. de Inst. des Hautes Études Chinoise*, XXII, tome 2.

Mattingly, Harold. 1967. *Christianity in the Roman Empire*. New York: Norton.

Miyakawa, Hisayuki 宮川尚志. 1964. *Rikuchōshi kenkyū shūkyōhen* 六朝史研究宗教篇. Kyoto: Heirakuji.

———. 1974. *Rikuchō shūkyōshi* 六朝宗教史. Toyko, Kobunto.

———. 1979. "Local Cults around Mount Lu at the Time of Sun En's Rebellion." In *Facets of Taoism*, ed. by H. Welch and A. Seidel, 83–101. New Haven: Yale University Press.

———. 1983. *Chūgoku shūkyōshi kenkyū* 中國宗教史研究 (一). Kyoto: Dōhōsha.

Mori, Mikisaburō 森三樹三郎. 1940. "Shinkan ni okeru minkan saishi no toitsu 秦漢における民間祭祀の統一." *Tōhō gakuhō* (Kyoto) 11, 1: 61–89.

Morris, J. 1987. *Burial and Ancient Society*. Cambridge: Cambridge University Press.

Mote, F. W. 1970. *Intellectual Foundations of China*. New York: Knopf.

Murakami Yoshimi 村上嘉實. 1961. "Kōsōden no shini ni tsuite 高僧傳の神異について." *Tōhō shūkyō* 17: 1–17.

———. 1956. *Chūgoku no sennin* 中國の仙人. Kyoto: Heiraku.

Nakahachi Masakazu 中鉢雅量. 1979. "Kodai shinwa ni okeru rakuen—Kōsen o chūshin to shite 古代神話における樂園——黃泉を中心として." *Tōhōgakku* 東方學 58: 42–56.

Nan-ching po-wu-yüan I-cheng po-wu-kuan ch'ou-pei pan-kung-shih 南京博物院儀征博物館籌備辦公室. 1992. "I-cheng Chang-chi-t'uan-shan hsi-Han-mu 儀征張集團山西漢墓." *KKHP* 1992, 4: 477–506.

Nan-ching po-wu-yüan 南京博物院. 1987. "Chiang-su I-cheng Yen-tai-shan Han-mu 江蘇儀征煙袋山漢墓." *KKHP* 1987, 4: 471–502.

Nan-yang shih po-wu-kuan 南陽市博物館. 1974. "Nan-yang fa-hsien tung-Han Hsü A-ch'ü mu-chih hua-hsiang-shih 南陽發現東漢許阿瞿墓志畫像石." *WW* 1974, 8: 73–75.

Needham, Joseph. 1956. *Science and Civilization in China*, vol. II. Cambridge: Cambridge University Press.

Ngo, Van Xuyet. 1976. *Divination, magie, et politique dans la Chine ancienne: Essai suivi de la traduction des "Biographies des Magiciens" tirés de l'Histoire des Han postérieurs*. Paris: Presses Universitaires de France.

Nilsson, Martin P. 1948. *Greek Piety*. London: Clarendon Press.

Nivison, David. 1983. "Dates of Western Chou." *HJAS* 43, 2: 481–579.

Nock, A. D. 1933. *Conversion—The Old and the New in Religion from Alexander the Great to Augustine of Hippo*. London: Oxford University Press.

———. 1944. "The Cult of Heroes." *Harvard Theological Review* 37: 141–174.

Nylan, Michael. 1982. "Ying Shao's 'Feng Su Tung Yi': An Exploration of Problems in Han Dynasty Political, Philosophical and Social Unity." Ph.D. dissertation, Princeton University.

Ōfuchi, Ninji 大淵忍爾. 1964. *Dōkyōshi no kenkyū* 道教史の研究. Okayama.

Ogilvie, R. M. 1969. *The Romans and Their Gods in the Age of Augustus*. New York: Norton.

Okushi, Atsuhiro 大節敦弘. 1986. "Unbō Shinkan Nissho ni mieru jun ni tsuite 雲夢秦簡日書にみえる困について." *Chūgoku—Shakai to bunka* 中國——社會と文化 2: 117–125.

Ong, Roberto K. 1985. *The Interpretation of Dreams in Ancient China*. Bochum: Studienverlag Brockmeyer.

O'Neil, Mary R. 1986. "From 'Popular' to 'Local' Religion: Issues in Early Modern European Religious History." *Religious Studies Review* 12, 3/4: 222–26.

Osing, J. 1977. *Der Tempel Sethos' I in Gurna*. Mainz: Phillip von Zabern.

Overmyer, Daniel L. 1986. *Religions of China*. San Francisco: Harper and Row.

———— et. al. 1995. "Chinese Religions—the State of the Field." Pt. I and II. *JAS* 54.1: 124–160; 54.2: 314–395.

Ozment, Steven. 1982. *Reformation Europe: A Guide to Research*. St. Louis: Center for Reformation Research.

Paper, Jordan. 1978. "The meaning of the 'T'ao-t'ieh'." *History of Religions* 18: 18–41.

————. 1986. "The Feng in Protohistoric Chinese Religion." *History of Religions* 26: 213–235.

————. 1995. *The Spirits are Drunk: Comparative Approaches to Chinese Religion*. Albany: State University of New York Press.

Pei-ching ta-hsüeh k'ao-ku shih-hsi-tui 北京大學考古實習隊. 1961. "Luo-yang Wang-wan i-chih fa-chüeh chien-pao 洛陽王灣遺址發掘簡報." *KK* 1961, 4: 175–178.

P'eng, Chung-to 彭仲鐸. 1935. "Ch'ü Yüan wei-wu k'ao 屈原爲巫考." *Hsüeh I* 學藝 14, 9: 1–8.

P'eng, Hao 彭浩. 1988. "Chen-mu-shou hsin-chieh 鎮墓獸新解." *Chiang-han k'ao-ku* 1988, 2: 66–68.

————. 1991. "Pao-shan erh-hao Ch'u-mu pu-shih ho ch'i-tao chu-chien te ch'u-pu yen-chiu 包山二號楚墓卜筮和祈禱竹簡的初步研究." In *Pao-shan Ch'u-chien*, ed. by Hu-pei-sheng Ching-sha-t'ieh-lu k'ao-ku-tui, 555–563. Peking: Wen-wu.

Peters, F. E. 1970. *The Harvest of Hellenism*. New York: Simon and Schuster.

Peters, Heather A. 1985. "The Role of the State of Chu in Eastern Zhou Period China: A Study of Interaction and Exchange in the South." Ann Arbor: University Microfilms Inc.

Peterson, J. O. 1989, 1990."The Early Traditions relating to the Han Dynasty Transmission of the Taiping jing." pt. 1, *Acta Orientalia* 50: 133–171; pt. 2, *Acta Orientalia* 51: 133–216.

P'ing-shuo k'ao-ku tui 平朔考古隊. 1987. "Shan-hsi Shuo-hsien Ch'in-Han mu fa-chüeh chien-pao 山西朔縣秦漢墓發掘簡報." *WW* 1987, 6: 1–52.

Pokora, Timotheus. 1975. *Hsin-lun (New Treatise) and Other Writings by Huan T'an (43 B.C.–28 A.D.)*. Ann Arbor: University of Michigan.

Poo, Mu-chou 蒲慕州. 1986. "Wu-ku chih-huo te cheng-chih i-i 巫蠱之禍的政治意."*BIHP* 57, 3: 511–38.

———. 1989. "Lun Chung-kuo ku-tai mu-tsang hsing-chih 論中國古代墓葬形制." *Bulletin of the College of Liberal Arts of National Taiwan University* 國立台灣大學文史哲學報 37: 235–279.

———. 1990. "Ideas Concerning Death and Burial in Pre-Han and Han China." *Asia Major* 3rd. series, vol. III, pt. 2: 25–62.

———. 1990a. "Shen-hsien yü kao-seng: Wei-Chin Nan-pei-ch'ao tsung-chiao hsin-t'ai shih-t'an 神仙與高僧: 魏晉南北朝宗敎心態試探." *Han-hsüeh yen-chiu* 漢學研究 8, 2 : 149–176.

———. 1992. "Shui-hu-ti Ch'in-chien jih-shu te shih-chieh 睡虎地秦簡日書的世界." *BIHP* 62, 4: 623–675.

———. 1993. "Popular Religion in Pre-imperial China: Observations on the Almanacs of Shui-hu-ti." *T'oung Pao* 79: 225–248.

———. 1993a. *Mu-tsang yü sheng-ssu: Chung-kuo ku-tai tsung-chiao chih hsing-ssu* 墓葬與生死: 中國古代宗敎之省思. Taipei: Lien-ching.

———. 1995. "The Images of Immortals and Eminent Monks: Religious Mentality in Early Medieval China." *Numen* 42: 172–196.

———. 1995a. *Wine and Wine-Offering in the Religion of Ancient Egypt*. London: Kegan Paul International.

Powers, Martin J. 1983. "Hybrid Omens and Public Issues in Early Imperial China." *BMFEA* 55: 1–55.

———. 1991. *Art and Political Expression in Ancient China*. New Haven and London: Yale University Press.

———. 1995. "The Figure in the Carpet: Reflections on the Discourse of Ornament in Zhou China." *Monumenta Serica* 43: 211–233.

Pritchard, J. B. 1955. *Ancient Near Eastern Texts Relating to the Old Testament*. Princeton: Princeton University Press.

P'u-yang-shih wen-wu kuan-li wei-yüan hui and P'u-yang-shih po-wu-kuan wen-wu tui 濮陽市文物管理委員會及濮陽市博物館文物隊. 1988. "P'u-yang Hsi-shui-p'o i-chih shih-chüeh chien-pao 濮陽西水坡遺址試掘簡報." *Chung-yüan wen-wu* 中原文物 1988, 1: 1–6.

Queen, Sarah A. 1991. "From Chronicle to Canon: The Hermeneutics of the Spring and Autumn Annals According to Tung Chung-shu." Ph.D. dissertation, Harvard University.

Rawson, Jessica. 1990. "Ancient Chinese Bronzes." In *Ancient Chinese and Ordos Bronzes*, ed. by J. Rawson and E. Bunker, 13–61. Hong Kong: Oriental Ceramic Society.

Rawson, J., and E. Bunker. 1990. *Ancient Chinese and Ordos Bronzes*. Hong Kong: Oriental Ceramic Society.

Redfield, R. 1956. *Peasant Society and Culture*. Chicago: University of Chicago.

Redford, D. B. 1984. *Akhenaten, The Heretic King*. Princeton: Princeton University Press.

Rice, D. G., and J. E. Stambaugh eds. 1979. *Sources for the Study of Greek Religion*. Missoula: Scholars Press.

Richardson, N. J. 1985. "Early Greek Views about Life after Death." In *Greek Religion and Society*, ed. by P. E. Easterling and J. V. Muir, 34–49. Cambridge: Cambridge University Press.

Riegel, Jeffrey K. 1982. "Early Chinese Target Magic." *Journal of Chinese Religion* 10: 1–18.

———. 1983. "The Songs of Possessed Children: A Survey of T'ung Yao in Chou and Han Dynasty Sources." Paper presented at the Workshop on Divination and Portent Interpretation in Ancient China, Berkeley, June 20–July 1, 1983.

———. 1989–90. "Kou-mang and Ju-shou." *Cahiers d'Extrême-Asie* 5: 55–83.

Rohde, E. 1925. *Psyche*. New York: Harcourt.

Sakai, Tadao 酒井忠夫. 1937. "Taizan shinkō no kenkyū 太山信仰の研究." *Shichō* 史潮 7, 2: 245–294.

Saleh, M. and H. Sourouzian. 1987. *The Egyptian Museum Cairo*, Official Catalogue. Mainz: Philipp von Zabern.

Salviati, F. 1994. "Bird and Bird-Related Motifs in the Iconography of the Liangzhu Culture." *Revista degli Studi Orientali* 58, 1/2: 133–160.

Sangren, P. Steven. 1984. "Great Tradition and Little Traditions Reconsidered: The Question of Cultural Integration in China. " *Journal of Chinese Studies* 1: 1–24.

309

———. 1987. *History and Magical Power in a Chinese Community*. Stanford: Stanford University Press.

Sawaguchi Takeo 澤口剛雄. 1966. "Kan no gakufu ni okeru shinsen Dōkā no shisō 漢の樂府における神仙道家の思想." *Tōhō Shūkyō* 27: 1–22.

Schafer, H. 1951. "Ritual Sacrifice in Ancient China." *HJAS* 11: 130–184.

Schiffeler, John Wm. 1978. *The Legendary Creatures of Shan-Hai Ching*. Taipei: Hwa Kang Press.

Schipper, Kristofer M. 1990. "The Cult of Pao-sheng Ta-ti and Its Spreading to Taiwan: A Case Study of Fen-hsiang." In *Development and Decline of Fukien Province in the 17th and 18th Centuries*, ed. by E. B. Vermeer, 397–416. Leiden: Brill.

———. 1993. *The Taoist Body*. Tr. by K. C. Duval. Berkeley: University of California Press.

Schnaufer, A. 1970. *Frühgriechischer Totenglaube: Untersuchungen zum Totenglauben der Mykenischen und Homerischen Zeit*. Hildesheim and New York: G. Olms.

Schwartz, Benjamin. 1985. *The World of Thought in Ancient China*. Cambridge: Harvard University. Press.

Seidel, Anna. 1978. *La divinisation de Lao tseu dans le taoisme des Han*. Paris: École Française d'Extrême-Orient.

———. 1987. "Traces of Han Religion in Funeral Texts Found in Tombs." In *Dōkyō to shūkyō bunka*, ed. by Akitsuki Kan'ei, 21–57.

———. 1989–90. "Chronicle of Taoist Studies in the West 1950–1990." *Cahiers d'Extrême-Asie* 5: 55–83.

Shan-tung-sheng po-wu-kuan 山東省博物館. 1972. "Shan-tung I-tu Ssu-fu-t'un i-hao nu-li hsün-tsang mu 山東益都蘇埠屯一號奴隸殉葬墓." *WW* 1972, 8: 17–30.

Shan-tung-sheng wen-wu kuan-li-ch'u and Chi-nan-shih po-wu-kuan eds. 山東省文物管理處、濟南市博物館. 1974. *Ta Wen K'ou* 大汶口. Peking: Wen-wu.

Shan-tung ta-hsüeh li-shih-hsi k'ao-ku chuan-yeh 山東大學歷史系考古專業. 1980. "Shan-tung ssu-shui I-chia-ch'eng ti-i-tz'u shih-chüeh 山東泗水尹家城第一次試掘." *KK* 1980,1: 13ff.

Sharpe, Eric J. 1986. *Comparative Religion, A History*. La Salle, Ill.: Open Court.

Shaughnessy, Edward L. 1991. *Sources of Western Zhou History: Inscribed Bronze Vessels*. Berkeley: University of California Press.

Shen, Yüan 沈元. 1962. "Chi-chiu-p'ien yen-chiu 急就篇研究." *Li-shih yen-chiu* 1962, 3: 61–87.

Shih, Chang-ju 石璋如. 1953. "Ho-nan An-yang Hsiao-t'un Yin-mu chung te tung-wu i-hai 河南安陽小屯殷墓中的動物遺骸." *Bulletin of the College of Liberal Arts of National Taiwan University* 5: 1–14.

Shih, Hsing-pang 石興邦. 1962. "Yu-kuan Ma-chia-yao wen-hua te i-hsieh wen-t'i 有關馬家窯文化的一些問題." *KK* 1962, 6: 318–329.

Shih, Sheng-han 石聲漢 ed. 1965. *Ssu-min yüeh-ling chiao-chu* 四民月令校注. Peking: Chung-hua.

Shirakawa, Shizuka. 白川靜, 1979. *Chūgoku kodai no bunka* 中國古代の文化. Tokyo: Kodansha.

Shui-hu-ti Ch'in-mu chu-chien cheng-li hsiao-tsu 睡虎地秦墓竹簡整理小組. 1990. *Shui-hu-ti Ch'in mu chu-chien* 睡虎地秦墓竹簡. Peking: Wen-wu.

Sinclair, A. 1967. *The Greek Anthology*. New York: MacMillan.

Smith, D. Howard. 1970. *Chinese Religion*. New York: Holt, Rinehart and Wilson.

Smith, Richard J. 1991. *Fortune-tellers and Philosophers: Divination in Traditional Chinese Society*. Boulder, San Francisco, Oxford: Westview Press.

———. 1992. *Chinese Almanacs*. Oxford: Oxford University Press.

Solmsen, F. 1979. *Isis among the Greeks and Romans*. Cambridge: Harvard University Press.

Spiro, M. E. 1963. "Religion: Problems of Definition and Explanation." In *Anthropological Approaches to the Study of Religion*, ed. by M. Banton, 85–126. New York: F. A. Praeger.

Spronk, K. 1986. *Beatific Afterlife in Ancient Israel and in the Ancient Near East*. Neukirchen-Vluyn: Verlag Butzon and Bercker Kevelaer.

Stein, Rolf A. 1979. "Religious Taoism and Popular Religion from the Second to Seventh Centuries." In *Facets of Taoism*, ed. by H. Welch and A. Seidel, 53–81. New Haven: Yale University Press.

Sun, I-jang 孫貽讓. 1974. *Mo-tzu hsien-ku* 墨子閒詁. Taipei: Shih-chieh.

Sun, Shou-tao 孫守道, and Kuo Ta-shun 郭大順. 1986. "Niu-ho-liang hung-shan wen-hua nü-shen t'ou-hsiang ti fa-hsien yü yen-chiu 牛河梁紅山文化女神頭像的發現與研究." *WW* 1986, 8: 18–24

Sun, Te-jun 孫德潤, and He Ya-i 賀雅宜. 1987. "Kung-chia-wai i-hao mu-tsang ch'ing-li chien-pao 龔家灣一號墓葬清理簡報." *K'ao-ku yü wen-wu* 1987, 1: 1–9.

Sun, Tso-yün 孫作雲. 1943. "Fei-lien k'ao: Chung-kuo ku-tai niao-tsu chih yen-chiu 飛廉考——中國古代鳥族之研究." *Hua-pei pien-i-kuan kuan-k'an* 華北編譯館館刊 2, 3: 6.1–6.29; 2, 4: 7.1–7.22.

———. 1945. "Chung-kuo ku-tai niao-shih-tsu chu-ch'iu-chang k'ao 中國古代鳥氏族諸酋長考." *Chung-kuo hsüeh-pao* 中國學報 3, 3: 18–36.

———. 1946. "Shuo Tan-Chu: Chung-kuo ku-tai ho-shih-tsu chih yen-chiu 說丹朱——中國古代鶴氏族之研究." *Li-shih yü k'ao-ku* 歷史與考古 vol. 1: 76–95.

———. 1947. "Shuo yü-jen 說羽人." *Shen-yang po-wu-kuan ch'ou-pei wei-yüan-hui hui-k'an* 瀋陽博物館籌備委員會彙刊 vol. 1: 29–75.

———. 1963. "Han-tai ssu-ming shen-hsiang te fa-hsien 漢代司命神像的發現." *Kuang-ming jih-pao* 光明日報 1963, 12, 4.

———. 1977. "Lo-yang hsi-Han Pu Ch'ien-ch'iu mu pi-hua k'ao-shih 洛陽西漢卜千秋墓壁畫考釋." *WW* 1977, 6: 17–22.

Sung, Kuang-yü 宋光宇. 1995. *Tsung-chiao yü she-hui* 宗教與社會. Taipei: Tung-ta.

Sung, Wen-hsün 宋文薰 *et al.* ed. 1991. *K'ao-ku yü li-shih wen-hua* 考古與歷史文化. Taipei: Cheng-chung.

Tai, T'ung-hsin 戴彤心, and Chia Mai-ming 賈麥明. 1988. "Hsi-pei ta-hsüeh i-yüan Han-mu ch'ing-li chien-pao 西北大學醫院漢墓清理簡報." *Wen-po* 文博, 3: 5–9.

T'ang, Ch'ih 湯池. 1994. "Shih-lun Luan-p'ing Hou-t'ai-tzu ch'u-t'u te shih-tiao nü-shen-hsiang 試論灤平后台子出土的石雕女神像." *WW* 1994, 3: 46–51.

T'ang, I-chieh 湯一介. 1988. *Wei-Chin Nan-pai-ch'ao shih-ch'ih te Tao-chiao* 魏晉南北朝時期的道教. Taipei: Tung-ta.

T'ang, Yung-t'ung 湯用彤. 1962. *Han-Wei Liang-Chin Nan-pei-ch'ao Fo-chiao shih* 漢魏兩晉南北朝佛教史. Taipei: Ting Wen.

———. 1983. "Tu T'ai-p'ing ching-shu so-chien 讀太平經書所見." In *T'ang Yung-t'ung hsüeh-shu lun-wen-chi* 湯用彤學術論文集. Peking: Chung-hua.

Taylor, R. 1990. "Official and Popular Religion and the Political Organization of Chinese Society in the Ming." In *Orthodoxy in Late Imperial China*, ed. by Kwang-Ching Liu, 126–157. Berkeley: University of California Press.

Teiser, Stephen E. 1988. *The Ghost Festival in Medieval China*. Princeton: Princeton University Press.

———. 1995. "Popular Religion." *JAS* 54.2: 378–395.

Teng, Shu-p'ing 鄧淑蘋. 1993. "Chung-kuo hsin-shih-ch'i shih-tai yü-ch'i shang-ti shen-mi fu-hao 中國新石器時代玉器上神祕符號." *Ku-kung hsüeh-shu chi-k'an* 故宮學術季刊 10, 3: 1–50.

Thompson, Laurence G. 1989. "On the Prehistory of Hell in China." *Journal of Chinese Religion* 17: 27–41.

Thote, A. 1992. "Aspects of the Serpent on Eastern Zhou Bronzes and Lacquerware." In *The Problem of Meaning in Early Chinese Ritual Bronzes*, ed. by R. Whitfield, 150–160.

Tou, Lien-jung 竇連榮, and Wang Kuei-chün 王桂鈞. 1989. "Ch'in-tai tsung-chiao chih li-ch'eng 秦代宗教之歷程." *Ning-hsia she-hui k'o-hsüeh* 寧夏社科學 1989, 3: 9–16.

Trombley, Frank R. 1994. *Hellenic Religion and Christianization C. 370–529*, 2 vols. Leiden: E.J. Brill.

Tseng, Chao-yü 曾昭燏. 1956. *I-nan ku-hua-hsiang-shih mu fa-chüeh pao-kao* 沂南古畫像石墓發掘報告. Shanghai: Wen-hua kuan-li-chu.

Tsien, Ch'un-hsün. 1962. *Written on Bamboo and Silk*. Chicago: University of Chicago. Revised ed.: *Chung-kuo ku-tai shu-shih* 中國古代書史. Hong Kong: Chinese University press. 1975.

Tsuda, Sokichi 津田左右吉. 1939. *Shinsen shiso no kenkyū* 神仙思想の研究. Tokyo: Iwanami.

Tu, Cheng-sheng 杜正勝. 1989. "Chou-li shen-fen-chih chih ch'üeh-ting chi ch'i liu-pien 周禮身份制之確定及其流變." *Ti-erh-chieh kuo-chi Han-hsüeh hui-i lun-wen-chi* 第二屆國際漢學會議論文集. Taipei: Academia Sinica.

———. 1990. *Pien-hu ch'i-min* 編戶齊民. Taipei: Lien-ching.

———. 1991. "Hsing-t'i ching-ch'i yü hun-p'o—Chung-kuo ch'uan-t'ung tui 'jen' jen-shih te hsing-ch'eng 形體、精氣與魂魄——中國傳統對「人」認識的形成." *Hsin-shih-hsüeh* 2, 3 : 1–65.

———. 1995. "Ch'ung mei-shou tao ch'ang-sheng 從眉壽到長生." *BIHP* 66, 2: 383–487.

Tu, Wen-lan 杜文瀾. 1986. *Ku Yao-yen* 古謠諺. Taipei: Hisn-wen-feng.

Tuan, Yü-ts'ai 段玉裁. 1988. *Shuo-wen chieh-tzu-chu* 說文解字注. Taipei: I-wen reprint.

T'ung, Shu-yeh 童書業. 1946. *Ch'un-ch'iu shih* 春秋史. Shanghai: K'ai-ming.

Twitchett, D. and Loewe, M. eds. 1986. *The Cambridge History of China*, vol. 1, 52–64. Cambridge: Cambridge University Press.

Uchino, Kumaichirō 內野熊一郎. 1983. "Shinkyō haito haimei shibun ni araware taru shinsen shini shinen no gensen ko 秦鏡背圖、背銘詩文に現われたる神仙、讖緯思念の源泉考." In *Shini shisō no sōgōteki kenkyū* 讖緯思想の綜合的研究, ed. by Yasui Kōzan, 3–18. Tokyo: Kokusho Kankōkai.

Unschuld, Paul U. 1985. *Medicine in China: A History of Ideas*. Berkeley: University of California Press.

Vandermeersch, L. 1980. "Note sur le Inscriptions Oraculaires de Fengch'u-ts'un." *Ikeda Suetoshi hakushi koki kinen Tōyōgaku ronshū* 池田末利博士古稀記念東洋學論集, 1–15. Hiroshima.

Veith, Ilza. 1949. *Huang Ti Nei Ching Su Wen*. Baltimore: Williams and Wilkins.

Vermeule, E. 1979. *Aspects of Death in Early Greek Art and Poetry*. Berkeley: University of California Press.

Vernant, Jean-Pierre. 1991. *Mortals and Immortals*. Princeton: Princeton University Press.

Vrijhof, P. H., and J. Waardenburg eds. 1979. *Official and Popular Religion, Analysis of a Theme for Religious Studies*. The Hague: Mouton.

Wagner, Rudolf G. 1988. "Imperial Dreams in China." In *Psycho-Sinology: The Universe of Dreams in Chinese Culture*, ed. by Carolyn T. Brown, 11–24. Washington D.C.: Woodrow Wilson International Center for Scholars.

Waley, Authur. 1937, 1952. *The Book of Songs*. London: Allen and Unwin.

Wang, Chen-chung 王震中. 1988. "Tung-shan-tsui yüan-shih chi-t'an yü chung-kuo ku-tai te she-ch'ung-pai 東山嘴原始祭壇與中國古代的社崇拜." *Shih-chieh tsung-chiao yen-chiu* 世界宗教研究 1988, 4: 82–81.

Wang, Fei 王飛. 1986. "Yung-ting chih-tu hsing-shuai i-i 用鼎制度興衰異議." *Wen-po* 1986, 6: 29–33.

Wang, Hsien-ch'ien 王先謙. 1971. *Hsün-tzu chi-chieh* 荀子集解. Taipei: Shih-chieh.

———. 1981. *Hou-Han-shu chi-chieh* 後漢書集解. Peking: Chung-hua.

Wang, Hsien-shen 王先愼. 1962. *Han-fei-tzu chi-chieh* 韓非子集解. Taipei: Shih-chieh.

Wang, Jui-ming 王瑞明. 1979. "Chen-mu-shou k'ao 鎮墓獸考." *WW* 1979, 6: 85–87.

Wang, Kuei-chün 王桂鈞. 1988. 'Jih-shu so-chien tsao-ch'i Ch'in-su fa-wei 日書所見早期秦俗發微." *Wen-po* 1988, 4: 63–70.

Wang, Kuo-liang 王國良. 1984. *Wei-Chin Nan-pei-ch'ao chih-kuai hsiao-shuo yen-chiu* 魏晉南北朝志怪小說研究. Taipei: Wen-shih-che.

Wang, Kuo-wei 王國維. 1959. "Sheng-pa ssu-pa k'ao 生霸死霸考." In *Kuan-t'ang chi-lin* 觀堂集林, vol. 1, 19–26. Peking: Chung-hua.

Wang, Li-ch'i 王利器. 1981. *Feng-su t'ung-i chiao-chu* 風俗通義校注. Peking: Chung-hua.

Wang, Ming 王明. 1960. *T'ai-p'ing-ching ho-chiao* 太平經合校. Peking: Chung-hua.

Wang, Pao-hsüan 王葆玹. 1992. "Hsi-Han kuo-chia tsung-chiao yü Huang-Lao hsüeh-p'ai te tsung-chiao ssu-hsiang 西漢國家宗教與黃老學派的宗教思想." In *Tao-chia wen-hua yen-chiu* 道家文化研究, ed. by Ch'en Ku-ying 陳鼓應, vol. 2, 193–208. Shang-hai: Ku-chi.

Wang, Tao. 1992. "A Textual Investigation on the Taotie." In *The Problem of Meaning*, ed. by R. Whitfield, 102–118. London: University of London.

Wang, Yü-ch'üan. 1949. "An Outline of the Central Government of the Former Han Dynasty." *HJAS* 12: 134–187.

Wang, Yü-ch'eng 王育成. 1991. "Tung-Han tao-fu shih-li 東漢道符釋例." *KKHP* 1991, 1: 45–55.

Wang, Yü-hsin 王宇信. 1986. "Hsi-chou chia-ku shu-lun 西周甲骨述論." In *Chia-ku-wen yü yin-shang-shih* 甲骨文與殷商史, ed. by Hu Hou-hsüan, vol. 2, 338–413. Shanghai: Ku-chi ch'u-pan-she.

Wang, Yün 王筠. 1988. *Shuo-wen chieh-tzu chu-tu* 說文解字句讀. Peking: Chung-hua reprint.

Wang, Zhongshu. 1982. *Han Civilization*. New Haven: Yale University Press.

Watson, Burton. 1962. *Early Chinese Literature*. New York: Columbia University Press.

———. 1963. *Hsün Tzu*. New York: Columbia University Press.

———. 1964. *Chuang Tzu: Basic Writings*. New York: Columbia University Press.

———. 1967. *Basic Writings of Mo Tzu, Hsun Tzu, and Han Fei Tzu*. New York: Columbia University Press.

———. 1989. *The Tso Chuan*. New York: Columbia University Press.

Watson, James L., and Evelyn S. Rawski eds. 1988. *Death Ritual in Later Imperial and Modern China*. Berkeley: University of California Press.

Watson, William. 1966. *Early Civilization in China*. London: Thames and Hudson.

Weber, Max. 1951. *The Religion of China*. Glencoe, Ill.: Free Press.

Wechsler, Howard J. 1985. *Offerings of Jade and Silk: Ritual and Symbol in the Legitimation of the T'ang Dynasty*. New Haven: Yale University Press.

Welch, H. 1965. *Taoism, The Parting of the Way*. Boston: Beacon Press.

Weller, Robert P. 1987. *Unities and Diversities in Chinese Religion*. London: Macmillan.

Wen, Ch'ung-i 文崇一. 1990. *Ch'u-wen-hua yen-chiu* 楚文化研究. Taipei: Tung-ta.

Wen, I-to 聞一多. 1975. "Shuo-yü 說魚." In *Shen-hua yü shih* 神話與詩, 117–138. Taipei: Lan-teng reprint.

———. 1975. "Shen-hsien k'ao 神仙考." In *Shen-hua yü shih*, 153–180.

Wen-po chien-hsün 文博簡訊. 1977. "Liao-ning Kai-hsien Chiu-lung-ti fa hsien tung-Han chi-nien chuan-mu 遼寧蓋縣九龍地發現東漢紀年磚墓." *WW* 1977, 9: 93.

Whitfield, Roderick ed. 1992. *The Problem of Meaning in Early Chinese Ritual Bronzes*. London: University of London.

Wilhelm, Richard tr. 1955. *The I Ching, or Book of Changes*. New York: Bollingen Foundation Inc.

Wolf, A. P. 1974. "Gods, Ghosts, and Ancestors." In *Religion and Ritual in Chinese Society*, ed. by A. P. Wolf, 131–182. Stanford: Stanford University Press.

Wright, A. F. 1954. "Biography and Hagiography: Hui-chiao's Lives of Eminent Monks." *Silver Jubilee Volume of the Zinbunkagaku Kenkyūsyo Kyoto University*, 383–432. Kyoto: Kyoto University Press.

———. 1959. *Buddhism in Chinese History*. Stanford: Stanford University Press.

Wu, Chiu-lung 吳九龍. 1985. *Yin-ch'üeh-shan Han-chien shih-wen* 銀雀山漢簡釋文. Peking: Wen-wu.

Wu, Hung. 1985. "Bird Motifs in Eastern Yi Art." *Orientations* 16, 10: 30–41.

———. 1989. "Han Ming Wei Wen te li-chih kai-ko yü Han-tai hua-hsiang i-shu chih sheng-shuai 漢明、魏文的禮制改革與漢代畫像藝術之盛衰." *Chiu-chou hsüeh-k'an* 九州學刊 3, 2: 31–44.

———. 1989a. *The Wu Liang Shrine: The Ideology of Early Chinese Pictorial Art*. Stanford: Stanford University Press.

———. 1992. "Art in a Ritual Context: Rethinking Mawangdui." *Early China* 17: 111–144.

———. 1995. *Monumentality in Early Chinese Art and Architecture*. Stanford: Stanford University Press.

Wu, Jung-tseng 吳榮曾. 1981. "Chen-mu-wen chung so chien-tao te tung-Han tao-wu kuan-hsi 鎮墓文中所見到的東漢道巫關係." *WW* 1981, 3: 56–63.

Wu, Tian-Ying 吳天穎. 1982. "Han-tai mai-ti-ch'üan k'ao 漢代買地券考." *KKHP* 1: 15–34.

Wu, Shu-p'ing 吳樹平. 1981. "Yün-meng Ch'in-chien so fan-ying te Ch'in-tai she-hui chieh-chi chuang-k'uang 雲夢秦簡所反映的秦代社會階級狀況." In *Yün-meng Ch'in-chien yen-chiu* 雲夢秦簡研究, ed. by Chung-hua shu-chü pien-chi-pu, 79–130. Peking: Chung-hua.

Yang, C. K. 1976. *Religion in Chinese Society*. Berkeley: University of California Press.

Yang, K'uan 楊寬. 1980. *Chan-kuo shih* 戰國史. Shanghai: Jen-min.

Yang, Shu-ta 楊樹達. 1989. *Han-tai hun-sang li-su k'ao* 漢代婚喪禮俗考. Shanghai: Shanghai.

Yang-chou po-wu-kuan 揚州博物館. 1987. "Chiang-su I-cheng Hsü-p'u no. 101 hsi-Han mu 江蘇儀征胥浦 101 號西漢墓." *WW* 1987, 1: 1–19.

Yasui, Kōzan 安居香山. 1984. *Shini shisō no sogōteki kenkyū* 讖緯思想の綜合的研究. Tokyo: Kokusho kankōkai.

Yasui, Kōzan and Shōhachi Nakamura 中村璋八. 1987. *Isho no kisoteki kenkyū* 緯書の基礎的研究. Tokyo: Kokusho kankōkai.

Yeh, Mao-lin 葉茂林. 1992. "Shan-hsi Chi-hsien Shih-tzu-t'an i-chih yen-hua pien-i 陝西桔縣獅子灘遺址岩畫辨異." *KK* 1992, 5: 431–433.

Yen, Ming 言明. 1988. "Kuan-yü P'u-yang Hsi-shui-p'o i-chih fa-chüeh chien-pao chi-ch'i yu-kuan-te liang-p'ien wen-chang chung jo-kan wen-t'i te shang-ch'üeh 關於濮陽西水坡遺址試掘簡報及其有關的兩篇文章中若干問題的商榷." *Hua-hsia k'ao-ku* 華夏考古 1988, 4: 50–70.

Yin, Hung-chi 尹弘基. 1989. "Lun Chung-kuo ku-tai feng-shui te ch'i-yüan ho fa-chan 論中國古代風水的起源和發展." *Tzu-jan k'o-hsüeh-shih yen-chiu* 自然科學史研究 8, 1: 84–89.

Yoshinami, Takashi 好並隆司. 1988. "Unbō Shinkan Nissho shōron 雲夢秦簡日書小論." In *Chūgoku Shakaishi no Sōshō* 中國社會史の諸相, ed. by Yokoyama Hide 橫山英 and Teraji Jun 寺地尊, 1–51. Tokyo: Keiso Shobō.

Yoyotte, Jean *et al.* 1961. *Le Jugement des Morts. Sources Orientales* 4, Paris: Éditions du Seuil.

Yu, Anthony C. 1987. "'Rest, Rest, Perturbed Spirit!' Ghosts in Traditional Chinese Prose Fiction." *HJAS* 47, 2: 397–434.

Yü, Wei-ch'ao 俞偉超. 1985. "Chou-tai yung-ting chih-tu yen-chiu 周代用鼎制度研究." *Hsien-Ch'in liang-Han k'ao-ku-hsüeh lun-chi* 先秦兩漢考古學論集, 62–107. Peking: Wen-wu.

Yü, Ying-shih 余英時. 1964–65. "Life and Immortality in the Mind of Han China." *HJAS* 25: 80–122.

———. 1980. *Chung-kuo chih-shih chieh-ts'eng shih-lun (ku-tai p'ien)* 中國知識階層史論 (古代篇). Taipei: Lien-ching.

———. 1981. "New Evidence on the Early Chinese Conception of Afterlife." *JAS* 41,1: 81–85.

———. 1987. *Chung-kuo ssu-hsiang ch'uan-t'ung te hsien-tai ch'üan-shih* 中國思想傳統的現代詮釋. Taipei: Lien-ching.

———. 1987a. "Chung-kuo ku-tai ssu-hou shih-chieh-kuan te yen-pien 中國古代死後世界觀的演變." In *Chung-kuo ssu-hsiang ch'uan-t'ung te hsien-tai ch'üan-shih*, 123–143.

———. 1987b. "Han-tai hsün-li yü wen-hua ch'uan-po 漢代循吏與文化傳播." In *Chung-kuo ssu-hsiang ch'uan-t'ung te hsien-tai ch'üan-shih*, 167–258.

———. 1987c. "O Soul Come Back! A Study in the Changing Conceptions of the Soul and Afterlife in Pre-Buddhist China." *HJAS* 47, 2: 363–395.

Yüan, K'o 袁珂. 1980. *Shan-hai-ching chiao-chu* 山海經校注. Shanghai: Ku-chi ch'u-pan-she.

———. 1987. *Chung-kuo shen-hua ch'uan-shuo tz'u-tien* 中國神話傳說辭典. Taipei: Hua shih.

———. 1988. *Chung-kuo shen-hua shih* 中國神話史. Shanghai: Wen-i.

Yün-meng Shui-hu-ti Ch'in-mu pien-hsieh tsu 雲夢睡虎地秦墓編寫組. 1981. *Yün-meng Shui-hu-ti Ch'in-mu* 雲夢睡虎地秦墓. Peking: Wen-wu.

Zandee, J. 1960. *Death as an Enemy*. Leiden: E. J. Brill.

Zürcher, E. 1972. *The Buddhist Conquest of China*, 2 vols. Leiden: E. J. Brill.

———. 1990. "Han Buddhism and the Western Region." In *Thought and Law in Qin and Han China*, ed. by W. L. Idema and E. Zürcher, 158–182. Leiden: E. J. Brill.

Index